Glorious DESSERTS

Glorious DESSERTS

More than 350 irresistibly sweet
temptations for after-dinner indulgence

MARTHA DAY

HERMES
HOUSE

This edition is published by Hermes House

Hermes House is an imprint of Anness Publishing Ltd
Hermes House, 88-89 Blackfriars road, London SE1 8HA
tel. 020 7401 2077; fax 020 7633 9499; info@anness.com

A CIP catalogue record for this book is available from the British Library.

Publisher: Joanna Lorenz
Project Editor: Finny Fox Davies
Designer: Ian Sandom
Recipes: Catherine Atkinson, Alex Barker, Michelle Berriedale-Johnson, Angela Boggiano, Janet Briinkworkth, Carla
Capalbo, Jacqueline Clark, Francis Cleary, Carol Clements, Roz Denny, Patrizia Diemling, Nicola Diggins, Joanna Farrow,
Christine France, Sarah Gates, Shirley Gill, Rosamund Grant, Carole Handslip, Deh-Ta Hsiung, Shehzad Husain, Sheila
Kimberley, Gilly Love, Norma MacMillan, Sue Maggs, Maggie Mayhew, Maggie Parnell, Anne Sheasby, Liz Trigg, Laura
Washburn, Stephen Wheeler, Kate Whiteman, Elizabeth Wolf-Cohen, Jeni Wright
Photographers: William Adams-Lingwood, Karl Adamson, Edward Allwright, David Armstrong, Stever Baxter, James
Duncan, Michelle Garrett, Amanda Heywood, David Jordan, Don Last, Patrick McLeavy, Michael Michaels, Thomas
Odulate

Previously published in two separate volumes, Best Ever Desserts and The Ultimate Fat-Free Dessert Cookbook

Printed in Singapore

1 3 5 7 9 10 8 6 4 2

NOTES

Standard spoon and cup measures are level.

Large eggs are used unless otherwise stated.

Portion sizes: The recipes in this book are generally for four people. They can be halved or quartered, depending on the
number of servings required.

Contents

Introduction

DESSERT RECIPES CAN RANGE from the lightest sorbet to the most rich chocolate cake, so there are several decisions to be made when planning a menu. Your choice of what to serve will be influenced by the season, the occasion and the dietary requirements of your guests. If you are serving a filling main course, you will invariably choose a light or fruity dessert to follow it; if you plan to make a rich, creamy dessert, you will deliberately pick a light main course. To help you maintain a healthy balance, this book includes a wide range of delicious low-fat desserts that can make the decision reassuringly easy.

Many of the desserts in this book can be made a day or two in advance, others can be started early in the day and finished just before you eat, while frozen desserts and ice creams can be made weeks in advance, ready to serve whenever you need them. If you are planning a festive meal or entertaining a large number of people make sure you leave plenty of time for preparation, choose one of the desserts that can be made in advance and do at least some of the work for the other courses earlier in the day. That way your guests *and you* can enjoy the meal.

All the recipes have clear instructions, so that even the potentially difficult desserts, such as soufflés and roulades, will be easy to make, and look and taste delicious. For the best results, read the recipe through before you start, and follow the step-by-step instructions.

The book is divided into two sections. *Best-ever Desserts* contains all the old favorites, such as Crème Caramel and English Trifle, along with some more unusual recipes that are destined to become favorites. There are chapters on hot desserts, cold desserts and everything in between, to make sure you serve a best-ever dessert for every occasion. The book also contains recipes that are just as delicious but carefully designed to fit into a healthy, lighter diet. Almost all of the recipes have no more than 5 grams of fat per portion, and many have fewer than 200 calories.

Best-ever Desserts

Desserts are irresistible at any time of day: with morning coffee or afternoon tea, as the perfect end to a lazy lunch, as a special indulgence or treat, or as the grand finale to a romantic evening. This section of the book presents recipes for the most luxurious, sumptuous desserts imaginable, including classics such as Peach Melba and Black Forest Gâteau, as well as innovative ideas such as Chocolate and Cherry Polenta Cake and Kiwi Ricotta Cheese Tart. There are six easy-to-use chapters that cover every kind of dessert for all occasions—hot and cold puddings, cakes and gâteaux, pastries and pies, custards and soufflés, fruit salads, ices and sorbets.

◆ ◆ ◆

Making Shortcrust Pastry

A crumbly pastry crust sets off any filling to perfection, whether sweet or savory. The fat content of the pastry dough can be made up of half butter or margarine and half white vegetable fat or with all one kind of fat.

INGREDIENTS

For a 9-inch pastry shell

2 cups all-purpose flour

¼ teaspoon salt

8 tablespoons fat, chilled and diced

1 Sift the flour and salt into a bowl. Add the fat. Rub it into the flour with your fingertips until the mixture is crumbly.

2 Sprinkle 3 tablespoons ice water on the mixture. With a fork, toss gently to mix and moisten it.

3 Press the dough into a ball. If it is too dry to hold together, gradually add another 1 tablespoon of ice water.

4 Wrap the ball of dough with plastic wrap or waxed paper and chill it for at least 30 minutes.

5 To make pastry in a food processor: combine the flour, salt and cubed fat in the work bowl. Process, turning the machine on and off, just until the mixture is crumbly. Add 3–4 tablespoons of ice water and process again briefly—just until the dough starts to pull away from the sides of the bowl. It should still look crumbly. Remove the dough from the process and gather it into a ball. Wrap and chill.

SHORTCRUST PASTRY VARIATIONS

For Nut Shortcrust
Add ¼ cup finely chopped walnuts or pecans to the flour mixture.

For Rich Shortcrust
Use 2 cups all-purpose flour and ¾ cup fat (preferably all butter), plus 1 tablespoon sugar if making a sweet pie. Bind with 1 egg yolk and 2–3 tablespoons water.

For a Two-crust Pie
Increase the proportions for these pastries by 50%. Thus the amounts needed for basic shortcrust pastry are: 3 cups all-purpose flour, ½ teaspoon salt, ¾ cup fat, 5–6 tablespoons water.

PASTRY MAKING TIPS

It helps if the fat is cold and firm, particularly if making the dough in a food processor. Cold fat has less chance of warming and softening too much when it is being rubbed into the flour, resulting in an oily pastry. Use stick margarine rather than the soft container-type for the same reason.

When rubbing the fat into the flour, if it begins to soften and feel oily, put the bowl in the refrigerator to chill for 20–30 minutes. Then continue to make the dough.

Liquids used should be ice-cold so that they will not soften or melt the fat.

Take care when adding the water: start with the smaller amount (added all at once, not in dribbles), and add more only if the mixture will not come together into a dough. Too much water will make the dough difficult to handle and will result in tough pastry.

When gathering the mixture together into a ball of dough, handle it as little as possible: overworked dough will again produce a tough pastry.

To avoid shrinkage, chill the pastry dough before rolling out and baking. This "resting time" will allow any elasticity developed during mixing to relax.

Making French Tart Pastry

The pastry for tarts and flans is made with butter or margarine, giving rich and crumbly results. The more fat used, the richer the pastry will be—almost like cookie dough— and the harder to roll out. If you have difficulty rolling it, you can press it into the pan instead, or roll it out between sheets of plastic wrap. Tart pastry, like shortcrust, can be made by hand or in a food processor. Tips for making, handling and using shortcrust pastry apply equally to this type of pastry.

INGREDIENTS

For a 9-inch tart shell

1¾ cups all-purpose flour

½ teaspoon salt

½ cup butter or margarine, chilled

1 egg yolk

¼ teaspoon lemon juice

1 Sift the flour and salt into a bowl. Add the butter or margarine. Rub into the flour until the mixture resembles fine bread crumbs.

2 In a small bowl, mix the egg yolk, lemon juice and 2 tablespoons of ice water. Add to the flour mixture. With a fork, toss gently to mix and moisten.

3 Press the dough into a rough ball. If it is too dry to come together, add 1 tablespoon more water. Turn onto the work surface or a pastry board.

4 With the heel of your hand, push small portions of dough away from you, smearing them on the surface.

5 Continue mixing the dough in this way until it feels pliable and can be peeled easily off the work surface or pastry board.

6 Press the dough into a smooth ball. Wrap in plastic wrap and chill for at least 30 minutes.

TART PASTRY VARIATIONS

For Sweet Tart Pastry
Reduce the amount of salt to ¼ teaspoon, add 1 tablespoon sugar with the flour.

For Rich Tart Pastry
Use 1¾ cups all-purpose flour, ½ teaspoon salt, 10 tablespoons butter, 2 egg yolks, and 1–2 tablespoons water.

For Rich Sweet Tart Pastry
Make rich tart pastry, adding 3 tablespoons sugar with the flour and, if desired, ½ teaspoon vanilla extract with the egg yolks.

Making Choux Pastry

Unlike other pastries, where the fat is rubbed into the flour, with choux pastry the butter is melted with water and then the flour is added, followed by eggs. The result is more of a paste than a pastry. It is easy to make, but care must be taken in measuring the ingredients.

INGREDIENTS

For 18 profiteroles or 12 éclairs

½ cup butter, cut into small pieces

2 teaspoons sugar (optional)

¼ teaspoon salt

1¼ cups all-purpose flour

4 eggs, beaten to mix

1 egg, beaten with 1 teaspoon cold water, for glaze

1 Preheat the oven to 425°F. Combine the butter, sugar, if using, salt and 1 cup of water in a large heavy saucepan. Bring to a boil over medium-high heat, stirring occasionally.

2 As soon as the mixture is boiling, remove the pan from heat. Add the flour all at once and beat vigorously with a wooden spoon to mix the flour smoothly into the liquid.

3 Return the pan to medium heat and cook, stirring, until the mixture will form a ball, pulling away from the side of the pan. This will take about 1 minute. Remove from heat again and let cool for 3–5 minutes.

4 Add a little of the beaten eggs and beat well to incorporate. Add a little more egg and beat in well. Continue beating in the eggs until the mixture becomes a smooth and shiny paste.

5 While still warm, shape choux puffs, éclairs, profiteroles or rings on a baking sheet lined with baking parchment.

6 Glaze with 1 egg beaten with 1 teaspoon of cold water. Put into the preheated oven, then reduce the heat to 400°F. Bake until puffed and golden brown.

SHAPING CHOUX PASTRY

For Large Puffs

Use two large spoons dipped in water. Drop the paste in 2–2½-inch wide blobs on the paper-lined baking sheet, leaving 1½ inches between each. Neaten the blobs as much as possible. Alternatively, for well-shaped puffs, pipe the paste using a piping bag fitted with a ¾-inch plain nozzle.

For Profiteroles

Use two small spoons or a piping bag fitted with a ½-inch nozzle and shape 1-inch blobs.

For Éclairs

Use a piping bag fitted with a ¾-inch nozzle. Pipe strips 4–5 inches long.

For a Ring

Draw a 12-inch circle on the paper. Spoon the paste in large blobs on the circle to make a ring. Or, pipe two rings around the circle and a third on top.

BAKING TIMES FOR CHOUX PASTRY	
Large puffs and éclairs	30–35 minutes
Profiteroles	20–25 minutes
Rings	40–45 minutes

Rolling Out and Lining a Pan

A neat pastry shell that doesn't distort or shrink in baking is the desired result. The key to success is handling the dough gently. Use the method here to line a round pie or tart pan that is about 2 inches deep.

Remove the chilled dough from the refrigerator and let it soften slightly at room temperature. Unwrap and put it on a lightly floured surface. Flatten the dough into a neat, round disk. Lightly flour the rolling pin.

1 Using even pressure, start rolling out the dough, working from the center to the edge each time and easing the pressure slightly as you reach the edge.

2 Lift up the dough and give it a quarter turn from time to time during the rolling. This will prevent the dough from sticking to the surface, and will help keep the thickness even.

3 Continue rolling out until the dough circle is about 2 inches larger all around than the pan. It should be about ⅛ inch thick.

4 Set the rolling pin on the dough, near one side of the circle. Fold the outside edge of the dough over the pin, then roll the pin over the dough to wrap the dough around it. Do this gently and loosely.

5 Hold the pin over the pan and gently unroll the dough so it drapes into the pan, centering it as much as possible.

6 With your fingertips, lift and ease the dough into the tin, gently pressing it over the bottom and up the side. Turn excess dough over the rim and trim it with a knife or scissors, depending on how you want to finish the edge.

Finishing the Edge

1 *For a forked edge*
Using a knife, trim the dough even with the rim and press it flat. Firmly and evenly press the prongs of a fork all around the edge. If the fork sticks, dip it in flour every so often.

2 *For a crimped edge*
Using scissors, trim the dough to leave an overhang of about ½ inch all round. Fold the extra dough under. Put the knuckle or tip of the index finger of one of your hands inside the edge, pointing directly out. With the thumb and index finger of your other hand, pinch the dough edge around your index finger into a "V" shape. Continue all the way around the edge.

3 *For a ruffled edge*
Using scissors, trim the dough to leave an overhang of about ½ inch all around. Fold the extra dough under. With the thumb and index finger of one hand about 1 inch apart, gently pinch the dough around the index finger of your other hand. Continue this all the way around the edge.

4 *For a cutout edge*
Using a knife, trim the dough even with the rim and press it flat. With a small pastry cutter, cut out decorative shapes from the dough trimmings. Moisten the edge of the pastry shell and press the cutouts in place, overlapping them slightly if desired.

5 *For a ribbon edge*
Using a knife, trim the dough even with the rim and press it flat. Cut long strips about ¾ inch wide from the dough trimmings. Moisten the edge and press one end of a strip onto it. Twist the strip gently and press it onto the edge again. Continue this all the way around the edge.

Preparing Fresh Fruit

PEELING AND TRIMMING FRUIT

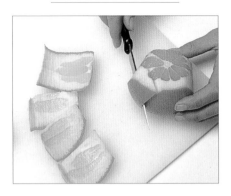

Citrus fruit

To peel completely: cut a slice from the top and from the bottom. Set the fruit bottom down on a work surface. Using a small sharp knife, cut off the peel lengthwise in thick strips. Take the colored zest and all the white pith (which has a bitter taste). Cut, following the curve of the fruit.

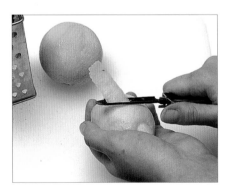

To remove zest: use a vegetable peeler to save off the zest in wide strips, taking none of the white pith. Use these strips whole or cut them into fine shreds with a sharp knife, according to recipe directions. Or rub the fruit against the fine holes of a metal grater, turning the fruit so you take just the colored zest and not the white pith. Or use a special tool, called a citrus zester, to take fine threads of zest. (Finely chop the threads as an alternative method to grating.)

Kiwi

Follow the citrus fruit technique, taking off the peel in thin lengthwise strips.

Apples, pears, quinces, mangoes, papayas

Use a small sharp knife or a vegetable peeler. Take off the peel in long strips, as thinly as possible.

Peaches, apricots

Cut a cross in the bottom. Immerse the fruit in boiling water. Leave for 10–30 seconds (according to ripeness), then drain and immerse in ice water. The skin should slip off easily.

Pineapple

Cut off the leafy crown. Cut a slice from the bottom and set the pineapple upright. With a sharp knife, cut off the peel lengthwise, cutting thickly to remove the brown "eyes" with it.

Bananas, lychees, avocados

Make a small cut and remove the peel with your fingers.

Passion fruit, pomegranates

Cut in half, or cut a slice off the top. With a spoon, scoop the flesh and seeds into a bowl.

Star fruit (carambola)

Trim off the tough, darkened edges of the five segments.

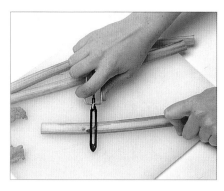

Rhubarb
Cut off the leaves and discard them (they are poisonous). Peel off any tough skin.

Fresh currants (red, black, white)
Pull each cluster through the prongs of a fork to remove the currants from the stems.

Fresh dates
Squeeze gently at the stem end to remove the rather tough skin.

CORING AND PITTING OR SEEDING FRUIT

Apples, pears, quinces
For whole fruit: use an apple corer to stamp out the whole core from stem end to bottom. Alternatively, working up from the bottom, use a melon baller to cut out the core. Leave the stem end intact.

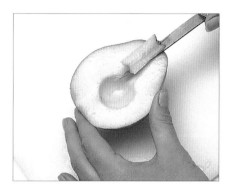

For halves: use a melon baller to scoop out the core. Cut out the stem and bottom using a small sharp knife.
For quarters: cut out the stem and core with a serrated knife.

Citrus fruit
With the tip of a pointed knife, nick out seeds from slices or segments.

Cherries
Use a cherry pitter to achieve the neatest results.

Peaches, apricots, nectarines, plums
Cut the fruit in half, cutting around the indentation. Twist the halves apart. Lift out the pit, or lever it out with the tip of a sharp knife.

Fresh dates
Cut the fruit lengthwise in half and lift out the pit. Or, if the fruit is to be used whole, cut in from the stem end with a thin-bladed knife to loosen the pit, then remove it.

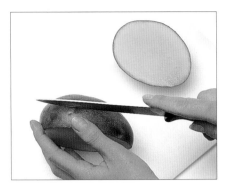

Apples, quinces

For rings: remove the core and seeds with an apple corer. Set the fruit on its side and cut across into thick or thin rings, as required.

Mangoes

Cut lengthwise on either side of the large flat pit in the center. Curve the cut slightly to follow the shape of the pit. Cut the flesh from the two thin ends of the pit.

Grapes

Cut the fruit lengthwise in half. Use a small knife to nick out the seeds. Alternatively, use the curved end of a sterilized bobby pin.

For slices: cut the fruit in half and remove core and seeds with a melon baller. Set one half cut-side down and cut it across into neat slices, thick or thin according to recipe directions. Or cut the fruit into quarters and remove core and seeds with a knife. Cut lengthwise into neat slices.

Papayas, melons

Cut the fruit in half. Scoop out the seeds from the central hollow, then scrape out any fibers.

Star fruit (carambola), watermelon

With the tip of a pointed knife, nick out seeds from slices.

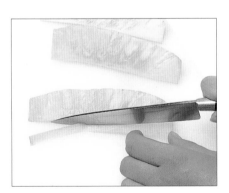

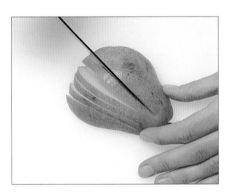

Pineapple

For spears and wedges: cut out the core neatly with a sharp knife.
For rings: cut out the core with a small pastry cutter.

Gooseberries

Use scissors to trim off the stem and flower ends.

Strawberries

Use a special huller to remove the leafy green top and central core. Or cut these out with a small sharp knife.

Avocado

Cut the fruit in half lengthwise. Stick the tip of a sharp knife into the pit and lever it out without damaging the surrounding flesh.

Pears

For fans: cut the fruit in half and remove the core and seeds with a melon baller. Set the halves cut-side down and cut lengthwise into thin slices, not cutting all the way through at the stem end. Gently fan out the slices so they are overlapping each other evenly. Transfer the pear fans to the plate or pastry shell using a spatula.
For slices: follow apple technique.

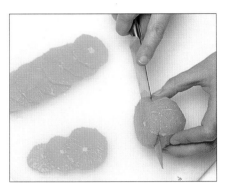

Citrus fruit
For slices: using a serrated knife, cut the fruit across into neat slices.

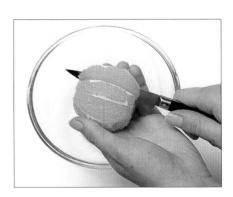

For segments: hold the peeled fruit in your cupped palm, over a bowl to catch the juice. Working from the side of the fruit to the center, slide the knife down one side of a separating membrane to free the flesh from it. Then slide the knife down the other side of that segment to free it from the membrane there. Drop the segment into the bowl. Continue cutting out the segments, folding back the membrane like the pages of a book as you work. When all the segments have been cut out, squeeze all the juice from the membrane.

Peaches, nectarines, apricots, plums
For slices: follow apple technique.

Papayas, avocados
For slices: follow apple technique. Or cut the unpeeled fruit into wedges, removing the central seeds or pit. Set each wedge peel side down and slide the knife down the length to cut the flesh off the peel.
For fans: follow pear technique.

Melon
For slices: follow papaya technique.
For balls: Use a melon baller.

Mangoes
Cut the peeled flesh into slices or cubes, according to recipe directions.

Pineapple
For spears: cut the peeled fruit lengthwise in half and then into quarters. Cut each quarter into spears and cut out the core.
For chunks: cut the peeled fruit into spears. Remove the core. Cut across each spear into chunks.
For rings: cut the peeled fruit across into slices. Stamp out the central core from each slice using a pastry cutter.

Kiwi, star fruit (carambola)
Cut the fruit across into neat slices; discard the ends.

Banana
Cut the fruit across into neat slices. Or cut in half and then lengthwise into quarters.

Gelatin

DISSOLVING GELATIN

It's important to dissolve gelatin correctly, or it can spoil the texture and set of your finished dessert.

1 Place 3 tablespoons of very hot water per envelope of gelatin in a small bowl.

2 Sprinkle the gelatin on the liquid. Always add the gelatin to the liquid, never the other way around.

3 Stir briskly until the gelatin is completely dissolved. There should be no visible crystals and the liquid should be clear. If necessary, stand the container in a pan of hot water over low heat until dissolved. Do not let the gelatin boil.

VEGETARIAN ALTERNATIVE

There is a vegetarian alternative to gelatin, which can be used in the appropriate recipes, if desired. Follow the instructions on the envelope, but in general you should sprinkle the alternative onto cold liquid and stir until completely dissolved. Next, heat the mixture to near boiling. (If setting proves difficult, add more of the gelatin alternative to the mixture and reheat.) It is now ready to be used as specified in the recipe, but should be allowed to set for about 1 hour or until firm and should always be allowed to cool.

Red Currant and Raspberry Coulis

A dessert sauce for the height of summer to serve with light meringues and fruit sorbets. Make it particularly pretty with a decoration of fresh flowers and leaves.

INGREDIENTS

Serves 6

2 cups red currants

2⅔ cups raspberries

½ cup confectioners' sugar

1 tablespoon cornstarch

juice of 1 orange

2 tablespoons heavy cream, to decorate

1 Strip the red currants from their stems using a fork. Place in a food processor or blender with the raspberries and sugar, and purée until it it smooth.

2 Press the mixture through a fine sieve into a bowl and discard the seeds and pulp.

3 Blend the cornstarch with the orange juice, then stir into the fruit purée. Transfer to a saucepan and bring to a boil, stirring continuously, and cook for 1–2 minutes, until smooth and thick. Set aside until cold.

4 Spoon the sauce onto each plate. Drip the cream from a teaspoon to make small dots evenly around the edge. Draw a toothpick through the dots to form heart shapes. Place the meringue or scoop sorbet into the middle and decorate with flowers.

Crème Anglaise

Here is the classic English custard, light, creamy and delicious—far superior to packaged versions. Serve hot or cold.

INGREDIENTS

Serves 4

1 vanilla bean

1⅞ cups milk

3 tablespoons sugar

4 egg yolks

1 Split the vanilla bean and place in a saucepan with the milk. Bring slowly to a boil. Remove from heat, then cover and infuse for 10 minutes before removing the bean.

2 Beat together the sugar and egg yolks until thick, light and creamy.

3 Slowly pour the warm, infused milk onto the egg mixture, stirring constantly.

4 Transfer to the top of a double boiler or place the bowl over a saucepan of hot water. Stir constantly over low heat for 10 minutes or until the mixture coats the back of the spoon. Remove from heat immediately, as curdling will occur if the custard is allowed to simmer.

5 Strain the custard into a bowl if serving hot or, if serving cold, strain into a bowl and cover the surface with buttered paper or plastic wrap.

VARIATION

Infuse a few strips of thinly pared lemon or orange zest with the milk, instead of the vanilla bean.

Sabayon

Serve this frothy sauce hot or chill and serve just as it is with cookies or whatever you prefer. Never let it stand for any length of time, as it will collapse.

INGREDIENTS

Serves 4–6

1 egg

2 egg yolks

⅔ cup sugar

⅔ cups sweet white wine

finely grated zest and juice of 1 lemon

1 Whisk the egg, yolks and sugar until they are pale and thick.

2 Stand the bowl over a saucepan of hot—not boiling—water. Add the wine and lemon juice, a little at a time, whisking vigorously and constantly.

3 Continue whisking until the mixture is thick enough to leave a trail. Whisk in the lemon zest. If serving hot serve immediately.

4 To serve cold, place over a bowl of ice water and whisk until chilled. Pour into small glasses and serve immediately.

Butterscotch Sauce

A deliciously sweet sauce that will be loved by adults and children alike! Serve with ice cream or with pancakes or waffles.

INGREDIENTS

Serves 4–6

6 tablespoons butter
¾ cup dark brown sugar
¾ cup evaporated milk
½ cup hazelnuts

1 Melt the butter and sugar in a heavy pan, bring to a boil and boil for 2 minutes. Cool for 5 minutes.

2 Heat the evaporated milk to just below the boiling point, then gradually stir into the sugar mixture. Cook over low heat for 2 minutes, stirring frequently.

3 Spread the hazelnuts on a baking sheet and toast under a hot broiler.

4 Put the nuts on a clean dish towel and rub them briskly to remove the skins.

5 Chop the nuts roughly and stir into the sauce. Serve hot, poured onto scoops of vanilla ice cream, or warm waffles or pancakes.

Brandy Butter

This is traditionally served with Christmas pudding and mince pies but a good spoonful on a hot baked apple is equally delicious.

INGREDIENTS

Serves 6

½ cup butter
½ cup confectioners' or light brown sugar
3 tablespoons brandy

1 Cream the butter until very pale and soft, then beat in the sugar gradually until mixed.

2 Add the brandy, a few drops at a time, beating continuously. Add enough for a good flavor but be sure it does not curdle.

3 Pile into a small serving dish and let harden. Alternatively, spread onto aluminum foil and chill until firm. Cut into shapes with small fancy cutters.

VARIATION

Cumberland Rum Butter
Use light brown sugar and rum instead of brandy. Grate the zest of 1 orange and beat in with the sugar, adding a good pinch of allspice.

Chocolate Fudge Sauce

A real treat if you're not counting calories. Fabulous with scoops of vanilla ice cream.

INGREDIENTS

Serves 6

⅔ cup heavy cream

4 tablespoons butter

¼ cup sugar

6 ounces semi-sweet chocolate

2 tablespoons brandy

VARIATIONS

White Chocolate and Orange Sauce:

3 tablespoons sugar, to replace
  ¼ cup sugar

6 ounces white chocolate, to replace semi-sweet chocolate

2 tablespoons orange liqueur, to replace brandy

finely grated zest of 1 orange

Coffee Chocolate Fudge:

¼ cup light brown sugar, to replace sugar

2 tablespoons coffee liqueur or dark rum, to replace brandy

1 tablespoon coffee extract

1 Heat the cream with the butter and sugar in the top of a double boiler or in a heatproof bowl over a saucepan of hot water. Stir until smooth, then cool.

2 Break the chocolate into the cream. Stir until it is melted and thoroughly combined.

3 Stir in the brandy a little at a time, then cool to room temperature.

4 For the White Chocolate and Orange Sauce, heat the cream and butter with the sugar and orange zest in the top of a double boiler, until dissolved. Then, follow the recipe to the end, but using white chocolate and orange liqueur instead.

5 For the Coffee Chocolate Fudge, follow the recipe, using light brown sugar and coffee liqueur or rum. Stir in the coffee extract at the end.

6 Serve the sauce over cream-filled profiteroles, and serve any that is left over separately.

Glossy Chocolate Sauce

Delicious poured onto ice cream or on hot or cold desserts, this sauce also freezes well. Pour into a freezer-proof container, seal, and keep for up to three months. Thaw at room temperature.

INGREDIENTS

Serves 6

½ cup sugar

6 ounces semi-sweet chocolate, broken into squares

2 tablespoons unsalted butter

2 tablespoons brandy or orange juice

1 Place the sugar and 4 tablespoons of water in a saucepan and heat gently, stirring occasionally, until the sugar has dissolved.

2 Stir in the chocolate, a few squares at a time, until melted, then add the butter in the same way. Do not let the sauce boil. Stir in the brandy or orange juice and serve warm.

Hot Desserts

✦✦✦

Warm Lemon Syrup Cake

The combination of pears and lemon syrup makes this a real winner. Drizzle with light cream for extra richness.

INGREDIENTS

Serves 8

3 eggs

¾ cup butter, softened

¾ cup sugar

1½ cups self-rising flour

½ cup ground almonds

¼ teaspoon freshly grated nutmeg

5 tablespoons candied lemon peel, finely chopped

grated zest of 1 lemon

2 tablespoons lemon juice

poached pears, to serve

For the syrup

¾ cup sugar

juice of 3 lemons

1 Preheat the oven to 350°F. Grease and bottom-line a deep, round 8-inch cake pan.

2 Place all the cake ingredients in a large bowl and beat well for 2–3 minutes, until the mixture is light and fluffy.

3 Put the batter into the prepared pan, spread level and bake for 1 hour or until golden and firm to the touch.

4 Meanwhile, make the syrup. Put the sugar, lemon juice and 5 tablespoons water in a pan. Heat gently, stirring until the sugar has dissolved, then boil, without stirring, for 1–2 minutes.

5 Turn out the cake onto a plate with a rim. Prick the surface of the cake all over with a fork, then pour on the hot syrup. Let soak for about 30 minutes. Serve the cake warm with thin wedges of poached pears.

Chocolate and Orange Pancakes

Fabulous baby pancakes in a rich creamy orange liqueur sauce.

INGREDIENTS

Serves 4

1 cup self-rising flour

2 tablespoons unsweetened cocoa powder

2 eggs

2 ounces semi-sweet chocolate, broken into squares

⅞ cup milk

finely grated zest of 1 orange

2 tablespoons orange juice

butter or oil for frying

4 tablespoons chocolate curls, for sprinkling

For the sauce

2 large oranges

2 tablespoons unsalted butter

3 tablespoons light brown sugar

1 cup crème fraîche

2 tablespoons Grand Marnier or Cointreau

chocolate curls, to decorate

1 Sift the flour and cocoa into a bowl and make a well in the center. Add the eggs and beat well, gradually incorporating the surrounding dry ingredients to make a smooth batter.

2 Mix the chocolate and milk in a saucepan. Heat gently until the chocolate has melted, then beat into the batter until smooth and bubbly. Stir in the grated orange zest and juice.

3 Heat a large heavy frying pan or griddle. Grease with a little butter or oil. Drop large spoonfuls of batter onto the hot surface. Cook over medium heat. When the pancakes are lightly browned underneath and bubbly on top, flip them over to cook the other side. Slide onto a plate and keep hot, then make more in the same way.

4 Make the sauce. Grate the zest of 1 of the oranges into a bowl and set aside. Peel both oranges, being careful to remove all the pith, then slice the flesh fairly thinly.

5 Heat the butter and sugar in a wide, shallow pan over low heat, stirring until the sugar dissolves. Stir in the crème fraîche and heat gently.

6 Add the pancakes and orange slices to the sauce, heat gently for 1–2 minutes, then spoon on the liqueur. Sprinkle with the reserved orange zest. Sprinkle on the chocolate curls and serve the pancakes immediately.

Gingerbread Upside-down Cake

Gingerbread is a big hit on a cold winter's day. This one is quite quick and easy to make and looks very impressive.

INGREDIENTS

Serves 4–6

sunflower oil, for brushing

1 tablespoon brown sugar

4 medium peaches, halved and pitted, or canned peach halves

8 walnut halves

For the base

generous 1 cup whole-wheat flour

½ teaspoon baking soda

1½ teaspoons ground ginger

1 teaspoon ground cinnamon

½ cup dark brown sugar

1 egg

½ cup skim milk

¼ cup sunflower oil

1 Preheat the oven to 350°F. For the topping, brush the bottom and sides of a 9-inch round spring-form cake pan with oil. Sprinkle the sugar on the bottom.

2 Arrange the peaches cut-side down in the pan with a walnut half in each.

3 Sift together the flour, baking soda, ginger and cinnamon, then stir in the sugar. Beat together the egg, milk and oil, then mix into the dry ingredients.

4 Pour the batter evenly on the peaches and bake for 35–40 minutes, until firm to the touch. Turn out and serve hot.

Rhubarb-Strawberry Crisp

Strawberries, cinnamon and ground almonds make this a luxurious and delicious version of rhubarb crisp.

INGREDIENTS

Serves 4

8 ounces strawberries, hulled

1 pound rhubarb, diced

½ cup sugar

1 tablespoon cornstarch

⅓ cup fresh orange juice

1 cup all-purpose flour

1 cup rolled oats

½ cup light brown sugar,
    firmly packed

½ teaspoon ground cinnamon

½ cup ground almonds

generous ½ cup cold butter

1 egg, lightly beaten

1 If the strawberries are large, cut them in half. Combine the strawberries, rhubarb and sugar in a 10-cup baking dish. Preheat the oven to 350°F.

2 In a small bowl, blend the cornstarch with the orange juice. Pour this mixture onto the fruit and stir gently to coat. Set the baking dish aside while making the topping.

3 In a bowl, toss together the flour, oats, brown sugar, cinnamon and ground almonds. With a pastry blender or two knives, cut in the butter until the mixture resembles coarse bread crumbs. Stir in the beaten egg.

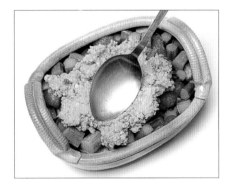

4 Spoon the oat mixture evenly on the fruit and press down gently. Bake until browned, 50–60 minutes, then serve warm.

Baked Apples with Caramel Sauce

The creamy caramel sauce turns this simple country dessert into a more sophisticated delicacy.

INGREDIENTS

Serves 6

3 Granny Smith apples, cored but
   not peeled
3 Red Delicious apples, cored but
   not peeled
¾ cup light brown sugar
½ teaspoon grated nutmeg
¼ teaspoon freshly ground black pepper
¼ cup walnut pieces
scant ¼ cup golden raisins
¼ cup butter or
   margarine, diced

For the caramel sauce
1 tablespoon butter or margarine
½ cup whipping cream

1 Preheat the oven to 375°F. Grease a baking dish just large enough to hold the apples.

2 With a small knife, cut at an angle to enlarge the core opening at the stem-end of each apple to about 1 inch in diameter. (The opening should resemble a funnel in shape.)

3 Arrange the apples in the prepared dish, stem-end up.

4 In a small saucepan, combine ¾ cup of water with the brown sugar, nutmeg and pepper. Bring the mixture to a boil, stirring. Boil for 6 minutes.

5 Mix the walnuts and golden raisins. Spoon some of this mixture into the opening in each apple.

6 Top each apple with some of the diced butter or margarine.

7 Spoon the brown sugar sauce over and around the apples. Bake, basting occasionally with the sauce, until the apples are just tender, 45–50 minutes. Transfer the apples to a serving dish, reserving the brown sugar sauce in the baking dish. Keep the apples warm.

8 For the caramel sauce, mix the butter or margarine, cream and reserved brown sugar sauce in a saucepan. Bring to a boil, stirring occasionally, and simmer until thickened, about 2 minutes. Let the sauce cool slightly before serving.

VARIATION

Use a mixture of firm red and gold pears instead of the apples, preparing them in the same way. Cook for 10 extra minutes.

British Cabinet Pudding

A rich, baked custard, flavored with candied and dried fruit.

INGREDIENTS

Serves 4

2½ tablespoons raisins, chopped

2 tablespoons brandy (optional)

2½ tablespoons candied
   cherries, halved

2½ tablespoons angelica, chopped

2 sponge cakes, diced

2 ounces macaroons, crushed

2 eggs

2 egg yolks

2 tablespoons sugar

1⅞ cups light cream or milk

few drops of vanilla extract

1 Soak the raisins in the brandy, if using, for several hours.

2 Butter a 3-cup charlotte mold and arrange some of the cherries and angelica in the bottom.

3 Mix the remaining cherries and angelica with the sponge cake, macaroons and raisins and brandy, if using, and spoon into the mold.

4 Lightly whisk together the eggs, egg yolks and sugar. Bring the cream or milk just to a boil, then stir into the egg mixture with the vanilla.

5 Strain the egg mixture into the mold, then let sit for 15–30 minutes.

6 Preheat the oven to 325°F. Place the mold in a roasting pan, cover with baking parchment and pour in boiling water to come halfway up the side of the mold. Bake for 1 hour or until set. Let sit for 2–3 minutes, then turn out onto a warm plate, to serve.

Eve's Dessert

The tempting apples beneath the sponge cake topping are the reason for this dessert's name.

INGREDIENTS

Serves 4–6

½ cup butter

generous ½ cup sugar

2 eggs, beaten

grated zest and juice of 1 lemon

scant 1 cup self-rising flour

⅓ cup ground almonds

scant ½ cup brown sugar

1½ pounds apples, cored and thinly sliced

¼ cup sliced almonds

1 Beat together the butter and sugar in a large mixing bowl until the mixture is very light and fluffy.

2 Gradually beat the eggs into the butter mixture, beating well after each addition, then fold in the lemon zest, flour and ground almonds.

3 Mix the brown sugar, apples and lemon juice, put in the dish, add the batter, then the sliced almonds. Bake for 40–45 minutes, until golden.

Chocolate Crêpes with Plums and Port

A good dinner party dessert, this dish can be made in advance and always looks impressive.

INGREDIENTS

Serves 6

2 ounces semi-sweet chocolate,
   broken into squares
⅞ cup milk
½ cup light cream
2 tablespoons unsweetened cocoa powder
1 cup all-purpose flour
2 eggs

For the filling

1¼ pounds red or golden plums
¼ cup sugar
2 tablespoons port
oil, for frying
¾ cup crème fraîche

For the sauce

5 ounces semi-sweet chocolate,
   broken into squares
¾ cup heavy cream
2 tablespoons port

1 Place the chocolate in a saucepan with the milk. Heat gently until the chocolate has dissolved. Pour into a blender or food processor and add the cream, cocoa powder, flour and eggs. Process until smooth, then put in a bowl and chill for 30 minutes.

2 Meanwhile, make the filling. Halve and pit the plums. Place them in a saucepan and add the sugar and 2 tablespoons of water. Bring to a boil, then lower the heat, cover, and simmer for about 10 minutes or until the plums are tender. Stir in the port and simmer for another 30 seconds. Remove the pan from heat and keep warm.

3 Have ready a sheet of nonstick baking parchment. Heat a crêpe pan, grease it lightly with a little oil, then pour in just enough batter to cover the bottom of the pan, swirling to coat it evenly.

4 Cook until the crêpe has set, then flip it over to cook the other side. Slide the crêpe out onto the sheet of paper, then cook 9–11 more crêpes in the same way.

5 Make the sauce. Combine the chocolate and cream in a saucepan. Heat gently, stirring until smooth. Add the port and heat gently, stirring, for 1 minute.

6 Divide the plum filling between the crêpes, add a dollop of crème fraîche to each and roll them up carefully. Serve in shallow plates, with the chocolate sauce spooned on top.

Pears in Chocolate Fudge Blankets

Warm poached pears coated in a rich chocolate fudge sauce—who could resist?

Serves 6

6 ripe pears

2 tablespoons lemon juice

scant ½ cup sugar

1 cinnamon stick

For the sauce

⅞ cup heavy cream

scant 1 cup light brown sugar

2 tablespoons unsalted butter

4 tablespoons golden or light corn syrup

½ cup milk

7 ounces dark chocolate, broken
  into squares

1 Peel the pears thinly, leaving the stems on. Scoop out the cores from the bottom. Brush the cut surfaces with lemon juice to prevent browning.

2 Place the sugar and 1¼ cups of water in a large saucepan. Heat gently until the sugar dissolves. Add the pears and cinnamon stick with any remaining lemon juice, and, if necessary, a little more water, so that the pears are almost covered.

3 Bring to a boil, then lower the heat, cover the pan and simmer the pears gently for 15–20 minutes.

4 Meanwhile, make the sauce. Place the cream, sugar, butter, golden or light corn syrup and milk in a heavy saucepan. Heat gently until the sugar has dissolved and the butter and syrup have melted, then bring to a boil. Boil, stirring constantly, for about 5 minutes or until thick and smooth.

5 Remove the pan from heat and stir in the chocolate until it has melted.

6 Using a slotted spoon, transfer the poached pears to a dish. Keep hot. Boil the syrup rapidly to reduce to about 3–4 tablespoons. Remove the cinnamon stick and gently stir the syrup into the chocolate sauce.

7 Serve the pears in individual bowls or on dessert plates, with the hot chocolate fudge sauce spooned on top.

Sticky Toffee Pudding

Filling, warming and packed with calories, but still the classic British dessert.

INGREDIENTS

Serves 6

1 cup toasted walnuts, chopped

¾ cup butter

scant 1 cup brown sugar

¼ cup light cream

2 tablespoons lemon juice

2 eggs, beaten

1 cup self-rising flour

1 Grease a 3¾-cup pudding mold and add half the walnuts.

2 Heat 4 tablespoons of the butter with 4 tablespoons of the sugar, the cream and 1 tablespoon lemon juice in a small pan, stirring until smooth. Pour half into the pudding mold, then swirl to coat it a little way up the sides.

3 Beat the remaining butter and sugar until light and fluffy, then gradually beat in the eggs. Fold in the flour and the remaining nuts and lemon juice and spoon into the bowl.

4 Cover the bowl with waxed paper with a pleat folded in the center, then tie securely with string.

5 Steam the pudding for about 1¼ hours, until it is set in the center.

6 Just before serving, gently warm the remaining sauce. Unmold the pudding onto a warm plate and pour on the warm sauce.

Chocolate and Orange Soufflé

The base of this soufflé is an easy-to-make semolina mixture, rather than the thick white sauce that most soufflés call for.

INGREDIENTS

Serves 4

2½ cups milk

generous ⅓ cup semolina

scant ¼ cup brown sugar

grated zest of 1 orange

6 tablespoons fresh orange juice

3 eggs, separated

2½ ounces semi-sweet chocolate, grated

confectioners' sugar, for sprinkling

1 Preheat the oven to 400°F. Butter a shallow 7½-cup ovenproof dish.

2 Pour the milk into a heavy saucepan and sprinkle on the semolina and brown sugar. Bring to a boil, stirring the mixture constantly, until thickened.

3 Remove the pan from heat, beat in the orange zest and juice, egg yolks and all but 1 tablespoon of the grated chocolate.

4 Whisk the egg whites until stiff, then lightly fold into the semolina mixture in three batches. Spoon into the buttered dish and bake for about 30 minutes, until just set in the center. Sprinkle with the reserved chocolate and the confectioners' sugar.

Queen of Puddings

This hot pudding was developed from a seventeenth-century recipe by Queen Victoria's chefs and named in her honor.

INGREDIENTS

Serves 4

1½ cups fresh bread crumbs

4 tablespoons sugar, plus 1 teaspoon

grated zest of 1 lemon

2½ cups milk

4 eggs

3 tablespoons raspberry jam, warmed

1 Preheat the oven to 325°F. Stir the bread crumbs, 2 tablespoons of the sugar and the lemon zest together in a bowl. Bring the milk to a boil in a saucepan, then stir into the bread crumb mixture.

2 Separate three of the eggs and beat the yolks with the whole egg. Stir into the bread crumb mixture, pour into a buttered baking dish and let stand for 30 minutes, then bake the pudding for 50–60 minutes, until set.

3 Whisk the three egg whites in a large, clean bowl until stiff but not dry, then gradually whisk in the remaining 2 tablespoons sugar, until the mixture is thick and glossy, being careful not to overwhip.

4 Spread the jam onto the pudding, then spoon on the meringue to cover the top completely. Sprinkle the remaining sugar on the meringue, then bake for another 15 minutes, until the meringue is beginning to turn a light golden color.

COOK'S TIP

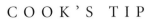

Use another flavored jam, lemon curd, marmalade or fruit purée.

Magic Chocolate Mud Cake

A popular favorite, which magically separates into a light and luscious cake and a velvety chocolate sauce.

Serves 4

¼ cup butter

generous 1 cup light brown sugar

2 cups milk

scant 1 cup self-rising flour

1 teaspoon ground cinnamon

5 tablespoons unsweetened cocoa powder

plain yogurt or vanilla ice cream,
   to serve

1 Preheat the oven to 350°F. Lightly grease a 6-cup ovenproof dish and place on a baking sheet.

2 Place the butter in a saucepan. Add ¾ cup of the sugar and ⅔ cup of the milk. Heat gently, stirring occasionally, until the butter has melted and all the sugar has dissolved. Remove the pan from heat.

COOK'S TIP

A soufflé dish will support the sponge as it rises above the sauce.

3 Sift the flour, cinnamon and 1 tablespoon of the cocoa powder into the pan and stir into the mixture, mixing evenly. Pour the mixture into the prepared dish and level the surface.

4 Sift the remaining sugar and cocoa powder into a bowl, mix well, then sprinkle on the pudding mixture.

5 Pour the remaining milk onto the pudding.

6 Bake for 45–50 minutes or until the sponge has risen to the top and is firm to the touch. Serve hot, with the yogurt or vanilla ice cream.

Christmas Pudding

*This recipe makes enough to fill one
5-cup basin or two 2½-cup basins. It
can be made up to a month before
Christmas and stored in a cool, dry
place. Steam the pudding for 2 hours
before serving. Serve with brandy or
rum butter, whiskey sauce, custard
or whipped cream, topped with a
decorative sprig of holly.*

INGREDIENTS

Serves 8

½ cup butter

1 heaping cup dark brown sugar

½ cup self-rising flour

1 teaspoon ground allspice

¼ teaspoon grated nutmeg

½ teaspoon ground cinnamon

2 eggs

2 cups fresh white bread crumbs

generous 1 cup golden raisins

generous 1 cup raisins

½ cup currants

3 tablespoons mixed candied peel,
    chopped finely

¼ cup chopped almonds

1 small apple, peeled, cored and
    coarsely grated

finely grated zest or 1 orange
    or lemon

juice of 1 orange or lemon,
    made up to ⅔ cup with brandy,
    rum or sherry

1 Cut a disk of waxed paper to fit
the bottom of the basin(s) and
butter the disk and basin(s).

2 Whisk the butter and sugar
together until soft. Beat in the
flour, spices and eggs. Stir in the
remaining ingredients thoroughly.
The mixture should have a soft
dropping consistency.

3 Turn the mixture into the
greased basin(s) and level the
top with a spoon.

4 Cover with another disk of
buttered waxed paper.

5 Make a pleat across the center
of a large piece of waxed paper
and cover the basin(s) with it,
tying it in place with string under
the rim. Cut off the excess paper.
Pleat a piece of aluminum foil in
the same way and cover the
basin(s) with it, tucking it around
the bowl neatly, under the waxed
frill. Tie another piece of string
around and across the top, as
a handle.

6 Place the basin(s) in a steamer
over a pan of simmering water
and steam for 6 hours.
Alternatively, put the basin(s) into
a large pan and pour in enough
boiling water to come halfway up
the basin(s) and cover the pan
with a tight-fitting lid. Check that
the water is simmering and add
boiling water as it evaporates.
When the pudding(s) have cooked,
let cool completely. Then remove
the foil and waxed paper. Wipe the
basin(s) clean and replace the
waxed paper and foil with clean
pieces, ready for reheating.

TO SERVE

Steam for 2 hours. Turn onto
a plate and let stand for 5 minutes,
before removing the pudding
basin (the steam will rise to the
top of the basin and help to loosen
the pudding). Decorate with a
sprig of holly.

Steamed Chocolate and Fruit Puddings

Some things always turn out well, including these wonderful little puddings. Dark, fluffy chocolate cake with tangy cranberries and apple is served with a honeyed chocolate syrup.

INGREDIENTS

Serves 4

⅔ cup dark brown sugar

1 apple

¾ cup cranberries, thawed if frozen

½ cup soft margarine

2 eggs

⅔ cup all-purpose flour

½ teaspoon baking powder

3 tablespoons unsweetened cocoa powder

For the chocolate syrup

4 ounces semi-sweet chocolate, broken into squares

2 tablespoons honey

1 tablespoon unsalted butter

½ teaspoon vanilla extract

1 Prepare a steamer or half fill a saucepan with water and bring it to a boil. Grease four individual pudding molds and sprinkle each one with a little of the brown sugar to coat well all over.

2 Peel and core the apple. Dice it into a bowl, add the cranberries and mix well. Divide equally among the prepared pudding molds.

3 Place the remaining brown sugar in a mixing bowl. Add the margarine, eggs, flour, baking powder and cocoa; beat until combined and smooth.

4 Spoon the mixture into the molds and cover each with a double thickness of aluminum foil. Steam for about 45 minutes, adding boiling water as needed, until the puddings are well risen and firm.

5 Make the syrup. Mix the chocolate, honey, butter and vanilla in a small saucepan. Heat gently, stirring, until melted and smooth.

6 Run a knife around the edge of each pudding to loosen it, then turn out onto individual plates. Serve immediately, with the chocolate syrup.

COOK'S TIP

The puddings can be cooked very quickly in the microwave. Use nonmetallic basins and cover with waxed paper instead of aluminum foil. Cook on High (100% power) for 5–6 minutes, then stand for 2–3 minutes before turning out.

Hot Chocolate Cake

This is wonderfully good served with a white chocolate sauce. The basic cake freezes well—thaw, then warm in the microwave before serving.

Makes 10–12 slices

1¾ cups self-rising whole-wheat flour

¼ cup unsweetened cocoa powder

pinch of salt

¾ cup soft margarine

¾ cup light brown sugar

few drops vanilla extract

4 eggs

3 ounces white chocolate,
    roughly chopped

chocolate leaves and curls, to decorate

For the white chocolate sauce

3 ounces white chocolate

⅔ cup light cream

2–3 tablespoons milk

1 Preheat the oven to 325°F. Sift the flour, cocoa powder and salt into a bowl, adding in the whole wheat flakes from the sieve.

2 Cream the margarine, sugar and vanilla extract together until light and fluffy, then gently beat in one egg.

3 Gradually stir in the remaining eggs, one at a time, alternately folding in some of the flour, until the mixture is blended in.

4 Stir in the white chocolate and spoon into a 1½–2-pound loaf pan or a 7-inch greased cake pan. Bake for 30–40 minutes or until just firm to the touch and shrinking away from the sides of the pan.

5 Meanwhile, prepare the sauce. Heat the white chocolate and cream very gently in a pan until the chocolate is melted. Add the milk and stir until cool.

6 Serve the cake sliced, in a pool of sauce and decorated with chocolate leaves and curls.

Bread Pudding with Pecans

A version of the British classic deliciously flavored with pecans and orange zest.

INGREDIENTS

Serves 6

1⅔ cups milk

1⅔ cups light or whipping cream

¾ cup sugar

3 eggs, beaten to mix

2 teaspoons grated orange zest

1 teaspoon vanilla extract

24 slices of day-old French bread,
   ½ inch thick

½ cup toasted pecans, chopped

confectioners' sugar, for sprinkling

whipped cream or sour cream and
   maple syrup, to serve

1 Put 1½ cups each of the milk and cream in a saucepan. Add the sugar. Warm over low heat, stirring to dissolve the sugar. Remove from heat and cool. Add the eggs, orange zest and vanilla and mix well.

2 Arrange half of the bread slices in a buttered 9–10-inch baking dish. Sprinkle two-thirds of the pecans on the bread. Arrange the remaining bread slices on top and sprinkle on the rest of the pecans.

3 Pour the egg mixture evenly on the bread slices. Soak for 30 minutes. Press the top layer of bread down into the liquid once or twice.

4 Preheat the oven to 350°F. If the top layer of bread slices looks dry and all the liquid has been absorbed, moisten with the remaining milk and cream.

5 Set the baking dish in a roasting pan. Add enough water to the pan to come halfway up the sides of the dish. Bring the water to a boil.

6 Transfer to the oven. Bake for 40 minutes or until the pudding is set and golden brown on top. Sprinkle the top of the pudding with sifted confectioners' sugar and serve warm, with whipped cream or sour cream and maple syrup, if desired.

Chocolate Chip and Banana Pudding

Hot and steamy, this superb light pudding tastes extra special served with chocolate sauce.

INGREDIENTS

Serves 4

1¾ cups self-rising flour

6 tablespoons unsalted butter
   or margarine

2 ripe bananas

⅓ cup sugar

¼ cup milk

1 egg, beaten

¼ cup semi-sweet chocolate chips or
   chopped chocolate

Glossy Chocolate Sauce (see Basic
   Techniques) and whipped cream, to serve

1 Prepare a steamer or half fill a saucepan with water and bring it to a boil. Grease a 4-cup pudding mold. Sift the flour into a bowl and rub in the butter or margarine until the mixture resembles bread crumbs.

2 Mash the bananas in a bowl. Stir them into the creamed mixture, with the sugar.

3 Whisk the milk with the egg in a bowl, then beat into the pudding batter. Stir in the semi-sweet chocolate chips or chopped chocolate.

4 Spoon the mixture into the prepared mold, cover closely with a double thickness of aluminum foil, and steam for 2 hours, adding water as needed during cooking.

5 Run a knife around the top of the pudding to loosen it, then turn it out onto a warm serving dish. Serve hot, with the chocolate sauce and a spoonful of whipped cream.

COOK'S TIP

If you have a food processor, make a quick-mix version by processing all the ingredients, except the chocolate, until smooth. Stir in the chocolate and proceed as in the recipe.

Hot Plum Pudding

Other fruits can be used instead of plums, depending on the season. Canned black cherries are a convenient substitute to keep on hand.

Serves 4

1 pound ripe red plums,
    quartered and pitted

⅞ cup skim milk

¼ cup nonfat dry milk

1 tablespoon light brown sugar

1 teaspoon vanilla extract

⅔ cup self-rising flour

2 egg whites

confectioners' sugar, to sprinkle

1 Preheat the oven to 425°F. Lightly oil a wide, shallow ovenproof dish and add the plums.

2 Pour the milk, milk powder, sugar, vanilla, flour and egg whites into a blender or food processor. Process until smooth.

3 Pour the batter onto the plums. Bake for 25–30 minutes or until puffed and golden. Sprinkle with confectioners' sugar and serve immediately.

C O O K ' S   T I P

If you don't have a food processor, then place the dry ingredients for the batter in a large bowl and gradually whisk in the milk and egg whites.

Glazed Apricot Cake

Desserts can be very high in saturated fat, but this healthy cake uses a minimum of oil and no eggs.

Serves 4

2 teaspoons golden or light corn syrup

14½-ounce can apricot halves in fruit juice

1¼ cups self-rising flour

1½ cups fresh bread crumbs

½ cup light brown sugar

1 teaspoon ground cinnamon

2 tablespoons sunflower oil

¾ cup skim milk

1 Preheat the oven to 350°F. Lightly oil a 3¾-cup pudding mold. Spoon in the syrup.

2 Drain the apricots and reserve the juice. Arrange about 8 halves in the mold. Purée the rest of the apricots with the juice and set aside.

3 Mix the flour, bread crumbs, sugar and cinnamon, then beat in the oil and milk. Spoon into the basin and bake for 50–55 minutes or until firm and golden. Turn out and serve with the puréed fruit as an accompaniment.

Crunchy Gooseberry Crumble

Gooseberries are perfect for traditional family desserts like this one. When gooseberries are not available, other fruits, such as apples, plums or rhubarb, could be used instead.

INGREDIENTS

Serves 4

5 cups gooseberries

¼ cup sugar

scant 1 cup rolled oats

⅔ cup whole-wheat flour

¼ cup sunflower oil

¼ cup brown sugar

2 tablespoons chopped walnuts

plain yogurt or custard, to serve

1 Preheat the oven to 400°F. Place the gooseberries in a pan with the sugar. Cover the pan and cook over low heat for about 10 minutes, until the gooseberries are just tender. Put the contents of the pan into an ovenproof dish.

2 To make the crumble, place the oats, flour and oil in a bowl and stir with a fork until evenly mixed.

3 Stir in the brown sugar and walnuts, then spread evenly onto the gooseberries. Bake for 25–30 minutes, until golden and bubbling. Serve hot with yogurt, or custard made with skim milk.

COOK'S TIP

The best gooseberries to use for cooking are the early, small, firm green ones.

Chocolate Amaretti Peaches

Quick and easy to prepare, this delicious dessert can also be made with fresh nectarines or apricots.

INGREDIENTS

Serves 4

4 ounces amaretti cookies, crushed

2 ounces semi-sweet chocolate, chopped

grated zest of ½ orange

1 tablespoon honey

¼ teaspoon ground cinnamon

1 egg white, lightly beaten

4 firm ripe peaches

⅔ cup white wine

1 tablespoon sugar

whipped cream, to serve

1 Preheat the oven to 375°F. Mix the crushed amaretti cookies, chocolate, orange zest, honey and cinnamon in a bowl. Add the beaten egg white and mix to bind the mixture together.

2 Halve and pit the peaches and fill the cavities with the chocolate mixture, mounding it up slightly.

3 Arrange the stuffed peaches in a lightly buttered, shallow ovenproof dish that will just hold the peaches comfortably. Pour the wine into a measuring cup and stir in the sugar.

4 Pour the wine mixture around the peaches. Bake for 30–40 minutes, until the peaches are tender. Serve immediately with a little of the cooking juices spooned on and the whipped cream.

Apple Fritters

Make sure you buy plenty of apples for this recipe. They taste so good you'll probably have to cook an extra batch.

INGREDIENTS

Serves 4–6

1⅓ cups all-purpose flour

2 teaspoons baking powder

¼ teaspoon salt

⅔ cup milk

1 egg, beaten

oil for deep-frying

¾ cup sugar

1 teaspoon ground cinnamon

2 large tart-sweet apples, peeled, cored, and cut in ¼-inch slices

confectioners' sugar, for dusting

1 Sift the flour, baking powder and salt into a bowl. Beat in the milk and egg with a wire whisk.

2 Heat at least 3 inches of oil in a heavy frying pan to 360°F or until a cube of bread browns in 1–2 minutes.

3 Mix the sugar and cinnamon in a shallow bowl or plate. Toss the apple slices in the sugar mixture to coat all over.

4 Dip the apple slices in the batter, using a fork or slotted spoon. Drain off excess batter. Fry, in batches, in the hot oil until golden brown on both sides, about 4–5 minutes. Drain the fritters on paper towels.

5 Sprinkle with confectioners' sugar, and serve hot.

Cherry Compote

Sweet cherries in syrup to serve with cream or ice cream.

INGREDIENTS

Serves 6

½ cup red wine

¼ cup light brown sugar, firmly packed

¼ cup sugar

1 tablespoon honey

1-inch strips of orange zest

¼ teaspoon almond extract

1½ pounds sweet fresh cherries, pitted

ice cream or whipped cream, for serving

1 Combine all the ingredients except the cherries in a saucepan with ½ cup of water. Stir over medium heat until the sugar dissolves. Raise the heat and boil until the liquid reduces slightly.

2 Add the cherries. Bring back to a boil. Reduce the heat slightly and simmer for 8–10 minutes. If necessary, skim off any foam.

3 Let cool to lukewarm. Spoon warm over vanilla ice cream, or refrigerate and serve cold with whipped cream, if desired.

Ginger Baked Pears

This simple French dessert is perfect to serve after Sunday lunch or a family supper. Try to find Comice or Anjou pears—this recipe is especially useful for slightly under-ripe fruit.

Serves 4

4 large pears
1¼ cups whipping cream
¼ cup sugar
½ teaspoon vanilla extract
¼ teaspoon ground cinnamon
pinch of freshly grated nutmeg
1 teaspoon grated fresh ginger root

1 Preheat the oven to 375°F. Lightly butter a large shallow baking dish.

2 Peel the pears, cut in half lengthwise and remove the cores. Arrange, cut-side down, in a single layer in the baking dish.

3 Mix the cream, sugar, vanilla, cinnamon, nutmeg and ginger and pour onto the pears.

4 Bake for 30–35 minutes, basting occasionally, until the pears are tender and browned on top and the cream is thick and bubbly. Cool slightly before serving.

Prunes Poached in Red Wine

Serve this simple dessert on its own, or with crème fraîche or vanilla ice cream.

Serves 8–10

1 unwaxed orange
1 unwaxed lemon
3 cups fruity red wine
¼ cup sugar, or to taste
1 cinnamon stick
pinch of freshly grated nutmeg
2 or 3 cloves
1 teaspoon black peppercorns
1 bay leaf
2 pounds large pitted prunes, soaked in cold water
strips of orange zest, to decorate
cream, to serve

1 Using a vegetable peeler, peel two or three strips of zest from both the orange and lemon. Squeeze the juice from both and put in a large saucepan.

2 Add the wine, sugar, spices, peppercorns, bay leaf, strips of zest to the pan and 2 cups of water.

3 Bring to a boil over medium heat, stirring occasionally to dissolve the sugar. Drain the prunes and add to the saucepan, reduce the heat to low and simmer, covered, for 10–15 minutes, until the prunes are tender. Remove from heat and set aside until cool.

4 Using a slotted spoon, transfer the prunes to a serving dish. Return the cooking liquid to medium-high heat and bring to a boil. Boil for 5–10 minutes, until slightly reduced and syrupy, then pour or strain over the prunes. Cool, then chill before serving with cream, decorated with strips of orange zest, if desired.

Apple Strudel

This Austrian dessert is traditionally made with paper-thin layers of buttered strudel pastry, filled with spiced apples and nuts. Ready-made phyllo pastry makes an easy substitute.

INGREDIENTS

Serves 4–6

¾ cup hazelnuts, chopped
    and roasted

2 tablespoons almonds,
    chopped and roasted

4 tablespoons sugar

½ teaspoon ground cinnamon

grated zest and juice of ½ lemon

2 large apples, peeled, cored and chopped

⅓ cup golden raisins

4 large sheets phyllo pastry

¼ cup unsalted butter, melted

confectioners' sugar, for dusting

cream, custard or yogurt, to serve

1 Preheat the oven to 375°F. In a bowl mix the hazelnuts, almonds, sugar, cinnamon, lemon zest and juice, apples and golden raisins. Set aside.

2 Lay one sheet of phyllo pastry on a clean dish towel and brush with melted butter. Lay a second sheet on top and brush again with melted butter. Repeat with the remaining two sheets.

3 Spread the fruit and nut mixture on the pastry, leaving a 3-inch border at the shorter ends. Fold the ends in over the filling. Roll up from one long edge, using the dish towel.

4 Transfer the strudel to a greased baking sheet, placing it seam-side down. Brush with butter and bake for 30–35 minutes, until golden and crisp. Dust with confectioners' sugar and serve hot with cream, custard or yogurt.

Chocolate Fruit Fondue

Fondues originated in Switzerland and this sweet treat is the perfect ending to any meal.

INGREDIENTS

Serves 6–8

16 fresh strawberries

4 rings fresh pineapple, cut into wedges

2 small nectarines, pitted and cut
    into wedges

1 kiwi, halved and thickly sliced

small bunch of black seedless grapes

2 bananas, chopped

1 small apple, cored and cut
    into wedges

lemon juice, for brushing

8 ounces semi-sweet chocolate

1 tablespoon butter

⅔ cup light cream

3 tablespoons Irish cream liqueur

1 tablespoon pistachios, chopped

1 Arrange the fruit on a serving platter and brush the banana and apple pieces with a little lemon juice. Cover and place in the refrigerator until ready to serve.

2 Place the chocolate, butter, cream and liqueur in a bowl over a pan of simmering water. Stir until melted and completely smooth.

3 Pour the mixture into a warmed serving bowl; sprinkle with pistachios. Guests help themselves by skewering fruits on forks and dipping in the hot sauce.

Crêpes Suzette

This is one of the best-known French desserts and is easy to make at home. You can make the crêpes in advance, then you will be able to put the dish together quickly at the last minute.

INGREDIENTS

Serves 6

1 cup all-purpose flour

¼ teaspoon salt

2 tablespoons sugar

2 eggs, lightly beaten

1 cup milk

2 tablespoons orange flower water or
  orange liqueur (optional)

2 tablespoons unsalted butter, melted,
  plus more for frying

For the orange sauce

6 tablespoons unsalted butter

¼ cup sugar

grated zest and juice of 1 large
  unwaxed orange

grated zest and juice of 1 unwaxed lemon

⅔ cup fresh orange juice

¼ cup orange liqueur, plus more for
  flaming (optional)

brandy, for flaming (optional)

orange segments, to decorate

1 In a medium bowl, sift together the flour, salt and sugar. Make a well in the center and pour in the beaten eggs. Using a whisk, beat the eggs, bringing in a little flour until it is all incorporated. Slowly whisk in the milk and 4 tablespoons water to make a smooth batter.

2 Whisk in the orange flower water or liqueur, if using, then strain the batter into a large bowl and set aside for 20–30 minutes. If the batter thickens, add a little milk or water to thin.

3 Heat a 7–8-inch crêpe pan over medium heat. Stir the melted butter into the crêpe batter. Brush the hot pan with a little extra melted butter and pour in about 2 tablespoons of batter. Quickly tilt and rotate the pan to cover the bottom with a thin layer of batter. Cook for about 1 minute until the top is set and the bottom is golden. With a spatula, carefully turn over the crêpe and cook for 20–30 seconds, just to set. Turn out onto a plate.

4 Continue cooking the crêpes, stirring the batter occasionally and brushing the pan with a little melted butter as and when necessary. Place a sheet of plastic wrap between each crêpe as they are stacked to prevent sticking.

5 To make the sauce, melt the butter in a large frying pan over medium-low heat, then stir in the sugar, orange and lemon zest and juice, the additional orange juice and the orange liqueur, if using.

6 Place a crêpe in the pan browned-side down, swirling gently to coat with the sauce. Fold it in half, then in half again to form a triangle and push to the side of the pan. Continue heating and folding the crêpes until all are warm and covered with the sauce.

7 To flame the crêpes, heat 2–3 tablespoons each of orange liqueur and brandy in a small saucepan over medium heat. Remove the pan from heat, carefully ignite the liquid with a match, then gently pour on the crêpes. Sprinkle on the orange segments and serve immediately.

Spiced Mexican Fritters

Hot, sweet and spicy fritters are popular in both Spain and Mexico for either breakfast or a snack.

INGREDIENTS

Makes 16 (serves 4)

1 cup raspberries

3 tablespoons confectioners' sugar

3 tablespoons orange juice

For the fritters

¼ cup butter

⅔ cup all-purpose flour, sifted

2 eggs, lightly beaten

1 tablespoon ground almonds

corn oil, for frying

1 tablespoon confectioners' sugar and
⅓ teaspoon ground cinnamon, for dusting

8 fresh raspberries, to decorate

1 Mash the raspberries with the confectioners' sugar, push through a sieve into a bowl to remove all the seeds. Stir in the orange juice and chill until ready to serve.

2 To make the fritters, place the butter and ⅔ cup water in a saucepan and heat gently until the butter has melted. Bring to a boil and, when boiling, add the sifted flour all at once and turn off the heat.

3 Beat until the mixture leaves the sides of the pan and forms a ball. Cool slightly, then beat in the eggs a little at a time, then add the almonds.

4 Spoon the mixture into a piping bag fitted with a large star nozzle. Half-fill a saucepan or deep-fat fryer with the oil and heat to 375°F.

5 Pipe about four 2-inch lengths at a time into the hot oil, cutting off the raw mixture with a knife as you go. Deep-fry for 3–4 minutes, turning occasionally, until puffed up and golden. Drain on paper towels and keep warm in the oven while frying the remainder.

6 When you have fried all the mixture, dust the hot fritters with confectioners' sugar and cinnamon. Serve three or four per person on serving plates drizzled with a little of the raspberry sauce, dust again with sieved confectioners' sugar and decorate with fresh raspberries.

Thai Fried Bananas

A very simple and quick Thai dessert—bananas fried in butter, brown sugar and lime juice, and sprinkled with toasted coconut.

INGREDIENTS

Serves 4

3 tablespoons butter

4 large slightly under-ripe bananas

1 tablespoon dry, shredded coconut

¼ cup light brown sugar

¼ cup lime juice

2 fresh lime slices, to decorate

thick and creamy yogurt, to serve

1 Heat the butter in a large frying pan or wok and fry the bananas for 1–2 minutes on each side or until they are lightly golden in color.

2 Meanwhile, dry-fry the coconut in a small frying pan until lightly browned, and reserve.

3 Sprinkle the sugar into the pan with the bananas, add the lime juice and cook, stirring until dissolved. Arrange bananas on a serving dish. Sprinkle the coconut on the bananas, decorate with lime slices and serve with the thick and creamy yogurt.

Apple and Lemon Risotto with Poached Plums

*Although it's entirely possible to
cook this by the conventional
risotto method—that is by adding
the liquid gradually—it makes
more sense to cook the rice with
the milk in the same way as for a
rice pudding.*

INGREDIENTS

Serves 4

1 cooking apple

1 tablespoon butter

scant 1 cup risotto rice

2½ cups creamy milk

¼ cup sugar

¼ teaspoon ground cinnamon

2 teaspoons lemon juice

3 tablespoons heavy cream

grated zest of 1 lemon, to decorate

For the poached plums

¼ cup light brown sugar

scant 1 cup apple juice

3 star anise

cinnamon stick

6 plums, halved and sliced

1 Peel and core the apple and cut
it into large chunks. Put the
chunks in a large, nonstick pan
and add the butter. Heat gently
until the butter melts.

2 Add the rice and milk and stir
well to mix. Bring to a boil
over medium heat, then simmer
very gently for 20–25 minutes,
stirring occasionally.

3 To make the poached plums,
dissolve the sugar in ⅔ cup
apple juice in a pan. Add the spices
and bring to a boil. Boil for
2 minutes. Add the plums and
simmer for 2 minutes. Set aside
until ready to serve.

4 Stir the sugar, cinnamon and
lemon juice into the risotto.
Cook for 2 minutes, stirring constantly, then stir in the cream. Taste
and add more sugar if necessary.
Decorate with the lemon zest and
serve hot with the poached plums.

Chocolate Risotto

If you've never tasted a sweet risotto, there's a treat in store for you: chocolate risotto is delectable.

Serves 4–6

scant 1 cup risotto rice

2½ cups milk

3 ounces semi-sweet chocolate, broken
into pieces

2 tablespoons butter

about ¼ cup sugar

pinch of ground cinnamon

4 tablespoons heavy cream

fresh raspberries and chocolate caraque,
to decorate

chocolate sauce, to serve

1 Put the rice in a nonstick pan. Pour in the milk and bring to a boil over low heat. Reduce the heat to the lowest setting and simmer for 20 minutes, stirring.

2 Stir in the chocolate, butter and sugar. Cook, stirring constantly over very low heat for 1–2 minutes, until the chocolate has melted.

3 Remove the pan from the heat and stir in the ground cinnamon and cream. Cover the pan and let stand for a few minutes.

4 Spoon the risotto into individual dishes or dessert plates, and decorate with fresh raspberries and chocolate caraque. Serve with chocolate sauce.

Caramel Rice Pudding

This rice pudding is delicious served with fresh fruit.

INGREDIENTS

Serves 4

1 tablespoon butter

¼ cup short-grain (pudding) rice

5 tablespoons sugar

14-ounce can evaporated milk made up to
    2½ cups with water

2 fresh baby pineapples

2 figs

1 apple

2 teaspoons lemon juice

salt

1 Preheat the oven to 300°F. Grease a soufflé dish lightly with a little of the butter. Put the rice in a sieve and wash it thoroughly under cold running water. Drain well and put into the soufflé dish.

2 Add 2 tablespoons of the sugar to the dish, with a pinch of salt. Pour on the diluted evaporated milk and stir gently.

3 Dot the surface of the rice with butter. Bake for 2 hours, then let cool for 30 minutes.

4 Meanwhile, quarter the pineapple and the figs. Cut the apple into segments and toss in the lemon juice. Preheat the broiler.

5 Sprinkle the remaining sugar evenly on the rice. Broil for 5 minutes or until the sugar has caramelized. Let the rice stand for 5 minutes to let the caramel harden, then serve warm with the fresh fruit.

Orange Rice Pudding

In Morocco, as in Spain, Greece and Italy, thick, creamy rice puddings are very popular, especially when sweetened with honey and flavored with orange.

INGREDIENTS

Serves 4

generous ¼ cup short-grain (pudding) rice

2½ cups milk

finely grated zest of ½ small orange

2–3 tablespoons honey

⅔ cup heavy cream

1 tablespoon chopped pistachios, toasted (optional)

grated orange zest, to garnish

1 Mix the rice with the milk and orange zest in a saucepan. Pour in the honey and stir well.

2 Bring to a boil, then lower the heat, cover and simmer very gently for about 1¼ hours, stirring frequently.

3 Remove the lid and continue cooking and stirring for 15–20 minutes, until the rice is creamy.

4 Pour in the cream, stirring constantly, then simmer for 5–8 more minutes. Spoon the rice pudding into warmed individual bowls. Sprinkle with the pistachios, if wished, garnish with the orange zest and serve hot.

Cold Desserts

◆ ◆ ◆

Boodles Orange Fool

This fool became the specialty of Boodles Club, a gentlemen's club in London's St. James's.

Serves 4

4 sponge cakes, cubed

1¼ cups heavy cream

2–4 tablespoons sugar

grated zest and juice of 2 oranges

grated zest and juice of 1 lemon

orange and lemon slices and zest,
    to decorate

1 Line the bottom and halfway up the sides of a large glass serving bowl or china dish with the cubed sponge cakes.

2 Whip the cream with the sugar until it starts to thicken, then gradually whip in the fruit juices, adding the fruit zests once most of the juices have been incorporated.

3 Carefully pour the cream mixture into the bowl or dish, taking care not to dislodge the sponge. Cover and chill for 3–4 hours. Serve decorated with orange and lemon slices and zest.

Apricot and Orange Gelatin

A light and refreshing dessert for a summer's day.

Serves 4

12 ounces well-flavored fresh ripe
    apricots, pitted

about ⅓ cup sugar

1¼ cups freshly squeezed orange juice

1 tablespoon powdered gelatin

light cream, to serve

finely chopped candied orange peel,
    to decorate

1 Heat the apricots, sugar and ½ cup of the orange juice, stirring until the sugar has dissolved. Simmer gently until the apricots are tender.

2 Press the apricot mixture through a nylon sieve into a small measuring cut using a spoon.

3 Pour 3 tablespoons of the orange juice into a small heatproof bowl, sprinkle on the gelatin and set aside for about 5 minutes, until softened.

4 Place the bowl over a saucepan of hot water and heat until the gelatin has dissolved. Slowly pour into the apricot mixture, stirring constantly. Make up to 2½ cups with the remaining orange juice.

5 Pour the apricot mixture into four individual dishes and chill until set. To serve, pour a thin layer of cream on the surface, and decorate with candied orange peel.

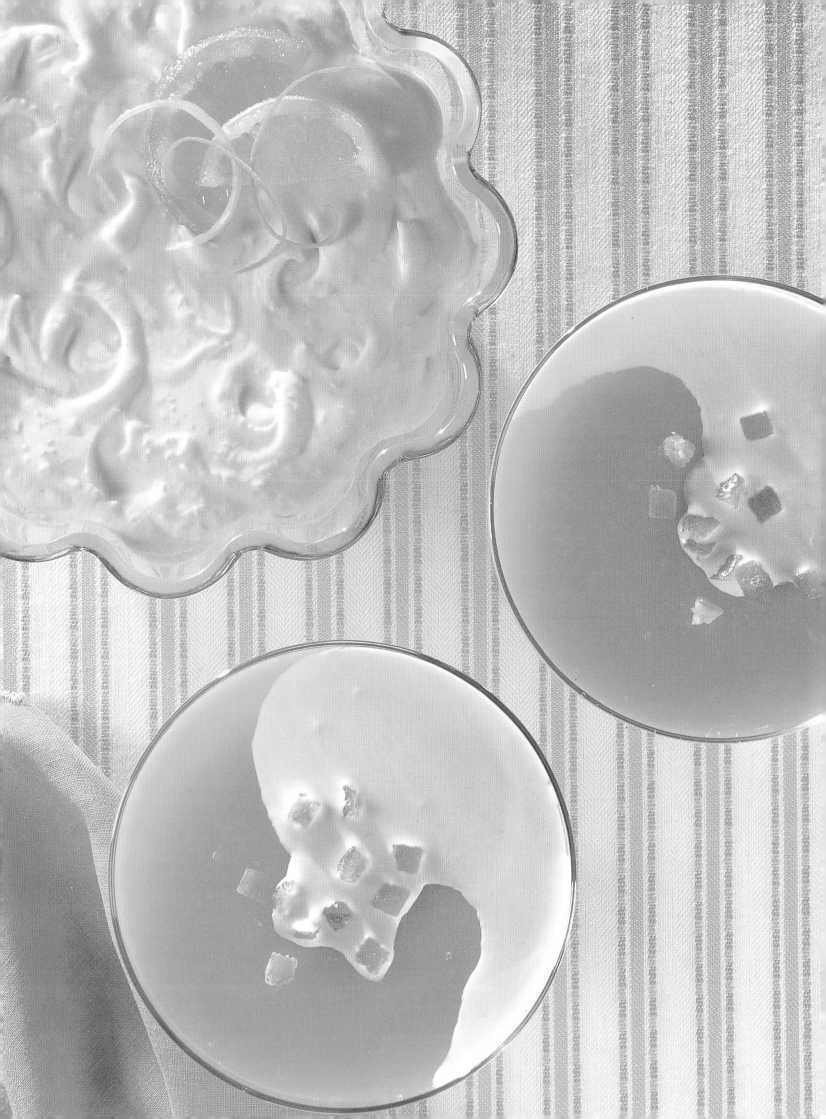

Peach Melba

The story that one of the great French chefs, Auguste Escoffier, created this dessert in honor of the opera singer Nellie Melba, is now forever enshrined in culinary, if not musical, history.

INGREDIENTS

Serves 6

¼ cup sugar

1 vanilla bean, split lengthwise

3 large peaches

For the sauce

2⅔ cups fresh or frozen
    raspberries

1 tablespoon lemon juice

2–3 tablespoons sugar

2–3 tablespoons raspberry liqueur
    (optional)

vanilla ice cream, to serve

mint leaves and fresh raspberries, to
    decorate (optional)

1 In a saucepan large enough to hold the peach halves in a single layer, combine 4 cups of water with the sugar and vanilla bean. Bring to a boil over medium heat, stirring occasionally to dissolve the sugar.

2 Cut the peaches in half and twist the halves to separate them. Using a small teaspoon, remove the peach pits. Add the peach halves to the poaching syrup, cut-sides down, adding more water, if needed, to cover the fruit. Press a piece of waxed paper against the surface, reduce the heat to medium-low, then cover and simmer for 12–15 minutes, until tender— the time will depend on the ripeness of the fruit. Remove the pan from heat and let the peaches cool in the syrup.

3 Remove the peaches from the syrup and peel off the skins. Place on several thicknesses of paper towel to drain (reserve the syrup for another use), then cover and chill.

4 Put the raspberries, lemon juice and sugar in a blender or food processor fitted with the metal blade. Process for 1 minute, scraping down the sides once. Press through a fine sieve into a small bowl, then stir in the raspberry liqueur, if using, and put in the refrigerator to chill.

5 To serve, place a peach half, cut-side up, on a dessert plate, fill with a scoop of vanilla ice cream and spoon the raspberry sauce onto the ice cream. Decorate with mint leaves and a few fresh raspberries, if using.

Gooseberry and Elderflower Cream

When elderflowers are available, instead of using the cordial, cook two to three elderflower heads with the gooseberries.

INGREDIENTS

Serves 4

1¼ pounds gooseberries, topped and tailed

1¼ cups heavy cream

about 1 cup confectioners' sugar, to taste

2 tablespoons elderflower cordial or orange flower water (optional)

mint sprigs, to decorate

almond cookies, to serve

2 Beat the cream until soft peaks form, then fold in half the gooseberries. Sweeten and add elderflower cordial or orange flower water, if using. Sweeten the remaining gooseberries.

3 Layer the cream mixture and the crushed gooseberries in four dessert dishes or tall glasses, then cover and chill. Decorate with mint sprigs and serve accompanied by almond cookies.

1 Place the gooseberries in a heavy saucepan, cover and cook over low heat, shaking the pan occasionally, until the gooseberries are tender. Put the gooseberries in a bowl, crush them, then let cool completely.

COOK'S TIP

If preferred, the cooked gooseberries can be puréed and sieved. An equivalent quantity of real custard can replace the cream.

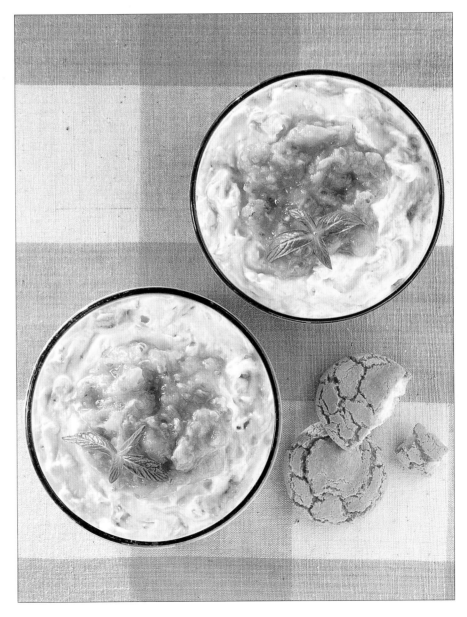

Apricots with Orange Cream

Mascarpone is a very rich cream cheese made from thick Lombardy cream. It is delicious flavored with orange as a topping for these poached, chilled apricots.

INGREDIENTS

Serves 4

2 cups dried apricots

strip of lemon peel

1 cinnamon stick

3 tablespoons sugar

⅔ cup sweet dessert wine (such as Muscat de Beaumes de Venise)

½ cup mascarpone cheese

3 tablespoons orange juice

pinch of ground cinnamon and fresh mint sprig, to decorate

1 Place the apricots, lemon peel, cinnamon stick and 1 tablespoon of the sugar in a pan and cover with 1⅞ cups cold water. Bring to a boil, cover and simmer gently for 25 minutes, until the fruit is tender.

2 Remove from heat and stir in the dessert wine. Let sit until cold, then chill for at least 3–4 hours or overnight.

3 Mix the mascarpone cheese, orange juice and the remaining sugar in a bowl and beat well until smooth, then chill.

4 Just before serving remove the cinnamon stick and lemon peel and serve with a spoonful of the orange cream sprinkled with cinnamon and decorated with a sprig of fresh mint.

Rhubarb and Orange Fool

Perhaps this traditional English pudding got its name because it is so easy to make that even a "fool" can attempt it.

INGREDIENTS

Serves 4

2 tablespoons orange juice

1 teaspoon finely shredded orange zest

2 pounds (about 10–12 stems) rhubarb, chopped

1 tablespoon red currant jelly

3 tablespoons sugar

⅔ cup thick and creamy custard

⅔ cup heavy cream, whipped

cookies, to serve

1 Place the orange juice and zest, the rhubarb, red currant jelly and sugar in a saucepan. Cover and simmer gently for about 8 minutes, stirring occasionally, until the rhubarb is just tender but not mushy.

2 Remove the pan from heat, transfer the rhubarb to a bowl and let cool completely.

3 Drain the cooled rhubarb to remove some of the liquid. Reserve a few pieces of the rhubarb and a little orange zest for decoration. Purée the remaining rhubarb in a food processor or blender, or push through a sieve.

4 Stir the custard into the purée, then fold in the whipped cream. Spoon the fool into individual bowls, cover and chill. Just before serving, top with the reserved fruit and zest. Serve with cookies.

Cherry Syllabub

This recipe follows the style of the earliest syllabubs from the sixteenth and seventeenth centuries, producing a frothy, creamy layer over a liquid one.

Serves 4

8 ounces ripe dark cherries, pitted and chopped

2 tablespoons kirsch

2 egg whites

scant ½ cup sugar

2 tablespoons lemon juice

⅔ cup sweet white wine

1¼ cups heavy cream

1 Divide the chopped cherries among six tall dessert glasses and sprinkle on the kirsch.

2 In a clean bowl, whisk the egg whites until stiff. Gently fold in the sugar, lemon juice and wine.

3 In a separate bowl (but using the same whisk), lightly beat the cream, then fold into the egg white mixture.

4 Spoon the cream mixture onto the cherries and chill overnight.

Rose Petal Cream

This is an old-fashioned junket set with rennet—don't move it while it is setting, or it will separate.

Serves 4

2½ cups milk

3 tablespoons sugar

several drops triple-strength rosewater

2 teaspoons rennet

4 tablespoons heavy cream

sugared rose petals, to decorate (optional)

1 Gently heat the milk and 2 tablespoons of the sugar, stirring continuously, until the sugar has melted and the temperature reaches 98.4°F, or the milk feels lukewarm.

2 Stir rosewater to taste into the milk, then remove the pan from heat before stirring in the rennet.

3 Pour the milk into a serving dish and let sit undisturbed for 2–3 hours, until the junket has set.

4 Stir the remaining sugar into the cream, then carefully spoon onto the junket. Decorate with sugared rose petals, if desired.

COOK'S TIP

Only use rose petals taken from bushes that have not been sprayed with chemicals of any kind.

Creole Ambrosia

A refreshing cold fruity dessert that can be made at any time of the year.

INGREDIENTS

Serves 6

6 oranges

1 coconut

2 tablespoons sugar

1 Peel the oranges removing all white pith, then slice thinly, picking out seeds with the point of a knife. Do this on a plate to catch the juice.

2 Pierce the "eyes" of the coconut and pour away the milk, then crack open the coconut with a hammer. (This is best done outside on a stone surface.)

COOK'S TIP

☙

Mangoes instead of oranges make the dessert more exotic but less authentically Creole.

3 Peel the coconut with a sharp knife, then grate half the flesh coarsely, either on a hand grater or on the grating blade of a blender or food processor.

4 Layer the coconut and orange slices in a glass bowl, starting and finishing with the coconut. After each orange layer, sprinkle on a little sugar and pour on some of the reserved orange juice.

5 Let the dessert stand for 2 hours before serving, either at room temperature or, in hot weather, in the refrigerator.

Chocolate and Chestnut Mousse

Prepared in advance, these are the perfect ending for a dinner party. Remove them from the refrigerator about 30 minutes before serving, to let them "ripen."

INGREDIENTS

Serves 6

9 ounces semi-sweet chocolate

¼ cup Madeira

2 tablespoons butter, diced

2 eggs, separated

scant 1 cup unsweetened chestnut purée

crème fraîche or whipped heavy cream,
    to decorate

1 Make a few chocolate curls for decoration, then break the rest of the chocolate into squares and melt it with the Madeira in a saucepan over low heat. Remove from heat and add the butter, a few pieces at a time, stirring until melted and smooth.

COOK'S TIP

If Madeira is not available, use brandy or rum instead. These chocolate mousses can be frozen successfully for up to 2 months.

2 Beat the egg yolks quickly into the mixture, then beat in the chestnut purée, mixing until smooth.

3 Whisk the egg whites in a clean, grease-free bowl until stiff. Stir about 1 tablespoon of the whites into the chestnut mixture to lighten it, then fold in the rest smoothly and evenly.

4 Spoon the mixture into six small ramekin dishes and chill until set. Serve the mousse topped with a generous spoonful of crème fraîche or whipped heavy cream and decorated with the chocolate curls.

Coffee, Vanilla and Chocolate Parfaits

This looks really special served in elegant wine glasses and tastes appropriately exquisite.

INGREDIENTS

Serves 6

1½ cups sugar

6 tablespoons cornstarch

3¾ cups milk

3 egg yolks

6 tablespoons unsalted butter,
    at room temperature

generous 1 tablespoon instant coffee
    granules

2 teaspoons vanilla extract

2 tablespoons unsweetened cocoa powder

whipped cream, to serve

1 To make the coffee layer, place ½ cup of the sugar and 2 tablespoons of the cornstarch in a heavy saucepan. Gradually add one-third of the milk, whisking until well blended. Over medium heat, whisk in one of the egg yolks and bring to a boil, whisking. Boil for 1 minute.

2 Remove the pan from heat. Stir in 2 tablespoons of the butter and the instant coffee powder. Set aside in the pan to cool slightly.

3 Divide the coffee mixture among six wine glasses. Smooth the tops before the mixture sets.

4 Wipe any dribbles on the insides and outsides of the glasses with damp paper towels.

5 To make the vanilla layer, place half of the remaining sugar and cornstarch in a heavy saucepan. Whisk in 1¼ cups of the milk. Over medium heat, whisk in another egg yolk and bring to a boil, whisking. Boil for 1 minute.

6 Remove the pan from heat and stir in 2 tablespoons of the butter and the vanilla. Let cool slightly, then spoon into the glasses on top of the coffee layer. Smooth the tops and wipe the glasses with paper towels.

7 To make the chocolate layer, place the remaining sugar and cornstarch in a heavy saucepan. Gradually whisk in the remaining milk and continue whisking until blended. Over medium heat, whisk in the last egg yolk and bring to a boil, whisking constantly. Boil for 1 minute. remove from heat, and stir in the remaining butter and the cocoa powder. Let cool slightly, then spoon into the glasses on top of the vanilla layer. Chill until set.

8 Pipe swirls of whipped cream on top of each dessert just before serving.

COOK'S TIP

For a special occasion, prepare the vanilla layer using a fresh vanilla bean. Choose a plump, supple bean and split it down the center with a sharp knife. Add to the mixture with the milk and discard the bean before spooning the mixture into the glasses. The flavor will be more pronounced and the dessert will have pretty brown specks from the vanilla seeds.

Chocolate Hazelnut Galettes

Chocolate rounds sandwiched with fromage frais. If only all sandwiches looked and tasted this good.

INGREDIENTS

Serves 4

6 ounces semi-sweet chocolate,
  broken into squares

3 tablespoons light cream

2 tablespoons chopped hazelnuts

4 ounces white chocolate,
  broken into squares

¾ cup fromage frais (8% fat)

1 tablespoon dry sherry

¼ cup finely chopped hazelnuts, toasted

Cape gooseberries, dipped in white
  chocolate, to decorate

1 Melt the semi-sweet chocolate in a heatproof bowl over hot water, then remove from heat and stir in the cream.

2 Draw 3-inch circles on sheets of nonstick baking parchment. Turn the paper over and spread the semi-sweet chocolate over each marked circle, covering in a thin, even layer. Sprinkle chopped hazelnuts on four of the circles, then let set.

3 Melt the white chocolate in a heatproof bowl over hot water, then stir in the fromage frais and dry sherry. Fold in the chopped, toasted hazelnuts. Let cool until the mixture holds its shape.

4 Remove the chocolate rounds carefully from the paper and sandwich them together in stacks of three, spooning the hazelnut cream between each layer and using the hazelnut-covered rounds on top. Chill before serving.

5 To serve, place the galettes on individual plates and decorate with chocolate-dipped cape gooseberries.

COOK'S TIP

∽

The chocolate could be spread on heart shapes instead, for a special Valentine's Day dessert.

Double Chocolate Snowball

This is an ideal party dessert, as it can be prepared at least one day ahead and decorated on the day.

INGREDIENTS

Serves 12–14

12 ounces semi-sweet chocolate, chopped

1½ cups sugar

1¼ cups unsalted butter, cut into
   small pieces

8 eggs

¼ cup orange-flavored liqueur or
   brandy (optional)

unsweetened cocoa powder for dusting

For the white chocolate cream

7 ounces fine quality white chocolate,
   broken into pieces

2 cups heavy or whipping cream

2 tablespoons orange-flavor liqueur
   (optional)

1 Preheat the oven to 350°F. Line a 1½-quart round ovenproof bowl with aluminum foil, smoothing the sides. In a bowl over a pan of simmering water, melt the semi-sweet chocolate. Add the sugar and stir until it dissolves. Strain into a medium bowl. With an electric mixer at low speed, beat in the butter, then the eggs, one at a time, beating well after each addition. Stir in the liqueur or brandy, if using, and pour into the prepared bowl. Tap gently to release any large air bubbles.

2 Bake for 1¼–1½ hours, until the surface is firm and slightly risen, but cracked. The center will still be wobbly: this will set on cooling. Remove to a rack to cool to room temperature. Cover with a plate, then cover completely with plastic wrap or foil and chill overnight. To unmold, remove plate and wrap or foil and invert mold onto a plate; shake firmly to release. Peel off foil. Cover until ready to decorate.

3 Process the white chocolate in a blender or food processor until fine crumbs form. In a small saucepan, heat ½ cup of the cream until just beginning to simmer. With the food processor running, pour cream through the feed tube and process until the chocolate is completely melted. Strain into a medium bowl and cool to room temperature, stirring occasionally.

4 Beat the remaining cream until soft peaks form, add the liqueur, if using, and beat for 30 seconds or until the cream just holds its shape. Fold a spoonful of cream into the chocolate, then fold in remaining cream. Spoon into a bag fitted with a star tip and pipe rosettes on the surface. If desired, dust with cocoa powder.

White Chocolate Parfait

Everything you could wish for in a dessert; white and dark chocolate in one mouthwatering slice.

Serves 10

8 ounces white chocolate, chopped

2½ cups whipping cream

½ cup milk

10 egg yolks

1 tablespoon sugar

scant ½ cup dry, shredded coconut

½ cup canned sweetened coconut milk

1¼ cups unsalted macadamia nuts

For the chocolate icing

8 ounces semi-sweet chocolate

6 tablespoons butter

generous 1 tablespoon golden or
    light corn syrup

¾ cup whipping cream

curls of fresh coconut, to decorate

1 Line the bottom and sides of a 6-cup terrine mold (10 x 4 inches) with plastic wrap.

2 Place the chopped white chocolate and ½ cup of the cream in the top of a double boiler or in a heatproof bowl set over hot water. Stir until melted and smooth. Set aside.

3 Put 1 cup of the cream and the milk in a pan and bring to the boiling point.

4 Meanwhile, whisk the egg yolks and sugar together in a large bowl, until thick and pale.

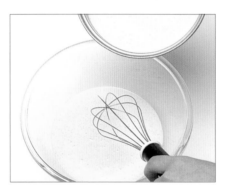

5 Add the hot cream mixture to the yolks, beating constantly. Pour back into the saucepan and cook over low heat for 2–3 minutes, until thickened. Stir constantly and do not boil. Remove the pan from heat.

6 Add the melted chocolate, dry, shredded coconut and coconut milk, then stir well and let cool.

7 Whip the remaining cream until thick, then fold into the chocolate and coconut mixture.

8 Put 2 cups of the parfait mixture in the prepared mold and spread evenly. Cover and freeze for about 2 hours, until just firm. Cover the remaining mixture and chill.

9 Sprinkle the macadamia nuts evenly on the frozen parfait. Pour in the remaining parfait mixture. Cover the terrine and freeze for 6–8 hours or overnight, until the parfait is firm.

10 To make the icing, melt the chocolate with the butter and syrup in the top of a double boiler set over hot water. Stir occasionally.

11 Heat the cream in a saucepan, until just simmering, then stir into the chocolate mixture. Remove the pan from heat and let cool until lukewarm.

12 To turn out the parfait, wrap the terrine in a hot towel and set it upside-down on a plate. Lift off the terrine mold, then peel off the plastic wrap. Place the parfait on a rack over a baking sheet and pour the chocolate icing evenly on top. Working quickly, smooth the icing down the sides with a spatula. Let set slightly, then freeze for another 3–4 hours. Cut into slices using a knife dipped in hot water. Serve, decorated with curls of fresh coconut.

White Chocolate Mousse with Dark Sauce

Creamy vanilla-flavored white chocolate mousse is served with a dark rum and chocolate sauce.

INGREDIENTS

Serves 6–8

7 ounces white chocolate, broken into squares

2 eggs, separated

¼ cup sugar

1¼ cups heavy cream

1 envelope powdered gelatin or alternative

⅔ cup plain yogurt

2 teaspoons vanilla extract

For the sauce

2 ounces semi-sweet chocolate, broken into squares

2 tablespoons dark rum

¼ cup light cream

1 Line a 4-cup loaf pan with nonstick baking parchment or plastic wrap. Melt the chocolate in a heatproof bowl over hot water, then remove from heat.

2 Whisk the egg yolks and sugar in a bowl until pale and thick, then beat in the melted chocolate.

3 Heat the cream in a small saucepan until almost boiling, then remove from heat. Sprinkle the powdered gelatin over, stirring gently until until it is completely dissolved.

4 Then pour onto the chocolate mixture, whisking vigorously to mix until smooth.

5 Whisk the yogurt and vanilla extract into the mixture. In a clean, grease-free bowl, whisk the egg whites until stiff, then fold them into the mixture. Pour into the prepared loaf pan, level the surface and chill until set.

6 Make the sauce. Melt the chocolate with the rum and cream in a heatproof bowl over barely simmering water, stirring occasionally, then let cool.

7 When the mousse is set, remove it from the pan with the aid of the paper or plastic wrap. Serve in thick slices with the cooled chocolate sauce poured around.

COOK'S TIP

Make sure the gelatin is completely dissolved in the cream before adding to the other ingredients.

Fluffy Banana and Pineapple Mousse

This light, low-fat mousse looks very impressive but is really very easy to make, especially with a food processor. To make it even simpler, use a 4-cup serving dish which will hold the mixture without a paper "collar."

INGREDIENTS

Serves 6

2 ripe bananas

1 cup cottage cheese

15-ounce can pineapple chunks or pieces
   in juice

1 envelope powdered gelatin,
   or alternative

2 egg whites

1 Tie a double band of nonstick baking parchment around a 2½-cup soufflé dish, to come 2 inches above the rim.

2 Peel and chop one banana and place it in a blender or food processor with the cottage cheese. Process them until smooth.

3 Drain the pineapple, reserving the juice, and reserve a few pieces or chunks for decoration. Add the rest to the mixture in the blender or food processor and process for a few seconds until finely chopped.

4 Dissolve the gelatin in 4 tablespoons of the reserved pineapple juice. Stir the gelatin quickly into the fruit mixture.

5 Whisk the egg whites until they hold soft peaks and fold them into the mixture. Pour the mousse mixture into the prepared dish, smooth the surface and chill, until set.

6 When the mousse is set, carefully remove the paper collar and decorate with the reserved banana and pineapple.

Portuguese Rice Pudding

This pudding is popular all over Portugal, and if you visit you're likely to find it on most menus. Traditionally it is served cold but is actually delicious warm as well.

INGREDIENTS

Serves 4–6

scant 1 cup short-grain (pudding) rice

2½ cups creamy milk

2 or 3 strips pared lemon zest

5 tablespoons butter, in pieces

½ cup sugar

4 egg yolks

salt

ground cinnamon, for dusting

lemon wedges, to serve

1 Cook the rice in plenty of lightly salted water for about 5 minutes.

2 Drain well, then return to the clean pan. Add the milk, lemon zest and butter. Bring to a boil over medium heat, then cover, reduce the heat to the lowest setting and simmer for about 20 minutes or until the rice is thick and creamy.

3 Remove the pan from heat and let the rice cool a little. Remove and discard the lemon zest, then stir in the sugar and the egg yolks. Mix well.

4 Divide among four to six serving bowls and dust with ground cinnamon. Serve cold, with lemon wedges.

Rice Conde Sundae

Cooking rice pudding on top of the stove instead of in the oven gives it a light, creamy texture, especially if you remember to stir it frequently. It is particularly good served cold with a topping of fruit and toasted nuts or a drizzle of hot chocolate sauce.

INGREDIENTS

Serves 4

generous ¼ cup short-grain
   (pudding) rice
1 teaspoon vanilla extract
½ teaspoon ground cinnamon
3 tablespoons sugar
2½ cups milk

For the topping
soft berries such as strawberries,
   raspberries and cherries
chocolate sauce and sliced toasted
   almonds (optional)

1 Mix the rice, vanilla, cinnamon and sugar in a saucepan. Pour in the milk. Bring to a boil, stirring constantly, then reduce the heat so that the mixture barely simmers.

2 Cook the rice over low heat for 30–40 minutes, stirring frequently. Add extra milk to the rice if it begins to dry out.

3 When the grains are soft, remove the pan from heat. Let the rice cool, stirring occasionally, then chill.

4 Before serving, stir the rice pudding and spoon it into four sundae dishes. Top with fresh fruits, and with chocolate sauce and almonds, if using.

VARIATION

For a special occasion, use light cream instead of milk, and glaze the fruit with a little melted red currant jelly. (Add a splash of port, if desired.)

Cherries Jubilee

Fresh cherries are wonderful cooked lightly to serve hot over ice cream. Children will love this dessert.

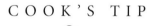

INGREDIENTS

Serves 4

1 pound red or black cherries

generous ½ cup sugar

pared zest of 1 lemon

1 tablespoon arrowroot

¼ cup Kirsch

vanilla ice cream, to serve

COOK'S TIP

∾

If you don't have a cherry pitter, simply push the pits through with a skewer. Remember to save the juice to use in the recipe.

1 Pit the cherries over a pan to catch the juice. Drop the pits into the pan as you work.

2 Add the sugar, lemon zest and 1¼ cups water to the pan. Stir over low heat until the sugar dissolves, then bring to a boil and simmer for 10 minutes. Strain the syrup, then return to the pan. Add the cherries and cook for 3–4 minutes.

3 Blend the arrowroot into a paste with 1 tablespoon cold water and stir into the cherries, after removing them from heat.

4 Return the pan to heat and bring to a boil, stirring constantly. Cook the sauce for a minute or two, stirring until it is thick and smooth. Heat the Kirsch in a ladle over a flame, ignite and pour onto the cherries. Spoon the cherries and hot sauce onto scoops of ice cream and serve immediately.

Apricots in Marsala

Make sure the apricots are completely covered by the syrup so that they don't discolor.

INGREDIENTS

Serves 4

12 apricots

¼ cup sugar

1¼ cups Marsala

2 strips pared orange zest

1 vanilla bean, split

⅔ cup heavy or whipping cream

1 tablespoon confectioners' sugar

¼ teaspoon ground cinnamon

⅔ cup plain yogurt

1 Halve and pit the apricots, then place in a bowl of boiling water for about 30 seconds. Drain well, then slip off their skins.

2 Place the sugar, Marsala, orange zest, vanilla bean and 1 cup water in a pan. Heat gently until the sugar dissolves. Bring to a boil, without stirring, then simmer for 2–3 minutes.

3 Add the apricot halves to the pan and poach for 5–6 minutes or until just tender. Using a slotted spoon, transfer the apricots to a serving dish.

4 Boil the syrup rapidly until reduced by half, then pour onto the apricots and let cool. Cover and chill. Remove the orange zest and vanilla bean.

5 Whip the cream with the confectioners' sugar and cinnamon until it forms soft peaks. Gently fold in the yogurt. Spoon into a serving bowl and chill. Serve with the apricots.

Poached Pears in Red Wine

This makes a very pretty dessert, as the pears take on a red blush from the wine.

INGREDIENTS

Serves 4

1 bottle red wine

¾ cup sugar

3 tablespoons honey

juice of ½ lemon

1 cinnamon stick

1 vanilla bean, split open lengthwise

2-inch piece of orange zest

1 clove

1 black peppercorn

4 firm, ripe pears

whipped cream or sour cream,
    to serve

1 Place the wine, sugar, honey, lemon juice, cinnamon stick, vanilla bean, orange zest, clove and peppercorn in a saucepan just large enough to hold the pears standing upright. Heat gently, stirring occasionally, until the sugar has completely dissolved.

2 Meanwhile, peel the pears, leaving the stem intact. Take a thin slice off the bottom of each pear so that it will stand square and upright in the pan.

3 Place the pears in the wine mixture, then simmer, uncovered, for 20–35 minutes depending on size and ripeness, until the pears are just tender; be careful not to overcook.

4 Carefully transfer the pears to a bowl using a slotted spoon. Continue to boil the poaching liquid until reduced by about half. Let cool, then strain the cooled liquid over the pears and chill for at least 3 hours.

5 Place the pears in four individual serving dishes and spoon on a little of the red wine syrup. Serve with whipped cream or sour cream.

Coffee Crêpes with Peaches and Cream

Juicy golden peaches and cream conjure up the sweet taste of summer. Here, they are delicious as the filling for these coffee crêpes.

INGREDIENTS

Serves 6

⅔ cup all-purpose flour

¼ cup buckwheat flour

¼ teaspoon salt

1 egg, beaten

scant 1 cup milk

1 tablespoon butter, melted

scant ½ cup strong coffee

sunflower oil, for frying

For the filling

6 ripe peaches

1¼ cups heavy cream

1 tablespoon Amaretto liqueur

1 cup mascarpone

generous ¼ cup sugar

2 tablespoons confectioners' sugar, for dusting

1 Sift the flours and salt into a bowl. Make a well and add the egg, half the milk and the melted butter. Beat into the flour until smooth, then beat in the remaining milk and coffee.

2 Heat a drizzle of oil in a 6–8-inch crêpe pan. Pour in just enough batter to thinly cover the bottom of the pan. Cook for 2–3 minutes, until the underneath is golden brown, then flip over and cook the other side.

3 Slide the crêpe out of the pan onto a plate. Continue making crêpes until all the mixture is used, stacking and interleaving with waxed paper. Keep the crêpes warm while you make the filling.

4 To make the filling, halve the peaches and remove the pits. Cut into thick slices. Whip the cream and Amaretto liqueur until they form into soft peaks. Beat the mascarpone with the sugar until smooth. Beat 2 tablespoons of the cream into the mascarpone, then fold in the remainder.

5 Spoon a little of the Amaretto cream onto one half of each pancake and top with peach slices. Gently fold over the pancake and dust with confectioners' sugar. Serve immediately while still warm.

Fruit Kebabs with Mango and Yogurt Sauce

These mixed fresh fruit kebabs make an attractive and healthy dessert.

INGREDIENTS

Serves 4

½ pineapple, peeled, cored and cubed

2 kiwis, peeled and cubed

1½ cups strawberries, hulled and cut in
    half, if large

½ mango, peeled, pitted and cubed

For the sauce

½ cup fresh mango purée,
    from 1–1½ peeled and pitted mangoes

½ cup thick plain yogurt

1 teaspoon sugar

few drops vanilla extract

1 tablespoon finely chopped
    mint leaves

1 To make the sauce, beat together the mango purée, yogurt, sugar and vanilla with an electric mixer.

2 Stir in the chopped mint. Cover the sauce and place in the refrigerator until needed.

3 Thread the prepared fruit onto twelve 6-inch wooden skewers, alternating the pineapple, kiwis, strawberries and mango cubes.

4 Arrange the kebabs on a large serving tray with the mango and yogurt sauce in the center.

Tropical Fruits in Cinnamon Syrup

A delicious glazed fruit salad, a simply prepared but satisfying end to any meal.

INGREDIENTS

Serves 6

2¼ cups sugar

1 cinnamon stick

1 large or 2 medium papayas (about
    1½ pounds), peeled, seeded and cut
    lengthwise into thin pieces

1 large or 2 medium mangoes (about
    1½ pounds), peeled, pitted and cut
    lengthwise into thin pieces

1 large or 2 small star fruit
    (about 8 ounces), thinly sliced

yogurt or crème fraîche, to serve

1 Sprinkle one-third of the sugar on the bottom of a large saucepan. Add the cinnamon stick and half the papaya, mango and star fruit pieces.

2 Sprinkle half of the remaining sugar onto the fruit pieces in the pan. Add all the remaining fruit and sprinkle with the rest of the sugar.

3 Cover the pan and cook the fruit over medium-low heat for 35–45 minutes, until the sugar melts completely. Shake the pan occasionally, but do not stir or the fruit will collapse.

4 Uncover the pan and simmer until the fruit begins to appear translucent, about 10 minutes. Remove the pan from heat and let cool.

5 Transfer the fruit and syrup to a bowl, cover and chill overnight. Serve with yogurt or crème fraîche.

Greek Figs with Honey

A quick and easy dessert made from fresh or canned figs topped with thick and creamy plain yogurt, drizzled with honey and sprinkled with pistachios.

INGREDIENTS

Serves 4

4 fresh or canned figs

2 cups plain yogurt, strained

4 tablespoons honey

2 tablespoons chopped pistachios

1 Chop the figs and place in the bottom of four stemmed wine glasses or deep, individual dessert bowls.

2 Top each glass or bowl of figs with ½ cup of the plain yogurt. Chill until ready to serve.

3 Just before serving drizzle 1 tablespoon of honey on each one and sprinkle with the pistachios.

COOK'S TIP

Try specialty honeys made from, clover, acacia or thyme.

Russian Fruit Compote

This fruit compote is traditionally called "Kissel" and is made from the thickened juice of stewed red or black currants. This recipe uses the whole fruit with an added dash of blackberry liqueur.

INGREDIENTS

Serves 4

2 cups red or black currants or a mixture of both

1⅓ cups raspberries

4 tablespoons sugar

1½ tablespoons arrowroot

1–2 tablespoons Crème de Mûre

plain yogurt, to serve

COOK'S TIP

Use Crème de Cassis instead of Crème de Mûre.

1 Place the red or black currants, raspberries and sugar in a pan with ⅔ cup of water. Cover the pan and cook gently over low heat for 12–15 minutes, until the fruit is soft.

2 Blend the arrowroot with a little water in a bowl and stir into the fruit. Bring back to a boil, stirring until thickened.

3 Remove from heat and cool slightly, then gently stir in the Crème de Mûre.

4 Pour into four serving bowls and leave until cold, then chill. Serve topped with spoonfuls of plain yogurt.

Floating Islands

Originally these oval-shaped meringues were poached in milk, and this was then used to make the rich custard sauce.

INGREDIENTS

Serves 4–6

1 vanilla bean

2½ cups milk

8 egg yolks

¼ cup sugar

For the meringues

4 egg whites

¼ teaspoon cream of tartar

1¼ cups sugar

For the caramel

¾ cup sugar

1 Split the vanilla bean lengthwise and scrape the seeds into a saucepan. Add the milk and bring just to a boil over medium heat, stirring frequently. Cover and set aside for 15–20 minutes.

2 In a medium bowl, whisk the egg yolks and sugar for 2–3 minutes, until thick and creamy. Whisk in the hot milk and return the mixture to the saucepan. With a wooden spoon, stir over medium-low heat until the sauce begins to thicken and coat the back of the spoon (do not let boil). Immediately strain into a chilled bowl, let cool, stirring occasionally and then chill.

3 Half-fill a large, wide frying pan or saucepan with water and bring just to the simmering point. In a clean, grease-free bowl, whisk the egg whites until frothy. Add the cream of tartar and continue whisking until they form soft peaks. Sprinkle on the sugar, about 2 tablespoons at a time, and whisk until the whites are stiff and glossy.

4 Using two tablespoons, form egg-shaped meringues and slide them into the water (you may need to work in batches). Poach them for 2–3 minutes, turning once until just firm. Using a large slotted spoon, transfer the cooked meringues to a baking sheet lined with paper towels to drain.

5 Pour the cold custard into individual serving dishes and arrange the meringues on top.

6 To make the caramel, put the sugar into a small saucepan with 3 tablespoons of water to moisten. Bring to a boil over high heat, swirling the pan to dissolve the sugar. Boil, without stirring, until the syrup turns a dark caramel color. Immediately drizzle the caramel on the meringues and custard sauce in a zig-zag pattern. Serve cold. (The caramel will soften if made too far ahead.)

Chestnut Delight

This is an Italian specialty, made during the months of October and November, when fresh sweet chestnuts are gathered.

INGREDIENTS

Serves 4–5

1 pound fresh sweet chestnuts

1¼ cups milk

½ cup sugar

2 eggs, separated, at room temperature

¼ cup unsweetened cocoa powder

½ teaspoon pure vanilla extract

½ cup confectioners' sugar, sifted

fresh whipped cream, to garnish

marrons glacés, to garnish

1 Cut a cross in the side of the chestnuts, and drop them into a pan of boiling water. Cook for 5–6 minutes. Remove with a slotted spoon, and peel while still warm.

2 Place the peeled chestnuts in a heavy or nonstick saucepan with the milk and half of the sugar. Cook over low heat, stirring occasionally, until soft. remove from heat and let cool. Press the contents of the pan through a strainer.

3 Preheat the oven to 350°F. Beat the egg yolks with the remaining sugar until the mixture is pale yellow and fluffy. Beat in the cocoa powder and the vanilla.

4 In a separate bowl, whisk the egg whites with a wire whisk or electric beater until they form soft peaks. Gradually beat in the sifted confectioners' sugar and continue beating until the mixture forms stiff peaks.

5 Fold the chestnut and egg yolk mixtures together. Fold in the egg whites. Turn the mixture into one large or several individual buttered pudding molds. Place on a baking sheet, and bake for 12–20 minutes, depending on the size. Remove from the oven, and let cool for 10 minutes before unmolding. Serve garnished with whipped cream and marrons glacés.

Bitter Chocolate Mousse

This is the quintessential French dessert— easy to prepare ahead, rich and extremely delicious. Use the darkest chocolate you can find for the most authentic and intense chocolate flavor.

INGREDIENTS

Serves 8

8 ounces semi-sweet chocolate, chopped

2 tablespoons orange liqueur or brandy

2 tablespoons unsalted butter,
    cut into small pieces

4 eggs, separated

6 tablespoons whipping cream

¼ teaspoon cream of tartar

3 tablespoons sugar

crème fraîche or sour cream and chocolate
    curls, to decorate

1 Place the chocolate and 4 tablespoons of water in a heavy saucepan. Melt over low heat, stirring until smooth. Remove the pan from heat and whisk in the liqueur and butter.

2 With an electric mixer, beat the egg yolks for 2–3 minutes, until thick and creamy, then slowly beat into the melted chocolate until well blended. Set aside.

3 Whip the cream until soft peaks form and stir a spoonful into the chocolate to lighten it. Fold in the remaining cream.

4 In a clean, grease-free bowl, using an electric mixer, beat the egg whites until frothy. Add the cream of tartar and continue beating until they form soft peaks. Gradually sprinkle on the sugar and continue beating until the whites are stiff and glossy.

5 Using a rubber spatula or large metal spoon, stir a quarter of the egg whites into the chocolate mixture, then gently fold in the remaining whites, cutting down to the bottom, along the sides and up to the top in a semicircular motion until they are just combined. (Don't worry about a few white streaks.) Gently spoon into an 8-cup dish or into eight individual dishes. Chill for at least 2 hours, until set and chilled.

6 Spoon a little crème fraîche or sour cream on the mousse and decorate with chocolate curls.

Brazilian Coffee Bananas

Rich, lavish and sinful-looking, this dessert takes only about two minutes to make!

INGREDIENTS

Serves 4

4 small ripe bananas

1 tablespoon instant coffee granules or powder

2 tablespoons dark brown sugar

1⅛ cups plain yogurt, strained

1 tablespoon toasted sliced almonds

1 Peel and slice one banana and mash the remaining three with a fork.

2 Dissolve the coffee in 1 tablespoon of hot water and stir into the mashed bananas.

3 Spoon a little of the mashed banana mixture into four serving dishes and sprinkle with sugar. Top with a spoonful of yogurt, then repeat until all the ingredients are used up.

4 Swirl the last layer of yogurt for a marbled effect. Finish with a few banana slices and almonds. Serve cold. Best eaten within about an hour of making.

VARIATION

For a special occasion, add a dash of dark rum or brandy to the bananas for extra richness.

Cakes
&
Gâteaux

◆ ✦ ◆

Raspberry Meringue Gâteau

A rich, hazelnut meringue sandwiched with whipped cream and raspberries makes an irresistible dessert for a special occasion.

INGREDIENTS

Serves 6

4 egg whites

1 cup sugar

a few drops of vanilla extract

1 teaspoon distilled malt vinegar

1 cup roasted and chopped hazelnuts, ground

1¼ cups heavy cream

2 cups raspberries

confectioners' sugar, for dusting

raspberries and mint sprigs, to decorate

For the sauce

1⅓ cups raspberries

3–4 tablespoons confectioners' sugar, sifted

1 tablespoon orange liqueur

1 Preheat the oven to 350°F. Grease two 8-inch cake pans and line the bottoms with waxed paper.

2 Whisk the egg whites in a large bowl until they hold stiff peaks, then gradually whisk in the sugar a tablespoon at a time, whisking well after each addition.

COOK'S TIP

~

You can buy roasted chopped hazelnuts at supermarkets. Otherwise toast whole hazelnuts under the broiler and rub off the flaky skins using a clean dish towel. To chop finely, process in a blender or food processor for a few moments.

3 Continue whisking the meringue mixture for a minute of two until very stiff, then fold in the vanilla, vinegar and ground hazelnuts.

4 Divide the meringue mixture between the prepared pans and spread level. Bake for 50–60 minutes, until crisp. Remove the meringues from the pans and let them cool on a wire rack.

5 While the meringues are cooling, make the sauce. Process the raspberries with the confectioners' sugar and orange liqueur in a blender or food processor, then press the purée through a fine nylon sieve to remove any seeds. Chill the sauce until ready to serve.

6 Whip the cream until it forms soft peaks, then gently fold in the raspberries. Sandwich the meringue rounds together with the raspberry cream.

7 Dust the top of the gâteau with confectioners' sugar. Decorate with mint sprigs and serve with the raspberry sauce.

VARIATION

Fresh red currants make a good alternative to raspberries. Pick over the fruit, then pull each sprig gently through the prongs of a fork to release the red currants. Add them to the whipped cream with a little confectioners' sugar, to taste.

Chocolate Layer Cake

The cake layers can be made ahead, wrapped and frozen for future use. Always defrost cakes completely before icing.

INGREDIENTS

Serves 10–12

unsweetened cocoa powder for dusting

8-ounce can cooked whole beets, drained and juice reserved

½ cup unsalted butter, softened

2½ cups light brown sugar, firmly packed

3 eggs

1 tablespoon vanilla extract

3 ounces unsweetened chocolate, melted

2¼ cups all-purpose flour

2 teaspoons baking powder

½ teaspoon salt

½ cup buttermilk

chocolate curls (optional)

For the chocolate ganache frosting

2 cups whipping or heavy cream

1¼ pounds fine quality, bittersweet or semi-sweet chocolate, chopped

1 tablespoon vanilla extract

1 Preheat oven to 350°F. Grease two 9-inch cake pans and dust the bottom and sides with cocoa powder. Grate beet and add to beet juice. With electric mixer, beat the butter, brown sugar, eggs and vanilla until pale and fluffy (3–5 minutes). Reduce the speed and beat in chocolate.

2 In a bowl, sift flour, baking powder and salt. With mixer on low speed, alternately beat in flour mixture in fourths and buttermilk in thirds. Add beets and juice and beat for 1 minute. Divide between pans and bake for 30–35 minutes or until a cake tester inserted in the center comes out clean. Cool for 10 minutes, then unmold and cool completely.

3 To make the frosting, in a heavy saucepan over medium heat, heat cream until it just begins to boil, stirring occasionally to prevent it from scorching.

4 Remove from heat and stir in chocolate, stirring constantly until melted and smooth. Stir in vanilla. Strain into a bowl and refrigerate, stirring every 10 minutes, until spreadable, about 1 hour.

5 Assemble the cake. Place one layer on a serving plate and spread with one-third of the ganache. Turn cake layer bottom side up and spread remaining ganache on top and side of cake. If using, top with the chocolate curls. Let ganache to set for 20–30 minutes, then refrigerate before serving.

Spiced Date and Walnut Cake

*A classic flavor combination,
which makes a very easy low fat,
high-fiber cake.*

INGREDIENTS

Makes 1 cake

2¾ cups whole-wheat
  self-rising flour
2 teaspoons allspice
1 cup chopped dates
½ cup chopped walnuts
4 tablespoons sunflower oil
½ cup dark brown sugar
1¼ cups skim milk
walnut halves, to decorate

1 Preheat the oven to 350°F.
Grease and then line a 2-pound
loaf pan with waxed paper.

2 Sift together the flour and
spice, adding back any bran
from the sieve. Stir in the dates
and walnuts.

3 Mix the oil, sugar and milk,
then stir evenly into the dry
ingredients. Spoon into the
prepared pan and arrange the
walnut halves on top.

4 Bake the cake for 45–50 minutes
or until golden brown and
firm. Turn out the cake, remove
the lining paper and let cool on a
wire rack.

VARIATION

Pecans can be used instead of the
walnuts in this cake.

Banana Orange Loaf

For the best banana flavor and a really good, moist texture, make sure the bananas are very ripe.

INGREDIENTS

Makes 1 loaf

generous ¾ cup whole-wheat flour

generous ¾ cup all-purpose flour

1 teaspoon baking powder

1 teaspoon ground allspice

3 tablespoons chopped hazelnuts, toasted

2 large ripe bananas

1 egg

2 tablespoons sunflower oil

2 tablespoons honey

finely grated zest and juice
  of 1 small orange

4 orange slices, halved

2 teaspoons confectioners' sugar

1 Preheat the oven to 350°F. Brush a 4-cup loaf pan with sunflower oil and line the bottom with nonstick baking parchment.

2 Sift the flours with the baking powder and spice into a bowl.

3 Stir the hazelnuts into the dry ingredients. Peel and mash the bananas. Beat in the egg, oil, honey and the orange zest and juice. Stir evenly into the dry ingredients.

4 Spoon into the prepared pan and smooth the top. Bake for 40–45 minutes or until firm and golden brown. Turn out and cool on a wire rack.

5 Sprinkle the orange slices with the confectioners' sugar and broil until golden. Use to decorate the cake.

COOK'S TIP

If you plan to keep the loaf for more than two or three days, omit the orange slices. Brush the cake with honey and sprinkle with hazelnuts.

Banana Bread

Banana bread improves with keeping. Store it in a covered container for up to two months.

INGREDIENTS

Makes 12 squares

1¾ cups all-purpose flour

2 teaspoons baking soda

2 teaspoons ground ginger

1¼ cups medium oatmeal

4 tablespoons dark brown sugar

6 tablespoons sunflower
  margarine

⅔ cup golden or light corn syrup

1 egg, beaten

3 ripe bananas, mashed

¾ cup confectioners' sugar

stem ginger, to decorate

1 Preheat the oven to 325°F. Grease and line a 7 x 11-inch cake pan.

2 Sift together the flour, baking soda and ginger, then stir in the oatmeal. Melt the sugar, margarine and syrup in a saucepan, then stir into the flour mixture. Beat in the egg and mashed bananas.

3 Spoon into the pan and bake for about 1 hour or until firm to the touch. Let cool in the pan, then turn out and cut into even-sized squares.

4 Sift the confectioners' sugar into a bowl and stir in just enough water to make a smooth, runny icing. Drizzle the icing on each square and top with pieces of stem ginger, if desired.

COOK'S TIP

This is a nutritious cake, ideal for packed lunches, as it doesn't break up too easily.

Greek Honey and Lemon Cake

The semolina in this recipe gives the cake an excellent texture.

INGREDIENTS

Makes 16 slices

3 tablespoons sunflower margarine

4 tablespoons honey

finely grated zest and juice of 1 lemon

⅔ cup skim milk

1¼ cups all-purpose flour

1½ teaspoons baking powder

½ teaspoon grated nutmeg

⅓ cup semolina

2 egg whites

2 teaspoons sesame seeds

1 Preheat the oven to 400°F. Lightly oil a 7½-inch square deep cake pan and line the bottom with nonstick baking parchment.

2 Place the margarine and 3 tablespoons of the honey in a saucepan and heat gently until melted. Reserve 1 tablespoon lemon juice, then stir in the rest with the lemon zest and milk.

3 Stir together the flour, baking powder and nutmeg, then beat in with the semolina. Whisk the egg whites until they form soft peaks, then fold evenly into the semolina mixture.

4 Spoon into the pan and sprinkle with sesame seeds. Bake for 25–30 minutes, until golden brown.

5 Mix the reserved honey and lemon juice and drizzle on the cake while warm. Cool in the pan, then cut into fingers to serve.

Strawberry Roulade

An attractive and delicious cake, perfect for a family supper.

INGREDIENTS

Serves 6

4 egg whites

scant ⅔ cup light brown sugar

⅔ cup all-purpose flour, sifted

2 tablespoons orange juice

sugar, for sprinkling

1 cup strawberries, chopped

¾ cup low-fat fromage frais

strawberries, to decorate

1 Preheat the oven to 400°F. Oil a 9 x 13-inch jelly roll pan and line with nonstick baking parchment.

2 Place the egg whites in a large clean bowl and whisk until they form soft peaks. Gradually whisk in the sugar. Fold in half of the sifted flour, then fold in the rest with the orange juice.

3 Spoon the mixture into the prepared pan, spreading evenly. Bake for 15–18 minutes or until golden brown and firm to the touch.

4 Meanwhile, spread out a sheet of nonstick baking parchment and sprinkle with sugar. Turn out the cake onto this and remove the lining paper. Roll up the cake loosely from one short side, with the paper inside. Cool.

5 Unroll and remove the paper. Stir the strawberries into the fromage frais and spread onto cake. Roll up and serve decorated with strawberries.

Classic Cheesecake

You can decorate this with fruit and serve it with cream, if desired, but it tastes delicious just as it is.

INGREDIENTS

Serves 8

½ cup graham cracker crumbs

2 pounds cream cheese

1¼ cups sugar

grated zest of 1 lemon

3 tablespoons fresh lemon juice

1 teaspoon vanilla extract

4 eggs, at room temperature

1 Preheat the oven to 325°F. Grease an 8-inch springform cake pan. Place on a round of aluminum foil 5 inches larger than the diameter of the pan. Press it up the sides to seal tightly.

2 Sprinkle the crumbs in the bottom of the pan. Press to form an even layer.

3 With an electric mixer, beat the cream cheese until smooth. Add the sugar, lemon zest and juice and vanilla, and beat until blended. Beat in the eggs, one at a time. Beat just enough to blend thoroughly.

4 Pour into the prepared pan. Set the pan in a larger baking tray and place in the oven. Pour enough hot water in the outer tray to come 1 inch up the side of the pan.

5 Bake until the top of the cake is golden brown, about 1½ hours. Let cool in the pan.

6 Run a knife around the edge to loosen, then remove the rim of the pan. Chill for at least 4 hours before serving.

Chocolate Cheesecake

This popular variation of the classic dessert is made with a cinnamon and chocolate crust.

INGREDIENTS

Serves 10–12

6 ounces semi-sweet chocolate squares

4 ounces bittersweet chocolate squares

2½ pounds cream cheese, at room temperature

1 cup sugar

2 teaspoons vanilla extract

4 eggs, at room temperature

¾ cup sour cream

For the crust

1½ cups chocolate wafer crumbs

6 tablespoons butter, melted

½ teaspoon ground cinnamon

1 Preheat the oven to 350°F. Grease a 9-inch springform cake pan.

2 For the crust, mix the chocolate wafer crumbs with the butter and cinnamon. Press evenly in the bottom of the pan.

3 Melt the semi-sweet and bittersweet chocolate in the top of a double boiler, or in a heatproof bowl set over hot water. Set aside.

4 With an electric mixer, beat the cream cheese until smooth, then beat in the sugar and vanilla. Add the eggs, one at a time, scraping the bowl with a spatula when necessary.

5 Add the sour cream. Stir in the melted chocolate.

6 Pour into the pan. Bake for 1 hour. Let cool in the pan; remove rim. Chill before serving.

Blueberry-hazelnut Cheesecake

The crust for this cheesecake is made with ground hazelnuts—a tasty and unusual alternative to a cookie crust.

INGREDIENTS

Serves 6–8

12 ounces blueberries

1 tablespoon honey

6 tablespoons sugar

juice of 1 lemon

¾ cup cream cheese,
    at room temperature

1 egg

1 teaspoon hazelnut liqueur (optional)

½ cup whipping cream

For the crust

1⅔ cups ground hazelnuts

⅔ cup all-purpose flour

pinch of salt

4 tablespoons butter, at room
    temperature

⅓ cup light brown sugar,
    firmly packed

1 egg yolk

1 For the crust, put the hazelnuts in a large bowl. Sift in the flour and salt, and stir to mix. Set aside.

2 Beat the butter with the brown sugar until light and fluffy. Beat in the egg yolk. Gradually fold in the nut mixture, in three batches, until well combined.

3 Press the dough into a greased 9-inch pie pan, spreading it evenly against the sides. Form a rim around the top edge that is slightly thicker than the sides. Cover and chill for at least 30 minutes.

4 Preheat the oven to 350°F. Meanwhile, for the topping, combine the blueberries, honey, 1 tablespoon of the sugar and 1 teaspoon lemon juice in a heavy saucepan. Cook the mixture over low heat, stirring occasionally, until the berries have given off some liquid but still retain their shape, 5–7 minutes. Remove from the heat and set aside.

5 Place the crust in the oven and bake for 15 minutes. Remove and let cool while making the filling.

6 Beat together the cream cheese and remaining sugar until light and fluffy. Add the egg, 1 tablespoon lemon juice, the liqueur, if using, and the cream and beat until thoroughly blended.

7 Pour the cheese mixture into the crust and spread evenly. Bake until just set, 20–25 minutes.

8 Let the cheesecake cool completely on a wire rack, then cover and chill for at least 1 hour.

9 Spread the blueberry mixture evenly on top of the cheesecake. Serve at room temperature.

COOK'S TIP

The cheesecake can be prepared 1 day in advance, but add the fruit shortly before serving.

Sponge Cake with Fruit and Cream

Called Génoise, this is the French cake used as the base for both simple and elaborate creations. You could simply dust it with confectioners' sugar, or layer it with seasonal fruits to serve as a seasonal dessert.

INGREDIENTS

Serves 6

1 cup all-purpose flour

pinch of salt

4 eggs, at room temperature

scant ⅔ cup sugar

½ teaspoon vanilla extract

4 tablespoons butter, melted or clarified
  and cooled

For the filling

1 pound fresh strawberries
  or raspberries

2–4 tablespoons sugar

2 cups whipping cream

1 teaspoon vanilla extract

1 Preheat the oven to 350°F. Lightly butter a 9-inch springform pan or deep cake pan. Line the bottom with nonstick baking parchment, and dust lightly with flour. Sift the flour and salt together twice.

2 Half-fill a medium saucepan with hot water and set over low heat (do not let the water boil). Put the eggs in a heatproof bowl that just fits into the pan without touching the water. Using an electric mixer, beat the eggs at medium-high speed, gradually adding the sugar, for 8–10 minutes, until the mixture is very thick and pale and leaves a ribbon trail when the beaters are lifted. Remove the bowl from the pan, add the vanilla and continue beating until the mixture is cool.

3 Fold in the flour mixture in three batches, using a balloon whisk or metal spoon. Before the third addition of flour, stir a large spoonful of the mixture into the melted or clarified butter to lighten it, then fold the butter into the remaining mixture with the last addition of flour. Work quickly, but gently, so the mixture does not deflate. Pour into the prepared pan, smoothing the top so the sides are slightly higher than the center.

4 Bake for 25–30 minutes, until the top of the cake springs back when touched and the edge begins to shrink away from the sides of the pan. Place the cake in its pan on a wire rack to cool for 5–10 minutes, then invert the cake onto the rack to cool completely. Peel off the baking parchment.

5 To make the filling, slice the strawberries, place in a bowl, sprinkle with 1–2 tablespoons of the sugar and set aside. Beat the cream with 1–2 tablespoons of the sugar and the vanilla until it holds soft peaks.

6 To assemble the cake (up to 4 hours before serving), split the cake horizontally, using a serrated knife. Place the top, cut-side up, on a serving plate. Spread with a third of the cream and cover with an even layer of sliced strawberries.

7 Place the bottom half of the cake, cut-side down, on top of the filling and press lightly. Spread the remaining cream on the top and sides of the cake. Chill until ready to serve. Serve the remaining strawberries with the cake.

Devil's Food Cake with Orange Frosting

Chocolate and orange are the ultimate combination. Can you resist the temptation?

INGREDIENTS

Serves 8–10

½ cup unsweetened cocoa powder

¾ cup butter, at room temperature

1½ cups dark brown sugar, firmly packed

3 eggs, at room temperature

2 cups all-purpose flour

1½ teaspoons baking soda

¼ teaspoon baking powder

¾ cup sour cream

orange zest strips, for decoration

For the frosting

1½ cups sugar

2 egg whites

4 tablespoons frozen orange juice concentrate

1 tablespoon fresh lemon juice

grated zest of 1 orange

1 Preheat the oven to 350°F. Line two 9-inch cake pans with waxed paper and grease. In a bowl, mix the cocoa powder and ¾ cup of boiling water until smooth. Set aside.

2 With an electric mixer, cream the butter and sugar until light and fluffy. Add the eggs, one at a time, beating well.

3 When the cocoa mixture is cooked to lukewarm, stir into the butter mixture.

4 Sift together the flour, baking soda and baking powder twice. Fold into the cocoa mixture in three batches, alternating with the sour cream.

5 Pour into the pans. Bake until the cakes pull away from the pan, 30–35 minutes. Stand for 15 minutes before unmolding.

6 Thinly slice the orange zest strips. Blanch in boiling water for 1 minute.

7 For the frosting, place all the ingredients in the top of a double boiler or in a bowl set over hot water. With an electric mixer, beat until the mixture holds soft peaks. Continue beating off the heat until thick enough to spread.

8 Sandwich the cake with frosting, then spread on the top and sides. Arrange the zest on top.

Black Forest Gâteau

This light chocolate cake, moistened with Kirsch and layered with cherries and cream, is still one of the most popular of all the chocolate gâteaux.

INGREDIENTS

Serves 8–10

6 eggs

scant 1 cup sugar

1 teaspoon vanilla extract

½ cup all-purpose flour

½ cup unsweetened cocoa powder

½ cup unsalted butter, melted

For the filling and topping

4 tablespoons Kirsch

2½ cups heavy or whipping cream

2 tablespoons confectioners' sugar

½ teaspoon vanilla extract

1½-pound jar pitted morello
   cherries, drained

To decorate

confectioners' sugar, for dusting

grated chocolate

chocolate curls

fresh or drained canned
   morello cherries

1 Preheat the oven to 350°F. Grease three 7½-inch sandwich cake pans and line the bottom of each with nonstick baking parchment. Whisk the eggs with the sugar and vanilla in a large bowl until pale and very thick—the mixture should hold a firm trail when the whisk is lifted.

2 Sift the flour and cocoa powder onto the mixture and fold in lightly and evenly. Stir in the melted butter. Divide the mixture among the prepared cake pans, smoothing them level.

3 Bake for 15–18 minutes, until risen and springy to the touch. Let cool in the pans for about 5 minutes, then turn out onto wire racks and let cool completely.

4 Prick each layer all over with a skewer or fork, then sprinkle with Kirsch. Whip the cream in a bowl until it starts to thicken, then beat in the confectioners' sugar and vanilla until the mixture begins to hold its shape.

5 To assemble, spread one cake layer with a thick layer of flavored cream and top with a quarter of the cherries. Spread a second cake layer with cream and cherries, then place it on top of the first layer. Top with the final layer.

6 Spread the remaining cream all over the cake. Dust a plate with confectioners' sugar; position the cake. Press grated chocolate on the sides and decorate with the chocolate curls and cherries.

Angel Food Cake

This cake is beautifully light. The secret? Sifting the flour over and over again to let plenty of air into it.

INGREDIENTS

Serves 12–14

1 cup sifted cake flour

1½ cups sugar

1¼ cups egg whites (about 10–11 eggs)

1¼ teaspoons cream of tartar

¼ teaspoon salt

1 teaspoon vanilla extract

¼ teaspoon almond extract

confectioners' sugar, for dusting

1 Preheat the oven to 325°F. Sift the flour before measuring, then sift it four times with ½ cup of the sugar. Transfer to a bowl.

2 With an electric mixer, beat the egg whites until foamy. Sift on the cream of tartar and salt and continue to beat until they hold soft peaks when the beaters are lifted.

3 Add the remaining sugar in three batches, beating well after each addition. Stir in the vanilla and almond extracts.

4 Add the flour mixture, ½ cup at a time, and fold in gently with a large metal spoon after each addition.

5 Transfer to an ungreased 10-inch straight-sided ring mold and bake until delicately browned on top, about 1 hour.

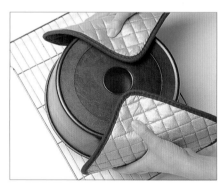

6 Turn the ring mold upside down onto a cake rack and let cool for 1 hour. If the cake does not unmold, run a spatula around the edge to loosen it. Invert onto a serving plate.

7 When cool, lay a star-shaped template on top of the cake, sift with confectioners' sugar, and lift off.

Chocolate and Cherry Polenta Cake

Polenta and almonds add an unusual nutty texture to this delicious cake.

INGREDIENTS

Serves 8

⅓ cup quick-cook polenta

7 ounces semi-sweet chocolate, broken into squares

5 eggs, separated

¾ cup sugar

1 cup ground almonds

4 tablespoons all-purpose flour

finely grated zest of 1 orange

½ cup candied cherries, halved

confectioners' sugar, for dusting

1 Place the polenta in a heatproof bowl and pour in just enough boiling water to cover, about ½ cup. Stir well, then cover the bowl and let stand for about 30 minutes, until the polenta has absorbed all the excess moisture.

2 Preheat the oven to 375°F. Grease a deep 8½-inch round cake pan and line the bottom with nonstick baking parchment. Melt the chocolate in a heatproof bowl over hot water.

3 Whisk the egg yolks with the sugar in a bowl until thick and pale. Beat in the chocolate, then fold in the polenta, ground almonds, flour and orange zest.

4 Whisk the egg whites in a clean bowl until stiff. Stir 1 tablespoon of the whites into the chocolate mixture, then fold in the rest. Finally, fold in the cherries.

5 Scrape the mixture into the prepared pan and bake for 45–55 minutes or until well risen and firm to the touch. Cool on a rack. Dust with confectioners' sugar to serve.

Lemon Coconut Layer Cake

The flavors of lemon and coconut complement each other beautifully in this light dessert cake.

INGREDIENTS

Serves 8–10

1 cup all-purpose flour

pinch of salt

8 eggs

1¾ cups sugar

1 tablespoon grated orange zest

grated zest of 2 lemons

juice of 1 lemon

½ cup dry, shredded coconut

2 tablespoons cornstarch

6 tablespoons butter

For the frosting

½ cup unsalted butter,
    at room temperature

1 cup confectioners' sugar

grated zest of 1 lemon

6–8 tablespoons fresh lemon juice

14 ounces dry, shredded coconut

1 Preheat the oven to 350°F. Line three 8-inch cake pans with baking parchment and grease. In a bowl, sift together the flour and salt and set aside.

2 Place six of the eggs in a large heatproof bowl set over hot water. With an electric mixer, beat until frothy. Gradually beat in ¾ cup of the sugar until the mixture doubles in volume and is thick enough to leave a ribbon trail when the beaters are lifted, which takes about 10 minutes.

3 Remove the bowl from the hot water. Fold in the orange zest, half the grated lemon zest and 1 tablespoon of the lemon juice until blended. Fold in the coconut.

4 Sift in the flour mixture in three batches, folding in thoroughly after each addition.

5 Divide the mixture between the prepared pans.

6 Bake until the cakes pull away from the sides of the pan, 25–30 minutes. Let stand 3–5 minutes, then unmold and transfer to a cooling rack.

7 In a bowl, blend the cornstarch with a little cold water to dissolve. Whisk in the remaining eggs until just blended. Set aside.

8 In a saucepan, combine the remaining lemon zest and juice, the remaining sugar, butter and 1 cup of water.

9 Over medium heat, bring the mixture to a boil. Whisk in the eggs and cornstarch, and return to a boil. Whisk continuously until thick, about 5 minutes. Remove from heat. Cover with baking parchment to stop a skin from forming and set aside.

10 For the frosting, cream the butter and confectioners' sugar until smooth. Stir in the lemon zest and enough lemon juice to obtain a thick, spreadable consistency.

11 Sandwich the three cake layers with the lemon custard mixture. Spread the frosting on the top and sides. Cover the cake with the coconut, pressing it in gently.

Carrot Cake with Maple Butter Frosting

A good, quick cake for a family supper.

INGREDIENTS

Serves 12

1 pound carrots, peeled

1½ cups all-purpose flour

2 teaspoons baking powder

½ teaspoon baking soda

1 teaspoon salt

2 teaspoons ground cinnamon

4 eggs

2 teaspoons vanilla extract

1 cup dark brown sugar,
    firmly packed

½ cup sugar

1¼ cups sunflower oil

1 cup walnuts,
    finely chopped

½ cup raisins

walnut halves, for decorating
    (optional)

For the frosting

6 tablespoons unsalted butter, at room
    temperature

3 cups confectioners' sugar

¼ cup maple syrup

1 Preheat the oven to 350°F. Line an 11 x 8-inch rectangular cake pan with nonstick baking parchment and grease. Grate the carrots and set aside.

2 Sift the flour, baking powder, baking soda, salt and cinnamon into a bowl. Set aside.

3 With an electric mixer, beat the eggs until blended. Add the vanilla, sugars and oil and beat well to incorporate.

4 Add the carrots, walnuts and raisins to the mixture, and fold in thoroughly.

5 Pour the batter into the prepared pan and bake until the cake springs back when touched lightly, 40–45 minutes. Let stand for 10 minutes, then unmold and transfer to a rack.

6 For the frosting, cream the butter with half the sugar until soft. Add the syrup, then beat in the remaining sugar until blended.

7 Spread the frosting on the top of the cake. Using a metal spatula, make decorative ridges in the frosting. Cut into squares. Decorate with walnut halves.

Black and White Pound Cake

A good cake for packed lunches and picnics, as it cuts into neat slices with no messy filling, or serve with custard for dessert.

INGREDIENTS

Serves 16

4 ounces semi-sweet chocolate,
   broken into squares
3 cups all-purpose flour
1 teaspoon baking powder
2 cups butter,
   at room temperature
3⅓ cups sugar
1 tablespoon vanilla extract
10 eggs, at room temperature
confectioners' sugar, for dusting

1 Preheat the oven to 350°F. Line the bottom of a 10-inch straight-sided ring mold with nonstick baking parchment and grease. Dust with flour spread evenly with a brush.

3 In a bowl, sift together the flour and baking powder. In another bowl, cream the butter, sugar and vanilla with an electric mixer until light and fluffy. Add the eggs, two at a time, then gradually incorporate the flour mixture on a low speed.

4 Spoon half of the batter into the prepared pan.

5 Stir the chocolate into the remaining batter, then spoon into the pan. With a metal spatula, swirl the two batters to create a marbled effect.

2 Melt the chocolate in the top of a double boiler, or in a heatproof bowl set over a pan of hot water. Stir occasionally. Set aside.

COOK'S TIP

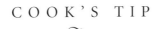

This is also known as Marbled Cake because of its distinctive appearance.

6 Bake until a cake tester inserted in the center comes out clean, about 1¾ hours. Cover with foil halfway through baking. Let stand for 15 minutes, then unmold and transfer to a cooling rack. To serve, dust with confectioners' sugar.

Chocolate Mousse Strawberry Layer Cake

The strawberries used in this cake can be replaced by raspberries or blackberries and the appropriate flavor liqueur.

INGREDIENTS

Serves 10

4 ounces fine quality white chocolate, chopped

½ cup whipping or heavy cream

½ cup milk

1 tablespoon rum or vanilla extract

½ cup unsalted butter, softened

generous ¾ cup sugar

3 eggs

2½ cups all-purpose flour

1 teaspoon baking powder

pinch of salt

1½ pounds fresh strawberries, sliced, plus extra for decoration

3 cups whipping cream

2 tablespoons rum or strawberry-flavor liqueur

For the white chocolate mousse

9 ounces fine quality white chocolate, chopped

1½ cups whipping or heavy cream

2 tablespoons rum or strawberry-flavor liqueur

1 Preheat oven to 350°F. Grease and flour two 9 x 2-inch cake pans. Line the bottoms of the pans with nonstick baking parchment. Melt chocolate and cream in a double boiler over low heat, stirring until smooth. Stir in milk and rum or vanilla, set aside to cool.

2 In a large bowl with an electric mixer, beat the butter and sugar until light and creamy. Add the eggs one at a time, beating well.

3 In a small bowl, stir together the flour, baking powder and salt. Alternately add flour and melted chocolate to the eggs in batches, just until blended. Pour the batter evenly into the pans.

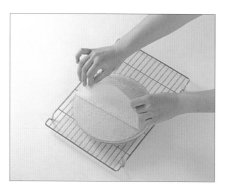

4 Bake for 20–25 minutes, until a cake tester inserted in the center comes out clean. Cool on a wire rack for 10 minutes. Turn cakes out onto wire rack, peel off paper and cool completely.

5 Prepare the mousse. In a medium saucepan over low heat, melt the chocolate and cream until smooth, stirring frequently. Stir in rum or strawberry-flavor liqueur and pour into a bowl. Chill until just set. With a wire whisk, whip lightly until mixture has a "mousse" consistency.

6 Slice both cake layers in half crosswise. Sandwich the four layers together with the mousse and strawberries.

7 Whip the cream with the rum or strawberry-flavor liqueur until firm peaks form. Spread half on the top and sides of the cake. Spoon remaining cream into a decorating bag with a star tip and pipe scrolls on top. Garnish with remaining strawberries.

Death by Chocolate

One of the richest chocolate cakes ever, so serve in thin slices.

INGREDIENTS

Serves 16–20

8 ounces dark chocolate,
　broken into squares
½ cup unsalted butter
⅔ cup milk
1¼ cups light brown sugar
2 teaspoons vanilla extract
2 eggs, separated
⅔ cup sour cream
2 cups self-rising flour
1 teaspoon baking powder

For the filling
4 tablespoons seedless raspberry jam
4 tablespoons brandy
14 ounces dark chocolate,
　broken into squares
scant 1 cup unsalted butter

For the topping
1 cup heavy cream
8 ounces dark chocolate,
　broken into squares
semi-sweet and white chocolate curls,
　to decorate
chocolate-dipped Cape gooseberries,
　to decorate (optional)

1 Preheat the oven to 350°F. Grease and bottom-line a deep 9-inch springform cake pan. Place chocolate, butter and milk in a saucepan. Heat gently until smooth. Remove from heat, beat in sugar and vanilla, then cool.

2 Beat the egg yolks and cream in a bowl, then beat into the chocolate mixture. Sift the flour and baking powder onto the surface and fold in. Whisk the egg whites in a grease-free bowl until stiff; fold into the mixture.

3 Scrape into the prepared pan and bake for 45–55 minutes or until firm to the touch. Cool in the pan for 15 minutes, then invert to a wire rack to cool.

4 Slice the cold cake across the middle to make three even layers. In a small saucepan, warm the jam with 1 tablespoon of the brandy, then brush on two of the layers. Heat the remaining brandy in a saucepan with the chocolate and butter, stirring, until smooth. Cool until beginning to thicken.

5 Spread the bottom layer of the cake with half the chocolate filling, taking care not to disturb the jam. Top with a second layer, jam side up, and spread with the remaining filling. Top with the final layer and press lightly. Let set.

6 To make the topping, heat the cream and chocolate together in a saucepan over low heat, stirring frequently, until the chocolate has melted. Pour into a bowl, let cool, then whisk until the mixture begins to hold its shape.

7 Spread the top and sides of the cake with the chocolate ganache. Decorate with plain and white chocolate curls and, if desired, chocolate-dipped Cape gooseberries.

Simple Chocolate Cake

An easy, everyday chocolate cake which can be filled with butter-cream, or with a rich chocolate ganache for a special occasion.

INGREDIENTS

Serves 6–8

4 ounces semi-sweet chocolate, broken
   into squares
3 tablespoons milk
⅔ cup unsalted butter or margarine,
   softened
scant 1 cup light brown sugar
3 eggs
1¾ cups self-rising flour
1 tablespoon unsweetened cocoa powder

For the buttercream
6 tablespoons unsalted butter or
   margarine, softened
1½ cups confectioners' sugar
1 tablespoon unsweetened cocoa powder
½ teaspoon vanilla extract
confectioners' sugar and unsweetened
   cocoa powder, for dusting

1 Preheat the oven to 350°F. Grease two 7-inch round cake pans and line the bottom of each with nonstick baking parchment. Melt the chocolate with the milk in a heatproof bowl set over a pan of simmering water.

2 Cream the butter or margarine with the sugar in a mixing bowl until pale and fluffy. Add the eggs one at a time, beating well after each addition. Stir in the chocolate mixture until it is well combined.

3 Sift the flour powder and cocoa powder over the mixture and fold in with a metal spoon until evenly mixed. Scrape into the prepared pans, smooth level and bake for 35–40 minutes or until well risen and firm. Turn out onto wire racks and let cool.

4 To make the buttercream, beat the butter or margarine, confectioners' sugar, cocoa powder and vanilla extract together in a bowl until the mixture is smooth.

5 Sandwich the cake layers together with the buttercream. Dust with a mixture of confectioners' sugar and cocoa powder just before serving.

Pineapple Upside-down Cake

This is a perennial favorite to serve in winter or summer.

Serves 8

½ cup butter

1 cup dark brown sugar,
   firmly packed

16-ounce can pineapple slices, drained

4 eggs, separated

grated zest of 1 lemon

pinch of salt

½ cup sugar

¾ cup all-purpose flour

1 teaspoon baking powder

1 Preheat the oven to 350°F. Melt the butter in an ovenproof cast-iron frying pan, about 10 inches in diameter. Remove 1 tablespoon of the melted butter and set aside.

2 Add the brown sugar to the frying pan and stir until blended. Place the drained pineapple slices on top in one layer. Set aside.

3 In a bowl, whisk together the egg yolks, reserved butter and lemon zest until smooth and well blended. Set aside.

4 With an electric mixer, beat the egg whites with the salt until stiff. Fold in the sugar, 2 tablespoons at a time. Fold in the egg yolk mixture.

5 Sift the flour and baking powder together. Fold into the egg mixture in three batches.

6 Pour the batter over the pineapple and smooth level.

7 Bake until a cake tester inserted in the center comes out clean, about 30 minutes.

8 While still hot, place a serving plate on top of the frying pan, bottom-side up. Holding them together with oven mitts, flip over. Serve hot or cold.

Raspberry and White Chocolate Cheesecake

Raspberries and white chocolate are an irresistible combination, especially when teamed with rich mascarpone on a crunchy ginger and pecan crust.

INGREDIENTS

Serves 8

4 tablespoons unsalted butter

2⅓ cups ginger cookies, crushed

½ cup chopped pecans
   or walnuts

For the filling

1¼ cups mascarpone cheese

¾ cup fromage frais

2 eggs, beaten

3 tablespoons sugar

9 ounces white chocolate,
   broken into squares

1⅓ cups fresh or frozen raspberries

For the topping

½ cup mascarpone cheese

⅓ cup fromage frais

white chocolate curls and raspberries,
   to decorate

1 Preheat the oven to 300°F. Melt the butter in a saucepan, then stir in the crushed cookies and nuts. Press into the bottom of a 9-inch springform cake pan.

2 Make the filling. Beat the mascarpone and fromage frais in a bowl, then beat in the eggs and sugar until evenly mixed.

3 Melt the white chocolate gently in a heatproof bowl over hot water.

4 Stir the chocolate into the cheese mixture with the raspberries.

5 Pour into the prepared pan and spread evenly, then bake for about 1 hour or until just set. Switch off the oven, but do not remove the cheesecake. Leave it until cold and completely set.

6 Release the pan and lift the cheesecake onto a plate. Make the topping by mixing the mascarpone and fromage frais in a bowl and spread onto the cheesecake. Decorate with chocolate curls and raspberries.

Marbled Jelly Roll

The combination of light chocolate cake and walnut chocolate buttercream is simply sensational.

INGREDIENTS

Serves 6–8

scant 1 cup all-purpose flour

1 tablespoon unsweetened cocoa powder

1 ounce semi-sweet chocolate, grated

1 ounce white chocolate, grated

3 eggs

generous ½ cup sugar

For the filling

6 tablespoons unsalted butter or
    margarine, softened

1½ cups confectioners' sugar

1 tablespoon unsweetened cocoa powder

½ teaspoon vanilla extract

3 tablespoons chopped walnuts

semi-sweet and white chocolate curls, to
    decorate (optional)

1 Preheat the oven to 400°F. Grease a 12 x 8-inch jelly roll pan and line with nonstick baking parchment. Sift half the flour with the cocoa powder into bowl. Stir in the grated semi-sweet chocolate. Sift the remaining flour into another bowl; stir in the grated white chocolate.

2 Whisk the eggs and sugar in a heatproof bowl; set over a saucepan of hot water until it holds its shape when the whisk is lifted.

3 Remove the bowl from heat and put half the mixture into a separate bowl. Fold the white chocolate mixture into one portion, then fold the semi-sweet chocolate mixture into the other. Stir 1 tablespoon boiling water into each half to soften the batters.

4 Place alternate spoonfuls of mixture in the prepared pan and swirl lightly together for a marbled effect. Bake for 12–15 minutes or until firm. Turn out onto a sheet of nonstick baking parchment.

5 Trim the edges to neaten and cover with a damp, clean dish towel. Cool.

6 For the filling, beat the butter or margarine, confectioners' sugar, cocoa powder and vanilla together in a bowl until smooth, then mix in the walnuts.

7 Uncover the cake, lift off the baking parchment and spread the surface with the buttercream. Roll up carefully from a long side and place on a serving plate. Decorate with semi-sweet and white chocolate curls, if desired.

Sachertorte

This glorious gâteau was created in Vienna in 1832 by Franz Sacher, a chef in the royal household.

INGREDIENTS

Serves 10–12

8 ounces dark chocolate,
   broken into squares
⅔ cup unsalted butter, softened
generous ½ cup sugar
8 eggs, separated
1 cup all-purpose flour

For the glaze
scant 1 cup apricot jam
1 tablespoon lemon juice

For the icing
8 ounces dark chocolate,
   broken into squares
1 cup sugar
1 tablespoon golden or light corn syrup
1 cup heavy cream
1 teaspoon vanilla extract
semi-sweet chocolate curls, to decorate

1 Preheat the oven to 350°F. Grease a 9-inch round springform cake pan and line with nonstick baking parchment. Melt the chocolate in a heatproof bowl over hot water, then remove from heat.

2 Cream the butter with the sugar in a mixing bowl until pale and fluffy, then add the egg yolks, one at a time, beating after each addition. Beat in the melted chocolate, then sift the flour onto the mixture and fold it in evenly.

3 Whisk the egg whites in a clean, grease-free bowl until stiff, then stir about a quarter of the whites into the chocolate mixture to lighten it. Fold in the remaining whites.

4 Put the mixture into the prepared cake pan and smooth level. Bake for 50–55 minutes or until firm. Turn out carefully onto a wire rack to cool.

5 Heat the apricot jam with the lemon juice in a small saucepan until melted, then strain through a sieve into a bowl. Once the cake is cold, slice in half across the middle to make two equal-size layers.

6 Brush the top and sides of each layer with the apricot glaze, then sandwich them together. Place on a wire rack.

7 Mix the icing ingredients in a heavy saucepan. Heat gently, stirring until thick. Simmer for 3–4 minutes, without stirring, until the mixture registers 200°F on a sugar thermometer. Pour quickly over the cake and spread evenly. Let set, then decorate with chocolate curls.

Australian Hazelnut Pavlova

Meringue topped with fresh fruit and cream—perfect for summer dinner parties.

INGREDIENTS

Serves 4–6

3 egg whites

generous ¾ cup sugar

1 teaspoon cornstarch

1 teaspoon white wine vinegar

5 tablespoons chopped roasted hazelnuts

1 cup heavy cream

1 tablespoon orange juice

2 tablespoons plain yogurt

2 ripe nectarines, pitted and sliced

1⅓ cups raspberries

1–2 tablespoons red currant jelly, warmed

1 Preheat the oven to 275°F. Lightly grease a baking sheet. Draw an 8-inch circle on a sheet of baking parchment. Place pencil-side down on the baking sheet.

2 Place the egg whites in a large, clean, grease-free bowl and whisk with an electric mixer until stiff. Whisk in the sugar 1 tablespoon at a time, whisking well after each addition.

3 Add the cornstarch, vinegar and hazelnuts and fold in carefully with a large metal spoon.

4 Spoon the meringue onto the marked circle and spread out, making a dip in the center.

5 Bake for 1¼–1½ hours, until crisp. Let cool, then transfer to a serving platter.

6 Whip the cream and orange juice until just thick, stir in the yogurt and spoon onto the meringue. Top with the fruit and drizzle on the red currant jelly. Serve immediately.

Pastries
&
Pies

◆ ◆ ◆

Chocolate Almond Meringue Pie

This dream dessert combines three very popular flavors: velvety chocolate filling on a light orange pastry crust, topped with fluffy white meringue.

INGREDIENTS

Serves 6

1½ cups all-purpose flour

⅓ cup ground rice

⅔ cup unsalted butter

finely grated zest of 1 orange

1 egg yolk

sliced almonds and melted dark chocolate,
    to decorate

For the filling

5 ounces dark chocolate,
    broken into squares

4 tablespoons unsalted butter, softened

⅓ cup sugar

2 teaspoons cornstarch

4 egg yolks

¾ cup ground almonds

For the meringue

3 egg whites

¾ cup sugar

1 Sift the flour and ground rice into a bowl. Rub in the butter until the mixture resembles bread crumbs. Stir in the orange zest. Add the egg yolk; bring the dough together. Roll out and use to line a 9-inch round tart pan. Chill for 30 minutes.

2 Preheat the oven to 375°F. Prick the pastry crust all over with a fork, cover with waxed paper weighed down with baking beans and bake blind for 10 minutes. Remove the pastry crust; take out the baking beans and paper.

3 Make the filling. Melt the chocolate in a heatproof bowl over hot water. Cream the butter with the sugar in a bowl, then beat in the cornstarch and egg yolks. Fold in the almonds, then the chocolate. Spread in the pastry crust. Bake for another 10 minutes.

4 Make the meringue. Whisk the egg whites until stiff, then gradually add half the sugar. Fold in remaining sugar.

5 Spoon the meringue onto the chocolate filling, lifting if up with the back of the spoon to form peaks. Reduce the oven temperature to 350°F and bake the pie for 15–20 minutes or until the topping is pale gold. Serve warm, with almonds sprinkled on top and drizzled with melted chocolate.

Red Berry Tart with Lemon Cream Filling

This tart is best filled just before serving so the pastry remains mouthwateringly crisp. Select red berries such as strawberries, raspberries and red currants.

INGREDIENTS

Serves 6–8

1¼ cups all-purpose flour

¼ cup cornstarch

5 tablespoons confectioners' sugar

7 tablespoons butter

1 teaspoon vanilla extract

2 egg yolks, beaten

sprig of mint, to decorate

For the filling

scant 1 cup cream cheese

3 tablespoons lemon curd

grated zest and juice of 1 lemon

confectioners' sugar, to sweeten (optional)

2 cups mixed red berries

3 tablespoons red currant jelly

1 Sift the flour, cornstarch and confectioners' sugar together, then rub in the butter until the mixture resembles bread crumbs.

2 Beat the vanilla into the egg yolks, then mix into the crumbs to make a firm dough, adding cold water if necessary.

3 Roll out the pastry and line a 9-inch round tart pan. Prick the bottom of the crust with a fork and let it rest in the refrigerator for 30 minutes.

4 Preheat the oven to 400°F. Line the crust with waxed paper and baking beans. Place the pan on a baking sheet and bake for 20 minutes, removing the paper and beans for the last 5 minutes. When cooked, cool and remove the pastry shell from the tart pan.

5 Cream the cheese, lemon curd and lemon zest and juice, adding confectioners' sugar to sweeten, if desired. Spread the mixture into the bottom of the crust.

6 Top with the berries. Gently warm the red currant jelly and drizzle it on the filling just before serving, decorated with a sprig of mint.

VARIATION

There are all sorts of delightful variations to this recipe. For instance, leave out the red currant jelly and sprinkle lightly with sugar or decorate with fresh strawberry leaves. Alternatively, top with sliced kiwi or bananas sprinkled with lemon juice.

Peach and Blueberry Pie

The unusual combination of fruits in this pie looks especially good with a lattice pastry topping.

INGREDIENTS

Serves 8

2 cups all-purpose flour

pinch of salt

2 teaspoons sugar

10 tablespoons cold butter
    or margarine

1 egg yolk

2 tablespoons milk, to glaze

For the filling

1 pound fresh peaches, peeled, pitted
    and sliced

2 cups fresh blueberries

¾ cup sugar

2 tablespoons fresh lemon juice

⅓ cup all-purpose flour

large pinch of grated nutmeg

2 tablespoons butter or margarine,
    cut into tiny pieces

1 To make the pastry, sift the flour, salt and sugar into a bowl. Rub the butter or margarine into the dry ingredients as quickly as possible until the mixture resembles coarse bread crumbs.

2 Mix the egg yolk with ¼ cup of ice water and sprinkle on the flour mixture. Combine with a fork until the dough holds together. If the dough is too crumbly, add a little more water, 1 tablespoon at a time. Gather the dough into a ball and flatten into a round. Place in a sealed plastic bag and chill for at least 20 minutes.

3 Roll out two-thirds of the pastry between two sheets of waxed paper to a thickness of about ⅛ inch. Use to line a 9-inch pie dish.

4 Trim the pastry all around, leaving a ½-inch overhang. Fold the overhang under to form the edge. Using a fork, press the edge to the rim of the pie dish.

5 Gather the trimmings and remaining pastry into a ball, and roll out to a thickness of about ¼ inch. Using a pastry wheel or sharp knife, cut into long, ½-inch wide strips. Chill both the pastry shell and the strips of pastry for 20 minutes. Meanwhile, preheat the oven to 400°F.

6 Line the pastry shell with waxed paper and fill with dried beans. Bake for 7–10 minutes, until the pastry is just set. Remove from the oven and carefully lift out the paper with the beans. Prick the bottom of the pastry shell with a fork, then return to the oven and bake for another 5 minutes. Let cool slightly before filling. Leave the oven on.

7 For the filling, place the peach slices and blueberries in a bowl and stir in the sugar, lemon juice, flour and nutmeg. Spoon the fruit mixture into the pastry shell. Dot the top with the pieces of butter or margarine.

8 Weave a lattice top with the chilled pastry strips, pressing the ends to the edge of the baked pastry shell. Brush the strips with the milk.

9 Bake the pie for 15 minutes. Reduce the oven temperature to 350°F, and continue baking for another 30 minutes, until the filling is tender and bubbling and the pastry lattice is golden. If the pastry becomes too brown, cover loosely with a piece of aluminum foil. Serve the pie warm or at room temperature.

COOK'S TIP

Don't over-chill the pastry strips. If they become too firm, they may crack and break as you weave them into a lattice.

Rhubarb Pie

Use a cookie cutter to cut out decorative pastry shapes and make this pie extra special.

INGREDIENTS

Serves 6

1½ cups all-purpose flour

½ teaspoon salt

2 teaspoons sugar

6 tablespoons cold butter or margarine

2 tablespoons light cream

light or heavy cream, to serve

For the filling

2¼ pounds fresh rhubarb,
  cut into 1-inch slices

2 tablespoons cornstarch

1 egg

1½ cups sugar

1 tablespoon grated orange zest

1 To make the pastry, sift the flour, salt and sugar into a bowl. Using a pastry blender or two knives, cut the butter or margarine into the dry ingredients as quickly as possible until the mixture resembles bread crumbs.

2 Sprinkle the flour mixture with about ¼ cup of ice water and mix until the dough just holds together. If the dough is too crumbly, add a little more water, 1 tablespoon at a time.

3 Gather the dough into a ball, flatten into a round, place in a plastic bag and put in the refrigerator for 20 minutes.

4 Roll out the pastry between two sheets of waxed paper to a ⅛-inch thickness. Use to line a 9-inch pie dish. Trim all around, leaving a ½-inch overhang. Fold the overhang under the edge and flute. Chill the shell and trimmings for 30 minutes.

5 To make the filling, put the rhubarb in a bowl, sprinkle with the cornstarch and toss to coat.

6 Preheat the oven to 425°F. Beat the egg with the sugar in a bowl until thoroughly blended, then mix in the orange zest.

7 Stir the sugar mixture into the rhubarb and mix well, then spoon the fruit into the prepared pastry shell.

8 Roll out the pastry trimmings. Stamp out decorative shapes with a cookie cutter.

9 Arrange the pastry shapes on top of the pie. Brush the shapes and the edge of the pastry case with cream.

10 Bake the pie for 30 minutes. Reduce the oven temperature to 325°F and continue baking for another 15–20 minutes, until the pastry is golden brown and the rhubarb is tender. Serve the pie hot with cream.

Chocolate Pecan Torte

This torte uses finely ground nuts instead of flour. Toast then cool the nuts before grinding finely in a blender or food processor. Do not over-grind the nuts, as the oils will form a paste.

INGREDIENTS

Serves 16

7 ounces bittersweet or semi-sweet
  chocolate, chopped

10 tablespoons unsalted butter, cut
  into pieces

4 eggs

½ cup sugar

2 teaspoons vanilla extract

1 cup ground pecans

2 teaspoons ground cinnamon

24 toasted pecan halves to decorate
  (optional)

For the chocolate honey glaze

4 ounces bittersweet or semi-sweet
  chocolate, chopped

¼ cup unsalted butter,
  cut into pieces

2 tablespoons honey

pinch of ground cinnamon

1 Preheat oven to 350°F. Grease an 8 x 2-inch springform pan; line with baking parchment then grease the paper. Wrap the bottom and sides of the pan with aluminum foil to prevent water seeping in. In a saucepan over low heat, melt the chocolate and butter, stirring until smooth. Remove from heat. In a mixing bowl with the electric mixer, beat the eggs, sugar and vanilla until frothy, 1–2 minutes. Stir in the melted chocolate, peanuts and cinnamon. Pour into the prepared pan.

2 Place the foil-wrapped pan in a large roasting pan and pour boiling water into the roasting pan, to come ¾ inch up the side of the springform pan. Bake for 25–30 minutes, until the edge of the cake is set, but center is soft. Remove from the water bath and remove foil. Cool on a rack.

3 Prepare glaze. In a small saucepan over low heat, melt the chocolate, butter, honey and cinnamon, stirring until smooth; remove from heat. Carefully dip toasted pecan halves halfway into the glaze and place on a nonstick baking parchment-lined baking sheet until it is set.

4 Remove side from springform pan and invert the cake onto wire rack. Remove the pan bottom and paper, so the bottom of the cake is now the top. Pour the thickened glaze on the cake, tilting the rack slightly to spread the glaze. Use a metal knife to smooth the sides. Arrange the glazed nuts on the outside edge of the torte and let the glaze set.

Key Lime Pie

Key limes come from Florida, but if they are not available, ordinary limes will do just as well.

INGREDIENTS

Serves 8

3 large egg yolks

14-ounce can sweetened condensed milk

1 tablespoon grated Key lime zest

½ cup fresh Key lime juice

green food coloring (optional)

½ cup whipping cream

For the crust

1¼ cups graham cracker crumbs

5 tablespoons butter or margarine, melted

1 Preheat the oven to 350°F. For the crust, place the crumbs in a bowl and add the butter or margarine. Mix to combine.

2 Press the crumbs evenly on the bottom and sides of a 9-inch pie dish. Bake for 8 minutes. Let cool.

3 Beat the yolks until thick. Beat in the milk, lime zest and juice, and coloring, if using. Pour into the prebaked pie crust and refrigerate until set, about 4 hours. To serve, whip the cream. Pipe a lattice pattern on top, or spoon dollops around the edge.

Fruit Tartlets

The chocolate pastry shells make a dramatic bottom to these tartlets.

INGREDIENTS

Makes 8

¾ cup red currant or grape jelly

1 tablespoon fresh lemon juice

¾ cup whipping cream

1½ pounds fresh fruit, such as strawberries, raspberries, kiwi, peaches, grapes or blueberries, peeled and sliced as necessary

For the pastry

⅔ cup cold butter, cut in pieces

⅓ cup dark brown sugar, firmly packed

3 tablespoons unsweetened cocoa powder

1½ cups all-purpose flour

1 egg white

1 For the pastry, combine the butter, brown sugar and cocoa powder over low heat. When the butter is melted, remove from heat and sift over the flour. Stir, then add just enough egg white to bind the mixture. Gather into a ball, wrap in waxed paper, and chill for at least 30 minutes.

2 Preheat the oven to 350°F. Grease eight 3-inch tartlet pans. Roll out the dough between two sheets of waxed paper and stamp out eight 4-inch rounds with a fluted cutter.

3 Line the tartlet pans with dough. Prick the bottoms. Chill for 15 minutes.

4 Bake until firm, 20–25 minutes. Let cool, then remove from the pans.

5 Melt the jelly with the lemon juice. Brush a thin layer in the bottom of the tartlets. Whip the cream and spread a thin layer in the tartlet shells. Arrange the fruit on top. Brush evenly with the glaze and serve.

Cherry Pie

The woven lattice is the perfect finishing touch, although you can cheat and use a lattice pastry roller if you prefer.

Serves 8

2 pounds fresh Morello cherries, pitted,
 or 2 1-pound cans or jars,
 drained and pitted
generous ¾ cup sugar
¼ cup all-purpose flour
1½ tablespoons fresh lemon juice
¼ teaspoon almond extract
2 tablespoons butter or margarine

For the pastry
2 cups all-purpose flour
1 teaspoon salt
¾ cup lard or vegetable fat

1 For the pastry, sift the flour and salt into a mixing bowl. Using a pastry blender, cut in the fat until the mixture resembles coarse bread crumbs.

2 Sprinkle in 4–5 tablespoons ice water, a tablespoon at a time, tossing lightly with your fingertips or a fork until the pastry forms a ball.

3 Preheat the oven to 425°F. Divide the pastry in half and shape each half into a ball. On a lightly floured surface, roll out one of the balls to a circle about 12 inches in diameter.

4 Use it to line a 9-inch pie pan, easing the pastry in and being careful not to stretch it. With scissors, trim off excess pastry, leaving a ½-inch overhang around the pie pan.

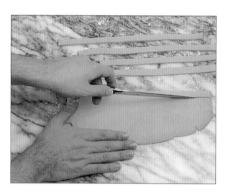

5 Roll out the remaining pastry to ⅛ inch thick. Cut out eleven strips ½ inch wide.

6 In a mixing bowl, combine the cherries, sugar, flour, lemon juice and almond extract. Spoon the mixture into the pastry shell and dot the top with the butter or margarine.

7 To make the lattice, place five of the pastry strips evenly across the filling. Fold every other strip back. Lay the first strip across in the opposite direction. Continue in this pattern, folding back every other strip each time you add a cross strip.

8 Trim the ends of the lattice strips even with the case overhang. Press together so that the edge rests on the pie-pan rim. With your thumbs, flute the edge. Chill for 15 minutes.

9 Bake the pie for 30 minutes, covering the edge of the pastry case with aluminum foil, if necessary, to prevent over-browning. Let cool, in the pan, on a wire rack.

Mince Pies with Orange Cinnamon Pastry

Homemade mince pies are so much better than store bought, especially with this tasty pastry.

INGREDIENTS

Makes 18

2 cups all-purpose flour

1½ ounces confectioners' sugar

2 teaspoons ground cinnamon

10 tablespoons butter

grated zest of 1 orange

⅔ cup mincemeat

1 beaten egg, to glaze

confectioners' sugar, to dust

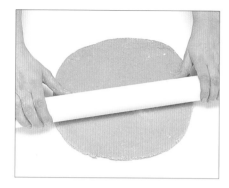

1 Sift together the flour, confectioners' sugar and cinnamon, then rub in the butter until it forms crumbs. (This can be done in a food processor.) Stir in the grated orange zest.

2 Mix into a firm dough with about 4 tablespoons ice cold water. Knead lightly, then roll out to a ¼-inch thickness.

3 Using a 2½-inch round cutter, cut out 18 circles, re-rolling as necessary. Then cut out 18 smaller 2-inch circles.

4 Line two muffin pans with the 18 larger circles—they will fill one and a half pans. Spoon a small spoonful of mincemeat into each pastry shell and top with the smaller pastry circles, pressing the edges lightly together to seal.

5 Glaze the tops of the pies with egg and let rest in the refrigerator for 30 minutes. Preheat the oven to 400°F.

6 Bake the pies for 15–20 minutes, until they are golden brown. Remove them to wire racks to cool. Serve just warm, dusted with confectioners' sugar.

Apple-cranberry Lattice Pie

Use fresh or frozen cranberries for this classic American pie.

INGREDIENTS

Serves 8

grated zest of 1 orange

3 tablespoons fresh orange juice

2 large, tart apples

1 cup cranberries

½ cup raisins

¼ cup walnuts, chopped

1 cup sugar

½ cup dark brown sugar

1 tablespoon quick-cooking tapioca

For the pastry

2 cups all-purpose flour

½ teaspoon salt

6 tablespoons cold butter, cut in pieces

4 tablespoons cold lard, cut in pieces

1 tablespoon sugar,
   for sprinkling

1 For the pastry, sift the flour and salt into a bowl. Add the butter and lard and rub in until the mixture resembles coarse crumbs. With a fork, stir in just enough ice water to bind the dough. Gather into two equal balls, wrap in waxed paper, and chill for at least 20 minutes.

2 Put the orange zest and juice into a mixing bowl. Peel and core the apples and grate them into the bowl. Stir in the cranberries, raisins, walnuts, sugar, brown sugar and tapioca.

3 Place a baking sheet in the oven and preheat to 400°F.

4 On a lightly floured surface, roll out one ball of dough about ⅛ inch thick. Transfer to a 9-inch pie pan and trim the edge. Spoon the cranberry and apple mixture into the shell.

5 Roll out the remaining dough to a circle about 11 inches in diameter. With a serrated pastry wheel, cut the dough into ten strips, ¾ inch wide. Place five strips horizontally across the top of the tart at 1-inch intervals. Weave in six vertical strips. Trim the edges. Sprinkle the top with 1 tablespoon of sugar.

6 Bake for 20 minutes. Reduce the heat to 350°F and bake until the crust is golden and the filling is bubbling, about 15 more minutes.

Lemon Meringue Pie

Serve this exactly as it is, hot, warm or cold. It doesn't need any accompaniment.

Serves 8
grated zest and juice of 1 large lemon
1 cup sugar
2 tablespoons butter
3 tablespoons cornstarch
3 eggs, separated
pinch of salt
⅛ teaspoon cream of tartar

For the pastry
1 cup all-purpose flour
½ teaspoon salt
⅓ cup cold lard, cut in pieces

1 For the pastry, sift the flour and salt into a bowl. Add the lard and cut in with a pastry blender until the mixture resembles coarse crumbs. With a fork, stir in just enough ice water to bind the dough (about 2 tablespoons). Gather the dough into a ball.

2 On a lightly floured surface, roll out the dough to ⅛ inch thick. Transfer to a 9-inch pie pan and trim the edge to leave a ½-inch overhang.

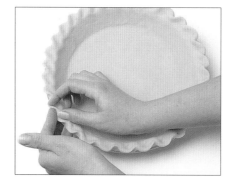

3 Fold the overhang under and crimp the edge. Chill the pie shell in the refrigerator for at least 20 minutes. Preheat the oven to 400°F.

4 Prick the dough all over with a fork. Line with waxed paper and fill with baking beans. Bake for 12 minutes. Remove the paper and beans and continue baking until golden, 6–8 more minutes.

5 In a saucepan, combine the lemon zest and juice, ½ cup of the sugar, butter and 1 cup of water. Bring the mixture to a boil.

6 Meanwhile, in a mixing bowl, dissolve the cornstarch in 1 tablespoon of cold water. Add the egg yolks.

7 Add the egg yolks to the lemon mixture and return to a boil, whisking continuously, until the mixture thickens, about 5 minutes.

8 Cover the surface with waxed paper to prevent a skin from forming and let cool.

9 For the meringue, using an electric mixer, beat the egg whites with the salt and cream of tartar until they hold stiff peaks. Add the remaining sugar and beat until glossy.

10 Spoon the lemon mixture into the pie shell and spread level. Spoon the meringue on top, smoothing it up to the edge of the crust to seal. Bake until golden, 12–15 minutes.

Chocolate Chiffon Pie

This light and creamy dessert is as luxurious as its name suggests.

Serves 8

6 ounces semi-sweet chocolate squares

1 ounce square bittersweet chocolate

1 cup milk

1 tablespoon gelatin, or alternative

⅔ cup sugar

2 eggs, separated

1 teaspoon vanilla extract

1½ cups whipping cream

pinch of salt

whipped cream and chocolate curls,
    to decorate

For the crust

1½ cups graham cracker crumbs

6 tablespoons butter, melted

1 Place a baking sheet in the oven and preheat to 350°F. For the crust, mix the crumbs and butter in a bowl. Press the crumbs evenly on the bottom and sides of a 9-inch pie pan. Bake for 8 minutes. Let cool.

2 Chop the chocolate, then grind in a food processor or blender. Set aside.

3 Place the milk in the top of a double boiler or in a heatproof bowl. Sprinkle on the gelatin. Let stand 5 minutes to soften.

4 Set the top of the double boiler or heatproof bowl over hot water. Add ⅓ cup of the sugar, the chocolate and egg yolks. Stir until dissolved. Add the vanilla.

5 Set the top of the double boiler in a bowl of ice and stir until the mixture reaches room temperature. Remove from the ice and set aside.

6 Whip the cream lightly. Set aside. With an electric mixer, beat the egg whites and salt until they hold soft peaks. Add the remaining sugar and beat only enough to blend.

7 Fold a dollop of egg whites into the chocolate mixture, then pour back into the whites and gently fold in.

8 Fold in the whipped cream and pour into the pastry shell. Put in the freezer until just set, about 5 minutes. If the center sinks, fill with any remaining mixture. Chill for 3–4 hours. Decorate with whipped cream and chocolate curls. Serve cold.

Coconut Cream Pie

Once you have made the pastry, the delicious filling can be put together in moments.

Serves 8

2½ cups shredded coconut

⅔ cup sugar

4 tablespoons cornstarch

pinch of salt

2½ cups milk

¼ cup whipping cream

2 egg yolks

2 tablespoons unsalted butter

2 teaspoons vanilla extract

For the pastry

1 cup all-purpose flour

¼ teaspoon salt

3 tablespoons cold butter, cut in pieces

2 tablespoons cold lard

1 For the pastry, sift the flour and salt into a bowl. Add the butter and lard and cut in with a pastry blender or two knives until the mixture resembles coarse bread crumbs.

2 With a fork, stir in just enough ice water to bind the dough (2–3 tablespoons). Gather into a ball, wrap in waxed paper and chill for at least 20 minutes.

3 Preheat the oven to 425°F. Roll out the dough ⅛ inch thick. Transfer to a 9-inch tart pan. Trim and flute the edges. Prick the bottom. Line with waxed paper and fill with baking beans. Bake for 10–12 minutes. Remove the paper and beans, reduce the heat to 350°F and bake until brown, 10–15 more minutes.

4 Spread 1 cup of the coconut on a baking sheet and toast until golden, 6–8 minutes, stirring often. Set aside for decorating.

5 Put the sugar, cornstarch and salt in a saucepan. In a bowl, whisk together the milk, cream and egg yolks. Add the egg mixture to the saucepan.

6 Cook over low heat, stirring constantly, until the mixture comes to a boil. Boil for 1 minute, then remove from heat. Add the butter, vanilla and remaining coconut.

7 Pour into the prebaked pastry shell. When the filling is cool, sprinkle toasted coconut in a ring in the center.

Peach Tart with Almond Cream

The almond cream filling should be baked until it is just turning brown. Take care not to overbake it, or the delicate flavors will be spoiled.

INGREDIENTS

Serves 8–10

4 large ripe peaches

⅔ cup blanched almonds

2 tablespoons all-purpose flour

7 tablespoons unsalted butter,
    at room temperature

scant ¾ cup sugar

1 egg

1 egg yolk

½ teaspoon vanilla extract,
    or 2 teaspoons rum

For the pastry

1¼ cups all-purpose flour

¾ teaspoon salt

7 tablespoons cold unsalted butter,
    cut in pieces

1 egg yolk

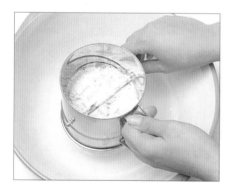

1 For the pastry, sift the flour and salt into a bowl.

2 Add the butter and cut in with a pastry blender until the mixture resembles coarse crumbs. With a fork, stir in the egg yolk and just enough ice water (2–3 tablespoons) to bind the dough. Gather into a ball, wrap in waxed paper and chill for at least 20 minutes. Place a baking sheet in the oven and preheat to 400°F.

3 On a lightly floured surface, roll out the pastry ⅛ inch thick. Transfer to a 10-inch tart pan. Trim the edge, prick the bottom and chill.

4 Score the bottoms of the peaches. Drop the peaches, one at a time, into boiling water. Leave for 20 seconds, then dip in cold water. Peel off the skins using a sharp knife.

5 Grind the almonds finely with the flour in a food processor, blender or nut grinder. With an electric mixer, cream the butter and ½ cup of the sugar until light and fluffy. Gradually beat in the egg and yolk. Stir in the almonds and vanilla or rum. Spread in the pastry shell.

6 Halve the peaches and remove the pits. Cut crosswise in thin slices and arrange on top of the almond cream like the spokes of a wheel; keep the slices of each peach-half together. Fan them out by pressing down gently at a slight angle.

7 Bake until the pastry begins to brown, 10–15 minutes. Lower the heat to 350°F and continue baking until the almond cream sets, about 15 more minutes. Ten minutes before the end of the cooking time, sprinkle with the remaining sugar.

VARIATION

For a Nectarine and Apricot Tart with Almond Cream, replace the peaches with nectarines, prepared and arranged the same way. Peel and chop three fresh apricots. Fill the spaces between the fanned-out nectarines with chopped apricots. Bake as above.

Raspberry Tart

This glazed fruit tart really does taste as good as it looks.

Serves 8

4 egg yolks

⅓ cup sugar

3 tablespoons all-purpose flour

1¼ cups milk

pinch of salt

½ teaspoon vanilla extract

1 pound fresh raspberries

5 tablespoons grape or red currant jelly

1 tablespoon fresh orange juice

For the pastry

1¼ cups all-purpose flour

½ teaspoon baking powder

¼ teaspoon salt

1 tablespoon sugar

grated zest of ½ orange

6 tablespoons cold butter, cut in pieces

1 egg yolk

3–4 tablespoons whipping cream

1 For the pastry, sift the flour, baking powder and salt into a bowl. Stir in the sugar and orange zest. Add the butter and mix until the mixture resembles coarse crumbs. With a fork, stir in the egg yolk and just enough cream to bind the dough. Gather into a ball, wrap in waxed paper and chill.

2 For the custard filling, beat the egg yolks and sugar until thick and lemon-colored. Gradually stir in the flour.

3 In a saucepan, bring the milk and salt just to a boil, and remove from heat. Whisk into the egg yolk mixture, return to the pan, and continue whisking over medium-high heat until just bubbling. Cook for 3 minutes to thicken. Transfer immediately to a bowl. Stir in the vanilla to blend.

4 Cover with waxed paper to prevent a skin from forming.

5 Preheat the oven to 400°F. On a lightly floured surface, roll out the dough about ⅛ inch thick, transfer to a 10-inch tart pan and trim the edge. Prick the bottom all over with a fork and line with waxed paper. Fill with baking beans and bake for 15 minutes. Remove the paper and baking beans. Continue baking until golden, 6–8 more minutes. Let cool.

6 Spread an even layer of the pastry cream filling in the tart shell and arrange the raspberries on top. Melt the jelly and orange juice in a pan over low heat and brush on top to glaze.

Kiwi Ricotta Tart

It is well worth taking your time arranging the kiwi topping in neat rows for this impressive-looking tart.

INGREDIENTS

Serves 8

½ cup blanched almonds

½ cup plus 1 tablespoon sugar

4 cups ricotta cheese

1 cup whipping cream

1 egg

3 egg yolks

1 tablespoon all-purpose
   flour

pinch of salt

2 tablespoons rum

grated zest of 1 lemon

2½ tablespoons lemon juice

¼ cup honey

5 kiwis

For the pastry

1¼ cups all-purpose flour

1 tablespoon sugar

½ teaspoon salt

½ teaspoon baking powder

6 tablespoons cold butter,
   cut in pieces

1 egg yolk

3–4 tablespoons whipping cream

1 For the pastry, sift the flour, sugar, salt and baking powder into a bowl. Cut in the butter until the mixture resembles coarse crumbs. Mix the egg yolk and cream. Stir in just enough to bind the dough.

2 Transfer to a lightly floured surface, flatten slightly, wrap in waxed paper and chill for 30 minutes. Preheat the oven to 425°F.

3 On a lightly floured surface, roll out the dough ⅛ inch thick and transfer to a 9-inch spring-form pan. Crimp the edge.

4 Prick the bottom of the dough all over with a fork. Line with waxed paper and fill with baking beans. Bake for 10 minutes. Remove the paper and beans and bake until golden, 6–8 more minutes. Let cool. Reduce the heat to 350°F.

5 Grind the almonds finely with 1 tablespoon of the sugar in a food processor or blender.

6 With an electric mixer, beat the ricotta until creamy. Add the cream, egg, yolks, remaining sugar, flour, salt, rum, lemon zest and 2 tablespoons of the lemon juice. Beat to combine.

7 Stir in the ground almonds until well blended.

8 Pour into the shell and bake until golden, about 1 hour. Let cool, then chill, loosely covered, for 2–3 hours. Unmold and place on a serving plate.

9 Combine the honey and remaining lemon juice for the glaze. Set aside.

10 Peel the kiwis. Halve them lengthwise, then cut crosswise into ¼-inch slices. Arrange the slices in rows across the top of the tart. Just before serving, brush with the glaze.

Lemon and Orange Tart

Refreshing citrus fruits in a crisp, nutty pastry shell.

INGREDIENTS

Serves 8–10

1 cup all-purpose flour, sifted

1 cup whole-wheat flour

3 tablespoons ground hazelnuts

3 tablespoons confectioners' sugar, sifted

pinch of salt

½ cup unsalted butter

4 tablespoons lemon curd

1¼ cups whipped cream or fromage frais

4 oranges, peeled and thinly sliced

1 Place the flours, hazelnuts, sugar, salt and butter in a food processor and process in short bursts until the mixture resembles bread crumbs. Add 2–3 tablespoons cold water and process until the dough comes together.

2 Turn out onto a lightly floured surface and knead gently until smooth. Roll out and line a 10-inch tart pan. Ease the pastry gently into the corners without stretching it. Chill for 20 minutes. Preheat the oven to 375°F.

3 Line the pastry with waxed paper and fill with baking beans. Bake blind for 15 minutes, remove the paper and beans and continue for another 5–10 minutes, until the pastry is crisp. Let cool.

4 Whisk the lemon curd into the cream or fromage frais and spread on the pastry. Arrange the orange slices on top and serve at room temperature.

Chocolate Pear Tart

Serve slices of this drizzled with light cream or with a scoop of vanilla ice cream for a special treat.

INGREDIENTS

Serves 8

4 ounces semi-sweet chocolate, grated

3 large firm, ripe pears

1 egg

1 egg yolk

½ cup light cream

½ teaspoon vanilla extract

3 tablespoons sugar

For the pastry

1 cup all-purpose flour

pinch of salt

2 tablespoons sugar

½ cup cold unsalted butter,
   cut into pieces

1 egg yolk

1 tablespoon fresh lemon juice

1 For the pastry, sift the flour and salt into a bowl. Add the sugar and butter. Cut in with a pastry blender until the mixture resembles coarse crumbs. With a fork, stir in the egg yolk and lemon juice until the mixture forms a dough. Gather into a ball, wrap in waxed paper, and chill for at least 20 minutes.

2 Place a baking sheet in the oven and preheat to 400°F. On a lightly floured surface, roll out the dough to ⅛ inch thick and trim the edge. Transfer to a 10-inch tart pan.

3 Sprinkle the bottom of the tart shell with the grated chocolate.

4 Peel, halve and core the pears. Cut in thin slices crosswise, then fan them out slightly.

5 Transfer the pear halves to the tart with the help of a metal spatula and arrange on top of the chocolate to resemble the spokes of a wheel.

6 Whisk together the egg and egg yolk, cream and vanilla extract. Ladle onto the pears, then sprinkle with sugar.

7 Bake for 10 minutes. Reduce the heat to 350°F and cook until the custard is set and the pears begin to caramelize, about 20 more minutes. Serve at room temperature.

Tarte au Citron

You can find this classic lemon tart in bistros all over France.

INGREDIENTS

Serves 8–10

12 ounces shortcrust or sweet shortcrust
  pastry
grated zest of 2 or 3 lemons
⅔ cup freshly squeezed lemon juice
½ cup sugar
4 tablespoons crème fraîche or
  heavy cream
4 eggs, plus 3 egg yolks
confectioners' sugar, for dusting

1 Preheat the oven to 375°F. Roll out the pastry thinly and use to line a 9-inch tart pan. Prick the pastry.

2 Line the pastry shell with aluminum foil and fill with baking beans. Bake for about 15 minutes, until the edges are set and dry. Remove the foil and beans and continue baking for another 5–7 minutes, until golden.

3 Place the lemon zest, juice and sugar in a bowl. Beat until combined and then gradually add the crème fraîche or heavy cream and beat until well blended.

4 Beat in the eggs, one at a time, then beat in the egg yolks and pour the filling into the pastry shell. Bake for 15–20 minutes, until the filling is set. If the pastry begins to brown too much, cover the edges with aluminum foil. Let cool. Dust with a little confectioners' sugar before serving.

Treacle Tart

*Quite a filling tart, so best served
after a light main course.*

INGREDIENTS

Serves 4–6

¾ cup golden syrup or light corn syrup

1½ cups fresh white bread crumbs

grated zest of 1 lemon

2 tablespoons fresh lemon juice

For the pastry

1¼ cups all-purpose flour

½ teaspoon salt

6 tablespoons cold butter, cut in pieces

3 tablespoons cold margarine,
   cut in pieces

1 For the pastry, combine the
   flour and salt in a bowl. Add
the butter and margarine and cut
in with a pastry blender until the
mixture resembles coarse crumbs.

2 With a fork, stir in just
   enough ice water (about
3–4 tablespoons) to bind the
dough. Gather into a ball, wrap in
waxed paper, and chill for at least
20 minutes.

3 On a lightly floured surface,
   roll out the dough ⅛ inch
thick. Transfer to an 8-inch tart
pan and trim off the overhang.
Chill for at least 20 minutes.
Reserve the trimmings for the
lattice top.

4 Place a baking sheet in the
   center of the oven and heat
to 400°F.

5 In a saucepan, warm the syrup
   until thin and runny.

6 Remove from heat and stir
   in the bread crumbs and
lemon zest. Let sit for 10 minutes
so the bread can absorb the syrup.
Add more bread crumbs if the
mixture is thin. Stir in the lemon
juice and spread evenly in the
pastry shell.

7 Roll out the pastry trimmings
   and cut into 10–12 thin strips.

8 Lay half the strips on the
   filling, then carefully arrange
the remaining strips to form a
lattice pattern.

9 Place on the hot sheet and
   bake for 10 minutes. Lower
the heat to 375°F. Bake until
golden, about 15 more minutes.
Serve warm or cold.

Rich Chocolate Berry Tart

*Use any berries you like to top this
delicious tart.*

Serves 10

½ cup unsalted butter, softened

½ cup sugar

½ teaspoon salt

1 tablespoon vanilla extract

½ cup unsweetened cocoa powder

1¾ cups all-purpose flour

1 pound fresh berries for topping

For the chocolate ganache filling

2 cups heavy cream

½ cup seedless blackberry preserves

8 ounces semi-sweet chocolate, chopped

2 tablespoons unsalted butter

For the blackberry sauce

8 ounces fresh or frozen blackberries
    or raspberries

1 tablespoon lemon juice

2 tablespoons sugar

2 tablespoons blackberry liqueur

1 Prepare the pastry. Place the butter, sugar, salt and vanilla in a food processor and process until creamy. Add cocoa powder and process for 1 minute. Add flour all at once and process for 10–15 seconds, until just blended. Place a piece of plastic wrap on a work surface. Turn out the dough onto the plastic wrap. Use more plastic wrap to help shape the dough into a flat disk and wrap tightly. Chill for 1 hour.

2 Lightly grease a 9-inch tart pan with a removable bottom. Roll out dough between two sheets of plastic wrap to an 11-inch round, about ¼ inch thick. Peel off top sheet of plastic wrap and invert the dough into the prepared pan. Ease the dough into the pan. Remove the plastic wrap.

3 With floured fingers, press the dough onto bottom and side of pan, then roll a rolling pin over the edge of the pan to cut off any excess dough. Prick the dough with a fork. Chill for 1 hour. Preheat the oven to 350°F. Line tart shell with aluminum foil or baking parchment; fill with dry beans or rice. Bake for 10 minutes; lift out foil with beans and bake for 5 more minutes, until just set (pastry may look underdone on the bottom but will dry out). Remove to a wire rack to cool.

4 Prepare filling. In a medium saucepan over medium heat, bring cream and blackberry preserves to a boil. Remove from heat and add chocolate, stirring until smooth. Stir in butter and strain into the cooled tart, smoothing the top. Cool tart completely.

5 Prepare sauce. In a food processor combine blackberries, lemon juice and sugar and process until smooth. Strain into a small bowl and add blackberry-flavor liqueur. If sauce is too thick, thin with a little water.

6 To serve, remove tart from pan. Place on serving plate and arrange the berries on top of the tart. With a pastry brush, brush berries with a little of the blackberry sauce to glaze lightly. Serve the remaining sauce separately.

Bakewell Tart

Although the pastry crust makes this a tart, the original recipe describes it as a pudding.

INGREDIENTS

Serves 4

8 ounces ready-made puff pastry
2 tablespoons raspberry or apricot jam
2 eggs
2 egg yolks
generous ½ cup sugar
½ cup butter, melted
½ cup ground almonds
few drops of almond extract
confectioners' sugar, for sifting

1 Preheat the oven to 400°F. Roll out the pastry on a lightly floured surface and use it to line a 7-inch pie pan or loose-bottomed tart pan. Spread the jam on the bottom of the pastry shell.

COOK'S TIP

Since this pastry shell isn't baked blind first, place a baking sheet in the oven while it preheats, then place the tart pan on the hot sheet. This will ensure that the bottom of the pastry cooks through.

2 Whisk the eggs, egg yolks and sugar together in a large bowl until thick and pale.

3 Gently stir the butter, ground almonds and almond extract into the mixture.

4 Pour the mixture into the pastry shell and bake for 30 minutes, until the filling is just set and browned. Sift confectioners' sugar on top before serving the tart hot, warm or cold.

VARIATION

Ground hazelnuts are increasingly available and make an interesting change from the almonds in this tart. If you are going to grind shelled hazelnuts yourself, first roast them for 10–15 minutes to bring out their flavor, then rub in a dish towel to remove skins.

Apple Pie

Delicious on its own, or with a dollop of heavy cream or ice cream.

INGREDIENTS

Serves 8

2 pounds tart apples

2 tablespoons all-purpose flour

½ cup sugar

1½ tablespoons fresh lemon juice

½ teaspoon ground cinnamon

½ teaspoon ground allspice

¼ teaspoon ground ginger

¼ teaspoon grated nutmeg

¼ teaspoon salt

4 tablespoons butter, diced

For the pastry

2 cups all-purpose flour

1 teaspoon salt

6 tablespoons cold butter, cut in pieces

4 tablespoons cold lard, cut in pieces

1 For the pastry, sift the flour and salt into a bowl.

2 Add the butter and lard and cut with a pastry blender or rub between your fingertips until the mixture resembles coarse crumbs. With a fork, stir in just enough ice water to bind the dough (4–8 tablespoons).

3 Gather into two balls, wrap in waxed paper and chill for 20 minutes.

4 On a lightly floured surface, roll out one dough ball to ⅛ inch thick. Transfer to a 9-inch pie pan and trim the edge. Place a baking sheet in the center of the oven and preheat to 425°F.

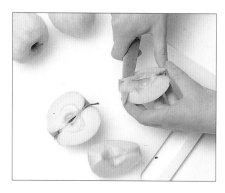

5 Peel, core and slice the apples into a bowl. Toss with the flour, sugar, lemon juice, spices and salt. Spoon into pie shell; dot with butter.

6 Roll out the remaining dough. Place on top of the pie and trim to leave a ¾-inch overhang. Fold the overhang under the bottom dough and press to seal. Crimp the edge.

7 Roll out the scraps and cut out leaf shapes and roll balls. Arrange on top of the pie. Cut steam vents.

8 Bake for 10 minutes. Reduce the heat to 350°F and bake until golden, 40–45 more minutes. If the pie browns too quickly, protect with aluminum foil.

Mississippi Pecan Pie

This fabulous dessert started life in the Deep South but has become an international favorite.

INGREDIENTS

Serves 6–8

For the pastry

1 cup all-purpose flour

4 tablespoons butter, cubed

2 tablespoons sugar

1 egg yolk

For the filling

½ cup golden or light corn syrup

⅓ cup dark brown sugar

4 tablespoons butter

3 eggs, lightly beaten

½ teaspoon vanilla extract

1¼ cups pecans

fresh cream or ice cream, to serve

1 Place the flour in a bowl and add the butter. Rub in the butter with your fingertips until the mixture resembles bread crumbs, then stir in the sugar, egg yolk and about 2 tablespoons cold water. Mix into a dough and knead lightly on a floured surface until smooth and free of lumps.

2 Roll out the pastry and use to line an 8-inch loose-bottomed fluted tart pan. Prick the pastry, then line with waxed paper and fill with baking beans. Chill for 30 minutes. Preheat the oven to 400°F.

3 Bake the pastry shell for 10 minutes. Remove the paper and beans and bake for 5 minutes. Reduce the oven temperature to 350°F.

4 Meanwhile, heat the syrup, sugar and butter in a pan until the sugar dissolves. Remove from heat and cool slightly. Whisk in the eggs and vanilla and stir in the pecans.

5 Pour into the pastry shell and bake for 35–40 minutes, until the filling is set. Serve with cream or ice cream.

Boston Banoffee Pie

There are many variations of this old-fashioned treat; this one is easy to make and tastes wonderful.

INGREDIENTS

Serves 6–8

1¼ cups all-purpose flour

1 cup butter

4 tablespoons sugar

½ 14-ounce can skim, sweetened condensed milk

⅔ cup light brown sugar

2 tablespoons golden or light corn syrup

2 small bananas, sliced

a little lemon juice

whipped cream, to decorate

1 teaspoon grated semi-sweet chocolate

1 Preheat the oven to 325°F. Place the flour and ½ cup of the butter in a food processor and blend until crumbed (or rub in with your fingertips). Stir in the sugar.

2 Squeeze the mixture together until it forms a dough. Press into an 8-inch loose-bottomed fluted tart pan. Bake for 25–30 minutes.

3 Place the remaining ½ cup of butter with the condensed milk, brown sugar and golden syrup or corn syrup in a large nonstick saucepan and heat gently, stirring, until the butter has melted and the sugar has dissolved.

4 Bring to a gentle boil and cook for 7 minutes, stirring constantly (to prevent burning), until the mixture thickens and turns a light caramel color. Pour onto the cooked pastry shell and leave until cold.

5 Sprinkle the bananas with lemon juice and arrange in overlapping circles on top of the caramel filling, leaving a gap in the center. Pipe a swirl of whipped cream in the center and sprinkle with the grated chocolate.

Chocolate Profiteroles

This mouthwatering dessert is served in cafés throughout France. Sometimes the profiteroles are filled with whipped cream instead of ice cream, but they are always drizzled with chocolate sauce.

Serves 4–6

10 ounces semi-sweet chocolate

3 cups vanilla ice cream

For the profiteroles

¾ cup all-purpose flour

¼ teaspoon salt

pinch of freshly grated nutmeg

6 tablespoons unsalted butter,
    cut into 6 pieces

3 eggs

1 Preheat the oven to 400°F and butter a baking sheet.

2 To make the profiteroles, sift together the flour, salt and nutmeg. In a medium saucepan, bring the butter and ¾ cup of water to a boil. Remove from heat and add the dry ingredients all at once. Beat with a wooden spoon for about 1 minute, until well blended and the mixture starts to pull away from the sides of the pan, then set the pan over low heat and cook the mixture for about 2 minutes, beating constantly. Remove from heat.

3 Beat one egg in a small bowl and set aside. Add the remaining eggs, one at a time, to the flour mixture, beating well. Add the beaten egg gradually until the dough is smooth and shiny; it should fall slowly when dropped from a spoon.

4 Using a tablespoon, drop the dough onto the baking sheet in 12 mounds. Bake for 25–30 minutes, until the pastry is well risen and browned. Turn off the oven and let the puffs cool with the oven door open.

5 To make the sauce, place the chocolate and ½ cup of warm water in a double boiler or in a bowl and melt, stirring occasionally over a pan of hot water.

6 Split the profiteroles in half and put a small scoop of ice cream in each. Arrange on a serving platter. Pour the sauce on top and serve immediately.

Pear and Almond Cream Tart

This tart is equally successful made with other kinds of fruit, and some variation can be seen at almost every good French pâtisserie. Try making it with nectarines, peaches, apricots or apples.

INGREDIENTS

Serves 6

12 ounces shortcrust or
    sweet shortcrust pastry

3 firm pears

lemon juice

1 tablespoon peach brandy or water

4 tablespoons peach preserves, strained

For the almond cream filling

¾ cup blanched whole almonds

¼ cup sugar

5 tablespoons butter

1 egg, plus 1 egg white

few drops almond extract

1 Roll out the pastry thinly and use to line a 9-inch tart pan. Chill the pastry shell while you make the filling. Put the almonds and sugar in a food processor and pulse until finely ground; they should not be pasty. Add the butter and process until creamy, then add the egg, egg white and almond extract and mix well.

2 Place a baking sheet in the oven and preheat to 375°F. Peel the pears, halve them, remove the cores and rub with lemon juice.

3 Put the pear halves cut-side down on a board and slice thinly crosswise, keeping the slices together.

4 Pour the almond cream filling into the pastry shell. Slide a spatula under one pear half and press the top with your fingers to fan out the slices. Transfer to the tart, placing the fruit on the filling like spokes of a wheel. If desired, remove a few slices from each half before arranging and use to fill in any gaps in the center.

5 Place on the baking sheet and bake for 50–55 minutes, until the filling is set and well browned. Cool on a rack.

6 Meanwhile, heat the brandy or water and the preserves in a small saucepan, then brush on top of the hot tart to glaze. Serve the tart warm.

Greek Chocolate Mousse Tartlets

The combination of white chocolate and plain yogurt makes an irresistibly light, but not too sweet, filling for these little tarts.

INGREDIENTS

Serves 6

1½ cups all-purpose flour

2 tablespoons unsweetened
   cocoa powder

2 tablespoons confectioners' sugar

½ cup butter

melted dark chocolate, to decorate

For the filling

7 ounces white chocolate, broken
   into squares

½ cup milk

2 teaspoons powdered gelatin

2 tablespoons sugar

1 teaspoon vanilla extract

2 eggs, separated

generous 1 cup plain yogurt

1 Preheat the oven to 375°F. Sift the flour, cocoa powder and confectioners' sugar into a large bowl.

2 Place the butter in a pan with 4 tablespoons water and heat gently until just melted. Cool, then stir into the flour to make a smooth dough. Chill until firm.

3 Roll out the pastry and line six deep 4-inch loose-bottomed tart pans.

4 Prick each pastry shell all over with a fork, cover with waxed paper weighed down with baking beans and bake blind for 10 minutes. Remove the baking beans and paper, return to the oven and bake for another 15 minutes or until the pastry is firm. Let cool in the pans.

5 Make the filling. Melt the chocolate in a heatproof bowl over hot water. Pour the milk into a saucepan, sprinkle on the gelatin and heat gently, stirring, until the gelatin has dissolved completely. Remove from heat and stir in the chocolate.

6 Whisk the sugar, vanilla and egg yolks in a large bowl, then beat in the chocolate mixture. Beat in the yogurt until evenly mixed.

7 Whisk the egg whites in a clean, grease-free bowl until stiff, then fold into the mixture. Divide among the pastry shells and leave to set.

8 Drizzle the melted white chocolate on the tartlets to decorate.

Tarte Tatin

This upside-down apple tart was first made by two sisters who served it in their restaurant in the Loire Valley in France.

INGREDIENTS

Serves 8–10

8 ounces puff or shortcrust pastry

10–12 large Golden Delicious apples

lemon juice

½ cup butter, cut into pieces

½ cup sugar

½ teaspoon ground cinnamon

crème fraîche or whipped cream, to serve

1 On a lightly floured surface, roll out the pastry into an 11-inch round less than ¼ inch thick. Transfer to a lightly floured baking sheet and chill.

2 Peel the apples, cut them in half lengthwise and core. Sprinkle them generously with lemon juice.

3 Preheat the oven to 450°F. In a 10-inch tarte tatin pan, cook the butter, sugar and cinnamon over medium heat until the butter has melted and sugar dissolved, stirring occasionally. Continue cooking for 6–8 minutes, until the mixture turns a medium caramel color, then remove the pan from heat and arrange the apple halves, standing on their edges, in the pan, fitting them in tightly, as they shrink during cooking.

4 Return the apple-filled pan to the heat and bring to a simmer over medium heat for 20–25 minutes, until the apples are tender and colored. Remove the pan from heat and cool slightly.

5 Place the pastry on top of the apple-filled pan and tuck the edges of the pastry inside the edge of the pan around the apples.

6 Pierce the pastry in two or three places, then bake for 25–30 minutes, until the pastry is golden and the filling is bubbling. Let the tart cool in the pan for 10–15 minutes.

7 To serve, run a sharp knife around edge of the pan to loosen the pastry. Cover with a serving plate and, holding them tightly, carefully invert the pan and plate together (do this over the sink in case any caramel drips). Lift off the pan and loosen any apples that stick with a spatula. Serve the tart warm with cream.

Jam Tart

Jam tarts are popular in Italy where they are traditionally decorated with pastry strips.

INGREDIENTS

Serves 6–8

1¾ cups all-purpose flour

pinch of salt

¼ cup sugar

½ cup butter or
   margarine, chilled

1 egg

¼ teaspoon grated lemon zest

1¼ cups jam, such as raspberry,
   apricot or strawberry

1 egg, lightly beaten with 2 tablespoons
   whipping cream, for glazing

1   Make the pastry by placing the flour, salt and sugar in a mixing bowl. Using a pastry blender or two knives, cut the butter or margarine into the dry ingredients as quickly as possible until the mixture resembles coarse crumbs.

2   Beat the egg with the lemon zest in a cup, and pour it over the flour mixture. Combine with a fork until the dough holds together. If it is too crumbly, mix in 1–2 tablespoons of water.

3   Gather the dough into two balls, one slightly larger than the other, and flatten into discs. Wrap in waxed paper, and put in the refrigerator for at least 40 minutes.

4   Lightly grease a shallow 9-inch tart pan, preferably with a removable bottom. Roll out the larger disc of pastry on a lightly floured surface to a thickness of about ⅛ inch.

5   Roll the pastry around the rolling pin and transfer to the prepared pan. Trim the edges evenly with a small knife. Prick the bottom with a fork. Chill for at least 30 minutes.

6   Preheat the oven to 375°F. Spread the jam thickly and evenly on the pastry. Roll out the remaining pastry.

7   Cut the pastry into strips about ¼ inch wide using a ruler as a guide. Arrange them on the jam in a lattice pattern. Trim the edges of the strips even with the edge of the pan, pressing them lightly onto the pastry shell. Brush the pastry with the egg and cream glaze. Bake for about 35 minutes or until the pastry is golden brown. Cool before serving.

Pumpkin Pie

The unofficial dish of Thanksgiving.

INGREDIENTS

Serves 4–6

1½ cups all-purpose flour

pinch of salt

6 tablespoons unsalted butter

1 tablespoon sugar

4 cups peeled fresh pumpkin, cubed, or
   2 cups canned pumpkin, drained

½ cup light brown sugar

¼ teaspoon salt

¼ teaspoon ground allspice

½ teaspoon ground cinnamon

½ teaspoon ground ginger

2 eggs, lightly beaten

½ cup heavy cream

whipped cream, to serve

1 Place the flour in a bowl with the salt and butter and rub with your fingertips until the mixture resembles bread crumbs (or use a food processor).

2 Stir in the sugar and add about 2–3 tablespoons water and mix into a soft dough. Knead the dough lightly on a floured surface. Flatten out into a round, wrap in a plastic bag and chill for 1 hour.

3 Preheat the oven to 400°F with a baking sheet inside. If you are using raw pumpkin for the pie, steam for 15 minutes, until quite tender, then let cool completely. Purée the steamed or canned pumpkin in a food processor or blender until it is very smooth.

4 Roll out the pastry quite thinly and use to line a 9½ inch (measured across the top) x 1 inch deep pie pan. Trim off any excess pastry and reserve for the decoration. Prick the pastry case with a fork.

5 Cut as many leaf shapes as you can from the excess pastry and make vein markings with the back of a knife on each. Brush the edge of the pastry with water and stick the leaves all around the edge. Chill.

6 In a large bowl mix the pumpkin purée, sugar, salt, spices, eggs and cream and pour into the prepared pastry shell. Smooth the top with a knife.

7 Place on the preheated baking sheet and bake for 15 minutes. Then reduce the temperature to 350°F and cook for another 30 minutes, or until the filling is set and the pastry golden. Serve the pie warm with a generous dollop of whipped cream.

Custards, Soufflés & Mousses

◆ ◆ ◆

Coffee Coeur à la Crème

These pretty heart-shaped creams, speckled with espresso-roasted coffee beans, are served with a fruit sauce.

INGREDIENTS

Serves 6

generous ¼ cup espresso-roasted
   coffee beans
1 cup ricotta or cottage cheese
1¼ cups crème fraîche
2 tablespoons sugar
finely grated zest of ½ orange
2 egg whites

For the red berry coulis
1 cup raspberries
2 tablespoons confectioners' sugar, sifted
⅔ cup small strawberries
   (or wild ones, if available), halved

1 Preheat the oven to 350°F. Spread the coffee beans onto a baking sheet and toast for 10 minutes. Cool, put in a large plastic bag and crush with a rolling pin.

2 Rinse 12 pieces of muslin in cold water and squeeze dry. Use to line six coeur à la crème molds with a double layer, letting the muslin overhang the edges.

3 Press the ricotta or cottage cheese through a fine sieve into a bowl. Stir the crème fraîche, sugar, orange zest and crushed roasted coffee beans together. Add to the cheese and mix well.

4 Whisk the egg whites until stiff and fold into the mixture. Spoon into the prepared molds, then bring the muslin up and over the filling. Drain and chill in the refrigerator overnight.

5 To make the red berry coulis, put the raspberries and confectioners' sugar in a food processor and blend until smooth. Push through a fine sieve to remove the seeds. Stir in the strawberries. Chill until you are ready to serve.

6 Unmold the hearts onto individual serving plates and carefully remove the muslin. Spoon on the coulis before serving.

Tiramisù

The name of this classic dessert translates as "pick me up," and is said to derive from the fact that it is so good that it literally makes you swoon when you eat it.

INGREDIENTS

Serves 4

1 cup mascarpone

¼ cup confectioners' sugar, sifted

⅔ cup strong coffee, chilled

1¼ cups heavy cream

3 tablespoons coffee liqueur such as
  Tia Maria, Kahlúa or Toussaint

4 ounces Savoiardi (ladyfinger) cookies

2 ounces bittersweet or semi-sweet
  chocolate, coarsely grated

unsweetened cocoa powder, for dusting

1 Lightly grease and line a 2-pound loaf pan with plastic wrap. In a large bowl, beat the mascarpone and confectioners' sugar for 1 minute. Stir in 2 tablespoons of the chilled coffee. Mix thoroughly.

2 Whip the cream and 1 tablespoon of the liqueur to soft peaks. Stir a spoonful into the mascarpone, then fold in the rest. Spoon half the mixture into the pan and smooth the top.

COOK'S TIP
∽

This dish also works well with a
single layer of ladyfingers.

3 Put the remaining strong brewed coffee and liqueur in a shallow dish just wider than the ladyfingers. Using half the cookies, dip one side of each into the coffee mixture, then arrange on top of the mascarpone mixture in a single layer.

4 Spoon the rest of the mascarpone mixture on the cookie layer and smooth the top.

5 Dip the remaining cookies in the coffee, arrange on top, and drizzle on any remaining coffee mixture. Cover with plastic wrap and chill for 4 hours. Turn the tiramisù out of the pan and sprinkle with grated chocolate and cocoa powder; serve cut into slices.

Hot Chocolate Zabaglione

This is a delicious chocolate-flavored variation of the classic Italian dessert.

Serves 6

6 egg yolks

¾ cup sugar

3 tablespoons unsweetened cocoa powder

⅞ cup Marsala

unsweetened cocoa powder or
confectioners' sugar, for dusting

almond cookies, to serve

1 Half-fill a medium saucepan with water and bring to the simmering point.

2 Place the egg yolks and sugar in a heatproof bowl and whisk until the mixture is pale and all the sugar has dissolved.

3 Add the cocoa powder and Marsala, then place the bowl over the simmering water. Whisk until the consistency of the mixture is smooth, thick and foamy.

4 Pour quickly into tall heatproof glasses, dust lightly with cocoa powder or confectioners' sugar and serve immediately with almond cookies.

Crème Caramel

Crème caramel, or crème renversée, is one of the most popular French desserts and is wonderful when freshly made. This is a slightly lighter modern version of the traditional recipe.

INGREDIENTS

Serves 6–8

1¼ cups sugar

4 tablespoons water

1 vanilla bean or

   2 teaspoons vanilla extract

1⅔ cups milk

1 cup whipping cream

5 large eggs

2 egg yolks

1 Put ⅞ cup of the sugar in a small heavy saucepan with 4 tablespoons of water to moisten. Bring to a boil over high heat, swirling the pan to dissolve the sugar. Boil, without stirring, until the syrup turns a dark caramel color (this will take about 4–5 minutes).

2 Immediately pour the caramel into a 4-cup soufflé dish. Holding the dish with oven mitts, quickly swirl the dish to coat the bottom and sides with the caramel and set aside. (The caramel will harden quickly as it cools.) Place the dish in a small roasting pan.

3 Preheat the oven to 325°F. With a small sharp knife, carefully split the vanilla bean lengthwise and scrape the black seeds into a medium saucepan. Add the milk and cream and bring just to a boil over medium-high heat, stirring frequently. Remove the pan from heat, cover and set aside for 15–20 minutes.

4 In a bowl, whisk the eggs and egg yolks with the remaining sugar for 2–3 minutes, until smooth and creamy. Whisk in the hot milk and carefully strain the mixture into the caramel-lined dish. Cover with aluminum foil.

5 Place the dish in a roasting pan and pour in enough boiling water to come halfway up the sides of the dish. Bake the custard for 40–45 minutes, until just set and a knife inserted about 2 inches from the edge comes out clean. Remove from the roasting pan and cool for at least 30 minutes, then chill overnight.

6 To turn out, carefully run a sharp knife around the edge of the dish to loosen the custard. Cover the dish with a serving plate and, holding them tightly, invert the dish and plate together. Gently lift one edge of the dish, letting the caramel run over the sides, then slowly lift off the dish.

Classic Coffee Crème Caramel

These lightly set coffee custards are served in a pool of caramel sauce. For a richer flavor, make them with half light cream, half milk.

INGREDIENTS

Serves 6

2½ cups milk

3 tablespoons ground coffee

¼ cup sugar

4 eggs

4 egg yolks

spun sugar, to decorate (optional)

For the caramel sauce

¾ cup sugar

4 tablespoons water

1 Preheat the oven to 325°F. To make the sauce, heat the sugar with the water in a heavy pan until it has dissolved.

2 Bring to a boil and boil rapidly until the syrup turns a rich golden brown. Quickly pour the hot syrup into six warmed ⅔-cup ramekins.

3 To make the coffee custard, heat the milk until almost boiling. Pour onto the ground coffee and let infuse for about 5 minutes. Strain through a fine sieve into a bowl.

4 In a bowl, whisk the sugar, eggs and yolks until light and creamy. Whisk the coffee-flavored milk into the egg mixture. Pour into the ramekins.

5 Put the ramekins in a roasting pan and add hot water to come two-thirds of the way up the dishes. Bake for 30–35 minutes, until just set. Remove the custards from heat and cool, then chill for 3 hours. To serve, invert onto plates and decorate.

COOK'S TIP

To make spun sugar, gently heat a scant ½ cup sugar, 1 teaspoon liquid glucose and 2 tablespoons water in a heavy pan, until the sugar dissolves. Boil the syrup to 325°F, then dip the bottom of the pan into cold water. Place waxed paper on the work surface and, holding two forks together, dip them in the syrup and flick rapidly back and forth over an oiled rolling pin.

Crème Brûlée

This dessert actually originated in Cambridge but has become associated with France and is widely eaten there. Add a little liqueur, if desired, but it is equally delicious without it.

INGREDIENTS

Serves 6

1 vanilla bean

4 cups heavy cream

6 egg yolks

½ cup sugar

2 tablespoons almond or orange liqueur (optional)

⅓ cup light brown sugar

1 Preheat the oven to 300°F. Place six ½-cup ramekins in a roasting pan and set aside.

2 With a small sharp knife, split the vanilla bean lengthwise and scrape the black seeds into a medium saucepan. Add the cream and bring just to a boil over medium heat, stirring. Remove from heat and cover. Set aside for 15–20 minutes.

3 In a bowl, whisk the egg yolks, sugar and liqueur, if using, until well blended. Whisk in the hot cream and strain into a large bowl. Divide the custard equally among the ramekins.

4 Pour enough boiling water into the roasting pan to come halfway up the sides of the ramekins. Cover the pan with aluminum foil and bake for about 30 minutes, until the custards are just set. Remove from the pan and let cool. Return to the dry roasting pan and chill.

5 Preheat the broiler. Sprinkle the sugar evenly on the surface of each custard and broil for 30–60 seconds, until the sugar melts and caramelizes. (Do not let the sugar burn or the custard curdle.) Place in the refrigerator to set the crust and chill completely before serving.

COOK'S TIP
~

To test if the custards are ready, push the point of a knife into center of one—if it comes out clean, the custards are cooked.

Coffee Cardamom Zabaglione

This warm Italian dessert is usually made with Italian Marsala wine. In this recipe coffee liqueur is used with freshly crushed cardamom.

INGREDIENTS

Serves 4

4 cardamom pods

8 egg yolks

4 tablespoons sugar

2 tablespoons strong brewed coffee

¼ cup coffee liqueur such as Tia Maria, Kahlúa or Toussaint

a few crushed roasted coffee beans, to decorate

1 Peel off the pale green outer husks from the cardamom pods and remove the black seeds. Crush these into a fine powder using a pestle and mortar.

2 Put the egg yolks, sugar and cardamom in a bowl and whisk until pale and creamy.

3 Gradually whisk the coffee and the liqueur into the egg yolk mixture until evenly combined.

4 Place the bowl over a saucepan of almost-boiling water and continue whisking for about 10 minutes.

5 Continue whisking until the mixture is very thick and fluffy and has doubled in volume, making sure the water doesn't boil—if it does the mixture will curdle. Remove the bowl from heat and carefully pour the zabaglione into four warmed glasses or dishes. Sprinkle with a few crushed roasted coffee beans and serve immediately.

Petits Pots de Cappuccino

These rich coffee custards, with a cream topping and a light dusting of cocoa powder, look wonderful presented in fine china coffee cups.

INGREDIENTS

Serves 6–8

1 cup roasted coffee beans

1¼ cups milk

1¼ cups light cream

1 whole egg and 4 egg yolks

4 tablespoons sugar

½ teaspoon vanilla extract

For the topping

½ cup whipping cream

3 tablespoons ice water

2 teaspoons unsweetened cocoa powder

1 Preheat the oven to 325°F. Put the coffee beans in a pan over low heat for 3 minutes, shaking frequently.

2 Pour the milk and cream over the beans. Heat until almost boiling; cover and infuse for 30 minutes. Whisk the egg and yolks, sugar and vanilla together. Return the milk to the boiling point and pour through a sieve onto the egg mixture. Discard the beans.

3 Pour the mixture into eight 5-tablespoon coffee cups or six ½-cup ramekins. Cover each with a piece of aluminum foil.

4 Put the coffee cups or ramekins in a roasting pan with hot water reaching about two-thirds of the way up the sides of the dishes. Bake for 30–35 minutes or until lightly set. Let cool. Chill in the refrigerator for at least 2 hours.

5 Whisk the whipping cream and ice water until thick and frothy and spoon on top of the custards. Dust with cocoa powder before serving.

Almost Instant Banana Pudding

Banana and ginger make a great combination in this very fast dessert.

INGREDIENTS

Serves 6–8

4 thick slices gingerbread

6 bananas

2 tablespoons lemon juice

1¼ cups whipping cream or fromage frais

4 tablespoons fruit juice

3–4 tablespoons brown sugar

1 Break up the cake into chunks and arrange in an ovenproof dish. Slice the bananas and toss in the lemon juice.

2 Whip the cream and, when firm, gently whip in the juice. (If using fromage frais, just gently stir in the juice.) Fold in the bananas and spoon the mixture onto the ginger cake.

3 Top with the brown sugar and place under a hot broiler for 2–3 minutes to caramelize. Chill to set again if desired, or serve later.

Ginger and Orange Crème Brûlée

This is a useful way of cheating at making crème brûlée! Most people would never know unless you overchill the custard, or keep it more than a day, but there's little risk of that!

INGREDIENTS

Serves 4–5

2 eggs, plus 2 egg yolks

1¼ cups light cream

2 tablespoons sugar

1 teaspoon powdered gelatin
   or alternative

finely grated zest and juice of ½ orange

1 large piece stem ginger, finely chopped

3–4 tablespoons sugar

orange segments and sprig of mint,
   to decorate

1 Whisk the eggs and yolks together until pale. Bring the cream and sugar to a boil, remove from heat and sprinkle on the gelatin. Stir until the gelatin has dissolved and then pour the cream mixture onto the eggs, whisking constantly.

3 Pour into four or five ramekins and chill until set.

4 Some time before serving, sprinkle the sugar generously on top of the custard and put under a very hot broiler. Watch closely for the couple of moments it takes for the tops to caramelize. Let cool before serving. Decorate with a few segments of orange and a sprig of mint.

2 Add the orange zest, a little juice to taste, and the chopped ginger to the mixture.

COOK'S TIP

For a milder ginger flavor, just add up to 1 teaspoon ground ginger instead of the stem ginger.

Chocolate Mandarin Trifle

Trifle is always a tempting treat, but when a rich chocolate and mascarpone custard is combined with amaretto and mandarin oranges, it becomes irresistible.

INGREDIENTS

Serves 6–8

4 layers sponge cake

14 amaretti cookies

4 tablespoons Amaretto di Saronno or
    sweet sherry

8 mandarin oranges

For the custard

7 ounces semi-sweet chocolate,
    broken into squares

2 tablespoons cornstarch or
    custard powder

2 tablespoons sugar

2 egg yolks

⅞ cup milk

generous 1 cup mascarpone cheese

For the topping

generous 1 cup fromage frais

chocolate shapes

mandarin slices

1 Break up the cake layers and place them in a large glass serving dish. Crumble the amaretti cookies on top and then sprinkle with amaretto or sweet sherry.

2 Squeeze the juice from two of the mandarins and sprinkle into the dish. Segment the rest and put in the dish.

3 Make the custard. Melt the chocolate in a heatproof bowl over hot water. In a separate bowl, mix the cornstarch or custard powder, sugar and egg yolks into a smooth paste.

4 Heat the milk in a small saucepan until almost boiling, then pour in a steady stream onto the egg yolk mixture, stirring constantly. Return to the clean pan and stir over low heat until the custard has thickened slightly and is smooth.

5 Stir the mascarpone until melted, then add the melted chocolate, mixing it thoroughly. Spread evenly on the trifle, cool, then chill until set.

6 To finish, spread the fromage frais on the custard, then decorate with chocolate shapes and the remaining mandarin slices just before serving.

COOK'S TIP

Always use the best chocolate, which has a high percentage of cocoa solids, and be careful not to overheat the chocolate when melting, as it will lose its gloss and look "grainy."

Tangerine Trifle

An unusual variation on a traditional trifle—of course, you can add a little alcohol if desired.

INGREDIENTS

Serves 4

5 sponge cake layers, halved lengthwise

2 tablespoons apricot jam

15–20 ratafia cookies

4¾-ounce package tangerine gelatin

11-ounce can mandarin oranges, drained, reserving juice

2½ cups ready-made (or homemade) custard

whipped cream and shreds of orange zest, to decorate

sugar, for sprinkling

1 Spread the halved sponge cakes with apricot jam and arrange in a deep serving bowl or glass dish. Sprinkle on the ratafia cookies.

2 Put the gelatin into a heatproof measuring cup, add the juice from the canned mandarins and dissolve in a pan of hot water or in the microwave. Stir until the liquid clears.

3 Make up to 2½ cups with ice cold water, stir well and let cool for up to 30 minutes. Sprinkle the mandarin oranges on the cakes and cookies.

4 Pour the gelatin on the mandarin oranges, cake and cookies and chill for 1 hour.

5 When the gelatin has set, pour the custard smoothly on top and chill again.

6 When ready to serve, pipe the whipped cream onto the custard. Wash the orange zest shreds, sprinkle them with sugar and use to decorate the trifle.

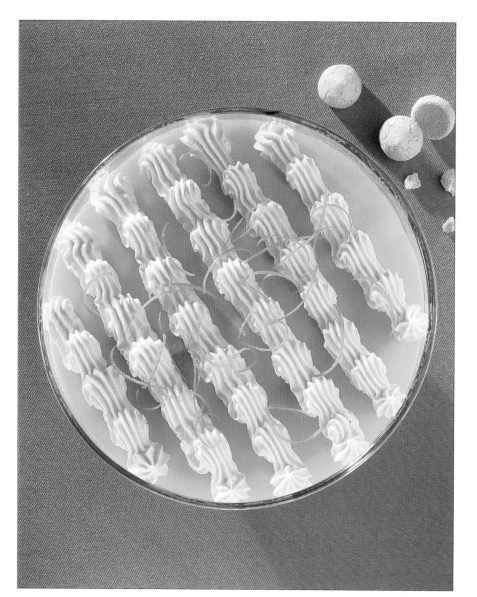

Raspberry Trifle

Use fresh or frozen raspberries for this ever-popular dessert.

Serves 6 or more

6 ounces sponge cake, or 1-inch cubes of
   sponge cake or coarsely crumbled
   ladyfingers

4 tablespoons medium sherry

4 ounces raspberry jam

1⅔ cups raspberries

scant 2 cups custard, flavored with
   2 tablespoons medium or sweet sherry

1¼ cups sweetened whipped cream

toasted sliced almonds and mint leaves,
   to decorate

1 Spread half of the cake pieces, cake cubes or ladyfingers on the bottom of a large serving bowl. (A glass bowl is best for presentation.)

2 Sprinkle half of the sherry on the cake to moisten it. Spoon on half of the jam, dotting it evenly on the cake cubes.

3 Reserve a few raspberries for decoration. Make a layer of half of the remaining raspberries on top.

4 Pour in half of the custard, covering the fruit and cake. Repeat the layers of moistened cake, jam, fruit and custard. Cover and chill for at least 2 hours.

5 Before serving, spoon the sweetened whipped cream evenly on top. To decorate, sprinkle with toasted sliced almonds and arrange the reserved raspberries and the mint leaves on top.

VARIATION

You can use other ripe summer fruit in the trifle, such as apricots, peaches, nectarines and strawberries, with different jams and fruit liqueurs to suit.

Coconut and Coffee Trifle

Dark coffee cake, laced with liqueur, coconut custard and a coffee cream topping, makes a rich dessert.

INGREDIENTS

Serves 6–8

For the coffee sponge cake
3 tablespoons strong-flavored ground coffee
3 tablespoons almost-boiling water
2 eggs
¼ cup dark brown sugar
⅓ cup self-rising flour, sifted
1½ tablespoons hazelnut or sunflower oil

For the coconut custard
1⅔ cups canned coconut milk
3 eggs
3 tablespoons sugar
2 teaspoons cornstarch

For the filling and topping
2 medium bananas
4 tablespoons coffee liqueur, such as Tia Maria
1¼ cups heavy cream
2 tablespoons confectioners' sugar, sifted
ribbons of fresh coconut, to decorate

1 Preheat the oven to 325°F. Oil and line a 7-inch square pan with waxed paper.

2 Put the ground coffee in a small bowl. Pour in the hot water and let infuse for 4 minutes. Strain the coffee, discarding the grounds.

3 Whisk the eggs and dark brown sugar in a large bowl until the whisk leaves a trail when lifted from the mixture.

4 Gently fold in the flour, 1 tablespoon of the coffee and the oil. Spoon the mixture into the pan and bake for 20 minutes. Turn out onto a rack, remove the paper and cool.

5 To make the coconut custard, heat the coconut milk in a saucepan until it is almost boiling.

6 Whisk the eggs, sugar and cornstarch until frothy, then whisk in the hot coconut milk. Add to the pan and heat gently, stirring for 1–2 minutes, until the custard thickens. Set aside to cool.

7 Cut the coffee sponge cake into 2-inch squares and arrange in a large glass bowl. Slice the bananas and arrange on the cake. Drizzle the coffee liqueur on top. Pour on the custard and chill until cold.

8 Whip the cream with the remaining coffee and confectioners' sugar until soft peaks form. Spoon the cream onto the custard. Cover and chill for several hours. Sprinkle with ribbons of fresh coconut.

COOK'S TIP

If fresh coconut is not available, use shredded coconut and toast until pale golden.

Jamaican Fruit Trifle

This trifle is actually based on a Caribbean fool that consists of fruit stirred into thick vanilla-flavored cream. This version is much less rich, redressing the balance with plenty of fruit, and with crème fraîche replacing some of the cream.

INGREDIENTS

Serves 8

1 large sweet pineapple, peeled and cored, about 12 ounces

1¼ cups heavy cream

scant 1 cup crème fraîche

4 tablespoons confectioners' sugar, sifted

2 teaspoons pure vanilla extract

2 tablespoons white or coconut rum

3 papayas, peeled, seeded and chopped

3 mangoes, peeled, pitted and chopped

thinly pared zest and juice of 1 lime

⅓ cup coarsely shredded coconut, toasted

1 Cut the pineapple into large chunks, place in a food processor or blender and process briefly until chopped. Put in a sieve placed over a bowl and let sit for 5 minutes to drain the juices from the fruit.

2 Whip the heavy cream into soft peaks. Fold in the crème fraîche, confectioners' sugar, vanilla and rum.

3 Fold the drained chopped pineapple into the cream mixture. Place the chopped papayas and mangoes in a large bowl and pour in the lime juice. Gently stir the fruit mixture to combine the ingredients. Shred the pared lime zest.

4 Divide the fruit mixture and the pineapple cream among eight dessert plates. Decorate with the lime shreds, toasted coconut and a few small pineapple leaves, if desired, and serve immediately.

Broiled Pineapple with Rum Custard

Freshly ground black pepper may seem an unusual ingredient to put with pineapple, until you realize that peppercorns are the fruit of a tropical vine. If the idea does not appeal, leave out the pepper.

INGREDIENTS

Serves 4

1 ripe pineapple
2 tablespoons butter
fresh strawberries, sliced, to serve
a few pineapple leaves, to decorate

For the sauce

1 egg
2 egg yolks
2 tablespoons sugar
2 tablespoons dark rum
½ teaspoon freshly ground black pepper

1 Remove the top and bottom from the pineapple with a serrated knife. Pare off the outer skin from top to bottom, remove the core and cut into slices.

2 Preheat the broiler to medium. Dot the pineapple slices with butter and broil for about 5 minutes.

3 To make the sauce, place all the ingredients in a bowl. Set over a saucepan of simmering water and whisk with a hand-held beater for 3–4 minutes or until foamy and cooked. Sprinkle the strawberries on the pineapple, decorate with a few pineapple leaves and serve with the sauce.

COOK'S TIP

The sweetest pineapples are picked and exported when ripe. Contrary to popular belief, pineapples do not ripen well after picking. Choose fruit that smells sweet and yields to firm pressure from your thumbs.

Banana and Passion Fruit Whip

This very easy and quickly prepared dessert is delicious served with crisp shortbread or ginger cookies.

INGREDIENTS

Serves 4

2 ripe bananas

2 passion fruit

6 tablespoons fromage frais

⅔ cup heavy cream

2 teaspoons honey

shortbread or ginger cookies, to serve

1 Peel the bananas, then mash them with a fork in a bowl into a smooth purée.

2 Halve the passion fruit and scoop out the pulp. Mix the pulp with the bananas and fromage frais. In a separate bowl, whip the cream with the honey until it forms soft peaks.

3 Carefully fold the cream and honey mixture into the fruit mixture. Spoon the whip into individual glass dishes and serve immediately with shortbread or ginger cookies.

Cappuccino Coffee Cups

Coffee-lovers will love this one—and it tastes rich and creamy, even though it's very light.

Serves 4

2 eggs

7.7-ounce can evaporated low-fat milk

1½ tablespoons instant coffee granules
    or powder

2 tablespoons sugar

2 teaspoons powdered gelatin,
    or alternative

4 tablespoons light crème fraîche

unsweetened cocoa powder or ground
    cinnamon, to decorate

1 Separate one egg and reserve the white. Beat the yolk with the whole remaining egg.

2 Put the evaporated milk, coffee granules, sugar and beaten eggs in a pan; whisk until evenly combined.

3 Put the pan over low heat and stir constantly until the mixture is hot, but not boiling. Cook, stirring constantly, without boiling, until the mixture is slightly thickened and smooth.

4 Remove the pan from heat. Sprinkle in the gelatin and whisk until the gelatin has completely dissolved.

5 Spoon the coffee custard into four individual dishes or glasses and chill them until set.

6 Whisk the reserved egg white until stiff. Whisk in the crème fraîche and then spoon the mixture onto the desserts. Sprinkle with cocoa powder or cinnamon and serve.

VARIATION

Plain yogurt can be used instead of the crème fraîche, if you prefer.

Vermont Baked Maple Custard

Try to find pure maple syrup for this custard, as it will really enhance the flavor.

COOK'S TIP

Baking delicate mixtures such as custards in a water bath helps protect them from uneven heating, which could make them rubbery.

INGREDIENTS

Serves 6

3 eggs

½ cup maple syrup

2½ cups milk

pinch of salt

pinch of grated nutmeg

1 Preheat the oven to 350°F. Combine all the ingredients in a large bowl and mix thoroughly.

2 Set individual custard cups or ramekins in a roasting pan half filled with hot water. Pour the custard mixture into the cups. Bake until the custards are set, 45 minutes–1 hour. Test by inserting the blade of a knife in the center: it should come out clean. Serve warm or chilled.

Mocha Cream Pots

The name of this rich baked custard, a classic French dessert, comes from the baking cups, called pots de crème. *The addition of coffee gives the dessert an unusual touch.*

INGREDIENTS

Serves 8

1 tablespoon instant coffee powder

2 cups milk

⅓ cup sugar

8 ounces semi-sweet chocolate, chopped

2 teaspoons vanilla extract

2 tablespoons coffee liqueur (optional)

7 egg yolks

whipped cream and crystallized mimosa balls, to decorate (optional)

1 Preheat the oven to 325°F. Place eight ½-cup *pots de crème* cups or ramekins in a roasting pan.

2 Put the instant coffee into a saucepan and stir in the milk, then add the sugar and set the pan over medium-high heat. Bring to a boil, stirring constantly, until both the coffee and sugar have dissolved.

3 Remove the pan from heat and add the chocolate. Stir until the chocolate has melted and the sauce is smooth. Stir in the vanilla and coffee liqueur, if using, until evenly combined.

4 In a bowl, whisk the egg yolks to blend them lightly. Slowly whisk in the chocolate mixture until well blended, then strain the mixture into a large bowl and divide equally among the cups or ramekins. Place them in a roasting pan and pour in enough boiling water to come halfway up the sides of the cups or ramekins. Cover the pan with aluminum foil.

5 Bake for 30–35 minutes, until the custard is just set and a knife inserted into a custard comes out clean. Remove the cups or ramekins from the roasting pan and let cool. Place on a baking sheet, cover and chill completely. Decorate with the whipped cream and crystallized mimosa balls, if using.

Plum and Custard Creams

This sophisticated dessert, prettily layered in glasses, will bring a smile to your face.

INGREDIENTS

Serves 6

1½ pounds red plums, pitted and sliced

grated zest and juice of 1 orange

¼ cup sugar

14-ounce carton ready-made
   custard sauce

1¼ cups heavy cream

2 tablespoons water

1 tablespoon powdered gelatin

1 egg white

plum slices and fresh mint sprigs,
   to decorate

1 Put the plums in a saucepan with the orange zest and juice and sugar. Heat, stirring constantly, until the sugar has dissolved. Cook the plums until tender. Let cool slightly, then process the plums into a smooth purée. Pass through a sieve into a bowl and cool.

2 Put the custard and half the cream in a saucepan, and heat until boiling. Pour the water into a heatproof bowl and sprinkle the gelatin on top; set aside for 5 minutes. Whisk the soaked gelatin into the hot custard, until dissolved, and let cool.

3 Whip the remaining cream and fold it into the custard mixture. In a grease-free bowl, whisk the egg white into soft peaks and fold into the custard. Set aside until just setting.

4 Quickly spoon alternate spoonfuls of the custard and plum purée into six tall dessert glasses. Marble the mixtures together. Chill for 2–3 hours or until the custard has set. Decorate each dessert with plum slices and fresh mint sprigs before serving.

Amaretto Soufflé

A mouthwatering soufflé with more than a hint of Amaretto liqueur.

Serves 6

6 amaretti cookies, coarsely crushed

4 tablespoons Amaretto liqueur

4 eggs, separated, plus 1 egg white

½ cup sugar

2 tablespoons all-purpose flour

1 cup milk

pinch of cream of tartar (if needed)

confectioners' sugar, for dusting

1 Preheat the oven to 400°F. Butter a 6¼-cup soufflé dish and sprinkle it with a little of the sugar.

2 Put the cookies in a bowl. Sprinkle them with 2 tablespoons of the Amaretto liqueur and set aside.

3 In another bowl, carefully mix the four egg yolks, 2 tablespoons of the sugar and all of flour.

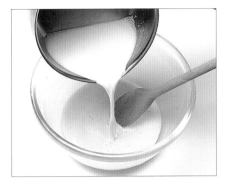

4 Heat the milk just to a boil in a heavy saucepan. Gradually add the hot milk to the egg mixture, stirring.

5 Pour the mixture back into the pan. Set over low heat and simmer gently for 3–4 minutes or until thickened, stirring occasionally.

6 Add the remaining Amaretto liqueur. Remove from heat.

7 In a scrupulously clean, grease-free bowl, whisk the five egg whites until they hold soft peaks. (If not using a copper bowl, add the cream of tartar as soon as the whites are frothy.) Add the remaining sugar and continue whisking until stiff.

8 Add about one-quarter of the whites to the liqueur mixture and stir in with a rubber spatula. Add the remaining whites and fold in gently.

9 Spoon half of the mixture into the prepared soufflé dish. Cover with a layer of the moistened amaretti cookies, then spoon the remaining soufflé mixture on top.

10 Bake for 20 minutes or until the soufflé is risen and lightly browned. Sprinkle with sifted confectioners' sugar and serve immediately.

Hot Quince Soufflés

These delicious fruits are more often picked than purchased, as they are seldom found at stores or markets. You can use pears instead.

INGREDIENTS

Serves 6

2 quinces, peeled and cored
4 tablespoons water
½ cup sugar
5 egg whites
melted butter, for greasing
confectioners' sugar, for dusting

For the pastry cream
1 cup milk
1 vanilla bean
3 egg yolks
⅓ cup sugar
¼ cup all-purpose flour
1 tablespoon Poire William liqueur

1 Cut the quinces into cubes. Place in a saucepan with the water. Stir in half the sugar and bring to a boil. Lower the heat, cover and simmer until tender. Remove the lid and boil until the liquid has almost evaporated.

2 Cool slightly, then purée the fruit in a blender or food processor. Press through a sieve into a bowl and set aside.

3 Make the pastry cream. Pour the milk into a small saucepan. Add the vanilla bean and bring to a boil over low heat. Meanwhile, beat the egg yolks, sugar and flour in a bowl until smooth.

4 Gradually strain the hot milk onto the yolks, whisking frequently until the mixture is smooth and free of lumps.

5 Discard the vanilla bean. Return the mixture to a clean pan and heat gently, stirring until thickened. Cook for another 2 minutes, whisking constantly, to ensure that the sauce is quite smooth and the flour is cooked.

6 Remove the pan from heat and stir in the quince purée and liqueur. Cover the surface of the pastry cream with plastic wrap to prevent it from forming a skin. Let cool slightly, while you prepare the ramekins.

7 Preheat the oven to 425°F. Place a baking sheet in the oven to heat. Butter six ramekins and sprinkle the insides with sugar. In a grease-free bowl, whisk the egg whites into stiff peaks. Slowly whisk in the remaining sugar, then carefully fold the egg whites into the pastry cream.

8 Divide the mixture among the prepared ramekins and level the surfaces. Carefully run a sharp knife around the sides of the ramekins, then place them on the hot baking sheet and bake for 8–10 minutes, until the tops of the soufflés are well risen and golden. Generously dust the tops with confectioners' sugar and serve the soufflés immediately.

COOK'S TIP

Kirsch, made from cherries, is a good alternative to Poire William.

Lemon Soufflé with Blackberries

The simple fresh taste of cold lemon mousse combines well with rich blackberry sauce, and the color contrast looks wonderful, too. Blueberries or raspberries make equally delicious alternatives to blackberries.

INGREDIENTS

Serves 6

grated zest of 1 lemon and juice of
   2 lemons
1 envelope powdered gelatin
5 eggs, separated
¾ cup sugar
few drops vanilla extract
1⅔ cups whipping cream

For the sauce
¾ cup blackberries
   (fresh or frozen)
2–3 tablespoons sugar
few fresh blackberries and blackberry
   leaves, to decorate

1 Place the lemon juice in a small pan and heat through. Sprinkle on the gelatin and let dissolve or heat more until clear. Let cool.

2 Put the lemon zest, egg yolks, sugar and vanilla into a large bowl and whisk until the mixture is very thick, pale and creamy.

3 Whisk the egg whites until stiff and almost peaky. Whip the cream until stiff.

4 Stir the gelatin mixture into the yolks, then fold in the whipped cream and lastly the egg whites. Turn into a 6-cup soufflé dish and freeze for about 2 hours.

5 To make the sauce, place the blackberries in a pan with the sugar and cook for 4–6 minutes, until the juices begin to run and all the sugar has dissolved. Pass through a sieve to remove the seeds, then chill.

6 When the soufflé is almost frozen, but still spoonable, scoop or spoon out onto individual plates and serve with the blackberry sauce, decorated with fresh blackberries and blackberry leaves.

Apple Soufflé Omelet

Apples sautéed until they are slightly caramelized make a delicious autumn filling—you could use fresh raspberries or strawberries when they are in season.

Serves 2

4 eggs, separated

2 tablespoons light cream

1 tablespoon sugar

1 tablespoon butter

confectioners' sugar, for dredging

For the filling

1 apple, peeled, cored and sliced

2 tablespoons butter

2 tablespoons light brown sugar

3 tablespoons light cream

1 To make the filling, sauté the apple slices in the butter and sugar until just tender. Stir in the cream and keep warm, while making the omelet.

2 Place the egg yolks in a bowl with the cream and sugar and beat well. Whisk the egg whites until they form stiff peaks, then fold into the yolk mixture.

3 Melt the butter in a large heavy frying pan, pour in the soufflé mixture and spread evenly. Cook for 1 minute, until golden underneath, then cover the pan handle with aluminum foil and place under a hot broiler to brown the top.

4 Slide the omelet onto a plate, add the apple mixture, then fold over. Sift the confectioners' sugar over thickly, then mark in a criss-cross pattern with a hot metal skewer. Serve immediately.

Hot Mocha Rum Soufflés

Serve these superb soufflés as soon as they are cooked for a fantastic finale to a dinner party.

INGREDIENTS

Serves 6

2 tablespoons unsalted butter, melted
generous ½ cup unsweetened
   cocoa powder
generous ⅓ cup sugar
4 tablespoons strong black coffee
2 tablespoons dark rum
6 egg whites
confectioners' sugar, for dusting

1 Preheat the oven with a baking sheet inside to 375°F. Grease six 1-cup soufflé dishes with the melted butter.

2 Mix 1 tablespoon of the cocoa powder with 1 tablespoon of the sugar in a bowl. Put the mixture in each of the dishes in turn, rotating them so that they are evenly coated.

3 Mix the remaining cocoa powder with the coffee and rum.

4 Whisk the egg whites in a clean, grease-free bowl until they form firm peaks. Whisk in the remaining sugar. Stir a generous spoonful of the whites into the cocoa mixture to lighten it, then gently fold in the remaining whites.

5 Spoon the mixture into the prepared dishes, smoothing the tops. Place on the hot baking sheet, and bake for 12–15 minutes or until well risen. Serve the soufflés immediately, lightly dusted with confectioners' sugar.

COOK'S TIP

When serving the soufflés at the end of a dinner party, prepare them just before the meal is served. Pop in the oven as soon as the main course is finished and serve freshly baked.

Cold Mango Soufflés with Toasted Coconut

Fragrant, fresh mango is one of the most delicious tropical fruits around, whether it is simply served in slices or used as the basis for an ice cream or soufflé.

INGREDIENTS

Makes 4

4 small mangoes, peeled, pitted
   and chopped

2 tablespoons water

1 tablespoon powdered gelatin

2 egg yolks

½ cup sugar

½ cup milk

grated zest of 1 orange

1¼ cups heavy cream

toasted shredded coconut,
   to decorate

1 Place a few pieces of mango in the bottom of four ramekins. Wrap a greased collar of nonstick baking parchment around the outside of each ramekin so that it stands about 2 inches above the rim the dish. Tape to secure, then tie with string.

2 Pour the water into a small heatproof bowl and sprinkle the gelatin on it. Leave for 5 minutes. Place the bowl in a pan of hot water. Stir until the gelatin has dissolved.

3 Whisk the egg yolks, sugar and milk in another heatproof bowl. Place the bowl over a saucepan of simmering water and whisk until the mixture is thick and frothy. Remove from heat and whisk continuously until the mixture cools. Whisk in the liquid gelatin.

4 Process the remaining mango pieces into a purée, then fold the purée into the egg yolk mixture with the orange zest. Set the mixture aside until it is starting to thicken.

5 Whip the heavy cream to form soft peaks. Reserve 4 tablespoons and keep refrigerated. Fold the rest into the mango mixture. Spoon into the ramekins until the mixture is 1 inch above the rim of each dish. Chill for 3–4 hours.

6 Carefully remove the paper collars from the soufflés. Spoon a little of the reserved cream on top of each soufflé and decorate with the coconut before serving.

Chocolate Soufflé Crêpes

A nonstick pan is ideal as it does not need greasing between each crêpe. Serve two crêpes per person.

INGREDIENTS

Makes 12 crepes

⅔ cup all-purpose flour

1 tablespoon unsweetened cocoa powder

1 teaspoon sugar

pinch of salt

1 teaspoon ground cinnamon

2 eggs

¾ cup milk

1 teaspoon vanilla extract

4 tablespoons unsalted butter, melted

confectioners' sugar, for dusting

raspberries, pineapple and mint sprigs,
    to decorate

For the pineapple syrup

½ medium pineapple, peeled, cored and
    finely chopped

2 tablespoons maple syrup

1 teaspoon cornstarch

½ cinnamon stick

2 tablespoons rum

For the soufflé filling

9 ounces semi-sweet or bittersweet
    chocolate

⅓ cup heavy cream

3 eggs, separated

2 tablespoons sugar

1 Prepare syrup. In a saucepan over medium heat, bring pineapple, ½ cup of water, maple syrup, cornstarch and cinnamon stick to a boil. Simmer for 2–3 minutes, until sauce thickens, whisking frequently. Remove from heat; discard cinnamon. Pour into a bowl, stir in rum and chill.

2 Prepare crêpes. In a bowl, sift flour, cocoa powder, sugar, salt and cinnamon. Stir to blend, then make a well in the center. In a bowl, beat eggs, milk and vanilla and gradually add to the well, whisking in flour from the side to form a smooth batter. Stir in half the melted butter and pour batter into a bowl. Let stand 1 hour.

3 Heat a 7–8-inch crêpe pan. Brush with butter. Stir the batter. Pour 3 tablespoons batter into the pan; swirl pan quickly to cover bottom with a thin layer. Cook over medium-high heat for 1–2 minutes, until bottom is golden. Turn over and cook for 30–45 seconds, then turn onto a plate. Stack crêpes between nonstick baking parchment and set aside.

4 Prepare filling. In a small saucepan, over medium heat, melt chocolate and cream until smooth, stirring frequently.

5 In a bowl, beat yolks with half the sugar for 3–5 minutes, until light and creamy. Gradually beat in the chocolate mixture. Let cool. In a large bowl, beat egg whites until soft peaks form. Gradually beat in remaining sugar until stiff. Beat in a spoonful of egg whites to the chocolate mixture, then fold in remaining whites.

6 Preheat the oven to 400°F. Lay a crêpe on a plate. Spoon a little soufflé mixture onto crêpe, spreading it to the edge. Fold the bottom half over the soufflé mixture, then fold in half again to form a filled "triangle." Place on a buttered baking sheet. Repeat with remaining crêpes.

7 Brush the tops with melted butter and bake for 15–20 minutes, until souffléd. Dust with confectioners' sugar and garnish with raspberries, pineapple, mint and a spoonful of pineapple syrup.

Chocolate Soufflés

These are easy to make and can be prepared in advance—the filled dishes can wait for up to one hour before baking. For best results, use good quality chocolate.

INGREDIENTS

Serves 6

6 ounces semi-sweet chocolate, chopped

⅔ cup unsalted butter, cut in small pieces

4 large eggs, separated

2 tablespoons orange liqueur (optional)

¼ teaspoon cream of tartar

3 tablespoons sugar

confectioners' sugar, for dusting

sprigs of red currants and white chocolate roses, to decorate

For the white chocolate sauce

3 ounces white chocolate, chopped

6 tablespoons whipping cream

1–2 tablespoons orange liqueur

grated zest of ½ orange

1 Generously butter six ⅓-cup ramekins. Sprinkle each with a little sugar and tap out any excess. Place the ramekins on a baking sheet.

2 In a heavy saucepan over very low heat, melt the chocolate and butter, stirring until smooth. Remove from heat and cool slightly, then beat in the egg yolks and orange liqueur, if using. Set aside, stirring occasionally.

3 Preheat the oven to 425°F. In a clean, grease-free bowl, whisk the egg whites slowly until frothy. Add the cream of tartar, increase the speed and whisk until they form soft peaks. Gradually sprinkle on the sugar, 1 tablespoon at a time, whisking until the whites are stiff and glossy.

4 Stir a third of the whites into the cooled chocolate mixture to lighten it, then pour the chocolate mixture onto the remaining whites. Using a rubber spatula or large metal spoon, gently fold the sauce into the whites. (Don't worry about a few white streaks.) Spoon into the prepared dishes.

5 To make the white chocolate sauce, put the chopped white chocolate and the cream into a small saucepan. Place over low heat and cook, stirring constantly, until melted and smooth. Remove from heat and stir in the liqueur and orange zest, then pour into a serving pitcher and keep warm.

6 Bake the soufflés for 10–12 minutes, until risen and set but still slightly wobbly in the center. Dust with confectioners' sugar and decorate with a sprig of red currants and a white chocolate rose. Serve the sauce separately.

Frozen Gin and Damson Plum Soufflés

For an unforgettable taste sensation, use sloe gin for these delicious individual frozen soufflés.

INGREDIENTS

Makes 6

1¼ pounds damson plums

1 cup water

1¼ cups sugar

2 tablespoons gin or sloe gin

4 large egg whites

1¼ cups heavy cream, whipped

fresh mint leaves, to decorate

4 Whisk the egg whites in a grease-free bowl until they form stiff peaks. Still whisking, slowly pour in the hot syrup until the meringue mixture is stiff and glossy. Fold in the whipped cream and fruit purée.

5 Spoon the mixture into the dishes to come 1 inch above the rim. Freeze until firm. Remove from the freezer 10 minutes before serving. Remove the collars, then decorate each with damson slices and mint leaves.

1 Wrap collars of greased nonstick baking parchment around the outside of six ramekins, so that they extend 2 inches above the rim. Tie in place with string.

2 Slice two damsons and reserve. Put the rest in a pan with half the water and ¼ cup of the sugar. Cover and simmer for about 7 minutes, until the damsons are tender. Sieve the pulp into a bowl to remove all the pits and skin, stir in the gin and set aside.

3 Combine the remaining sugar and water in the clean pan and heat gently until the sugar has dissolved. Bring to a boil and cook the syrup until it registers 238°F on a candy thermometer, or until a small amount of the mixture dropped into a cup of cold water can be molded into a soft ball.

Chilled Coffee and Praline Soufflé

A smooth coffee soufflé with a crushed praline topping that is spectacular and easy.

Serves 6

¾ cup sugar

5 tablespoons water

generous 1 cup blanched almonds, plus
   extra, for decoration

½ cup strong brewed coffee

1 tablespoon powdered gelatin

3 eggs, separated

scant ½ cup light brown sugar

1 tablespoon coffee liqueur,
   such as Tia Maria

⅔ cup heavy cream

about ⅔ cup heavy cream,
   for decoration (optional)

1 Make a collar from a double layer of waxed paper, 2 inches deeper than a 3¾ cup soufflé dish. Wrap around the dish and tie in place with string. Refrigerate.

2 Oil a baking sheet. Heat the sugar with the water in a heavy pan until dissolved. Boil rapidly until pale golden. Add the almonds and boil until golden.

3 Pour onto the baking sheet and let set hard. Break into pieces, reserving ½ cup, transfer the remainder to a plastic bag and crush with a rolling pin.

4 Pour half the coffee into a bowl; sprinkle on the gelatin and soak for 5 minutes, then place the bowl over hot water and stir until completely dissolved.

5 Over a pan of simmering water whisk the egg yolks, light brown sugar, remaining coffee and liqueur, until thick, then whisk in the gelatin.

6 Whip the cream until thick, then whisk the egg whites until stiff. Fold the praline into the cream, then fold into the coffee mixture. Finally, fold in the egg whites, half at a time.

7 Spoon into the soufflé dish and smooth the top; chill for at least 2 hours. Put in the freezer for 15–20 minutes before serving. Remove the paper collar by running a warmed spatula between the soufflé and the paper. Whisk the cream, if using, and place large spoonfuls on top. Decorate with the reserved praline pieces and blanched almonds.

Twice-baked Mocha Soufflé

The perfect way to end a meal, these mini mocha soufflés can be made up to 3 hours ahead, then reheated just before you serve them.

Serves 6

6 tablespoons unsalted butter, softened

3½ ounces bittersweet or semi-sweet chocolate, grated

2 tablespoons ground coffee

1⅔ cups milk

⅓ cup all-purpose flour, sifted

2 tablespoons unsweetened cocoa powder, sifted

3 eggs, separated

¼ cup sugar

¾ cup creamy chocolate or coffee liqueur, such as Crème de Caçao, Sheridans

1 Preheat the oven to 400°F. Brush six ⅔-cup dariole molds or pudding basins with 2 tablespoons of the butter. Coat with 2 ounces of the grated chocolate.

2 Put the coffee in a small bowl. Heat the milk until almost boiling and pour over the coffee. Infuse for 4 minutes and strain.

3 Melt the remaining butter in a pan. Stir in the flour and cocoa powder to make a roux. Cook for 1 minute, then add the coffee and milk, stirring constantly to make a thick sauce. Simmer for 2 minutes. Remove from heat and stir in the yolks.

4 Cool for 5 minutes, then stir in the chocolate. Whisk the egg whites until stiff, then gradually whisk in the sugar. Stir half into the sauce, then fold in the remainder.

5 Spoon the mixture into the dariole molds and place them in a roasting pan. Pour in hot water to come two-thirds of the way up the sides of the pan.

6 Bake the soufflés for 15 minutes. Turn them out onto a baking tray and let cool.

7 Before serving, spoon 1 tablespoon chocolate or coffee liqueur on each soufflé and reheat in the oven for 6–7 minutes. Serve on individual plates with the remaining liqueur poured on them.

Lemon Soufflé with Caramelized Almonds

This attractive and refreshing dessert soufflé is light and luscious, with a deliciously crunchy caramelized nut topping.

INGREDIENTS

Serves 6

oil, for greasing

grated zest and juice of 3 large lemons

5 large eggs, separated

½ cup sugar

1½ tablespoons powdered gelatin

scant 2 cups heavy cream

For the decoration

¾ cup sliced almonds

¾ cup confectioners' sugar

3 Cape gooseberries

1 Make the soufflé collar. Cut a strip of nonstick baking parchment to fit around a 3¾-cup soufflé dish and extending 3 inches above the rim. Fit the strip around the dish, tape, then tie it around the top of the dish with string. Brush the inside of the paper lightly with oil.

2 Put the lemon zest and egg yolks in a bowl. Add 6 tablespoons of the sugar and whisk until light and creamy.

3 Place the lemon juice in a bowl and sprinkle the gelatin on it. Soak for 5 minutes, then place the bowl over a pan of simmering water. Stir until the gelatin has dissolved. Cool, then stir the gelatin into the egg yolk mixture. In a separate bowl, lightly whip the cream to soft peaks. Fold into the egg yolk mixture and set aside.

4 Whisk the egg whites in a grease-free bowl until stiff. Gradually whisk in the sugar, then lightly fold the whites into the yolk mixture. Pour into the prepared dish, smooth the surface and chill for 4–5 hours.

5 Preheat the broiler. Lightly oil a baking sheet and sprinkle the almonds and sifted confectioners' sugar over it. Broil until the sugar has caramelized and the nuts are golden. Let cool, then remove from the tray and break into pieces.

6 Peel the paper off the soufflé and decorate with the caramelized almonds and Cape gooseberries.

Fruit Salads, Ices & Sorbets

◆ ◆ ◆

Frudités with Honey Dip

A colorful and tasty variation on the popular savory crudités. Quick to prepare from ingredients to hand, it's idea for impromptu entertaining.

INGREDIENTS

Serves 4

1 cup plain yogurt

3 tablespoons honey

selection of fresh fruit for dipping
  such as apples, pears, tangerines,
  grapes, figs, cherries, strawberries
  and kiwis

1 Place the yogurt in a dish, beat until smooth, then partially stir in the honey, leaving a little marbled effect.

2 Cut the various fruits into wedges or bite-sized pieces or leave whole.

3 Arrange the fruits on a platter with the bowl of dip in the center. Serve chilled.

COOK'S TIP

Sprinkle the apple and pear wedges with lemon juice to prevent discoloring.

Watermelon, Ginger and Grapefruit Salad

This pretty, pink combination is very light and refreshing for any summer meal.

INGREDIENTS

Serves 4

2 cups diced watermelon flesh

2 ruby or pink grapefruit

2 pieces stem ginger in syrup

2 tablespoons stem ginger syrup

whipped cream, to serve

1 Remove any seeds from the watermelon and cut into bite-sized chunks.

2 Using a small sharp knife, cut away all the peel and white pith from the grapefruit and carefully lift out the segments, catching any juice in a bowl.

COOK'S TIP
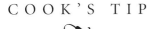

Toss the fruits gently—grape-fruit segments will break up easily and the appearance of the dish will be spoiled.

3 Finely chop the stem ginger and place in a serving bowl with the melon cubes and grapefruit segments, adding the reserved juice.

4 Spoon over the ginger syrup and toss the fruits lightly to give them an equal coating. Chill before serving with a bowl of whipped cream.

Fruits of the Forest with Chocolate Creams

Colorful berries make a fantastic accompaniment to a delightfully creamy white chocolate mousse.

INGREDIENTS

Serves 4

3 ounces white cooking chocolate, in squares

⅔ cup heavy cream

2 tablespoons crème fraîche

1 egg, separated

1 teaspoon powdered gelatin

2 tablespoons cold water

a few drops of pure vanilla extract

1 cup small strawberries, sliced

½ cup raspberries

¾ cup blueberries

3 tablespoons sugar

5 tablespoons white coconut rum

strawberry leaves, to decorate (optional)

1 Melt the chocolate in a heatproof bowl set over a pan of hot water. Heat the cream in a separate pan until almost boiling, then stir into the chocolate with the crème fraîche. Cool slightly, then beat in the egg yolk.

2 Sprinkle the gelatin over the cold water in another heatproof bowl and set aside for a few minutes to swell.

3 Set the bowl in a pan of hot water until the gelatin has dissolved completely. Stir the dissolved gelatin into the chocolate mixture and add the vanilla extract. Set aside until starting to thicken and set.

4 Oil four dariole molds or small soufflé dishes and line the bottom of each with nonstick baking parchment.

5 In a grease-free bowl, whisk the egg white to soft peaks, then fold into the chocolate mixture.

6 Spoon the mixture into the prepared molds or soufflé dishes, then level the surface of each and chill for 2–3 hours or until firm.

7 Meanwhile, place the fruits in a bowl. Add the sugar and coconut rum and stir gently to mix. Cover and chill until required.

8 Ease the chocolate cream away from the rims of the molds or dishes and turn out onto dessert plates. Spoon the fruits around the outside. Decorate with the strawberry leaves, if desired, then serve immediately.

Fruit Salad with Passion Fruit Dressing

Passion fruit juice makes a superb dressing for any fruit, but really brings out the flavor of exotic varieties in particular.

INGREDIENTS

Serves 6

1 mango

1 papaya

2 kiwis

coconut or vanilla ice cream,
   to serve

For the dressing

3 passion fruit

thinly pared zest and juice of 1 lime

1 teaspoon hazelnut or walnut oil

1 tablespoon honey

1 Peel the mango, cut it into three slices, then cut the flesh into chunks and place it in a large bowl. Peel the papaya and cut it in half. Scoop out the seeds, then chop the flesh.

2 Cut both ends off each kiwi, then stand them on a board. Using a small sharp knife, cut off the skin from top to bottom. Cut each kiwi in half lengthways, then cut into thick slices. Combine all the fruit in a large bowl.

3 Cut each passion fruit in half and scoop the seeds into a sieve, over a bowl. Press well to extract all the juices. Lightly whisk the remaining dressing ingredients into the juice, then pour over the fruit. Mix gently and chill for 1 hour before serving with coconut or vanilla ice cream.

Frozen Pear Terrine with Chocolate Sauce

This terrine, based on a classic French dessert, makes a refreshing and impressive end to any meal.

INGREDIENTS

Serves 8

3–3½ pounds ripe Williams pears

juice of 1 lemon

½ cup sugar

10 whole cloves

6 tablespoons water

julienne strips of orange zest, to decorate

For the sauce

7 ounces semi-sweet chocolate

4 tablespoons hot strong black coffee

scant 1 cup heavy cream

2 tablespoons Calvados or brandy

1 Peel, core and slice the pears. Put in a pan with the lemon juice, sugar, cloves and water. Cover and simmer for 10 minutes. Remove the cloves and cool.

2 Process the pears and juice in a processor or blender until smooth. Pour into a freezerproof bowl, cover and freeze until firm.

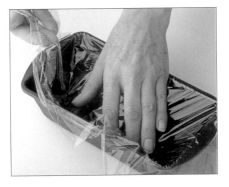

3 Meanwhile line a 2-pound loaf pan with plastic wrap, allowing plenty of overlap. Spoon the frozen pear purée into a food processor or blender. Process until smooth. Pour into the prepared pan, cover and freeze until firm.

4 Break the chocolate into a large heatproof bowl and place over a saucepan of hot water. When the chocolate has melted, stir in the coffee until smooth. Gradually stir in the cream and then the Calvados or brandy. Set the sauce aside.

5 20 minutes before serving, remove the pan from the freezer. Invert the terrine on to a plate, lift off the plastic wrap and place in the refrigerator to soften slightly. To serve, warm the sauce over hot water. Place a slice of terrine on each dessert plate and spoon over some sauce. Decorate with julienne strips of orange zest.

Chocolate Sorbet with Berries

The chill that thrills—that's chocolate sorbet. For a really fine texture, it helps to have an ice cream maker, which churns the mixture as it freezes, but you can make it by hand quite easily.

INGREDIENTS

Serves 6

2 cups water

3 tablespoons honey

½ cup sugar

¾ cup unsweetened cocoa powder

2 ounces bittersweet chocolate, broken into squares

14 ounces berries, such as raspberries, red currants or strawberries

1 Place the water, honey, sugar and cocoa powder in a saucepan. Heat gently, stirring occasionally, until the sugar has completely dissolved.

2 Remove from heat, add the chocolate and stir until melted. Let cool.

3 Put into an ice cream maker and churn until frozen. Alternatively, pour into a freezer-proof container, freeze until slushy, whisk until smooth, then freeze again. Whisk for a second time before the mixture hardens.

4 Remove from the freezer 10–15 minutes before serving, so that the sorbet softens slightly. Serve in scoops, with a mixture of berries, or with just one variety.

COOK'S TIP

This sorbet looks attractive if served in small oval scoops— simply scoop out the sorbet with one tablespoon, then use another to smooth it off and transfer it to the plate.

Lemon Sorbet

This is probably the most classic sorbet of all. It is refreshingly tangy and yet deliciously smooth.

INGREDIENTS

Serves 6

1 cup sugar

1¼ cups water

4 lemons, well scrubbed

1 egg white

sugared lemon zest to decorate

1 Put the sugar and water into a saucepan and bring to a boil, stirring occasionally, until the sugar has just dissolved.

2 Using a swivel vegetable peeler, pare the zest thinly from two of the lemons so that it falls straight into the pan. Simmer for 2 minutes without stirring, then take the pan off the heat, let cool, then chill.

3 Squeeze the juice from the lemons and add to the syrup. Strain the syrup and lemon juice and churn in an ice cream maker until thick. Alternatively, freeze and whisk as in the previous recipe.

4 In a small bowl, whisk the egg white lightly with a fork.

5 Using an ice cream maker, add the egg white to the mixture and continue to churn for 10–15 minutes until firm enough to scoop.

6 Scoop into bowls or glasses and decorate with sugared lemon zest to serve.

COOK'S TIP

Cut one third off the top of the lemon and retain as a lid. Squeeze the juice out of the larger portion. Remove any membrane and use the shell as a ready-made container. Scoop or pipe sorbet into the shell, top with the lid and add lemon leaves or small bay leaves.

Mango Sorbet

A light and refreshing dessert that's surprisingly easy to make.

INGREDIENTS

Serves 6

¾ cup sugar

a large strip of orange zest

1 large mango, peeled, pitted and cubed

4 tablespoons orange juice

mint sprigs, to decorate

1 Combine the sugar, orange zest and ¾ cup of water in a saucepan. Bring to a boil, stirring to dissolve the sugar. Let the syrup cool.

2 Purée the mango cubes with the orange juice in a blender or food processor. There should be about 2 cups of purée.

3 Add the purée to the cooled sugar syrup and mix well. Strain, then chill.

4 When cold, put into a freezer container and freeze until firm around the edges.

5 Spoon the semi-frozen mixture into the food processor and process until smooth. Return to the freezer and freeze until solid. Allow the sorbet to soften slightly at room temperature for 15–20 minutes before serving, decorated with mint sprigs.

VARIATIONS

For Banana Sorbet: peel and cube 4–5 large bananas. Purée with 2 tablespoons lemon juice to make 2 cups. If liked, replace the orange zest in the sugar syrup with 2–3 whole cloves, or omit the zest.

For Papaya Sorbet: peel, seed and cube 1½ pounds papaya. Purée with 3 tablespoons lime juice to make 2 cups. Replace the orange zest with lime zest.

For Passion Fruit Sorbet: halve 16 or more passion fruit and scoop out the seeds and pulp (there should be about 2 cups). Work in a blender or food processor until the seeds are like coarse pepper. Omit the orange juice and zest. Add the passion fruit to the sugar syrup, then press through a wire sieve before freezing.

Lime Sherbet

This light, refreshing sherbet is a good dessert to serve after a substantial main course.

Serves 4

1¼ cups granulated sugar

grated zest of 1 lime

¾ cup freshly squeezed
   lime juice

1–2 tablespoons fresh lemon juice

confectioners' sugar, to taste

slivers of lime zest, to decorate

1 In a small heavy saucepan, dissolve the granulated sugar in 2½ cups of water, without stirring, over medium heat. When the sugar has dissolved, boil for 5-6 minutes. Remove from heat and let cool.

2 Combine the cooled sugar syrup and lime zest and juice in a measuring cup or bowl. Stir well. Taste and adjust the flavor by adding lemon juice or some confectioners' sugar, if necessary. Do not over-sweeten.

3 Freeze the mixture in an ice cream maker, following the manufacturer's instructions.

4 If you do not have an ice cream maker, pour the mixture into a metal or plastic freezer container and freeze until softly set, for about 3 hours.

5 Remove from the container and chop roughly into 3-inch pieces. Place in a food processor and process until smooth. Return the mixture to the freezer container and freeze again until set. Repeat this freezing and chopping process two or three times, until a smooth consistency is obtained.

6 Serve in scoops decorated with slivers of lime zest.

COOK'S TIP

If using an ice cream maker for these sherbets, check the manufacturer's instructions to find out the freezing capacity. If necessary, halve the recipe quantities.

Ruby Orange Sherbet in Ginger Baskets

This superb frozen dessert is perfect for people without ice cream makers who can't be bothered with the freezing and stirring that home-made ices normally require. It is also ideal for serving at a special dinner party as both the sherbet and ginger baskets can be made in advance, leaving you to simply assemble the dessert between courses.

INGREDIENTS

Serves 6

grated zest and juice of 2 blood oranges
1½ cups confectioners' sugar
1¼ cups heavy cream
scant 1 cup plain natural yogurt
blood orange segments, to
    decorate (optional)

For the ginger baskets

2 tablespoons unsalted butter
1 tablespoon golden syrup or light
    corn syrup
2 tablespoons sugar
¼ teaspoon ground ginger
1 tablespoon finely chopped mixed
    citrus peel
1 tablespoon all-purpose flour

1 Place the orange zest and juice in a bowl. Sift the confectioners' sugar over the top and set aside for 30 minutes, then stir until smooth.

2 Whisk the heavy cream in a large bowl until the mixture forms soft peaks, then carefully fold in the yogurt.

3 Gently stir in the orange juice, then pour into a freezerproof container. Cover, freeze until firm.

4 Make the baskets. Preheat the oven to 350°F. Place the butter, syrup and sugar in a heavy saucepan and heat gently until melted.

5 Add the ground ginger, mixed citrus peel and flour and stir until the mixture is smooth.

> ### COOK'S TIP
> ∾
> It is essential to have the greased tins or cups ready and to work quickly. If the cookies firm up before you have made them all, a few seconds in the oven will soften them.

6 Lightly grease two baking sheets. Drop three portions of the ginger dough on to each baking sheet, using about 2 teaspoons of the mixture at a time; space well apart. Spread each one to a 2-inch circle, then bake for 12–14 minutes until dark golden.

7 Remove the cookies from the oven and let stand on the baking sheets for 1 minute to firm slightly. Lift off with a spatula and drape over six greased mini muffin tins or upturned cups; flatten the top (which will become the bottom) and flute the edges to form a basket shape.

8 When cool, lift the baskets off the tins or cups and place on individual dessert plates. Arrange scoops of the frozen sherbet in each basket. Decorate each portion with a few orange segments, if you like.

Apple and Cider Sorbet

This very English combination has a subtle apple flavor with just a hint of cider. As the apple purée is very pale, almost white, add a few drops of green food coloring to echo the pale green skin of the Granny Smith apples.

INGREDIENTS

Serves 6

1¼ pounds Granny Smith apples

¾ cup sugar

1¼ cups water

1 cup strong dry cider

few drops of green food coloring
  (optional)

strips of thinly pared lime zest,
  to decorate

1 Quarter, core and roughly chop the apples. Put them into a saucepan. Add the sugar and half the water. Cover and simmer for 10 minutes or until the apples are soft.

COOK'S TIP

Add the food coloring gradually, making the mixture a little darker than you would like the finished sorbet to be, as freezing lightens the color slightly.

2 Press the mixture through a sieve placed over a bowl. Discard the apple skins and seeds. Stir the cider and the remaining water into the apple purée and add a little coloring, if desired.

3 If making by hand, pour the mixture into a shallow plastic container and freeze for 6 hours, beating with a fork once or twice to break up the ice crystals. If you have an ice cream maker, churn the mixture until it is firm enough to scoop.

4 Scoop into dishes and decorate with twists of thinly pared lime zest.

Gooseberry and Clotted Cream Ice Cream

The delicious, slightly tart flavor of gooseberries goes particularly well with melt-in-your-mouth meringues.

INGREDIENTS

Serves 4–6

4 cups gooseberries, trimmed

4 tablespoons water

6 tablespoons sugar

⅔ cup whipping cream

a few drops of green food coloring
    (optional)

½ cup clotted cream

fresh mint sprigs, to decorate

meringues, to serve

1 Put the gooseberries in a saucepan and add the water and sugar. Cover and simmer for 10 minutes or until soft.

2 Transfer to a food processor or blender and process into a smooth purée. Press through a sieve placed over a bowl. Cool, then chill.

3 Chill the purée in a plastic container. Whip the cream until it is thick but still falls from a spoon. Fold into the purée with the green food coloring, if using. Freeze for 2 hours, then beat with a fork, electric mixer or in a food processor, to break up. Return to the freezer for 2 hours.

4 If making by hand, beat the ice cream again, then fold in the clotted cream. Freeze for 2–3 hours. If using an ice cream maker, mix the chilled purée with the whipping cream, add a few drops of green food coloring, if using, and churn until thickened and semi-frozen. Add the clotted cream and continue to churn until thick enough to scoop.

5 To serve, scoop the ice cream into dishes or small plates, decorate with fresh mint sprigs and add a few small meringues to each serving.

Banana and Toffee Ice Cream

The addition of sweetened condensed milk helps to bring out the natural flavor of the bananas and, surprisingly, the ice cream is not excessively sweet.

INGREDIENTS

Serves 4–6

3 ripe bananas

juice of 1 lemon

12½-ounce can sweetened condensed milk

⅔ cup whipping cream

5 ounces toffees

chopped toffees, to decorate

1 Process the bananas into a purée in a food processor or blender, then add the lemon juice and process briefly to mix. Scrape the purée into a plastic or similar freezerproof container.

2 Pour in the condensed milk, stirring with a metal spoon, then add the cream. Mix well, cover and freeze for 4 hours or until mushy.

3 Unwrap the toffees and chop them finely, using a sharp knife. If this proves difficult, put them in a double plastic bag and hit them with a rolling pin.

4 Beat the semi-frozen ice cream with a fork or electric mixer to break up the ice crystals, then stir in the toffees. Return the ice cream to the freezer for 3–5 hours or until firm. Scoop onto a plate or into a bowl and decorate with chopped toffees. Serve immediately.

COOK'S TIP

To reduce the initial freezing time, start chilling the mixture in a stainless steel roasting pan, transferring to a plastic container only after adding the toffees. If you are making this ice cream for small children, you may prefer to leave the toffees out or use chopped chocolate instead.

Strawberry Semi-freddo

Serve this quick strawberry and ricotta dessert semi-frozen to enjoy the flavor at its best.

INGREDIENTS

Serves 4–6

generous 2 cups strawberries

scant ½ cup strawberry jam

generous 1 cup ricotta cheese

scant 1 cup plain yogurt

1 teaspoon pure vanilla extract

3 tablespoons sugar

extra strawberries and mint or lemon
    balm, to decorate

1 Put the strawberries in a bowl and mash them with a fork until broken into small pieces but not completely puréed. Stir in the strawberry jam. Drain off any whey from the ricotta.

2 Put the ricotta into a bowl and stir in the yogurt, vanilla and sugar. Using a spoon gently fold the mashed strawberries into the ricotta mixture until rippled.

3 Spoon into individual freezerproof dishes and freeze for at least 2 hours, until almost solid. Alternatively, freeze until completely solid, then transfer the ice cream to the refrigerator for about 45 minutes to soften before serving. Serve in small bowls with extra strawberries and decorated with mint or lemon balm.

COOK'S TIP

Don't mash the strawberries too much or they'll become too liquid. Freeze in a large freezer container if you don't have suitable small dishes. Transfer to the refrigerator to thaw slightly, then scoop into glasses.

Mango and Passion Fruit Gelato

Fresh and fruity, this tropical ice cream has a delicate perfume. Passion fruit tend to vary in size. If you can locate the large ones, four will be plenty for this dish.

Serves 4

4 large mangoes

grated zest and juice of 1 lime

¼ cup sugar

1¼ cups whipping cream

4–6 passion fruit

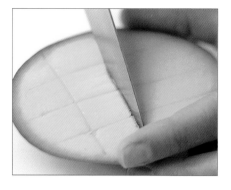

1 Cut a thick slice from either side of the pit on each unpeeled mango. Make criss-cross cuts in the flesh, cutting down as far as the skin.

2 Turn the slices inside out so that the pieces of mango stand out from the skin, then scoop them into a food processor or blender.

3 Process the mango flesh until smooth, then add the grated lime zest, lime juice and sugar and process briefly.

4 If making by hand, whip the cream until it is just thick but will still fall from a spoon. Fold in the puréed mango and lime mixture, then pour into a plastic or similar freezerproof container. Freeze for 4 hours until semi-frozen. If using an ice cream maker, churn the fruit mixture for 10–15 minutes, then add the cream and continue to churn until the mixture is thick but still too soft to scoop. Scrape it into a plastic container.

5 Cut the passion fruit in half and scoop the seeds and pulp into the ice cream mixture, mix well and freeze for 2 hours until firm enough to scoop.

Fresh Strawberry Ice Cream

You can make the ice cream by hand if you freeze it for several hours, whisking it every hour or so, but the texture won't be as good.

Serves 6

1¼ cups milk

1 vanilla bean

3 large egg yolks

1½–2 cups strawberries

juice of ½ lemon

¾ cup confectioners' sugar

1¼ cups heavy cream

sliced strawberries, to serve

3 Meanwhile, purée the strawberries with the lemon juice in a food processor or blender. Press the strawberry purée through a sieve into a bowl. Stir in the confectioners' sugar and set aside. In a separate bowl whip the cream until it forms soft peaks.

4 Gently fold the cream into the custard with the strawberry purée. Pour the mixture into an ice cream maker. Churn for 20–30 minutes, or until the mixture holds its shape. Transfer the ice cream to a freezerproof container, cover and freeze until firm. Soften briefly before serving decorated with sliced strawberries.

1 Put the milk and vanilla bean into a pan and slowly bring to a boil. Remove from heat and leave for 20 minutes. Strain the warm milk into a bowl containing the egg yolks and whisk well.

2 Return the mixture to a clean pan and heat, stirring constantly, until the custard just coats the back of the spoon. Pour into a clean bowl, cover with plastic wrap and set aside to cool.

Chocolate Ice Cream

Use good quality semi-sweet chocolate for the best flavor.

INGREDIENTS

Makes about 3¾ cups

3 cups milk

4-inch piece of vanilla bean

4 egg yolks

8 ounces semi-sweet chocolate, melted

¾ cup granulated sugar

1 To make the custard, heat the milk with the vanilla bean in a small saucepan. Remove from heat as soon as small bubbles start to form. Do not boil.

2 Beat the egg yolks with a wire whisk or electric beater. Gradually incorporate the sugar, and continue beating for about 5 minutes, until the mixture is pale yellow. Strain the milk. Slowly add it to the egg mixture drop by drop.

3 Pour the mixture into a double boiler with the melted chocolate. Stir over medium heat until the water in the pan is boiling and the custard thickens enough to lightly coat the back of a spoon. Remove from heat and let cool.

4 Freeze in an ice cream maker or, if you do not have an ice cream maker, pour the mixture into a metal or plastic freezer container and freeze until set, about 3 hours. Remove from the container and chop roughly into 7.5cm/3in pieces. Place in the bowl of a food processor and process until smooth. Return to the freezer container, and freeze again until firm. Repeat the freezing-chopping process 2 or 3 times, until a smooth consistency is reached.

Buttermilk Vanilla Ice Cream

Enriched with just a little heavy cream, this unusual ice cream tastes far more luxurious than it really is.

INGREDIENTS

Serves 6

1 cup buttermilk

4 tablespoons heavy cream

1 vanilla bean or ½ teaspoon
   vanilla extract

2 eggs

2 tablespoons honey

fresh fruit purée, to serve

1 Place the buttermilk and cream in a pan with the vanilla bean, if using, and heat gently over a low heat until the mixture is almost boiling. Remove the vanilla bean.

2 Place the eggs in a bowl over a pan of hot water and whisk until they are pale and thick. Add the heated buttermilk in a thin stream, while whisking hard. Continue whisking over the hot water until the mixture has thickened slightly.

> ### COOK'S TIP
>
> This basic vanilla ice cream can be used as a base for other flavors: stir in puréed fruit, citrus ring or coffee.

3 Whisk in the honey and vanilla, if using. Spoon the mixture into a freezer-proof container and freeze until firm.

4 Spoon the firm ice cream onto a sheet of nonstick baking parchment. Roll it up in the paper to form a cylinder and freeze again until firm. Serve the ice cream on plates in slices.

Frozen Strawberry Mousse Cake

Children love this pretty dessert—it tastes just like an ice cream.

INGREDIENTS

Serves 4–6

15-ounce can strawberries in syrup

1 envelope powdered gelatin

6 sponge cakes

3 tablespoons strawberry jam

⅞ cup crème fraîche

⅞ cup whipped cream,
   to decorate

1 Strain the syrup from the strawberries into a large heatproof bowl. Sprinkle on the gelatin and stir well. Stand the bowl in a pan of hot water and stir until the gelatin has dissolved.

2 Let cool, then chill for just under 1 hour, until beginning to set. Meanwhile, cut the sponge cakes in half lengthwise and spread the cut surfaces with the strawberry jam.

3 Carefully whisk the crème fraîche into the strawberry jelly, then whisk in the canned strawberries. Line a deep, 8-inch loose-bottomed cake pan with nonstick baking parchment.

4 Pour half the strawberry mousse mixture into the pan, arrange the sponge cakes on the surface, and then spoon on the remaining mousse mixture, pushing down any sponge cakes that rise up.

5 Freeze for 1–2 hours until firm. Remove the cake from the pan and carefully peel off the lining paper. Transfer to a serving plate. Decorate the mousse with whirls of whipped cream and a few strawberry leaves and a fresh strawberry, if you have them.

Hazelnut Ice Cream

This popular flavor goes very well served with scoops of chocolate and vanilla ice creams.

INGREDIENTS

Serves 4–6

½ cup hazelnuts

6 tablespoons granulated sugar

2 cups milk

4-inch piece of vanilla bean

4 egg yolks

1 Spread the hazelnuts on a baking sheet and place under the broiler for about 5 minutes, shaking the pan frequently to turn the nuts over. Remove from heat and let cool slightly. Place the nuts on a clean dish towel, and rub them with a cloth to remove their dark outer skin. Chop very finely or grind in a food processor with 2 tablespoons of the sugar.

2 Make the custard. Heat the milk with the vanilla bean in a small saucepan. Remove from heat as soon as small bubbles start to form on the surface.

3 Beat the egg yolks with a wire whisk or an electric beater. Gradually add the remaining sugar and continue beating until the mixture turns a pale yellow. Discard the vanilla bean and, stirring constantly, very gradually add the milk, pouring it through a strainer.

4 Pour the mixture into a double boiler, or into a bowl placed over a pan of simmering water. Add the chopped nuts. Stir over medium heat until the water in the pan is boiling and the custard thickens enough to lightly coat the back of a spoon. Remove from heat and let cool.

5 Freeze in an ice cream maker, or transfer the mixture to a freezerproof container and freeze for 5–6 hours. During the freezing time beat twice with a fork, electric beater or in a food processor until a smooth consistency has been reached. Serve in scoops.

Coffee Ice Cream with Caramelized Pecans

Coffee and sweetened nuts make a mouthwatering combination.

INGREDIENTS

Serves 4–6

For the ice cream

1¼ cups milk

1 tablespoon light brown sugar

6 tablespoons finely ground coffee or
    1 tablespoon instant coffee granules

1 egg plus 2 yolks

1¼ cups heavy cream

1 tablespoon sugar

For the pecans

1 cup pecan halves

4 tablespoons dark brown sugar

1 Heat the milk and light brown sugar in a small pan to boiling point. Remove from heat and sprinkle on the coffee. Let stand for 2 minutes, then stir, cover and let cool.

2 In a heatproof bowl, beat the egg and extra yolks until the mixture is thick and pale.

3 Strain the coffee mixture into a clean pan, heat to boiling point, then pour onto the eggs in a steady stream, beating hard.

4 Set the bowl over a pan of gently simmering water and stir until it thickens. Cool, then chill in the refrigerator.

5 Whip the cream with the sugar. Fold it into the coffee custard and freeze in a covered container. Beat twice at hourly intervals, then let freeze firm.

6 To caramelize the nuts, preheat the oven to 350°F. Spread the nuts on a baking sheet in a single layer. Put them into the oven for 10–15 minutes to toast, until they release their fragrance.

7 On top of the stove, dissolve the brown sugar in 2 tablespoons water in a heavy pan, shaking it over low heat until the sugar dissolves completely and the syrup clears.

8 When the syrup begins to bubble, add the toasted pecans and cook for a minute or two over medium heat until the syrup coats and clings to the nuts.

9 Spread the nuts on a lightly oiled baking sheet, separating them with the tip of a knife, and let cool. Store when cold in an airtight pan if they are not to be eaten on the same day.

10 Transfer the ice cream from the freezer to the refrigerator 30 minutes before scooping it into portions and serving with caramelized pecans.

COOK'S TIP

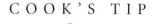

You can enhance good-quality bought ice cream with the same nutty garnish.

Brown Bread Ice Cream

Delicious on its own and irresistible served with this black currant coulis, brown bread ice cream is a classic British treat.

INGREDIENTS

Serves 6

½ cup roasted and chopped hazelnuts, ground

1¼ cups whole-wheat bread crumbs

4 tablespoons brown sugar

3 egg whites

½ cup sugar

1¼ cups heavy cream

few drops of vanilla extract

For the sauce

2 cups black currants

6 tablespoons sugar

1 tablespoon creme de cassis

fresh mint to decorate

1 Combine the hazelnuts and bread crumbs on a baking sheet, then sprinkle on the sugar. Place under a medium broiler and toast, stirring, until the mixture is crisp and evenly browned. Let cool.

2 Whisk the egg whites in a bowl until stiff, then gradually whisk in the caster sugar until thick and glossy. Whip the cream until it forms soft peaks and fold into the meringue with the bread crumb mixture and vanilla extract.

3 Spoon the mixture into a 5-cup loaf pan. Smooth the top level, then cover and freeze for several hours or until firm.

4 Meanwhile, make the sauce. Strip the black currants from their stems using a fork and put them in a small bowl with the sugar. Toss gently to mix and leave for 30 minutes.

5 Purée the black currants in a blender or food processor, then press through a nylon sieve until smooth. Add the crème de cassis and chill well.

6 To serve, turn out the ice cream onto a plate and cut into slices. Arrange each slice on a serving plate, spoon on a little sauce and decorate with fresh mint sprigs.

Indian Ice Cream (Kulfi)

Kulfi-wallahs (ice cream vendors) have always made kulfi, and continue to this day, without using modern freezers. Try this method— it works extremely well in an ordinary freezer. You will need to start making kulfi the day before you want to serve it.

INGREDIENTS

Serves 4–6

3 14-fluid-ounce cans evaporated milk

3 egg whites, whisked until peaks form

3 cups confectioners' sugar

1 teaspoon cardamom powder

1 tablespoon rose water

1½ cups pistachios, chopped

generous ½ cup golden raisins

¾ cup sliced almonds

2 tablespoons candied cherries, halved

1 Remove the labels from the cans of evaporated milk and lay the cans down in a pan with a tight-fitting cover. Fill the pan with water to reach three-quarters up the cans. Bring to a boil, cover and simmer for 20 minutes. When cool, remove and chill the cans in the refrigerator for 24 hours.

2 Open the cans and empty the milk into a large, chilled bowl. Whisk until it doubles in quantity, then fold in the whisked egg whites and confectioners' sugar.

3 Gently fold in the remaining ingredients, seal the bowl with cling film and leave in the freezer for 1 hour.

4 Remove the ice cream from the freezer and mix well with a fork. Transfer to a freezer container and return to the freezer for a final setting. Remove from the freezer 10 minutes before serving in scoops.

Turkish Delight Ice Cream

Not strictly a traditional Middle Eastern recipe, but a delicious way of using Turkish Delight. Sprinkle rose petals, if you have them.

Serves 6

4 egg yolks

½ cup sugar

1¼ cups milk

1¼ cups heavy cream

1 tablespoon rose water

6 ounces rose flavored Turkish
  Delight, chopped

1 Beat the egg yolks and sugar together until pale and thick. In a pan, bring the milk to a boil. Add to the yolks and sugar, stirring, then return to the pan.

2 Continue stirring over low heat, until the custard is thick enough to coat the back of a spoon. Do not boil, or it will curdle. Let cool, then stir in the cream and rose water.

3 Put the Turkish Delight in a pan with 2–3 tablespoons water. Heat gently, until almost melted, but with just a few small lumps. Remove from heat and stir into the cool custard mixture.

4 Let the mixture cool completely, then pour into a shallow freezer container. Freeze for 3 hours, until just frozen all over. Transfer the mixture into a mixing bowl.

5 Using a whisk, beat the mixture until smooth, return to the freezer container and freeze for 2 more hours. Repeat the beating process, then return to the freezer for about 3 hours or until firm. Remove the ice cream from the freezer 20–25 minutes before serving. Serve with thin almond cookies or meringues.

Pineapple Ice Cream

Tropically flavored, this ice cream can be made at any time of the year, but it is particularly good when made with fresh pineapple.

INGREDIENTS

Serves 8–10

8 eggs, separated

½ cup sugar

½ teaspoon vanilla extract

2½ cups whipping cream

4 tablespoons confectioners' sugar

15-ounce can pineapple chunks

¼ cup pistachios, chopped

wafer cookies to serve

1 Place the egg yolks in a bowl, add the sugar and vanilla and beat until thick and pale yellow.

2 In a separate bowl, whip the cream and confectioners' sugar to soft peaks. Add to the egg yolk mixture.

3 Whisk the egg whites in a separate large bowl until they are firm and hold stiff peaks. Gently fold the egg whites into the cream mixture and blend well.

COOK'S TIP

Use a small fresh pineapple when available. Remove the rough skin and core, then chop into chunks.

4 Cut the pineapple into very small pieces, add the pistachios and stir into the cream mixture, mixing well with a spoon.

5 Pour the mixture into an ice cream container and place in the freezer for a few hours until it is set and firm, stirring it once or twice during the freezing time.

6 Cut into thick slices and serve in a pretty glass dish decorated with wafer cookies.

Coconut Ice Cream

An easy-to-make ice cream that is quite heavenly and will be loved by all for its fresh tropical taste.

INGREDIENTS

Serves 8

14-ounce can evaporated milk

14-ounce can condensed milk

14-ounce can coconut milk

freshly grated nutmeg

1 teaspoon almond extract

lemon balm sprigs, lime slices and
    shredded coconut, to decorate

1 Mix the evaporated, condensed and coconut milks in a freezerproof bowl and stir in the nutmeg and almond extract.

2 Put in the freezer and chill for an hour or two until the mixture is semi-frozen.

3 Remove from the freezer and whisk the mixture with a hand or electric beater until it is fluffy and almost doubled in volume.

4 Pour into a freezer container, then cover and freeze until firm. Before serving, let the ice cream soften slightly at room temperature. Decorate with a sprig of lemon balm, lime slices and shredded coconut.

Cinnamon and Coffee Swirl Ice Cream

Light ice cream subtly spiced with cinnamon and rippled with a sweet coffee syrup.

INGREDIENTS

Serves 6

1¼ cups light cream

1 cinnamon stick

4 egg yolks

¾ cup sugar

1¼ cups heavy cream

For the coffee syrup

3 tablespoons ground coffee

3 tablespoons almost-boiling water

½ cup sugar

¼ cup water

1 Slowly bring to a boil the cream and cinnamon stick. Turn off the heat, cover and infuse for 30 minutes. Bring back to a boil and remove the cinnamon.

2 Whisk the yolks and sugar until light. Pour the hot cream over the egg mixture, whisking. Return to the pan and stir over low heat for 1–2 minutes, until it thickens. Let the mixture cool.

3 Whip the heavy cream until peaks form and fold into the custard. Pour into a container and freeze for 3 hours.

4 Meanwhile, put the coffee in a bowl and pour the hot water over. Let infuse for 4 minutes, then strain through a sieve. Discard the coffee grounds.

5 Gently heat the sugar and cold water in a pan until completely dissolved. Bring to a boil and gently simmer for 5 minutes. Cool, then stir in the coffee.

6 Turn the ice cream into a chilled bowl and briefly whisk to break down the ice crystals.

7 Spoon a third back into the container and drizzle on some coffee syrup. Repeat until it is all used.

8 Drag a skewer through the mixture a few times to achieve a marbled effect. Freeze for 4 hours, or until solid. Let soften slightly before serving.

Mint Ice Cream

This ice cream is best served slightly softened at room temperature, so take it out of the freezer 20 minutes before you want to serve it. For a special occasion, this looks spectacular served in an ice bowl.

INGREDIENTS

Serves 8

8 egg yolks

6 tablespoons sugar

2½ cups light cream

1 vanilla bean

4 tablespoons chopped fresh mint

1 Place the egg yolks and sugar in a bowl and beat, using a hand-held electric beater or a balloon whisk, until it is pale and slightly thick. Transfer the mixture to a saucepan.

2 Pour the cream into a separate saucepan and add the vanilla bean. Over medium heat gently bring the cream just to a boil.

3 Remove the vanilla bean and pour the hot cream onto the egg mixture, whisking briskly.

4 Continue whisking to ensure that the eggs are thoroughly mixed into the cream.

5 Gently heat the mixture until the custard thickens enough to coat the back of a wooden spoon. Let cool.

6 Stir in the mint and place in an ice cream maker to churn and freeze (about 3–4 hours). If you don't have an ice cream maker, freeze the ice cream until mushy and then whisk it well again, to break down the ice crystals. Freeze for another 3 hours, until it is softly frozen and whisk again. Finally, freeze the ice cream until hard, preferably overnight.

COOK'S TIP

To make an ice bowl, place a few ice cubes in the bottom of a freezerproof bowl, adding a few sprigs of the herb for decoration. Place a smaller bowl inside, to give a gap of ½-inch, level and secure with tape. Fill the gap with cooled boiled water and freeze until solid. To unmold, pour a little hot water into the inner bowl, then dip briefly in hot water to release the ice bowl.

VARIATION

For an equally refreshing alternative use lemon balm, borage or rose geranium instead of mint. Gather enough sprigs of the chosen herb to make 4 tablespoons of chopped herb and use in the recipe in exactly the same way.

Rocky Road Ice Cream

For chills and thrills, there's nothing to beat this classic sweet ice cream. A perennial favorite, packed with flavor and contrasting textures.

INGREDIENTS

Serves 6

4 ounces semi-sweet chocolate broken
    into squares

⅔ cup milk

1¼ cups heavy cream

½ cup marshmallows, chopped

¼ cup glace cherries, chopped

1 cup crumbled shortbread cookies

2 tablespoons chopped walnuts

1 Melt the chocolate in the milk in a saucepan over low heat, stirring from occasionally. Let cool.

2 Whip the cream in a bowl until it just holds it shape. Beat in the chocolate mixture.

3 Put the chocolate cream mixture into an ice cream maker and churn until thick and almost frozen. Alternatively, pour into a container suitable for use in the freezer, freeze until ice crystals form around the edges, then whisk until completely smooth.

4 Stir the marshmallows, cherries, crushed cookies and nuts into the mixture, then return to the freezer and freeze until firm.

5 Let the ice cream soften at room temperature for 15–20 minutes before serving in scoops.

> ### COOK'S TIP
>
> For a quick version, simply stir the flavorings into bought soft-serve chocolate ice cream and freeze until firm.

Brandied Fruit and Rice Ice Cream

Based on a favorite Victorian ice cream, this rich dessert combines spicy rice pudding with a creamy egg custard flecked with brandy-soaked fruits. The mixture is then frozen until it is just firm enough to serve in scoops.

INGREDIENTS

Serves 4–6

¹/₄ cup pitted prunes

¹/₄ cup dried apricots

¹/₄ cup candied cherries

2 tablespoons brandy

²/₃ cup light cream

For the rice mixture

generous ¹/₄ cup pudding rice

scant 2 cups whole milk

1 cinnamon stick, halved, plus extra
    cinnamon sticks, to decorate

4 cloves

For the custard

4 egg yolks

6 tablespoons sugar

1 teaspoon cornstarch

1¹/₄ cups whole milk

1 Chop the prunes, apricots and cherries finely and put them in a bowl. Pour in the brandy. Cover and let soak for 3 hours or overnight if possible.

COOK'S TIP

As the brandy-soaked fruits are so soft, it is better to remove the ice cream from the ice cream maker, fold in the fruits and then freeze the mixture in a tub until firm enough to scoop.

---

2 Put the rice, milk and whole spices in a saucepan. Bring to a boil, then simmer gently for 30 minutes, stirring occasionally, until most of the milk has been absorbed. Lift out the spices and let the rice cool.

3 Whisk the egg yolks, sugar and cornflower in a bowl until thick and creamy. Heat the milk in a heavy pan, then gradually pour it on the yolks, whisking constantly. Pour back into the pan and cook, stirring until the custard thickens. Let cool, then chill.

4 Mix the chilled custard, rice and cream together. Pour into a plastic container or similar freezer-proof container and freeze for 4–5 hours, until mushy. Beat the ice cream lightly with a fork to break up the ice crystals.

5 Fold in the fruits, then freeze for 2–3 hours, until firm enough to scoop.

6 Scoop the ice cream into individual dishes and decorate with cinnamon sticks.

Praline Ice Cream in Baskets

Praline, a delicious crunchy caramel and nut mixture, is a very popular flavoring in France—it can be made with almonds or hazelnuts or a mixture of the two, if you prefer.

INGREDIENTS

Serves 6–8

½ cup blanched almonds
  or hazelnuts
⅞ cup sugar
4 tablespoons water
1 cup heavy cream
6 egg yolks
2 cups milk

For the cookies baskets

½ cup whole blanched almonds, lightly
  toasted
½ cup sugar
3 tablespoons unsalted
  butter, softened
2 egg whites
½ teaspoon almond extract
¼ cup all-purpose flour, sifted

1 Lightly brush a baking sheet with oil. Put the nuts in a saucepan with ⅓ cup of the sugar and the water. Bring to a boil over high heat, swirling the pan to dissolve the sugar, then boil, without stirring, for 4–5 minutes until the syrup and nuts begin to pop. Immediately pour onto the baking sheet (do not touch the hot caramel). Set aside to cool completely then break into pieces.

2 Finely grind the praline in a food processor, using the metal blade. Or, put in a strong plastic bag and crush with a rolling pin.

3 Pour the cream into a cold bowl and set aside. In another bowl whisk the egg yolks and remaining sugar until thick and creamy. Meanwhile, bring the milk just to a simmer over medium heat, then whisk into the eggs and return the mixture to the saucepan.

4 With a wooden spoon, stir over a low heat for 3–4 minutes until the sauce thickens and coats the back of the spoon, then strain the custard into the bowl of cream. Cool, then chill until cold. Stir in the praline and freeze in an ice cream maker, or in the freezer, beating once or twice until smooth.

5 Preheat the oven to 400°F. Butter two baking sheets. To make the baskets, put the almonds and 2 tablespoons of the sugar in a food processor and finely grind with the metal blade. Beat the butter until creamy.

6 Add the remaining sugar to the butter and beat until light and fluffy, then gradually beat in the egg whites and the almond extract. Sift the flour onto the butter mixture, fold in, then fold in the ground almond mixture.

7 Drop tablespoon of mixture about 8 inches apart on to the prepared baking sheets. With the back of a wet spoon, spread into paper-thin rounds 4 inches across.

8 Bake the cookies, for 4–5 minutes, until the edges are golden and the centers are still pale. Transfer to a wire rack and, working quickly, loosen the edge of a hot cookie and carefully transfer to an upturned drinking glass or ramekin, pressing gently over the base to form a fluted basket shape. If the cookies become too crisp to shape, soften them in the oven for 15–30 seconds. Repeat with the remaining cookies. Set aside to cool completely before transferring to a wire rack.

9 To serve, ;let the ice cream soften at room temperature for 5–10 minutes. Place the baskets on dessert plates and fill with scoops of the ice cream.

Black Forest Sundae

Here is a truly indulgent variation on the classic Black Forest gâteau, but this one is spectacularly served in a sundae glass.

INGREDIENTS

Serves 4

14-ounce can pitted black cherries
   in syrup
1 tablespoon cornstarch
3 tablespoons kirsch
1 tablespoon confectioners' sugar
⅔ cup whipping cream
2½ cups chocolate
   ice cream
4 ounces chocolate cake
8 fresh cherries, to decorate
vanilla ice cream, to serve

2 Over medium heat, bring the syrup in the saucepan to a boil. Add the cornstarch and syrup mixture, stirring until it is well blended, and then simmer briefly to thicken, stirring continuously.

5 Place a spoonful of cherries in the bottom of four sundae glasses. Add a layer of ice cream, then chocolate cake, whipped cream and more cherries, continue until the glasses are full.

1 Strain all but 2 tablespoons of the cherry syrup into a saucepan. Measure the cornstarch into a small bowl with the remaining syrup and mix until smooth and creamy.

3 Add the cherries, stir in the kirsch and then spread onto a metal tray to cool.

6 To finish the sundaes add a piece of chocolate cake, two scoops of ice cream and another spoonful of cream. Place in the freezer for 5–10 minutes to firm the ice cream, and serve decorated with fresh cherries.

4 Sift the confectioners' sugar onto the cream, fold in and then whip until the mixture is thick and holds its shape.

COOK'S TIP

Bottled black cherries often have better flavor than canned, especially if the pits are left in. You don't need to remove the pits—but remember to tell your guests.

Ice Cream Strawberry Shortcake

This is an American classic and couldn't be easier to make. Fresh juicy strawberries, store-bought shortcakes and rich vanilla ice cream are all you need to create an irresistible feast of a dessert.

INGREDIENTS

Serves 4

6-inch shortcakes

5 cups vanilla or
    strawberry ice cream

1½ pound hulled fresh strawberries

confectioners' sugar, for dusting

1 If using store-bought short-cakes, trim the raised edges level with the base, using a serrated knife or bread knife.

2 Start with the shortcake and place one-third of the ice cream and the strawberries on top. Spread them evenly to make a level base. Add another layer of shortcake and another third of the ice cream and the strawberries. Then the final layer of shortcake.

3 Arrange the remaining ice cream on top and finish with the strawberries. Chill in the freezer before serving dusted with confectioners' sugar.

COOK'S TIP

Don't worry if the shortcake falls apart when you cut into it. Messy cakes are best. Ice Cream Strawberry Shortbread can be assembled up to 1 hour in advance and kept in the freezer without spoiling the fruit.

Chocolate Mint Ice Cream Pie

This colorful dessert uses ready-made ice cream, and it looks and tastes really professional.

INGREDIENTS

Serves 8

3 ounces semi-sweet chocolate chips

1½ ounces butter or margarine

2 ounces crisped rice cereal

1¼-pint mint-chocolate-chip ice cream

3 ounces chocolate, for curls

1 In a heatproof bowl set over a pan of barely simmering water, melt the chocolate chips and the butter or margarine.

2 Remove the bowl from heat and gradually stir in the cereal. Let it cool for 5 minutes.

3 Line a 9-inch pie pan with aluminum foil and place a round of waxed paper over the foil in the bottom of the pan. Press the chocolate and cereal mixture over the bottom and around the sides of the lined pan, forming a rim. Refrigerate until set hard.

4 Carefully remove the cereal crust from the pan and peel off the foil and waxed paper. Return the base to the pie pan.

5 Remove the ice cream from the freezer and let soften for 10 minutes.

6 Spread the ice cream evenly in the crust, then freeze for about 1 hour until firm.

7 For the decoration, use the heat of your hands to soften the chocolate slightly. Draw the blade of a swivel-headed vegetable peeler along the smooth surface of the chocolate to shave off short, wide curls. Refrigerate the curls until needed.

8 Just before serving, sprinkle the chocolate curls on the ice cream to cover the surface.

Pistachio and Nougat Torte

Pistachios, nougat, honey and rosewater make a perfect blend of flavors in this quick and easy frozen torte.

INGREDIENTS

Serves 6–8

¾ cup pistachios

5 ounces nougat

1¼ cups whipping cream

6 tablespoons honey

2 tablespoons rosewater

generous 1 cup fromage frais

8 sponge cakes

confectioners' sugar, for dusting

fresh raspberries, poached apricots or
    cherries, to serve (optional)

1 Soak the pistachios in boiling water for 2 minutes. Drain them thoroughly, then rub them between pieces of paper towel to remove the skins. Peel off any skins that remain, then chop the pistachios roughly.

2 Using a small sharp knife or scissors, cut the nougat into small pieces.

3 Pour the cream into a bowl, add the honey and rosewater and whip until it is just beginning to hold its shape. Stir in the fromage frais, chopped pistachios and nougat.

4 Slice the sponge cakes horizontally into three very thin layers.

5 Line a 6–6½-inch square loose-based cake pan with waxed paper or plastic wrap. Arrange a layer of cake on the bottom of the pan, trimming the pieces to fit.

6 Pack the pistachio and nougat filling into the pan and level the surface. Cover with the remaining cake, then cover with plastic wrap and freeze overnight.

7 To serve, invert the torte onto a serving plate and dust with confectioners' sugar. Serve with fresh raspberries, poached apricots or cherries, if desired.

Coffee and Chocolate Bombe

This impressive dessert is known in Italy as zuccotto, meaning pumpkin. A wide pudding mold gives the most authentic shape, but it will taste delicious whatever shape it is.

INGREDIENTS

Serves 6-8

¾ cup sweet Marsala

15–18 savoiardi (Italian ladyfingers)

3 ounces amaretti cookies

about 2 cups coffee ice cream, softened

about 2 cups vanilla ice cream, softened

2 ounces bittersweet or semi-sweet chocolate, grated

chocolate curls and sifted unsweetened cocoa powder or confectioners' sugar, to decorate

1 Line a 4-cup pudding mold with a large piece of damp muslin. Pour the Marsala into a shallow dish and dip a ladyfinger, turning it quickly to saturate it. Place against the side of the mold, sugared-side out. Repeat with the remaining ladyfingers, to line the mold.

2 Fill the base and any gaps around the side with any trimmings of ladyfingers cut to fit. Chill for about 30 minutes.

3 Put the amaretti cookies in a large bowl and crush them with a large rolling pin. Add the coffee ice cream and any remaining Marsala and beat until mixed. Spoon the mixture into the ladyfinger-lined basin.

4 Press the ice cream against the cake to form an even layer with a hollow. Freeze for 2 hours.

5 Put the vanilla ice cream and grated chocolate in a bowl and beat until evenly mixed. Spoon into the hollow in the center of the mold. Smooth the top, then cover with the overhanging muslin. Place in the freezer overnight.

6 To serve, run a spatula between the muslin and the basin, then unfold the top of the muslin. Place a chilled serving plate on top of the bombe, then invert them so that the bombe is upside down on the plate. Carefully peel off the muslin. Decorate the bombe with the chocolate curls, then sift on cocoa powder or confectioners' sugar. Serve immediately.

Maple Coffee and Pistachio Bombes

Real maple syrup tastes infinitely better than the synthetic varieties and is well worth searching for.

INGREDIENTS

Serves 6

For the pistachio ice cream

¼ cup sugar

¼ cup water

6-ounce can evaporated milk, chilled

½ cup shelled and skinned pistachios, finely chopped

drop of green food coloring (optional)

scant 1 cup whipping cream

For the maple coffee centers

2 tablespoons ground coffee

⅔ cup light cream

¼ cup maple syrup

2 egg yolks

1 teaspoon cornstarch

⅔ cup whipping cream

1 Put six ¾-cup mini pudding molds or dariole molds into the freezer to chill. Put the sugar and water in a heavy saucepan and heat gently until dissolved. Bring to a boil and simmer for 3 minutes. Cool.

2 Stir in the evaporated milk, nuts and coloring, if using. Lightly whip the cream into soft peaks and blend into the mixture.

3 Pour into a freezerproof container and freeze for at least 2 hours. Whisk the ice cream until smooth, then freeze for another 2 hours or until frozen, but not completely solid.

4 Put the ground coffee in a bowl. Heat the light cream to almost-boiling , pour over the coffee and infuse for 4 minutes. Whisk the maple syrup, egg yolks and cornstarch together. Strain the hot coffee cream over the egg mixture, whisking continuously. Return to the pan and cook gently for 1–2 minutes, until the custard thickens. Let cool, stirring occasionally.

5 Meanwhile, line the molds right up to the rim with an even thickness of the ice cream. Freeze until the ice cream is firm.

6 Beat the cream to soft peaks, and fold into the custard. Spoon into the middle of the molds. Cover and freeze for 2 hours. Serve immediately.

Frozen Coffee and Nut Meringue

This impressive frozen dessert may seem difficult but is actually very easy to prepare.

INGREDIENTS

Serves 8–10

scant 1 cup hazelnuts, toasted

1⅓ cups sugar

5 egg whites

pinch of cream of tartar

4 cups coffee ice cream

For the chocolate cream

2 cups whipping cream

2 tablespoons coffee liqueur

10 ounces semi-sweet chocolate, melted
  and cooled

white chocolate curls and fresh
  raspberries, to decorate

3 Let the ice cream soften for 15–20 minutes and then beat until smooth. Spread half the ice cream onto one meringue layer, and continue layering ice cream and meringue, finishing with the last meringue layer on top. Press down gently, then wrap and freeze for at least 4 hours, until firm.

4 To make the chocolate cream, beat the whipping cream until soft peaks form. Quickly fold in the liqueur and melted chocolate. Unwrap the frozen meringue and spread the chocolate cream on the top and sides; return to the freezer, rewrapping when firm. To serve, soften slightly before slicing.

1 Preheat the oven to 350°F. Line three baking sheets with nonstick baking parchment. Using a plate as a guide, mark an 8-inch circle on each and turn the paper over. Process the hazelnuts in a food processor until roughly chopped. Add a third of the sugar and process again until finely ground.

2 Whisk the egg whites until frothy, add the cream of tartar and whisk until they form soft peaks. Spoon the mixture onto the paper and spread within the marked circles. Bake for 1 hour, until firm and dry. Let cool in a turned off oven. Peel off the paper.

Frozen Praline Torte

Make this elaborate torte several days ahead, decorate it and return it to the freezer until you are nearly ready to serve it. Let the torte stand at room temperature for an hour before serving, or put it in the refrigerator overnight to soften.

INGREDIENTS

Serves 8

1 cup almonds or hazelnuts

8 tablespoons sugar

²⁄₃ cup raisins

6 tablespoons rum or brandy

4 ounces dark chocolate, broken
    into squares

2 tablespoons milk

1⅞ cups heavy cream

2 tablespoons strong black coffee

16 ladyfingers

To finish

²⁄₃ cup heavy cream

½ cup sliced almonds, toasted

½ ounce dark chocolate, melted

1 To make the praline, have ready an oiled cake pan or baking sheet. Put the nuts into a heavy pan with the sugar and heat gently until the sugar melts. Swirl the pan to coat the nuts in the hot sugar. Cook slowly until the nuts brown and the sugar caramelizes. Transfer the nuts quickly to the pan or tray and let them cool completely. Break them up and grind them to a fine powder in a blender or food processor.

2 Soak the raisins in 3 tablespoons of the rum or brandy for an hour (or better still overnight), so they soften and absorb the rum. Melt the chocolate with the milk in a bowl over a pan of hot, but not boiling water. Remove and let cool. Lightly grease a 5-cup loaf pan and line it with waxed paper.

3 Whisk the cream in a bowl until it holds soft peaks. Whisk in the cold chocolate. Then fold in the praline and the soaked raisins, with any liquid.

4 Mix the coffee and remaining rum or brandy in a shallow dish. Dip in the ladyfingers and arrange half in a layer on the bottom of the prepared loaf pan.

5 Cover with the chocolate mixture and add another layer of soaked ladyfingers. Leave in the freezer overnight.

6 Whip the heavy cream for the topping. Dip the pan briefly into warm water to loosen it and turn the torte out onto a serving plate. Cover with the whipped cream, sprinkle the top with toasted sliced almonds and drizzle the melted chocolate on the top. Return the torte to the freezer until it is needed.

> ### COOK'S TIP
> Make the praline in advance and store it in an airtight jar until needed.

Chocolate Fudge Sundaes

These look impressive, taste fantastic and only take minutes to make.

Serves 4

4 scoops each vanilla and coffee ice cream

2 small ripe bananas, sliced

whipped cream

toasted sliced almonds

For the sauce

¼ cup soft light brown sugar

½ cup golden syrup or light corn syrup

3 tablespoons strong black coffee

1 teaspoon ground cinnamon

5 ounces semi-sweet chocolate, chopped

⅓ cup whipping cream

3 tablespoons coffee liqueur (optional)

1 To make the sauce, place the sugar, syrup, coffee and cinnamon in a heavy saucepan. Bring to a boil, then boil for about 5 minutes, stirring the mixture constantly.

2 Turn off the heat and stir in the chocolate. When melted and smooth, stir in the cream and liqueur, if using. Let the sauce cool slightly. If made ahead, reheat the sauce gently until just warm.

3 Fill four glasses with one scoop of vanilla and another of coffee ice cream.

4 Sprinkle the sliced bananas on the ice cream. Pour the warm fudge sauce onto the bananas, then top each sundae with a generous swirl of whipped cream. Sprinkle toasted almonds on the cream and serve immediately.

VARIATION

For a change, choose other flavors of ice cream, such as strawberry, toffee or chocolate. In the summer, substitute raspberries or strawberries for the bananas, and sprinkle chopped roasted hazelnuts on top instead of the sliced almonds.

Frosted Raspberry and Coffee Terrine

A white chocolate and raspberry layer and contrasting smooth coffee layer, which is jeweled with whole raspberries, makes this attractive dessert doubly delicious.

INGREDIENTS

Serves 6–8

2 tablespoons flavored ground coffee

1 cup milk

4 eggs, separated

¼ cup sugar

2 tablespoons cornstarch

⅔ cup heavy cream

5 ounces white chocolate,
  roughly chopped

⅔ cup raspberries

shavings of white chocolate and unsweetened cocoa powder, to decorate

1 Line a 6¼-cup loaf pan with plastic wrap and chill. Put the ground coffee in a bowl. Heat scant ½ cup of the milk to near to the boiling point and pour over the coffee.

2 Blend the egg yolks, sugar and cornstarch in a pan and whisk in the remaining milk and cream. Bring to a boil, stirring, until the mixture has thickened.

3 Divide the mixture between two bowls and add the white chocolate to one, stirring until melted. Strain the coffee through a fine sieve into the other bowl and mix. Cool, stirring occasionally.

4 Whisk two egg whites until stiff and fold into the coffee custard. Spoon into the pan and freeze for 30 minutes. Whisk the remaining whites and fold into the the chocolate mixture with the fruit.

5 Spoon into the pan and level. Freeze for 4 hours. Turn out onto a flat serving plate and peel off the plastic wrap. Cover with chocolate shavings and dust with cocoa powder before serving.

Café Glace

A perfect finish to a summer meal, this delicious dessert is not only very quick and easy to prepare in advance, it needs only minutes to finish and serve. This must be the ultimate no-fuss dessert that looks as good as it tastes.

INGREDIENTS

Serves 4–6

2½ cups water

2–3 tablespoons instant dried coffee

1 tablespoon sugar

2½ cups milk

ice cubes

vanilla ice cream

4–6 chocolate sprinkles

8–12 crisp ice cream cookies,
    to serve

1 Bring ½ cup of the water to a boil, then transfer to a small bowl and stir in the coffee. Add the sugar and stir to dissolve. Chill for 2 hours. Mix the milk and remaining water in a large bowl. Add the chilled coffee and stir well.

2 Pour the coffee mixture into long glasses until they are three quarters full. Add ice cubes and the ice cream to the top of each glass and decorate with the chocolate sprinkles. To serve, place the long glasses on plates with the cookies to the side.

COOK'S TIP

You'll need to provide straws and long spoons for eating this dessert. Adjust the amount of coffee and sugar to suit your own taste.

Mint and Chocolate Cooler

*Many chocolate drinks are warm
and comforting, but this one is really
refreshing and ideal for a hot
summer's day.*

INGREDIENTS

Serves 4

4 tablespoons hot chocolate powder

1⅔ cups chilled milk

⅔ cup plain yogurt

½ teaspoon peppermint extract

4 scoops chocolate ice cream

mint leaves and chocolate shapes
  to decorate

1 Place the hot chocolate powder
in a small saucepan and stir in
½ cup of the milk. Heat gently,
stirring continuously, until almost
boiling, then remove from heat and
let cool.

COOK'S TIP

Use cocoa powder instead of hot
chocolate powder if you prefer,
but add sugar to taste.

2 Pour the cool chocolate milk
into a large bowl or jug and
whisk in the remaining milk, the
yogurt and peppermint extract.

3 Pour the mixture into tall
glasses and top each one with a
scoop of ice cream. Decorate with
mint leaves and chocolate shapes
and serve immediately.

Blushing Pina Colada

This is good with or without the rum. Don't be tempted to put roughly crushed ice into the blender; it will not be smooth and will ruin the blades. Make sure you crush it well first.

INGREDIENTS

Serves 2

1 banana, peeled and sliced

1 thick slice pineapple, peeled

4½ tablespoons pineapple juice

1 scoop strawberry ice cream or sorbet

1½ tablespoons coconut milk

2 tablespoons grenadine

wedges of pineapple and steamed
    maraschino cherries to decorate

1 Roughly chop the banana. Cut two small wedges from the pineapple for decoration and reserve. Cut up the remainder of the pineapple and place in the blender with the chopped banana. Place two large cocktail glasses in the refrigerator to chill.

VARIATION

For classic pina colada use vanilla ice cream and 1 measure white rum. For a passionate encounter, blend 2 scoops passion fruit sorbet and 1 tablespoon coconut milk with a measure each of pineapple and apricot juice.

2 Add the pineapple juice to the blender and process until the mixture is a smooth paste.

3 Add the strawberry ice cream or sorbet, and the coconut milk plus a small scoop of finely crushed ice, and process until very smooth.

4 Take the chilled cocktail glasses and pour in the mixture, being careful not to splash the sides of the glass.

5 Pour the grenadine syrup slowly on top of the pina colada; it will filter through the drink in a dappled effect.

6 Decorate each glass with a wedge of pineapple and a stemmed cherry and serve immediately with drinking straws.

COOK'S TIP

To crush the ice, place ice cubes into a clean kitchen cloth or a heavy duty plastic bag. Wrap up the cloth or seal the plastic bag, making sure that the ice cubes are quite secure and cannot come out. Place on a firm surface and crush with a wooden rolling pin until the cubes are in tiny pieces.

Low-fat Desserts

All too often, desserts are the downfall of anyone trying to follow a low-fat diet. After a sensible appetizer and a main course of grilled fish or chicken and fresh vegetables, there's an almost irresistible temptation to award yourself a large portion of dessert. The good news is that you can. You don't have to give up lovely, luscious desserts— provided that you stick to the recipes in this section of the book. Here you will find low-fat versions of old favorites such as Bread Pudding, Fruit Crumble and Angel Cake, together with new and exotic ideas such as Papaya Baked with Ginger and Tropical Fruit Pancakes.

◆ ◆ ◆

Facts About Fats

We all know we need to cut down on the amount of fat we eat—it would be difficult to live in the developed world and be unaware of that fact—but before making changes in our diet, it may be helpful to find out a bit more about the fats that we eat: some types are believed to be less harmful than others.

Fats are essential for the proper functioning of the body. However, we need the right kind of fat and the right amount. The average Western diet contains far too much of the "wrong" type of fat—saturated fat—which leads to obesity, heart problems and strokes. The daily recommended maximum amount of calories that should come from fat is between 30% and 35%. Unfortunately, too many Westerners obtain well over 40% of their calories from fat, often in the form of sweet treats and desserts and pastries.

Fats in our food are made up of different types of fatty acids and glycerol. Fats may be saturated or unsaturated, with unsaturated fat further categorized as mono-unsaturated or polyunsaturated.

Saturated fats

To appreciate the difference between saturated and unsaturated fatty acids, it is necessary to understand a little about their molecular structure. Put very simply, fatty acids are made up of chains of carbon atoms. A common analogy is to a string of beads. Unlike beads, however, which are linked only to each other, the carbon atoms are also able to link up—or bond—with one or more other atoms. In a saturated fat, all these potential linkages have been made: the carbon atoms are linked to each other and each is also linked to two hydrogen atoms. No further linkages are possible, and the fat is therefore said to be saturated.

Saturated fat is mainly found in foods of animal origin: meat and dairy products such as butter, which is solid at room temperature. However, there are also some saturated fats of vegetable origin, notably coconut oil and also palm oil which is the main vegetable oil used in hard margarines.

Unsaturated fats

Unsaturated fatty acids differ from saturated fatty acids in their structure—not all of the linkages or bonds are complete. Some of the carbon atoms are linked to only one hydrogen atom instead of the usual two, and some of the carbon atoms may be joined to each other by a double bond. Depending on how many double bonds there are, the fatty acid is described as mono-unsaturated (one double bond) or polyunsaturated (many double bonds). The different molecular structures need not concern us here—suffice it to say that unsaturated fats are generally more healthy than saturated fats.

Mono-unsaturated fats

These are found in foods such as olive oil, rapeseed oil, some nuts, oily fish and avocados. Mono-unsaturated fats are believed to be neutral, neither raising nor lowering blood cholesterol levels. This, plus the lower saturated fat intake as well as the higher fruit and vegetable intake, which are high in antioxidants, could explain the low incidence of heart disease in the Mediterranean countries.

Left: A bottle of sunflower oil (left) contains mostly polyunsaturated fats (68%), while olive oil is made of up mainly mono-unsaturated fats (70%).

Above: Many common foods contain some fats. Cheese, butter, milk, cream and nuts—all of which are frequently used in desserts—should be strictly limited, unless fat-free or very low-fat.

Polyunsaturated fats

Polyunsaturated fat has two types. The first (omega 6) is found in vegetable and seed oils, such as sunflower or almond oil, and the second (omega 3) comes from oily fish, green leaves and some seed oils, including rapeseed or canola oil.

Polyunsaturated fats are liquid at room temperature. When vegetable oils are used in soft margarine, they have to be hardened artificially. During this process, the composition of some of the unsaturated fatty acids changes. In the body, these altered or "trans" fatty acids are treated like saturated fats, so, although an oil such as sunflower oil may be high in polyunsaturated fatty acids which lowers cholesterol levels, the same is not necessarily true of a margarine made from that oil.

Although unsaturated fats are healthier then saturated ones, most experts agree that what matters more is reducing our total intake of fat.

A Guide to Low-fat Dessert Ingredients

Watching your fat intake doesn't mean you have to forgo creamy desserts. A wide range of low-fat and virtually fat-free products are on sale at supermarkets, some of them backed by alluring advertising. Clever packaging can sometimes persuade the impulse buyer to make an unwise choice, however, so always check the statistical data printed on the label.

Low-fat spreads have become very popular. These have a high water content so, while they are perfectly acceptable for spreading on bread they are not necessarily suitable for cooking. When baking or making cakes, look for a spread with a fat content of around 40%. If substituting a reduced-fat spread for butter in a conventional recipe, be prepared to experiment a little, as the results will not necessarily be the same.

Try to avoid using saturated fats such as butter and hard margarine. Oils that are high in polyunsaturates, such as sunflower, corn or safflower, are the healthier option. Cakes and baked goods made with oil are often excellent. If you must use margarine, choose a brand that is low in saturates and high in polyunsaturates.

Skim milk works well in batters and baked goods, although you may get a better result using 2%. Yogurt and fromage frais make excellent alternatives to cream, and when combined with honey, liqueur or other flavorings, they make delicious fillings or toppings for cheesecakes and fruit desserts. Many delectable desserts are based on soft cheeses. Cream cheese used to be the preferred option, but low-fat alternatives work just as well and are often easier to mix. If you're not familiar with it already, experiment with Quark, a virtually fat-free cheese product that is very versatile.

Oils and low-fat spreads

Corn oil: A polyunsaturated oil, this has a slight flavor, so it is not as good as sunflower oil for baking. Fried foods should be avoided completely if you are trying to limit your fat intake, but if you must fry this is a good choice if used sparingly, as it can reach high temperatures without smoking.

Sunflower oil spread: High in polyunsaturates, this light, delicately flavored oil is a good choice for desserts, as is safflower oil. Both can be used in cakes and baked goods and are particularly good in muffins.

Sunflower light spread: Like reduced-fat butter, this contains about 38% fat, plus emulsified milk solids and water. The flavor is mild.

Olive oil reduced-fat spread: With a fat content of around 63%, this spread is richer than many low-fat spreads, but it has an excellent flavor. It can be used for cooking.

Low-fat spread (rich buttermilk blend): This product is made with a high proportion of buttermilk, which is naturally low in fat. Low-fat spreads with a fat content of around 40% can

Left: A selection of cooking oils and low-fat spreads. Always check the packaging when buying low-fat spreads—if you are going to use them for cooking, they must have a fat content of about 40%.

be used for cooking: check the label.
Very low-fat spread: This contains about 20–30% fat and has a high water content; it is not suitable for cooking.

Low-fat milks

Buttermilk: This is the liquid that remains after cream has been churned into butter. Buttermilk produced in this way has a light flavor, similar to skim milk. Commercial buttermilk is made by adding a bacterial culture to skim milk. This gives it a slightly sharper taste than traditional buttermilk. It is very low in fat (0.5%).
Powdered skim milk: This is a useful, low-fat standby. You can make as little or as much as you need. Always follow the instructions on the package. Alone, the powder has quite a high fat content, so if you use too much, the drink will not be the low-fat alternative you wanted.
2% milk: With a fat content of only 2%, this milk doesn't taste as rich as full-cream milk. It is favored by many people for everyday use for precisely this reason. 2% milk can be used in all recipes calling for whole milk.
Skim milk: This milk has had virtually all the fat removed, leaving 0.1%. It is ideal for those wishing to reduce their intake of fats.

Low-fat cream substitutes

Crème Fraîche: Look for half-fat versions of this thick sour cream, where the normal fat content of 40% is reduced to 15%. Crème fraîche has a mild, lemony taste and is ideal as a dessert topping.
Plain yogurt: This thick, creamy yogurt is made from whole milk with a fat content of 9.1%. A low-fat version is also available.

Above: Almost all dairy products now come in low-fat or reduced-fat versions.

Low-fat yogurt: With a fat content of only about 1%, low-fat yogurt is a gift to the dessert cook. Use it instead of cream, as a topping or as an accompaniment. Drizzle a little honey on top if desired.

Low-fat cheeses

Cottage cheese: This low-fat cheese is also available in a half-fat form. Cottage cheese can be used instead of cream cheese in cheesecakes—press it through a sieve to remove the lumps.
Ricotta cheese: This low-fat soft cheese is generally made from skim or low-fat milk. A simple version can be made at home, using low-fat yogurt. Use ricotta cheese instead of cream cheese.
Edam: Hard cheeses are not widely used in desserts, except in some baked cheesecakes. If a recipe does call for grated hard cheese, however, this is a

good choice, as it is lower in fat than standards like Cheddar or Cheshire. If you prefer the taste of Cheddar, choose a half-fat version, where the fat will be reduced to 15%.
Fromage frais: This is a fresh, soft cheese with a very mild flavor. It is available in two grades: virtually fat-free (0.2% fat), and a more creamy variety (7.1% fat). Fromage frais is too soft to use on its own as a cheesecake filling, but it can be mixed with ricotta cheese.
Quark: Perfect for many different types of dessert, this soft white cheese is virtually fat-free. It is made from fermented skim milk.

Fat and Calorie Counts per 100g

The chart below lists both full-fat and low or reduced-fat typical dessert ingredients, so that you can see the savings at a glance if you choose the healthier option.

Ingredient	Fat (g)	Energy	Ingredient	Fat (g)	Energy
Oils and Spreads			Ricotta cheese	11.7	173 cals
Butter	81.7	737 cals	Edam	25	333 cals
Corn oil	99.9	899 cals	Fromage frais (plain)	7.1	113 cals
Low-fat spread	40.5	390 cals	Half-fat cheddar	15	261 cals
Margarine	81.6	739 cals	Quark	1.4	86 cals
Olive oil	99.9	899 cals	Reduced-fat cottage cheese	1.4	78 cals
Olive oil reduced-fat spread	63	571 cals	Very low-fat fromage frais	0.2	58 cals
Safflower oil	99.9	899 cals			
Sunflower oil	99.9	899 cals	*Eggs*		
Sunflower light spread	38	357 cals	about 2 (medium)	10.9	147 cals
Very low-fat spread	27	259 cals	Egg white	trace	36 cals
			Egg yolk	30.5	339 cals
Milk					
Buttermilk	0.5	37 cals	*Baking Products and Preserves*		
Low-fat Milk	2.0	46 cals	Chocolate (milk)	30.3	520 cals
Skim milk	0.1	33 cals	Chocolate (semi-sweet)	29.2	510 cals
Skim milk powder	0.6	348 cals	Cocoa powder	21.7	359 cals
Whole milk	3.9	66 cals	Fat-free sponge cake	6.1	294 cals
			Honey	0	288 cals
Cream/Cream Substitutes			Sugar (white)	0	394 cals
Crème fraîche	40	380 cals			
Heavy cream	48	449 cals	*Fruit and Nuts*		
Plain yogurt	9.1	115 cals	Almonds	55.8	612 cals
Half-fat crème fraîche	15	166 cals	Apples	0.1	47 cals
Low-fat yogurt (plain)	0.8	56 cals	Bananas	0.3	95 cals
Reduced-fat yogurt	5.0	80 cals	Brazil nuts	68.2	682 cals
Light cream	19.1	198 cals	Dried mixed fruit	0.4	268 cals
Whipping cream	39.3	373 cals	Hazelnuts	63.5	650 cals
			Oranges	0.1	37 cals
Cheeses			Peaches	0.1	33 cals
Cheddar	34.4	412 cals	Peanut butter (smooth)	53.7	623 cals
Cottage cheese (plain)	3.9	98 cals	Pears	0.1	40 cals
Cream cheese	47.7	439 cals	Pine nuts	68.6	688 cals

Information from *The Composition of Foods* (5th edition 1991) is reproduced with the permission of the Controller of Her Majesty's Stationery Office.

Making Desserts the Fat-free Way

To many people, dessert means lots of cream, butter and chocolate. Nowadays, however, it is perfectly possible for a host to trick guests into thinking they are having a luscious, creamy treat, when all the while, the ingredients are fat-free or low in fat.

Many ingredients are available in full-fat and reduced-fat or very low-fat forms. In every supermarket you will find a huge array of low-fat products, such as milk, cream, yogurt, hard and soft cheeses and fromage frais, reduced-fat sweet or chocolate cookies; low-fat, half-fat or very low-fat spreads; as well as reduced-fat ready-made desserts. Some ingredients work better than others in cooking, but often a simple substitution will spell success. In a crumb crust, for instance, reduced-fat cookies work just as well as classic graham crackers.

Some of the most delicious desserts are based on fruit. Serve fresh or dried fruit in a salad or compote, and there's no need to introduce fats.

If you are making a baked or steamed pudding, or pan-frying fruit such as bananas or pineapple rings, you can get away with using the merest slick of polyunsaturated oil, especially if you use a nonstick pan. Alternatively, use spray oil: a one-second spray of sunflower oil has 4.6 cals and just over half the fat of conventional cooking oil. Spray oil is particularly useful for lightly coating frying pans when making pancakes.

When seeking inspiration for the dessert course for that special dinner

Right: This sumptuous pineapple and strawberry meringue looks and tastes delicious even though it is very low in fat.

party, remember that there are plenty of ingredients that naturally contain very little fat. Rice, flour, oats, bread and cornflakes can all be used to make desserts and toppings, and there's no fat in wine, sherry, sugar or honey, although you may wish to restrict these for other reasons! Meringues are among the most popular desserts—topped with fresh fruit and yogurt or fromage frais, they are irresistible to eat and look great.

Spices and extracts add plenty of extra flavor and color to desserts, while decorations like rose petals, mint leaves or curls of pared citrus zest improve the appearance and stimulate the appetite.

Low-fat spreads in cooking

Some low-fat spreads can safely be substituted for butter or margarine in baked desserts, but others are only suitable for spreading. The limiting factor is the amount of water in the product. Very low-fat spreads achieve levels of fat of around 20% by virtue of their high water content and cannot be melted successfully. Spreads with a fat content of around 40% are suitable for spreading and for some cooking methods. The information on the label will indicate its suitability. When using low-fat spreads for cooking, the fat may behave slightly differently from full-fat products such as butter or margarine. Be prepared to

Left: Fresh fruit can be used to make simply superb sweet dishes, and there's no need at all to add any fat.

experiment a little—the results may surprise you. Some recipes actually work better with low-fat ingredients. For example, choux pastry made with half- or low-fat spread is often slightly crisper and lighter in texture than traditional choux pastry. A cheesecake cookie crust made with melted half- or low-fat spread combined with crumbs from reduced-fat cookies may be slightly softer in texture and less crisp than one made using melted butter, but it will still be very good.

Quick Tips for Fat-Free Cooking

• Use heavy or nonstick pans—that way you won't need as much fat for cooking.

• When baking low-fat or reduced-fat cakes, it is advisable to use good quality cookware that doesn't need greasing before use, or line the pan with nonstick paper and only grease very lightly before filling.

• Look for nonstick coated fabric sheeting. This reusable material will not stick and is amazingly versatile. It can be cut to size and used to line cake pans, baking sheets or frying pans. Heat resistant to 550°F and microwave safe, it will last for up to 5 years.

• Bake fruit in a loosely sealed parcel of waxed paper, moistening it with wine, fruit juice or liqueur instead of butter before sealing the parcel.

• When broiling fruit, the naturally high moisture content means that it is often unnecessary to add fat. If the fruit looks a bit dry, brush lightly and sparingly with a polyunsaturated oil such as sunflower or corn oil.

• Fruit cooked in the microwave seldom needs additional fat; add spices for extra color and flavor.

• Poach fresh or dried fruit in natural juice or syrup—there's no need to add any fat.

• Become an expert at cooking with phyllo pastry. Of itself, phyllo is extremely low in fat, and if you brush the sheets sparingly with melted low-fat spread, it can be used to make delicious desserts that will not significantly damage a low-fat diet and will replace other high-fat pastries.

• Avoid cooking with chocolate, which is high in fat. If you can't bear to abandon your favorite flavor, use cocoa powder instead.

• Get to know the full range of low- or reduced-fat products, including yogurt, crème fraîche and fromage frais. Low-fat yogurt can be used for making "creamy" sauces, but needs to be treated with a little more care as it can curdle when heated. Stabilize it by stirring in a little cornstarch, mixed to a paste with water or skim milk.

• Use skim milk rather than whole milk in rice pudding, semolina pudding and batters.

Above: Many delicious desserts can be made in moments if you have a well-stocked pantry.

When heating low-fat spreads, never let them get too hot. Always use a heavy pan over low heat to avoid the product burning, spitting or spoiling, and stir constantly. Half-fat or low-fat spreads cannot be used for shallow- or deep-frying, traditional pastry making, rich fruit cakes, shortbread and preserves such as lemon curd.

Baked goods, such as cakes, pies and pastries, made using reduced- or low-fat spreads will not keep as well as cakes made using butter; this is due to the lower fat content.

Fruit purées

One way of reducing the fat content of a recipe is to replace all or part of the fat with a fruit purée. This is particularly successful with breads, probably because the amount of fat is usually relatively small, and it also works well with some cookies and bars, such as brownies.

To make a dried fruit purée for this purpose, roughly chop 2/3 cup dried fruit and put it in a blender or food processor. Add 5 tablespoons water and blend into a fairly smooth purée. Scrape into a bowl, cover and keep in the refrigerator for up to 3 days. When baking, simply substitute the same weight of this dried fruit purée for all or just some of the fat in the recipe. You may need to experiment a little to find the proportions that work best. If preferred, you can purée a single variety of dried fruit, such as prunes, apricots, peaches or apples, or substitute mashed fresh fruit, such as ripe bananas or lightly cooked apples. If you choose to purée fresh fruit, omit the water.

Useful Techniques

Cooked or prepared in the right way, delicious desserts like meringues, fruit-filled pancakes and gelatins are actually very low in fat. Follow the simple techniques on these pages for certain success.

WHISKING EGG WHITES

1 Place the egg whites in a completely clean, grease-free bowl. If even a speck of egg yolk is present, you will not be able to beat the whites successfully. Use one half of the shell to remove any traces of yolk.

2 Use a balloon whisk in a wide bowl for the greatest volume (egg whites can increase their volume by about eight times), but an electric hand whisk will also do an efficient job. Purists swear that eggs whisked in a copper bowl give the greatest volume.

3 Whisk the whites until they are firm enough to hold either soft or stiff peaks when you lift the whisk—see individual recipes. For stiffly whisked whites, you should be able to hold the bowl upside down without their sliding out, but this is a risky test!

MAKING CRÊPES

1 Apply a light, even coat of spray oil to an 8-inch crêpe pan, then heat it gently. Pour in about 3 tablespoons of the batter, then quickly tilt the pan so that the batter spreads to cover the bottom thinly and evenly.

2 Cook the crêpe for 30–45 seconds, until it has set. Carefully lift the edge with a spatula; the bottom of the crêpe should have browned lightly. Shake the pan to loosen the crêpe, then turn it over with the spatula or flip it with a quick twist of your wrist.

3 Cook the other side of the crêpe for about 30 seconds, then slide the crêpe out onto a plate. Make more crêpes in the same way, then spread them with your chosen filling before rolling them or folding them neatly into triangles.

DISSOLVING GELATIN

1 Powdered gelatin is very easy to use. For every 1 tablespoon of gelatin in the recipe, place 3 tablespoons of very hot water in a small bowl.

2 Holding the bowl steady, sprinkle the powdered gelatin lightly and evenly on the hot liquid. Always add the gelatin to the liquid; never the other way around.

3 Stir until the gelatin has dissolved completely and the liquid is clear, with no visible crystals. You may need to stand the bowl in a pan of hot water.

UNMOLDING GELATIN

1 Have ready a serving plate that has been rinsed with cold water. Shake it but leave it damp—this will make it easier to center the gelatin. Run the tip of a knife around the molded mixture, to loosen it.

2 Dip the mold briefly into a bowl of hot water. One or two seconds is usually enough—if you leave it for too long, the mixture will start to melt around the edges. If the gelatin is stuck, dip again. Several short dips are better than one long one.

3 Quickly invert the plate over the mold. Holding mold and plate together, turn both over. Shake firmly to dislodge the gelatin; as soon as you feel it drop, lift the mold. If it does not lift, give it another shake.

QUICK TIPS FOR GELATIN

Some recipes require gelatin to be dissolved in a cold liquid, such as apple or orange juice. In this case, pour the liquid into a small heatproof bowl and sprinkle the gelatin on top. Leave until the liquid has absorbed the gelatin and looks spongy, then place the bowl over very hot water until the gelatin has dissolved completely. You could either use a *bain marie* or simply a pan full of boiling water.

Techniques for Tasty Toppings

Although whipped cream is taboo on a low-fat diet, there are some excellent alternatives. Whipped "cream" can be made from nonfat dry milk or yogurt, with very good results. Neither will hold the shape indefinitely, however, so use them as soon as possible after making. Strained yogurt and ricotta cheese are simple to make at home, and tend to be lower in fat than commercial varieties. Serve strained yogurt with desserts instead of cream, sweetening it with a little honey, if desired. Ricotta cheese can be used instead of sour cream, cream cheese or butter. Apricot glaze is very useful for brushing on a large variety of fresh fruit toppings. It gives the fruit a lovely shiny appearance.

LOW-FAT WHIPPED CREAM

INGREDIENTS

Makes ²/₃ cup

¹/₂ teaspoon powdered gelatin

5 tablespoons water

¹/₄ cup nonfat dry milk

1 tablespoon sugar

1 tablespoon lemon juice

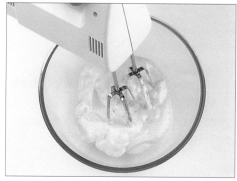

1 Sprinkle the powdered gelatin on 1 tablespoon cold water in a small bowl and let "sponge" for 5 minutes. Place the bowl over a pan of hot water and stir until dissolved. Let cool.

2 Whisk the dry milk, sugar, lemon juice and remaining water until frothy. Add the dissolved gelatin and whisk. Chill for 30 minutes.

3 Using an electric hand whisk, whisk the chilled mixture again until it holds its shape and is very thick and frothy. Serve within 30 minutes of making.

YOGURT PIPING CREAM

INGREDIENTS

Makes a scant 2 cups

2 teaspoons powdered gelatin

3 tablespoons water

1¹/₄ cups strained yogurt

1 tablespoon fructose

¹/₂ teaspoon vanilla extract

1 egg white

1 Sprinkle the gelatin on the water in a small bowl and let "sponge" for 5 minutes. Place the bowl over a saucepan of hot water and stir until dissolved. Let cool.

2 Mix the yogurt, fructose and vanilla extract. Stir in the gelatin. Chill in the refrigerator for 30 minutes or until just beginning to set around the edges.

3 Whisk the egg white until stiff, then carefully fold it into the yogurt mixture. Spoon into a piping bag fitted with a piping nozzle and use immediately.

STRAINED YOGURT AND SIMPLE RICOTTA CHEESE

INGREDIENTS

Makes 1¼ cups strained yogurt or ½ cup ricotta cheese

2½ cups low-fat yogurt

1 For strained yogurt, line a nylon or stainless steel sieve with a double layer of muslin. Put it over a bowl and carefully pour in the low-fat yogurt.

2 Let drain in the refrigerator for 3 hours, by which time it will have separated into thick strained yogurt and watery whey. Discard the whey.

3 For ricotta cheese, let drain in the refrigerator for 8 hours or overnight. Spoon the ricotta cheese into a serving bowl, cover and keep chilled.

APRICOT GLAZE

1 Place a few spoonfuls of apricot jam in a small pan and add a squeeze of lemon juice. Heat the jam, stirring until it has melted and is runny.

2 Set a wire sieve over a heatproof bowl. Pour the jam into the sieve, then stir it with a wooden spoon to help it go through the mesh.

3 Return the strained jam to the pan. Keep the glaze warm until needed, then brush it generously onto the fresh fruit until evenly coated.

Decorating with Citrus Zest Shreds

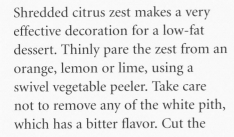

Shredded citrus zest makes a very effective decoration for a low-fat dessert. Thinly pare the zest from an orange, lemon or lime, using a swivel vegetable peeler. Take care not to remove any of the white pith, which has a bitter flavor. Cut the

strips of pared zest into very fine shreds with a sharp knife. Boil the shreds for a couple of minutes in water or sugar syrup to soften them.

Right: Shredded citrus zest adds extra color and appeal to this simple gelatin.

Hot Low-fat Desserts

◆ ◆ ◆

Spiced Pear and Blueberry Parcels

This combination makes a delicious dessert for a summer's evening and can be cooked on a grill or in the oven.

INGREDIENTS

Serves 4

4 firm, ripe pears

2 tablespoons lemon juice

1 tablespoon low-fat spread, melted

1 1/4 cups blueberries

4 tablespoons light brown sugar

freshly ground black pepper

NUTRITIONAL NOTES

Per portion:

Calories	146
Fat, total	1.8g
Saturated fat	0.37g
Cholesterol	0.2mg
Fiber	4g

1 Prepare the grill or preheat the oven to 400°F. Peel the pears thinly. Cut in half lengthwise. Scoop out the core from each half. Brush the pears with lemon juice, to stop them from browning. Cut four squares of double-thick aluminum foil, each large enough to wrap a pear.

2 Brush the aluminum foil squares with melted spread. Place two pear halves on each, cut-side upward. Gather the foil around them, to hold them level.

3 Mix the blueberries and sugar and spoon them on top of the pears. Sprinkle with black pepper. Close the foil and grill for 20–25 minutes or bake.

Fruit and Spice Bread Pudding

An easy-to-make fruity dessert with a hint of spice, this is delicious served either hot or cold.

2 Mix the golden raisins, apricots, sugar and spice and sprinkle half the fruit mixture on the bread in the dish.

3 Top with the remaining bread triangles and then the fruit.

4 Beat the eggs, milk and lemon zest together and pour onto the bread. Set aside for about 30 minutes, to let the bread absorb some of the liquid. Bake for 45–60 minutes, until lightly set and golden brown. Serve hot or cold.

INGREDIENTS

Serves 4

6 medium slices whole-wheat bread

2 ounces apricot or strawberry jam

low-fat spread, for greasing

1/3 cup golden raisins

1/4 cup dried apricots, chopped

1/3 cup light brown sugar

1 teaspoon ground allspice

2 eggs

2 1/2 cups skim milk

finely grated zest of 1 lemon

1 Preheat the oven to 325°F. Remove and discard the crusts from the bread. Spread the bread slices with jam and cut into small triangles. Place half the bread triangles in a lightly greased ovenproof dish.

NUTRITIONAL NOTES

Per portion:

Calories	305
Fat, total	4.51g
Saturated fat	1.27g
Cholesterol	99.3mg
Fiber	3.75g

Fruity Bread Pudding

A delicious family favorite from grandmother's kitchen, with a lighter, healthier touch for today.

NUTRITIONAL NOTES	
Per portion:	
Calories	190
Fat, total	0.89g
Saturated fat	0.21g
Cholesterol	0.75mg
Fiber	1.8g

2 Remove the pan from heat and stir in the bread cubes, spice and banana. Spoon the mixture into a shallow 5-cup ovenproof dish and pour in the milk.

3 Sprinkle with brown sugar and bake for 25–30 minutes, until firm and golden brown. Serve hot or cold, with yogurt, if desired.

INGREDIENTS

Serves 4

1/2 cup mixed dried fruit

2/3 cup unsweetened apple juice

3–4 slices day-old brown or white bread, cubed

1 teaspoon allspice

1 large banana, sliced

2/3 cup skim milk

1 tablespoon brown sugar

low-fat plain yogurt, to serve (optional)

1 Preheat the oven to 400°F. In a small pan, bring the dried fruit and apple juice to a boil.

Baked Apples with Red Wine

Special-occasion baked apples include a delicious filling of golden raisins soaked in spiced red wine.

INGREDIENTS

Serves 6

scant 1/2 cup golden raisins

1 1/2 cups red wine

pinch of grated nutmeg

pinch of ground cinnamon

1/4 cup sugar

pinch of grated lemon zest

7 teaspoons low-fat spread

6 apples of even size

1 Put the golden raisins in a small bowl and pour in the wine. Stir in the grated nutmeg, ground cinnamon, sugar and lemon zest. Cover and let stand for approximately 1 hour.

2 Preheat the oven to 375°F. Use a little of the low-fat spread to grease a baking dish. Core the apples, without cutting through to the bottom.

3 Divide the golden raisin mixture among the apples. Spoon in a little extra spiced wine. Arrange the apples in the prepared baking dish.

4 Pour the remaining wine around the apples. Top the filling in each apple with 1 teaspoon of the low-fat remaining spread. Bake for 40–50 minutes or until the apples are soft but not mushy. Serve hot or at room temperature.

NUTRITIONAL NOTES

Per portion:

Calories	187
Fat, total	2.7g
Saturated fat	0.61g
Cholesterol	0.4mg
Fiber	2.6g

Baked Apples with Apricot Nut Filling

This is an interesting version of an old favorite. Omit the low-fat spread if you want to reduce the fat content even more.

Serves 6

1/2 cup chopped dried apricots

3 tablespoons chopped walnuts

1 teaspoon grated lemon zest

1/4 teaspoon ground cinnamon

2/3 cup light brown sugar

2 tablespoons low-fat spread

6 Bramley or other apples

3 Stand the apples in a baking dish just large enough to hold them comfortably side by side.

4 Melt the remaining spread and brush it on the apples. Bake for 40–45 minutes, until tender. Serve hot.

1 Preheat the oven to 375ºF. In a bowl, combine the apricots, walnuts, lemon zest and cinnamon. Add the sugar and rub in two-thirds of the low-fat spread until thoroughly combined.

2 Core the apples, without cutting all the way through to the bottom. Peel the top third of each apple. With a small knife, widen the top of each cavity by about 1½ inches for the filling. Spoon the filling into the apples.

NUTRITIONAL NOTES

Per portion:

Calories	263
Fat, total	4.9g
Saturated fat	0.89g
Cholesterol	0.3mg
Fiber	4.3g

Baked Apples in Honey and Lemon

A classic combination of flavors in a traditional family dessert. Serve warm, with skim-milk custard, if desired.

Serves 4

4 Bramley or other apples

1 tablespoon honey

grated zest and juice of 1 lemon

1 tablespoon low-fat spread

skim milk custard, to serve (optional)

NUTRITIONAL NOTES
Per portion:

Calories	78
Fat, total	1.7g
Saturated fat	0.37g
Cholesterol	0.2mg
Fiber	2.4g

2 With a cannelle knife or a narrow bladed, sharp knife, cut lines through the apple skin at intervals. Stand the apples in an ovenproof dish.

3 Mix the honey, lemon zest, juice and low-fat spread.

1 Preheat the oven to 350ºF. Remove the cores from the apples, being careful not to cut through the bottoms of the apples.

4 Spoon the mixture into the apples and cover the dish with aluminum foil or a lid. Bake for 40–45 minutes or until the apples are tender. Serve with skim-milk custard, if desired.

Date, Chocolate and Walnut Pudding

Dessert is not totally taboo when you're reducing your fat intake—this one is just within the rules!

2 Separate the whole egg and place the yolk in a heatproof bowl. Add vanilla and sugar. Place over a pan of hot water and whisk to thicken.

3 Sift the flour and cocoa powder into the mixture and fold in. Stir in the milk. Whisk the egg whites and fold in.

INGREDIENTS

Serves 4

low-fat spread, for greasing
1 tablespoons chopped walnuts
2 tablespoons chopped dates
1 egg plus 1 egg white
1 teaspoon pure vanilla extract
2 tablespoons sugar
3 tablespoons whole-wheat flour
1 tablespoon unsweetened cocoa powder
2 tablespoons skim milk

1 Preheat the oven to 350ºF. Grease a 5-cup pudding mold and place a small circle of waxed or nonstick baking parchment in the bottom. Spoon in the walnuts and dates.

NUTRITIONAL NOTES
Per portion:

Calories	126
Fat, total	4.9g
Saturated fat	1.15g
Cholesterol	48.3mg
Fiber	1.3g

4 Spoon the mixture into the mold and bake for 40–45 minutes, until the pudding has risen and is firm to the touch. Run a knife around the pudding, then turn it out and serve hot.

Golden Raisin and Couscous Puddings

Most couscous is the pre-cooked variety, which hardly needs cooking, but check the package instructions first.

INGREDIENTS

Serves 4

1/3 cup golden raisins

2 cups unsweetened apple juice

scant 1 cup couscous

1/2 teaspoon allspice

skim milk custard, to serve (optional)

NUTRITIONAL NOTES

Per portion:

Calories	132
Fat, total	0.4g
Saturated fat	0.09g
Cholesterol	0mg
Fiber	0.3g

1 Lightly grease four 1-cup pudding molds. Place the golden raisins and apple juice in a pan.

2 Bring the apple juice to a boil, then lower the heat and simmer the mixture gently for 2–3 minutes, to plump up the fruit. Place about half the fruit in the bottom of the molds.

3 Add the couscous and allspice to the pan and bring the liquid back to a boil, stirring. Cover and leave over low heat for 8–10 minutes or until all the liquid has been absorbed.

4 Spoon the couscous into the molds, spread it level, then cover the molds tightly with aluminum foil. Place the molds in a steamer over boiling water, cover and steam for about 30 minutes. Run a knife around the edges, turn the puddings out carefully and serve hot, with skim milk custard, if desired.

COOK'S TIP

These puddings can also be cooked in the microwave. Use microwave-safe molds or teacups, cover, and cook on High for 8–10 minutes.

Blackberry Cobbler

Cobblers are easy to make—this one has a juicy blackberry compote under a delicious blanket.

INGREDIENTS

Serves 8

7 cups blackberries

generous 1 cup granulated sugar

3 tablespoons all-purpose flour

grated zest of 1 lemon

1/4 teaspoon grated nutmeg

For the topping

2 cups all-purpose flour

1 cup sugar

1 tablespoon baking powder

pinch of salt

1 cup skim milk

6 tablespoons low-fat spread, melted

1 Preheat the oven to 350°F. In a large mixing bowl, combine the blackberries with 1 cup of the sugar. Add the flour and lemon zest. Using a large spoon, stir gently to blend. Transfer to an 8-cup baking dish.

2 Make the topping. Sift the flour, sugar, baking powder and salt into a large bowl. Set aside. In bowl, combine the milk and melted low-fat spread.

3 Gradually stir the milk mixture into the dry ingredients and stir until the batter is just smooth.

4 Spoon the batter onto the berries. Mix the remaining sugar with the nutmeg, then sprinkle the mixture on the berries. Bake for about 50 minutes, until the topping is set. Serve hot.

NUTRITIONAL NOTES

Per portion:

Calories	427
Fat, total	4.5g
Saturated fat	1g
Cholesterol	1.2mg
Fiber	4.1g

Peach Cobbler

All the flavor of the traditional and popular version, with less fat than a conventional cobbler.

INGREDIENTS

Serves 6

5 cups peaches, peeled and sliced

3 tablespoons sugar

2 tablespoons peach brandy

1 tablespoon fresh lemon juice

1 tablespoon cornstarch

For the topping

1 cup all-purpose flour

1¹/₂ teaspoons baking powder

¹/₄ teaspoon salt

¹/₄ cup ground almonds

2¹/₂ ounces sugar

2 tablespoons low-fat spread

5 tablespoons skim milk

¹/₄ teaspoon almond extract

ice cream, to serve (optional)

1 Preheat the oven to 425°F. In a bowl, toss the peaches with the sugar, peach brandy, lemon juice and cornstarch. Spoon the peach mixture into a 2-quart baking dish.

2 Using a fine sieve, sift the flour, baking powder and salt into a mixing bowl. Add the ground almonds and 2 ounces of the sugar. With 2 knives, cut in the spread until the mixture resembles coarse crumbs.

3 Add the milk and almond extract. Stir until the mixture is combined.

4 Drop the almond mixture onto the peaches and sprinkle with the sugar.

5 Bake for 30–35 minutes, until piping hot. The cobbler topping should be lightly browned. Serve hot, with ice cream, if desired.

NUTRITIONAL NOTES
Per portion:

Calories	393
Fat, total	4.4g
Saturated fat	0.68g
Cholesterol	0.6mg
Fiber	4g

Apple Brown Betty

A traditional favorite, this tasty dessert is good served with low-fat yogurt or fromage frais.

INGREDIENTS

Serves 6

1 cup fresh white bread crumbs

low-fat spread, for greasing

1 cup light brown sugar

1/2 teaspoon ground cinnamon

1/4 teaspoon ground cloves

1/4 teaspoon grated nutmeg

2 pounds apples

juice of 1 lemon

2 tablespoons low-fat spread

3 tablespoons finely chopped walnuts

1 Preheat the broiler. Spread the bread crumbs on a baking sheet and toast under the broiler until golden, stirring so that they color evenly. Set aside.

2 Preheat the oven to 375ºF. Grease a 8-cup baking dish. Mix the sugar with the cinnamon, cloves and nutmeg in a medium-sized mixing bowl.

3 Peel, core and slice the apples. Toss the slices with the lemon juice to prevent them from turning brown.

4 Sprinkle about 3 tablespoons of the bread crumbs on the bottom of the prepared dish. Cover with one-third of the apples and sprinkle one-third of the sugar-spice mixture on top.

5 Add another layer of bread crumbs and dot with one-quarter of the spread. Repeat the layers two more times, ending with a layer of bread crumbs. Sprinkle with the nuts, and dot with the remaining spread.

6 Bake for 35–40 minutes, until the apples are tender and the top is golden brown. Serve warm.

NUTRITIONAL NOTES
Per portion:

Calories	257
Fat, total	4.7g
Saturated fat	0.73g
Cholesterol	0.3mg
Fiber	2.9g

Blueberry Buckle

This fruity dessert is delicious and can be served with low-fat yogurt, if desired.

INGREDIENTS

Serves 8

low-fat spread, for greasing

2 cups all-purpose flour

2 teaspoons baking powder

1/2 teaspoon salt

2 tablespoons low-fat spread

3/4 cup sugar

1 egg

1/2 teaspoon pure vanilla extract

3/4 cup skim milk

4 cups fresh blueberries

low-fat plain yogurt, to serve (optional)

For the topping

2/3 cup light brown sugar

1/2 cup all-purpose flour

1/2 teaspoon salt

1/2 teaspoon ground allspice

3 tablespoons low-fat spread

2 teaspoons skim milk

1 teaspoon pure vanilla extract

1 Preheat the oven to 375ºF. Grease a 9-inch round gratin dish or shallow baking dish. Sift the flour, baking powder and salt into a bowl. Set aside.

2 Cream the low-fat spread and sugar. Beat in the egg and vanilla. Add the flour mix and milk alternately, beginning and ending with flour.

3 Pour the mixture into the prepared dish and sprinkle onto the blueberries.

4 Make the topping. Mix the brown sugar, flour, salt and allspice in a bowl. Rub in the spread until the mixture resembles coarse crumbs.

NUTRITIONAL NOTES
Per portion:

Calories	338
Fat, total	4.9g
Saturated fat	1.14g
Cholesterol	25.1mg
Fiber	2.1g

5 Mix the milk and vanilla together. Drizzle onto the flour mixture and mix with a fork. Sprinkle the topping onto the blueberries. Bake for 45 minutes or until an inserted skewer comes out clean. Serve warm, with low-fat plain yogurt, if desired.

Apple and Walnut Crumble

Another favorite, combining delicious apples with crunchy walnuts, for a simple, but tasty, dessert.

INGREDIENTS

Serves 6

low-fat spread, for greasing

2 pounds apples, peeled and sliced

grated zest of ¹/2 lemon

1 tablespoon fresh lemon juice

¹/2 cup light brown sugar

³/4 cup all-purpose flour

¹/4 teaspoon salt

¹/4 teaspoon grated nutmeg

¹/2 teaspoon ground cardamom

¹/2 teaspoon ground cinnamon

2 tablespoons low-fat spread

3 tablespoons walnut pieces, chopped

1 Preheat the oven to 350°F. Grease a 9-inch shallow baking dish. Toss the apples with the lemon zest and juice. Arrange them evenly in the bottom of the dish.

2 In a mixing bowl, combine the brown sugar, flour, salt, nutmeg, cardamom and cinnamon. Rub in the spread until the mixture resembles coarse crumbs. Mix in the walnuts.

3 Sprinkle the crumble mixture evenly onto the apples. Cover with aluminum foil and bake for 30 minutes.

4 Remove the foil and continue baking for about 30 more minutes, until the apples are tender and the crumble topping is crisp. Serve warm.

NUTRITIONAL NOTES

Per portion:

Calories	240
Fat, total	4.7g
Saturated fat	0.76g
Cholesterol	0.3mg
Fiber	3.1g

Strawberry and Apple Crumble

A high-fiber, low-fat version of apple crumble. Fresh or frozen raspberries can be used instead of strawberries.

2 Toss together the apples, strawberries, sugar, cinnamon and orange juice. Put the mixture into a 5-cup ovenproof dish.

3 Make the crumble. Combine the flour and oats in a bowl and mix in the low-fat spread with a fork.

4 Sprinkle the crumble evenly onto the fruit. Bake for 40–45 minutes, until golden brown and bubbling. Serve warm, with low-fat custard or yogurt, if desired.

INGREDIENTS

Serves 4

1 pound apples

1¼ cups strawberries, hulled

2 tablespoons sugar

½ teaspoon ground cinnamon

2 tablespoons orange juice

low-fat custard or yogurt, to serve (optional)

For the crumble

3 tablespoons plain whole-wheat flour

⅔ cup oats

2 tablespoons low-fat spread

1 Preheat the oven to 350°F. Peel, core and cut the apples into approximately ¼-inch-size slices. Halve the strawberries.

NUTRITIONAL NOTES

Per portion:

Calories	173
Fat, total	3.9g
Saturated fat	0.85g
Cholesterol	0.4mg
Fiber	3.5g

Blackberry Charlotte

This delicious classic dessert is the perfect reward for an afternoon's blackberry picking.

INGREDIENTS

Serves 4

2 tablespoons low-fat spread

3 cups fresh white bread crumbs

1/4 cup light brown sugar

4 tablespoons golden syrup or light corn syrup

finely grated zest and juice of 2 lemons

1 pound cooking apples

4 cups blackberries

NUTRITIONAL NOTES

Per portion:

Calories	346
Fat, total	4.2g
Saturated fat	0.74g
Cholesterol	0.5mg
Fiber	6.3g

1 Preheat the oven to 350ºF. Melt the spread in a pan with the bread crumbs. Sauté for 5–7 minutes, until the crumbs are golden and fairly crisp. Let cool slightly.

2 Heat the sugar, syrup, lemon zest and juice gently in a small saucepan. Add the crumbs and mix well.

3 With a sharp knife, cut the apples in quarters, peel them and remove the cores. Slice the wedges thinly.

4 Arrange a thin layer of blackberries in a baking dish. Top with a thin layer of crumbs, then a thin layer of apple, topping the fruit with another thin layer of crumbs. Repeat the process with another layer of blackberries, followed by another layer of crumbs.

5 Continue until you have used up all the ingredients, finishing with a layer of crumbs.

6 Bake for 30 minutes, until the crumbs are golden and the fruit is soft.

Peach Cobbler

On chilly days, try this delicious hot fruit cobbler with its tantalizing, feather-light sponge cake topping.

INGREDIENTS

Serves 4

14-ounce can peach slices in natural juice

¼ cup low-fat spread

¼ cup light brown sugar

1 egg, beaten

½ cup whole-wheat flour

½ cup all-purpose flour

1 teaspoon baking powder

½ teaspoon ground cinnamon

4 tablespoons skim milk

½ teaspoon vanilla extract

2 teaspoons confectioners' sugar, for dusting

low-fat, ready-to-serve custard, to serve

NUTRITIONAL NOTES
Per portion:

Calories	255
Fat, total	6.78g
Saturated fat	1.57g
Cholesterol	0.5mg
Fiber	2.65g

1 Preheat the oven to 350°F. Drain the peaches and put into a 4-cup pie dish with 2 tablespoons of the juice.

2 Put all the remaining ingredients, except the confectioners' sugar, into a mixing bowl. Beat for 3–4 minutes, until thoroughly combined.

3 Spoon the sponge cake mixture onto the peaches and level the top. Cook in the oven for 35–40 minutes, until springy to the touch. Lightly dust the top with confectioners' sugar before serving hot with the custard.

Chunky Baked Apples

This filling, economical family dessert is a good way of using up bread that is a day or so old.

INGREDIENTS

Serves 4

1 pound Bramley or other apples

3 ounces whole-wheat bread, about 3 slices, without crusts

1/2 cup low-fat cottage cheese

3 tablespoons light brown sugar

scant 1 cup skim milk

1 teaspoon brown sugar

1 Preheat the oven to 425°F. Peel the apples, cut them in quarters and remove the cores.

VARIATION

You could experiment with other types of bread such as oat, rye or white. Pears could be used instead of apples.

NUTRITIONAL NOTES

Per portion:

Calories	158
Fat, total	1g
Saturated fat	0.38g
Cholesterol	2.4mg
Fiber	2.3g

2 Using a sharp knife, roughly chop the apples into even-size pieces, about 1/2 inch in width and depth.

3 Cut the bread into 1/2-inch cubes. Do not use crusts, as these will be too thick for the mixture.

4 Put the apples in a bowl and add the bread cubes, cottage cheese and brown sugar. Toss lightly and mix thoroughly.

5 Stir in the skim milk and then put the mixture into a wide ovenproof dish. Sprinkle brown sugar on top of the mixture.

6 Bake for 30–35 minutes or until golden brown and bubbling. Serve hot.

COOK'S TIP

You may need to adjust the amount of milk used, depending on the dryness of the bread; the more stale the bread, the more milk it will absorb. The texture should be very moist but not falling apart.

Apple Couscous Pudding

This unusual mixture makes a delicious family pudding with a rich fruity flavor, but virtually no fat.

INGREDIENTS

Serves 4

2¹/₂ cups unsweetened
   apple juice

²/₃ cup couscous

¹/₄ cup golden raisins

¹/₂ teaspoon allspice

2 large Bramley or other apples

2 tablespoons brown sugar

low-fat plain yogurt, to serve

NUTRITIONAL NOTES
Per portion:

Calories	194
Fat, total	0.58g
Saturated fat	0.09g
Cholesterol	0mg
Fiber	0.75g

1 Preheat the oven to 400°F. Boil the apple juice, couscous, golden raisins and spice in a pan, stirring. Lower heat, cover and simmer.

COOK'S TIP
~

Couscous is a pre-cooked grain that is widely available at supermarkets .

2 Spoon half the couscous mix into a 5-cup ovenproof dish. Peel, core and slice the apples and arrange half the slices on top, then add the remaining couscous.

3 Arrange the remaining apple slices on top and sprinkle with brown sugar. Bake for 25–30 minutes or until golden brown. Serve while still hot, with low-fat yogurt.

Baked Fruit Compote

This medley of dried fruit looks good, tastes even better and is quick and easy to make.

INGREDIENTS

Serves 6

2/3 cup dried figs

1/2 cup dried apricots

1/2 cup apple rings

1/4 cup prunes

1/2 cup dried pears

1/2 cup dried peaches

1¼ cups unsweetened apple juice

1¼ cups unsweetened orange juice

6 cloves

1 cinnamon stick

a few toasted sliced almonds, to decorate

2 Mix the unsweetened apple and orange juices and pour evenly over the fruit, thoroughly coating all the fruit with the apple and orange juices. Add the cloves and cinnamon stick and stir gently to mix.

3 Bake for about 30 minutes, until the fruit mixture is hot, stirring once or twice during cooking. Set aside and soak for 20 minutes, then discard the cloves and cinnamon stick.

4 Spoon into serving bowls and serve warm or cold, decorated with toasted sliced almonds.

COOK'S TIP

Pineapple and orange or grape and apple juice can be used instead.

1 Preheat the oven to 350°F. Place the figs, apricots, apple rings, prunes, pears and peaches in a shallow ovenproof dish and stir to mix.

NUTRITIONAL NOTES

Per portion:

Calories	174
Fat, total	0.8g
Saturated fat	0.05g
Cholesterol	0mg
Fiber	5.16g

Kumquat Compote

Warm, spicy and full of sun-ripened ingredients, this is the perfect winter dessert to remind you of summer days.

2 Pare the orange zest and add to the pan. Peel and grate the ginger and add to the pan. Crush the cardamom pods and add the seeds to the mixture, with the cloves.

3 Reduce the heat, cover, and simmer gently for 30 minutes, until the fruit is tender, stirring occasionally.

4 Add the squeezed orange juice to the compote. Sweeten with the honey, sprinkle with the almonds and serve warm.

INGREDIENTS

Serves 4

2 cups kumquats

scant 1 cup dried apricots

2 tablespoons golden raisins

1²/₃ cups water

1 orange

1-inch piece of fresh ginger root

4 cardamom pods

4 cloves

2 tablespoons honey

1 tablespoon sliced almonds, toasted

1 Wash the kumquats, and, if they are large, cut them in half. Place them in a pan with the apricots, golden raisins and water. Bring to a boil.

NUTRITIONAL NOTES
Per portion:

Calories	198
Fat, total	2.9g
Saturated fat	0.25g
Cholesterol	0mg
Fiber	6.9g

Russian Black Currant Pudding

This Russian pudding is traditionally made from the thickened juice of stewed red or black currants.

INGREDIENTS

Serves 4

2 cups red or black currants or
   a mixture of both

2 cups raspberries

2/3 cup water

1/4 cup sugar

1 1/2 tablespoons arrowroot

1 tablespoon crème de mûre

low-fat plain yogurt, to serve (optional)

1 Place the currants and raspberries, water and sugar in a pan. Cover the pan and cook over low heat for 12–15 minutes, until the fruit is soft.

2 Blend the arrowroot into a paste with a little water in a small bowl and stir into the hot fruit mixture. Bring the fruit mixture back to a boil, stirring constantly until thickened and smooth.

3 Remove the pan from heat and let the fruit compote cool slightly, then gently stir in the crème de mûre.

4 Pour the compote into four glass serving bowls and leave until cold, then chill until needed. Serve solo or with low-fat plain yogurt.

NUTRITIONAL NOTES
Per portion:

Calories	105
Fat, total	0.2g
Saturated fat	0g
Cholesterol	0mg
Fiber	3.3g

COOK'S TIP

Crème de mûre is a blackberry liqueur available at large supermarkets—you could use crème de cassis instead, if you prefer.

Cornflake-topped Peach Crisp

With a few staple ingredients, this golden, crisp-crusted dessert can be rustled up in next to no time.

INGREDIENTS

Serves 4

14 1/2-ounce can peach slices in juice
2 tablespoons golden raisins
1 cinnamon stick
strip of pared orange zest
2 tablespoons low-fat spread
1 1/2 cups cornflakes
2 teaspoons sesame seeds

1 Preheat the oven to 400°F. Drain the peaches, reserving the juice in a saucepan. Arrange the peaches in a shallow ovenproof dish.

2 Bring to a boil the golden raisins, cinnamon, orange zest and juice. Lower the heat and simmer, to reduce the liquid by half. Remove the zest and cinnamon and spoon onto the peaches.

3 Melt the low-fat spread in a small pan; stir in the cornflakes and sesame seeds.

4 Spread the cornflake mixture onto the fruit. Bake for 15–20 minutes or until the topping is crisp and golden. Serve hot.

NUTRITIONAL NOTES
Per portion:

Calories	150
Fat, total	4.6g
Saturated fat	1g
Cholesterol	0.5mg
Fiber	1.3g

Rhubarb Spiral Cobbler

*The tangy taste of rhubarb combines
perfectly with the ginger in this
unusual dessert.*

3 Roll out the dough on a floured
surface to a 10-inch square. Mix
the orange zest, brown sugar and
ginger, then sprinkle this onto the dough.

4 Roll up quite tightly, then cut into
about 10 slices using a sharp knife.
Arrange the slices on the rhubarb.

5 Bake for 20–25 minutes or until
the spirals are well risen and
golden brown. Serve warm.

INGREDIENTS

Serves 4

1½ pounds rhubarb, sliced

3 tablespoons unsweetened orange juice

6 tablespoons sugar

1¾ cups self-rising flour

about 1 cup low-fat plain yogurt

grated zest of 1 orange

2 tablespoons brown sugar

1 teaspoon ground ginger

1 Preheat the oven to 400°F. Mix
the rhubarb, orange juice and
4 tablespoons of the sugar in a pan.
Cover and cook over low heat for
10 minutes or until tender. Put into an
ovenproof dish.

2 To make the topping, mix the flour
and remaining sugar in a bowl,
then stir in enough of the yogurt to
bind into a soft dough.

NUTRITIONAL NOTES

Per portion:

Calories	320
Fat, total	1.2g
Saturated fat	0.34g
Cholesterol	2mg
Fiber	3.92g

COOK'S TIP

In the summer you could substitute
halved plums, sliced nectarines or
peaches for the rhubarb, if you prefer.

Plum, Apple and Banana Scone Pie

This is one of those simple, satisfying desserts that everyone enjoys. Serve hot or cold with low-fat plain yogurt.

INGREDIENTS

Serves 4

1 pound plums

1 Bramley or other apple

1 large banana

2/3 cup water

1 cup whole-wheat flour, or half whole-wheat
    and half all-purpose flour

2 teaspoons baking powder

3 tablespoons raisins

about 4 tablespoons sour milk or
    low-fat plain yogurt

low-fat plain yogurt, to serve (optional)

2 Mix the fruit in a saucepan. Pour in the water. Bring to the simmering point and cook gently for 15 minutes or until the fruit is completely soft.

5 Transfer the scone dough to a lightly floured surface and divide it into 6–8 portions, then pat them into flattish scones.

1 Preheat the oven to 350ºF. Cut the plums in half and ease out the pits. Peel, core and chop the apple, then slice the banana.

3 Spoon the fruit mixture into a pie dish. Level the surface.

4 Mix the flour, baking powder and raisins in a bowl. Add the sour milk or low-fat yogurt and mix into a very soft dough.

6 Cover the plum and apple mixture with the scones. Bake the pie for 40 minutes, until the scone topping is cooked through. Serve the pie hot with yogurt, or leave it until cold.

NUTRITIONAL NOTES

Per portion:

Calories	195
Fat, total	1g
Saturated fat	0.2g
Cholesterol	0.6mg
Fiber	5.2g

COOK'S TIP

To prevent the banana from discoloring before cooking, dip each slice in fresh lemon juice.

Pancakes with Mulled Plums

These light little pancakes, with their rich, spicy plum sauce, can just as easily be cooked on the stove as on the grill.

Serves 6

1¼ pounds red plums

6 tablespoons light brown sugar

1 cinnamon stick

2 whole cloves

1 piece star anise

6 tablespoons unsweetened apple juice

low-fat plain yogurt or fromage frais,
   to serve (optional)

For the pancakes

½ cup all-purpose flour

2 teaspoons baking powder

pinch of salt

½ cup fine cornmeal

2 tablespoons light brown sugar

1 egg, beaten

1¼ cups skim milk

1 tablespoon corn oil

1 Halve, pit and quarter the plums. Place them in a pan, with the sugar, spices and apple juice.

COOK'S TIP

Use spray oil on the griddle if you prefer, and cut the fat content even more.

2 Place on a hot grill or stove and bring to a boil. Lower heat, cover and simmer gently for 8–10 minutes, stirring, until the plums are soft. Remove the spices and keep warm.

3 For the pancakes, sift the flour, baking powder and salt into a large bowl and stir in the cornmeal and sugar.

4 Make a well in the center and add the egg; gradually beat in the milk. Beat with a wooden spoon into a smooth batter. Beat in 1 teaspoon of the oil.

5 Heat a griddle or a heavy frying-pan on a hot grill or stove. When it is very hot, brush with oil and then drop tablespoons of batter onto it. Cook the pancakes for about a minute, until bubbles appear on the surface and the underside is golden.

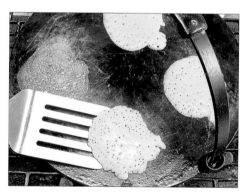

6 Turn the pancakes over and cook the other side for another minute or until golden. Bake the other pancakes. Serve hot with the mulled plums. Add a spoonful of low-fat yogurt or fromage frais, if desired.

NUTRITIONAL NOTES

Per portion:

Calories	159
Fat, total	3.3g
Saturated fat	0.58g
Cholesterol	33.1mg
Fiber	1.7g

Grilled Bananas with Spicy Vanilla Spread

Grilled bananas are easy because they cook in their own skins and need no preparation at all.

2 Meanwhile, split the cardamom pods, remove the seeds and crush them lightly in a pestle and mortar.

3 Split the vanilla bean lengthwise and scrape out the tiny seeds. Mix with the cardamom, orange zest, sugar brandy and spread, to make a paste.

4 Slit the skin of each banana, open out slightly and spoon in a little of the paste. Serve immediately.

INGREDIENTS

Serves 4

4 bananas

6 green cardamom pods

1 vanilla bean

finely grated zest of 1 small orange

2 tablespoons brandy

4 tablespoons light brown sugar

3 tablespoons low-fat spread

COOK'S TIP

If making this for children, use orange juice instead of the brandy or, if the fat content is no object, drizzle melted chocolate onto the cooked bananas.

1 Place the bananas, in their skins, on the hot grill and leave for 6–8 minutes, turning occasionally, until they are turning brownish-black.

NUTRITIONAL NOTES
Per portion:

Calories	215
Fat, total	4.9g
Saturated fat	1.22g
Cholesterol	0.7mg
Fiber	1.1g

Hot Spiced Bananas

Baking bananas in a rum and fruit syrup makes for a dessert with negligible fat and maximum flavor.

Serves 6

low-fat spread, for greasing

6 ripe bananas

generous 1 cup light brown sugar

1 cup unsweetened pineapple juice

1/2 cup dark rum

2 cinnamon sticks

12 whole cloves

NUTRITIONAL NOTES

Per portion:

Calories	290
Fat, total	0.3g
Saturated fat	0.11g
Cholesterol	0mg
Fiber	1.1g

3 Mix the sugar and pineapple juice in a saucepan. Heat gently until the sugar has dissolved, stirring. Add the rum, cinnamon and cloves. Bring to a boil, then remove from heat.

4 Pour the hot pineapple and spice mixture onto the bananas in the baking dish. Bake for 25–30 minutes, until the bananas are tender. Serve while still hot.

1 Preheat the oven to 350ºF. Grease a 9-inch shallow baking dish.

2 Peel the bananas and cut them diagonally into 1-inch pieces. Arrange the banana pieces to spread evenly on the bottom of the prepared baking dish.

Rum and Raisin Bananas

Choose almost-ripe bananas with evenly colored skins, either all yellow or just green at the tips.

INGREDIENTS

Serves 4

1/4 cup seedless raisins

5 tablespoons dark rum

1 tablespoon low-fat spread

4 tablespoons light brown sugar

4 ripe bananas, peeled and
    halved lengthwise

1/4 teaspoon grated nutmeg

1/4 teaspoon ground cinnamon

1 tablespoon slivered almonds, toasted

low-fat fromage frais or low-fat vanilla
    ice cream, to serve (optional)

1 Put the raisins in a bowl and pour in the rum. Let them soak for about 30 minutes, until plump.

2 Melt the spread in a frying pan, add the sugar and stir until it has completely dissolved. Add the bananas and cook for a few minutes, until tender, turning occasionally.

3 Sprinkle the spices onto the bananas, then pour on the rum and raisins. Carefully set on fire using a long-handled match; stir gently to mix.

4 Sprinkle on the slivered almonds and serve immediately with low-fat fromage frais or low-fat vanilla ice cream, if desired.

COOK'S TIP

For an accompaniment that won't add too much fat, make your own frozen yogurt by churning extra low-fat yogurt in an ice-cream maker.

NUTRITIONAL NOTES
Per portion:

Calories	263
Fat, total	4.1g
Saturated fat	0.51g
Cholesterol	0.2mg
Fiber	1.6g

Caribbean Bananas

Tender baked bananas in a rich and spicy sauce of ground allspice and ginger—a dessert for those with a sweet tooth!

INGREDIENTS

Serves 4

2 tablespoons low-fat spread

8 firm ripe bananas

juice of 1 lime

1/2 cup dark brown sugar

1 teaspoon ground allspice

1/2 teaspoon ground ginger

seeds from 6 cardamoms crushed

2 tablespoons rum

pared lime zest, to decorate

low-fat crème fraîche, to serve (optional)

1 Preheat the oven to 400°F. Use a little of the spread to grease a shallow baking dish large enough to hold the bananas snugly in a single layer.

2 Peel the bananas and cut them in half lengthwise. Arrange the bananas in the dish and pour in the lime juice.

3 Mix the sugar, allspice, ginger and crushed cardamom seeds in a bowl. Sprinkle the mixture onto the bananas. Dot with the remaining low-fat spread. Bake, basting once, for 15 minutes or until the bananas are soft.

4 Remove the dish from the oven. Warm the rum in a small pan or metal soup ladle, pour it onto the bananas and set it on fire.

5 As soon as the flames die down, decorate the dessert with the pared lime zest. Serve while still hot and add a dollop of low-fat crème fraîche to each portion, if desired.

VARIATION

For a version that will appeal more to children, use orange juice instead of lime and leave out the rum.

NUTRITIONAL NOTES

Per portion:

Calories	310
Fat, total	3.2g
Saturated fat	0.87g
Cholesterol	0.4mg
Fiber	2.2g

Grilled Pineapple Boats with Rum Glaze

Pineapple is even more full of flavor when grilled; this spiced rum glaze turns it into a special dessert.

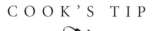

INGREDIENTS

Serves 4

1 medium pineapple, about 1 pound, 6 ounces

2 tablespoons dark brown sugar

1 teaspoon ground ginger

3 tablespoons low-fat spread, melted

2 tablespoons dark rum

COOK'S TIP

For an easier version, cut off the skin and then slice the whole pineapple into thick slices and cook as above.

1 With a large, sharp knife, cut the pineapple lengthwise into quarters. Cut out and discard the hard center core from each quarter. Be careful when handling the rough outer skin.

2 Cut between the flesh and skin, to release the flesh, but not cut the skin. Slice the flesh across, into chunks.

3 Push a bamboo skewer lengthwise through each quarter and into the stem, to hold the chunks in place.

4 Mix the sugar, ginger, melted spread and rum and brush onto the pineapple. Cook the quarters on a hot grill for 3–4 minutes; pour the remaining glaze on top and serve.

NUTRITIONAL NOTES
Per portion:

Calories	155
Fat, total	4.9g
Saturated fat	1.14g
Cholesterol	0.7mg
Fiber	1.8g

Broiled Nectarines with Amaretto

Amaretto, the sweet almond-flavored liqueur from Italy, adds a touch of luxury to these low-fat broiled nectarines.

INGREDIENTS

Serves 4

6 ripe nectarines

2 tablespoons honey

4 tablespoons Amaretto

half-fat crème fraîche, to serve (optional)

NUTRITIONAL NOTES

Per portion:

Calories	150
Fat, total	0.2g
Saturated fat	0g
Cholesterol	0mg
Fiber	2.7g

1 Cut the nectarines in half by running a small sharp knife down the side of each fruit from top to bottom, cutting right through to the pit. Gently ease the nectarine apart and remove the pit. Handle the fruit carefully, as nectarines bruise easily.

2 Place the nectarines cut-side up in an ovenproof dish and drizzle ½ teaspoon honey and 1 teaspoon Amaretto on each half. Preheat the broiler until very hot and then broil the fruit until slightly charred. Serve with a little half-fat crème fraîche, if desired.

Nectarines with Marzipan and Yogurt

A luscious dessert that few can resist; marzipan and nectarines are a wonderful combination.

INGREDIENTS

Serves 4

4 firm, ripe nectarines or peaches

3 ounces marzipan

5 tablespoons low-fat plain yogurt

3 amaretti cookies, crushed

1 Cut the nectarines or peaches in half, removing the pits.

2 Cut the marzipan into eight pieces and press one piece into the pit cavity of each nectarine half. Preheat the broiler, unless you are cooking on the grill.

COOK'S TIP

If the pit does not pull out easily when you halve the fruit, use a small, sharp knife to cut around it.

3 Spoon the low-fat yogurt on top. Sprinkle the crushed amaretti cookies onto the yogurt.

4 Place the fruits on a hot grill or under a hot broiler. Cook for 3–5 minutes, until the yogurt starts to melt.

NUTRITIONAL NOTES

Per portion:

Calories	176
Fat, total	4.3g
Saturated fat	0.98g
Cholesterol	3.2mg
Fiber	2.3g

Spiced Nectarines with Fromage Frais

This easy dessert is good at any time of year—use canned peach halves if fresh nectarines are not available.

2 Arrange the fruit, cut-side upward, in a wide flameproof dish or on a baking sheet.

3 Stir the sugar into the fromage frais. Using a teaspoon, spoon the mixture into the hollow of each half.

4 Sprinkle the fruit with the ground star anise or allspice. Place under a medium-hot broiler for 6–8 minutes or until the fruit is hot and bubbling. Serve warm.

INGREDIENTS

Serves 4

4 ripe nectarines or peaches

1 tablespoon light brown sugar

1/2 cup low-fat fromage frais

1/2 teaspoon ground star anise or
   allspice

1 With a sharp knife cut the nectarines or peaches in half and remove the pits.

NUTRITIONAL NOTES

Per portion:

Calories	108
Fat, total	3.3g
Saturated fat	2g
Cholesterol	14.4mg
Fiber	1.5g

Grilled Orange Parcels

This is one of the most delicious ways of ending a grilled meal. Serve on their own, or with low-fat fromage frais.

Serves 4

2 tablespoons low-fat spread, plus extra, melted, for brushing

4 oranges

2 tablespoons maple syrup

2 tablespoons Cointreau or Grand Marnier liqueur

low-fat fromage frais, to serve (optional)

1 Cut four double-thick squares of aluminum foil, large enough to wrap the oranges. Melt about 2 teaspoons of the low-fat spread and brush it on the center of each piece of foil.

2 Remove some shreds of orange zest, for the decoration. Blanch and dry them and set aside. Peel the oranges, removing the white pith and peel and catching the juice in a bowl.

3 Slice the oranges crosswise into thick slices. Reassemble, and place each orange on a square of aluminum foil.

4 Create a cup shape by tucking the foil up high around the oranges. This will keep them in shape, but leave the foil open at the top.

5 Mix the reserved orange juice, maple syrup and liqueur and spoon the mixture onto the oranges.

6 Add a dab of low-fat spread to each parcel and fold over the foil, to seal in the juices. Place the parcels on a hot grill for 10–12 minutes, until hot. Serve topped with shreds of orange zest and fromage frais, if desired.

NUTRITIONAL NOTES
Per portion:

Calories	127
Fat, total	3.2g
Saturated fat	0.74g
Cholesterol	0.5mg
Fiber	2.7g

COOK'S TIP

To make the orange shreds for the decoration, slice off several pieces of orange zest, taking care to avoid the bitter white pith, then cut them into thin matchsticks. Add to a small pan of boiling water, for 1 minute, then drain and dry on paper towels.

Apples and Raspberries in Rose Syrup

Inspiration for this dessert stems from the fact that the apple and the raspberry belong to the rose family.

INGREDIENTS

Serves 4

1 teaspoon rose pouchong tea

3³⁄₄ cups boiling water

1 teaspoon rose-water (optional)

¹⁄₄ cup sugar

1 teaspoon lemon juice

5 apples

1¹⁄₂ cups fresh raspberries

1 Warm a large tea pot. Add the rose pouchong tea, then pour on the boiling water, together with the rose-water, if using. Let stand and infuse for 4 minutes.

2 Measure the sugar and lemon juice into a stainless steel saucepan. Strain in the tea and stir to dissolve the sugar.

3 Peel and core the apples, then cut into quarters.

4 Poach the apples in the syrup for about 5 minutes.

5 Transfer the apples and syrup to a large metal tray and let cool to room temperature.

6 Pour the cooled apples and syrup into a bowl, add the raspberries and mix to combine. Spoon into individual dishes or bowls and serve while still warm.

NUTRITIONAL NOTES

Per portion:

Calories	125
Fat, total	0.4g
Saturated fat	0g
Cholesterol	0mg
Fiber	3.6g

Papaya Baked with Ginger

Ginger enhances the flavor of papaya in this recipe, which takes no more than ten minutes to prepare.

Serves 4

2 ripe papayas

2 pieces stem ginger in syrup, drained, plus
   1 tablespoon syrup from the jar

8 cookies, coarsely crushed

3 tablespoons raisins

shredded, finely pared zest and juice
   of 1 lime

1 tablespoon light brown sugar

4 tablespoons low-fat plain yogurt,
   plus extra to serve (optional)

1 tablespoon finely chopped unsalted
   pistachios

COOK'S TIP

Don't overcook papaya, or the flesh
will become very watery.

1 Preheat the oven to 400°F. Cut the papayas in half and scoop out their seeds. Place the halves in a baking dish and set aside. Cut the stem ginger into fine matchsticks.

2 Make the filling. Combine the crushed cookies, stem ginger matchsticks and raisins in a bowl. Make sure they are all mixed well.

3 Stir in the lime zest and juice, then add the sugar and the yogurt. Mix well.

4 Fill the papaya halves and drizzle with the ginger syrup. Sprinkle with the pistachios.

5 Bake for about 25 minutes or until tender. Serve hot, with extra low-fat yogurt, if desired.

NUTRITIONAL NOTES

Per portion:

Calories	218
Fat, total	4.2g
Saturated fat	1.23g
Cholesterol	6mg
Fiber	3.8g

Baked Peaches with Raspberry Sauce

Pretty as a picture—that's the effect when you serve these tasty stuffed peaches to delighted dinner party guests.

INGREDIENTS

Serves 6

2 tablespoons low-fat spread

1/4 cup sugar

1 egg, beaten

1/4 cup ground almonds

6 ripe peaches

glossy leaves and plain or frosted raspberries,
   to decorate

For the sauce

2 cups raspberries

1 tablespoon confectioners' sugar

NUTRITIONAL NOTES

Per portion:

Calories	137
Fat, total	4.7g
Saturated fat	0.81g
Cholesterol	32.3mg
Fiber	2.8g

1 Preheat the oven to 350°F. Beat the low-fat spread and sugar together, then beat in the egg and ground almonds.

2 Cut the peaches in half and remove the pits. With a spoon, scrape out some of the flesh from each peach half, slightly enlarging the hollow left by the pit. Save the excess peach for the sauce.

3 Stand the peach halves on a baking sheet, supporting them with crumpled foil to keep them steady. Fill each peach hollow with the almond mixture. Bake for 30 minutes or until the almond filling is puffed and golden and the peaches are very tender.

4 Meanwhile, process the raspberries, confectioners' sugar and the reserved peach flesh in a food processor or blender, until smooth. Press through a strainer over a bowl to remove fibers and seeds.

5 Let the peaches cool slightly. Spoon the sauce on each plate and arrange two peach halves on top. Decorate with the leaves and raspberries and serve immediately.

COOK'S TIP

For a special occasion, stir about 1 tablespoon framboise or peach brandy into the raspberry sauce.

Stuffed Peaches with Almond Liqueur

Together amaretti cookies and amaretto liqueur have an intense almond flavor, and make a natural partner for peaches.

Serves 4

4 ripe but firm peaches

1/2 cup amaretti cookies

2 tablespoons low-fat spread

2 tablespoons sugar

1 egg yolk

4 tablespoons almond liqueur

low-fat spread, for greasing

1 cup dry white wine

8 tiny sprigs of fresh basil, to decorate

low-fat ice cream, to serve (optional)

1 Preheat the oven to 350ºF. Cut the peaches in half and remove the pits. With a spoon, scrape out some of the flesh from each peach half, slightly enlarging the hollow. Chop this flesh and set it aside.

2 Put the amaretti cookies in a bowl and crush them finely with the end of a rolling pin.

3 Cream the low-fat spread and sugar together in a separate bowl until smooth. Stir in the reserved chopped peach flesh, the egg yolk and half the liqueur with the amaretti crumbs. Lightly grease a baking dish that is just large enough to hold the peach halves in a single layer.

NUTRITIONAL NOTES

Per portion:

Calories	232
Fat, total	5g
Saturated fat	1.37g
Cholesterol	54.7mg
Fiber	1.9g

4 Stand the peaches in the dish and spoon the stuffing into them. Mix the remaining liqueur with the wine, pour onto the peaches and bake for 25 minutes or until the peaches feel tender. Decorate with basil and serve immediately, with low-fat ice cream, if desired.

Coconut Dumplings with Apricot Sauce

These delicate little dumplings are simple to make. The sharp flavor of the sauce offsets the creamy dumplings.

INGREDIENTS

Serves 4

6 tablespoons low-fat cottage cheese

1 egg white

1 tablespoon low-fat spread

1 tablespoon light brown sugar

2 tablespoons self-rising whole-wheat flour

finely grated zest of ¹/₂ lemon

1 tablespoon dry, shredded coconut, toasted

For the sauce

8-ounce can apricot halves in
    natural juice

1 tablespoon lemon juice

2 Beat together the cottage cheese, egg white and low-fat spread until they are evenly mixed.

3 Stir in the sugar, flour, lemon zest and coconut, mixing everything evenly into a fairly firm dough.

4 Place 8–12 spoonfuls of the mixture in the steamer or on the plate, leaving a space between them.

5 Cover the steamer or pan tightly with a lid or a plate and steam for about 10 minutes, until the dumplings have risen and are firm to the touch.

6 Meanwhile make the sauce. Purée the can of apricots and stir in the lemon juice. Pour into a small pan and heat until boiling, then serve with the dumplings. Sprinkle with extra coconut to serve, if you can afford the extra fat.

1 Half-fill a steamer with boiling water and put it on to boil. If you do not own a steamer, place a heatproof plate or shallow dish over a pan of boiling water.

NUTRITIONAL NOTES
Per portion:

Calories	112
Fat, total	4.3g
Saturated fat	2.56g
Cholesterol	1.2mg
Fiber	1.7g

COOK'S TIP

The mixture should be quite stiff; if it is not stiff enough to hold its shape, stir in a little more flour.

Pineapple Flambé

Flambéing means adding alcohol and then burning it off so that the flavor is not too overpowering.

INGREDIENTS

Serves 4

1 large, ripe pineapple, about 1 pound, 6 ounces

2 tablespoons low-fat spread

1/4 cup light brown sugar

4 tablespoons fresh orange juice

2 tablespoons brandy or vodka

1 tablespoons sliced almonds, toasted

1 Cut away the top and bottom of the pineapple. Then cut down the sides, removing all the dark "eyes."

2 Cut the pineapple into thin slices. Using an apple corer, remove the hard, central core from each slice.

VARIATION

Try this with nectarines, peaches or cherries. Omit the almonds if you want to reduce the fat content a little.

3 Melt the spread in a frying pan, with the sugar. Add the orange juice. Stir until hot, then add as many pineapple slices as the pan will hold. Cook for 1–2 minutes, turning once. Remove each slice as it browns.

4 Return all the pineapple slices to the pan, heat briefly, then pour over the brandy or vodka and light with a long-handled match. Let the flames die down, then sprinkle with the almonds. Serve immediately.

NUTRITIONAL NOTES
Per portion:

Calories	171
Fat, total	5g
Saturated fat	0.62g
Cholesterol	0.4mg
Fiber	2.1g

Warm Pears in Cider

*Serve these pears with low-fat Greek
yogurt or fromage frais if you must, but
they are very good on their own.*

INGREDIENTS

Serves 4

1 lemon

1/4 cup sugar

a little grated nutmeg

1 cup sweet cider

4 firm, ripe pears

NUTRITIONAL NOTES

Per portion:

Calories	11
Fat, total	0g
Saturated fat	0g
Cholesterol	0mg
Fiber	3.3g

1 Using a potato peeler remove the
zest from the lemon in thin strips,
leaving any white pith behind.

2 Squeeze the juice from the lemon
and pour it into a saucepan. Add
the lemon zest, sugar, grated nutmeg
and cider and heat gently until the
sugar has completely dissolved.

3 Peel the pears, leaving the stems
on if possible, and place in the pan
of cider. Poach for 10–15 minutes until
almost tender, turning them frequently.

4 Transfer the pears to individual
serving dishes using a slotted
spoon. Simmer the liquid over high
heat until it reduces slightly and
becomes syrupy. Pour the warm syrup
over the pears. Serve immediately.

COOK'S TIP

To make sure that the pears are firm
enough for this dish, buy them
slightly under-ripe and then wait a
day or more.

Fanned Poached Pears in Port Syrup

The perfect choice for autumn dining, this simple dessert has a beautiful rich color and fantastic flavor.

INGREDIENTS

Serves 4

2 ripe, firm pears

pared zest of 1 lemon

3/4 cup port

1/4 cup sugar

1 cinnamon stick

4 tablespoons cold water

low-fat crème fraîche, to serve (optional)

To decorate

1 tablespoon sliced hazelnuts, toasted

fresh mint, pear or rose leaves

NUTRITIONAL NOTES
Per portion:

Calories	173
Fat	2.5g
Saturated fat	0.17g
Cholesterol	0mg
Fiber	1.9g

1 Peel the pears, cut them in half and remove the cores. Place the lemon zest, port, sugar, cinnamon stick and water in a shallow pan. Bring to a boil over low heat. Add the pears, cover and poach for 5 minutes. Let the pears cool in the syrup.

2 When the pears are cold, transfer them to a bowl with a slotted spoon. Return the syrup to the heat. Boil rapidly until it has reduced to form a syrup. Remove the cinnamon stick and lemon zest and let the syrup cool.

3 To serve, place each pear half on a board, cut-side down. Keeping it intact at the stem end, slice lengthwise. Carefully lift it off, using a spatula, and place on a dessert plate. Press gently to fan out the pears. Spoon in the port syrup, top with a few hazelnuts and decorate with fresh mint, pear or rose leaves. Serve with half-fat crème fraîche, if desired.

Mulled Pears with Ginger and Brandy

The flavors improve with keeping, so you can mull the pears several days before you want to serve them.

INGREDIENTS

Serves 8

2¹/2 cups red wine

1 cup sugar

1 cinnamon stick

6 cloves

finely grated zest of 1 orange

2 teaspoons grated fresh ginger root

8 even-sized firm pears, with stems

1 tablespoon brandy

¹/4 cup almonds or hazelnuts, toasted,
    to decorate

low-fat whipped cream, to serve (optional)

3 Gently remove the pears from the syrup with a slotted spoon, being very careful not to dislodge the stems. Put the cooked pears in a serving bowl or individual bowls, if you prefer.

NUTRITIONAL NOTES	
Per portion:	
Calories	246
Fat, total	1.9g
Saturated fat	0.13g
Cholesterol	0mg
Fiber	3.5g

4 Boil the syrup until it thickens and reduces. Cool slightly, add the brandy and strain over the pears. Decorate with toasted nuts. Serve with whipped cream, if desired.

1 Put all the ingredients except the pears, brandy and nuts into a large pan and heat slowly until the sugar has dissolved. Simmer for 5 minutes.

2 Peel the pears, leaving the stems on. Arrange them upright in the pan. Cover and simmer until tender, for 45–50 minutes, depending on size.

Poached Pears in Maple-yogurt Sauce

Poach the pears in advance, and have the cooled syrup ready to spoon on to the plates just before you serve.

INGREDIENTS

Serves 6

6 firm pears

1 tablespoon lemon juice

1 cup sweet white wine or cider

thinly pared zest of 1 lemon

1 cinnamon stick

2 tablespoons maple syrup

1/2 teaspoon arrowroot

2/3 cup low-fat
   plain yogurt

1 Peel the pears thinly, leaving them whole and with the stems. Brush them with lemon juice, to prevent them from browning. Use a potato peeler or small knife to scoop out the core from the bottom of each pear.

2 Place them in a wide, heavy pan and add the wine or cider, with cold water to almost cover the pears.

3 Add the lemon zest and cinnamon stick and bring to a boil. Reduce the heat, cover and simmer gently for 30–40 minutes, or until tender. Turn the pears so that they cook evenly. Lift out carefully, draining them well.

4 Boil the liquid uncovered to reduce to about 1/2 cup. Strain into a jug and add the maple syrup. Blend a little of the liquid with the arrowroot, then return the mixture to the jug; mix well. Return to the pan and cook, stirring, until thick and clear. Cool.

COOK'S TIP

The cooking time will vary, depending upon the type and ripeness of the pears. They should be ripe, but firm, soft pears will not keep their shape.

5 Slice each pear about three-quarters of the way through, leaving the slices attached at the stem end. Fan each pear out on a serving plate.

6 Stir 2 tablespoons of the cooled syrup into the yogurt and spoon it around the pears. Drizzle with the remaining syrup and serve immediately.

NUTRITIONAL NOTES

Per portion:

Calories	136
Fat, total	1.4g
Saturated fat	0.79g
Cholesterol	1.8mg
Fiber	3.3g

Blushing Pears

Pears poached in rosé wine and sweet spices absorb all the subtle flavors and turn a soft pink color.

Serves 6

6 firm pears

1¼ cups rosé wine

⅔ cup cranberry juice
    or apple juice

strip of thinly pared orange zest

4 whole cloves

1 cinnamon stick

1 bay leaf

5 tablespoons sugar

small bay leaves, to decorate

1 Thinly peel the pears with a sharp knife or vegetable peeler, leaving the stems attached.

2 Pour the wine and cranberry or apple juice into a large heavy saucepan. Add the orange zest, cloves, cinnamon stick, bay leaf and sugar.

3 Heat gently, stirring all the time until the sugar has dissolved. Add the pears and stand them upright in the pan. Pour in enough cold water to barely cover them. Cover and cook very gently for 20–30 minutes, or until just tender, turning and basting occasionally to ensure even cooking.

4 Using a slotted spoon, gently lift the pears out of the syrup and transfer to a serving dish.

5 Bring the syrup to a boil and boil rapidly for 10–15 minutes, or until it has reduced by half.

6 Strain the syrup and pour over the pears. Serve hot, decorated with bay leaves.

NUTRITIONAL NOTES
Per portion:

Calories	148
Fat, total	0.16g
Saturated fat	0g
Cholesterol	0mg
Fiber	1.9g

COOK'S TIP

Check the pears by piercing with a skewer or sharp knife toward the end of the poaching time and carefully lift out any that have cooked more quickly than others.

Char-grilled Apples on Cinnamon Toasts

This yummy treat makes a fabulous finale to a summer barbecue, but it can also be cooked under the broiler.

INGREDIENTS

Serves 4

4 sweet apples

juice of ½ lemon

4 individual muffins

1 tablespoon low-fat spread, melted

2 tablespoons light brown sugar

1 teaspoon ground cinnamon

low-fat plain yogurt, to serve (optional)

1 Core the apples and cut them horizontally in three or four thick slices. Sprinkle with lemon juice.

VARIATION

Other fruit in season could be used for this recipe. Try pears, peaches or pineapple for variety. Nutmeg or all-spice could also replace the cinnamon.

NUTRITIONAL NOTES
Per portion:

Calories	241
Fat, total	4.9g
Saturated fat	1.63g
Cholesterol	0.2mg
Fiber	3.0g

2 Cut the muffins into thick slices. Brush sparingly with melted low-fat spread on both sides.

3 Mix together the sugar and ground cinnamon. Preheat the broiler if not using the grill.

4 Place the apple and muffin slices on the hot grill or under the broiler and cook them for 3–4 minutes, turning once, until they are beginning to turn golden brown.

5 Sprinkle half the cinnamon sugar over the apple slices and toasts and cook for 1 more minute, until they are a rich golden brown.

6 To serve, arrange the apple slices over the toasts and sprinkle them with the remaining cinnamon sugar. Serve hot, with low-fat plain yogurt, if desired.

COOK'S TIP

To keep the quantity of fat within acceptable levels, make this simple, scrumptious dessert with muffins, but for a rare splurge, use brioche or a similar sweet bread.

Banana, Maple and Lime Crêpes

Crêpes are a treat any day of the week, and they can be made in advance and stored in the freezer for convenience.

INGREDIENTS

Serves 4

1 cup all-purpose flour

1 egg white

1 cup skim milk

4 tablespoons cold water

spray oil, for frying

shreds of lime zest, to decorate

For the filling

4 bananas, sliced

3 tablespoons maple syrup or golden syrup

2 tablespoons fresh lime juice

1 Make the crêpe batter by beating together the flour, egg white, milk and water in a bowl until smooth and bubbly. Cover and chill until needed.

2 Apply a light coat of spray oil to a nonstick frying pan. Heat the pan, then pour a little batter, swirling it around the pan to coat evenly.

3 Cook the crêpe until golden, then toss and cook the other side. Slide onto a plate, cover with aluminum foil and keep hot while cooking all the crêpes.

4 Make the filling. Mix the bananas, syrup and lime juice in a pan and simmer gently for 1 minute. Spoon into the crêpes and fold into quarters. Decorate with lime zest.

NUTRITIONAL NOTES

Per portion:

Calories	282
Fat, total	2.79g
Saturated fat	0.47g
Cholesterol	1.25mg
Fiber	2.12g

COOK'S TIP

Pancakes freeze well. To store for later use, interleave them with non-stick baking parchment, wrap and freeze for up to 3 months.

Chinese Chestnut Pancakes

Thin Chinese pancakes, spread with chestnut purée and fried in a little oil, make a deliciously different dessert.

INGREDIENTS

Serves 4

3 ounces canned sweetened chestnut purée

1 tablespoon vegetable oil, for frying

sugar, to serve

For the pancakes

1¼ cups all-purpose flour,
    plus extra for dusting

about 7 tablespoons boiling water

½ teaspoon vegetable oil

1 Make the pancakes. Sift the flour and then pour in the boiling water, stirring as you pour. Mix in the oil and knead the mixture into a dough. Cover with a damp towel and let stand for 30 minutes.

2 Knead the dough until smooth, then roll it out into a long "sausage," cut into eight pieces and roll each into a ball. Flatten each piece, then roll it to a 6-inch pancake.

NUTRITIONAL NOTES
Per portion:

Calories	192
Fat, total	3.8g
Saturated fat	0.47g
Cholesterol	0mg
Fiber	1.8g

3 Heat an ungreased frying pan until hot, then reduce the heat to low and place the pancakes, one at a time, in the pan. Turn them when small brown spots appear on the underside. Keep under a damp cloth until all are cooked.

4 Spread about 1 tablespoon of the chestnut purée over each pancake, then roll it up.

5 Heat the oil in a nonstick wok or frying pan. Add the rolls in batches and fry them briefly until golden brown, turning once.

6 Cut each pancake roll into three or four pieces and sprinkle with sugar. Serve immediately.

Tropical Fruit Crêpes

Fresh fruit, coated with a citrus and honey sauce, makes the perfect pancake filling for this light and tasty dessert.

INGREDIENTS

Serves 4

1 cup self-rising flour

pinch of grated nutmeg

1 tablespoon sugar

1 egg

1¼ cups skim milk

1 tablespoon melted low-fat spread

1 tablespoon dry, shredded coconut (optional)

light sunflower spray oil for frying

confectioners' sugar, for dusting

low-fat plain yogurt, to serve (optional)

For the filling

8 ounces ripe, firm mango

2 bananas

2 kiwis

1 large orange

1 tablespoon lemon juice

2 tablespoons unsweetened orange juice

1 tablespoon honey

1 Sift the flour, nutmeg and sugar into a large bowl. In a separate bowl, beat the egg lightly, then beat in most of the milk. Add to the flour mixture and beat to make a thick, smooth batter. Add the remaining milk, melted spread and coconut, if using, and continue beating until the batter is smooth and of a fairly thin, dropping consistency.

2 Spray a large nonstick frying pan with a very thin coating of oil. Heat, then pour in a little batter to cover the bottom. Fry until golden brown, then toss or turn with a spatula.

3 Repeat Step 2 with the remaining mixture to make about eight crêpes. Dice the mango, chop the bananas and slice the kiwi. Peel the orange and cut into segments.

4 Place the fruit in a bowl. Mix the lemon and orange juices and honey, then pour over the fruit.

5 Spoon a little fruit down the center of a crêpe and fold over each side. Repeat with the remaining crêpes. Dust with confectioners' sugar and serve solo or with low-fat plain yogurt.

NUTRITIONAL NOTES

Per portion:

Calories	303
Fat, total	4.7g
Saturated fat	0.98g
Cholesterol	49.9mg
Fiber	4.2g

Blueberry Pancakes

These fairly thick pancakes are popular as a breakfast option, but are equally good as a dessert.

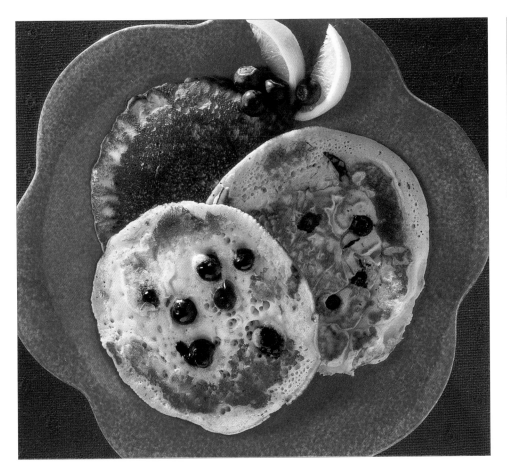

3 Heat a few drops of oil in a pancake pan or heavy frying pan until just hazy. Pour on about 2 tablespoons of the batter and swirl it around until it makes a neat pancake.

4 Cook for 2–3 minutes. When almost set on top, sprinkle on 1–2 tablespoons of the blueberries. As soon as the bottom is loose and golden brown, turn the pancake over.

5 Cook on the second side for only about 1 minute, until golden and crisp. Slide the pancake on to a plate and keep warm while you make 17 more pancakes in the same way. Serve drizzled with maple syrup, if desired, and offer lemon wedges for squeezing, if using.

INGREDIENTS

Serves 6

1 cup self-rising flour

pinch of salt

3 tablespoons sugar

2 eggs

1/2 cup skim milk

1 tablespoon vegetable oil

4 ounces fresh or frozen blueberries

maple syrup and miniature lemon wedges, to serve (optional)

1 Sift the flour and salt into a bowl. Add the sugar. In a separate bowl, beat the eggs thoroughly. Make a well in the flour and stir in the eggs.

2 Gradually blend in a little of the milk to make a smooth batter. Whisk in the rest of the milk for 1–2 minutes. Rest for 20–30 minutes.

COOK'S TIP

Instead of blueberries you could use fresh or thawed and drained frozen blackberries or raspberries.

NUTRITIONAL NOTES

Per portion:

Calories	146
Fat, total	3.9g
Saturated fat	0.76g
Cholesterol	64.6mg
Fiber	0.9g

Apple and Black Currant Crêpes

These crêpes are made with a whole-wheat batter and are filled with a delicious fruit mixture.

INGREDIENTS

Serves 4

1 cup whole-wheat flour

1¼ cups skim milk

1 egg, beaten

1 tablespoon sunflower oil

spray oil, for greasing

half-fat crème fraîche, to serve (optional)

toasted nuts or sesame seeds,
    for sprinkling (optional)

For the filling

1 pound Bramley or other cooking apples

2 cups black currants

2–3 tablespoons water

2 tablespoons light brown sugar

1 Make the crêpe batter. Place the flour in a mixing bowl and make a well in the center.

2 Add a little of the milk with the egg and the oil. Whisk the flour into the liquid, then gradually whisk in the rest of the milk, keeping the batter smooth. Cover the batter and put it in the refrigerator while you prepare the filling.

3 Quarter, peel and core the apples. Slice them into a pan and add the black currants and water. Cook over low heat for 10–15 minutes until the fruit is soft. Stir in enough light brown sugar to sweeten.

4 Apply a light, even coat of spray oil to a crêpe pan. Heat the pan, pour in about 2 tablespoons batter, swirl it around and cook for about 1 minute. Flip the crêpe over with a spatula and cook the other side. Keep the crêpe hot while cooking the remaining crêpes (unless cooking to order).

5 Fill the crêpes with the apple and black currant mixture and fold or roll them up. Serve with a dollop of crème fraîche, if using, and sprinkle with nuts or sesame seeds, if desired.

NUTRITIONAL NOTES

Per portion:

Calories	120
Fat, total	3g
Saturated fat	0.5g
Cholesterol	25mg
Fiber	0g

Cherry Crêpes

These crêpes are virtually fat-free, and lower in calories and higher in fiber than traditional ones.

INGREDIENTS

Serves 4

1/2 cup all-purpose flour

1/2 cup whole-wheat flour

pinch of salt

1 egg white

2/3 cup skim milk

2/3 cup water

spray oil for frying

For the filling

15-ounce can black cherries in syrup

1 1/2 teaspoons arrowroot

2 Apply a light coat of spray oil to a nonstick frying pan. Heat the pan, then pour a little batter, swirling the pan to cover the bottom evenly.

3 Cook until the crêpe is set and golden, then turn to cook the other side. Slide on to paper towels and cook the remaining 8 crêpes.

4 Drain the cherries, reserving the syrup. Mix about 2 tablespoons of the syrup with the arrowroot in a saucepan. Stir in the rest of the syrup. Heat gently, stirring, until the mixture boils, thickens and clears. Add the cherries and stir until heated. Spoon the cherries into the crêpes and fold them in quarters. Serve immediately.

1 Sift the flours and salt into a bowl, adding any bran left in the sieve to the bowl at the end. Make a well in the center of the flour and add the egg white, then the milk and water. Beat with a wooden spoon, gradually incorporating the surrounding flour mixture, then whisk the batter hard until it is smooth and bubbly.

NUTRITIONAL NOTES
Per portion:

Calories	190
Fat, total	1.7g
Saturated fat	0.23g
Cholesterol	0.8mg
Fiber	2.2g

Summer Berry Crêpes

The delicate flavor of these crêpes contrasts beautifully with tangy summer berries.

INGREDIENTS

Serves 4

1 cup self-rising flour

1 large egg

1 1/4 cups skim milk

a few drops of pure vanilla extract

spray oil, for greasing

confectioners' sugar, for dusting

For the fruit

1 tablespoon low-fat spread

1/4 cup sugar

juice of 2 oranges

thinly pared zest of 1/2 orange

3 cups mixed summer berries, such as sliced
   strawberries, yellow raspberries, blueberries
   and red currants

3 tablespoons Grand Marnier or other
   orange-flavored liqueur

1 Preheat the oven to 300°F. To make the crêpes, sift the flour into a large bowl and make a well in the center. Break in the egg and gradually whisk in the milk to make a smooth batter. Stir in the vanilla . Set the batter aside in a cool place for up to half an hour.

2 Apply a light, even coat of spray oil to a 7-inch nonstick frying pan. Whisk the batter, then pour a little of it into the hot pan, swirling to cover the bottom evenly. Cook until the mixture comes away from the sides and the crêpe is golden underneath.

3 Flip over the crêpe with a large spatula and cook the other side briefly until golden. Slide the crêpe onto a heatproof plate. Make seven more crêpes in the same way. Cover the crêpes with foil or another plate and keep them hot in a warm oven.

4 Melt the spread in a heavy frying pan, stir in the sugar and cook gently. Add the orange juice and zest and cook until syrupy. Then add the berries and warm through (reserve some for decoration), add the liqueur and set it on fire. Shake the pan until the flames die down.

5 Fold the pancakes into quarters and arrange two on each plate. Spoon on the berry mixture and dust with confectioners' sugar. Serve the remaining fruit separately.

COOK'S TIP

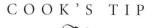

For safety, when igniting a mixture for flambéing, use a long taper or long wooden match and stand back.

NUTRITIONAL NOTES

Per portion:

Calories	285
Fat, total	5g
Saturated fat	1.06g
Cholesterol	59.5mg
Fiber	3.5g

Blueberry and Orange Crêpe Baskets

Impress your guests with these fruit-filled crêpes. When blueberries are out of season, try raspberries.

Serves 6

1¼ cups all-purpose flour

pinch of salt

2 egg whites

scant 1 cup skim milk

⅔ cup orange juice

spray oil, for greasing

For the filling

4 medium-size oranges

2 cups blueberries

NUTRITIONAL NOTES
Per portion:

Calories	165
Fat, total	1.4g
Saturated fat	0.16g
Cholesterol	0.7mg
Fiber	3.2g

1 Preheat the oven to 400ºF. Sift the flour and salt into a bowl. Make a well in the center and add the egg whites, milk and orange juice. Beat the liquid, gradually incorporating the surrounding flour mixture, then whisk the batter until it is smooth and bubbly.

2 Apply a light, even coat of spray oil to a heavy or nonstick crêpe pan and heat it. Pour in just enough batter to cover the bottom of the pan, swirling it to cover the pan evenly.

3 Cook until the pancake has set and is golden underneath and then turn it to cook on the other side. Slide the pancake onto a sheet of paper towel. Cook the remaining batter, to make six pancakes.

4 Invert six small ovenproof bowls or molds on a baking sheet and drape a pancake over each. Bake them for about 10 minutes, until they are crisp and set into shape. Carefully lift the "baskets" off the molds and set aside.

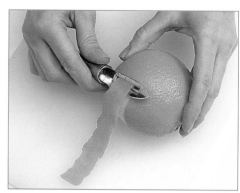

5 Pare a thin piece of orange zest from one orange and cut it in fine strips. Blanch the strips in boiling water for 30 seconds, rinse them in cold water and drain well. Cut all the peel and white pith from the oranges.

6 Cut the oranges into segments, working over a bowl to catch the juice. Add the segments and juice to the blueberries in a pan and warm through gently. Spoon the fruit into the baskets and sprinkle the shreds of zest on top.

COOK'S TIP

Don't fill the baskets until you are ready to serve them, because they will absorb the fruit juice and begin to soften.

Ginger and Honey Syrup

Particularly good for winter desserts, this virtually fat-free sauce can be served hot or cold with fruit salad.

Serves 4

1 lemon

4 green cardamom pods

1 cinnamon stick

2/3 cup honey

3 pieces stem ginger, plus
    2 tablespoons syrup from the jar

4 tablespoons water

3 Place the lemon zest, cardamoms, cinnamon stick, honey, ginger syrup and water in a saucepan. Boil, then simmer for 2 minutes.

4 Chop the ginger and stir it into the sauce with the lemon juice. Pour onto a winter fruit salad or try it with a baked fruit compote. Chill to serve.

1 Thinly pare two strips of zest from the lemon with a potato peeler.

2 Lightly crush the cardamom pods with the back of a heavy-bladed knife. Cut the lemon in half. Reserve half for another recipe and squeeze the juice from the remaining half. Set the juice aside.

NUTRITIONAL NOTES

Per portion:

Calories	145
Fat, total	0.1g
Saturated fat	0g
Cholesterol	0mg
Fiber	0g

Lemon and Lime Sauce

This tangy sauce goes well with crêpes or fruit tarts, or as an accompaniment to an orange or mandarin cheesecake.

Serves 4

1 lemon

2 limes

¼ cup sugar

1½ tablespoons arrowroot

1¼ cups water

freshly made crêpes, to serve

fresh lemon balm or mint leaves, to decorate

NUTRITIONAL NOTES

Per portion:

Calories	75
Fat, total	0.1g
Saturated fat	0g
Cholesterol	0mg
Fiber	0g

1 Using a citrus zester, pare the zests thinly from the lemon and limes. Squeeze the juice from the fruit.

VARIATION

This sauce can also be made with orange and lemon zest, if you prefer.

2 Place all the zest in a pan, cover with water and bring to a boil. Drain through a sieve and set it aside.

3 Mix a little sugar and the arrowroot with enough water to make a smooth paste. Add to the remaining water, heat, and stir until the sauce boils and thickens.

4 Stir in the remaining sugar, the citrus juice and the reserved zest. Serve hot with freshly made crêpes. Decorate with lemon balm or mint.

Cold Low-fat Desserts

✦

Rich Black Currant Coulis

There can be few more impressive desserts than this—port wine jelly with swirled cream hearts.

Serves 8

6 sheets of leaf gelatin

2 cups water

2 cups black currants

1 cup sugar

²/3 cup ruby port

2 tablespoons crème de cassis

¹/2 cup light cream, to decorate

1 In a small bowl, soak the gelatin in 5 tablespoons of the water until soft. Place the black currants, sugar and 1¹/4 cups of the remaining water in a large saucepan. Bring to a boil, lower the heat and simmer for 20 minutes.

2 Strain through a sieve and reserve the cooking liquid in a large bowl. Put the black currants in a bowl and pour in 4 tablespoons of the reserved cooking liquid.

3 Squeeze the water out of the gelatin and place in a saucepan with the port, cassis and remaining water. Heat gently to dissolve the gelatin. Stir the gelatin mixture into the black currant liquid.

4 Run 6–8 molds under cold water, drain and place in a roasting pan. Fill with the port mixture. Chill for at least 6 hours until set. Put the black currants into a food processor, purée until smooth, then pass through a fine sieve.

5 Run a fine knife around each gelatin. Dip each mold in hot water for 5–10 seconds, then turn out onto your hand. Place on a plate and spoon the coulis around the gelatin.

6 To decorate, drop a little cream at intervals onto the coulis. Draw a toothpick through the cream dots, dragging each into a heart shape.

NUTRITIONAL NOTES

Per portion:

Calories	276
Fat, total	3.8g
Saturated fat	2.4g
Cholesterol	11mg
Fiber	2.7g

Raspberry Muesli Layer

As well as being a delicious, low-fat dessert, this muesli can be served for a quick, healthy breakfast.

INGREDIENTS

Serves 4

2 cups fresh or frozen and thawed raspberries
1 cup low-fat yogurt
1/2 cup Swiss-style muesli

3 Sprinkle a layer of Swiss-style muesli onto the yogurt.

4 Continue the layers until all the ingredients have been used. Top each dessert with a whole raspberry.

1 Reserve four raspberries to decorate, then spoon a few raspberries into four stemmed glasses or glass dishes.

2 Top the raspberries in each glass with a spoonful of yogurt.

NUTRITIONAL NOTES
Per portion:

Calories	114
Fat, total	1.7g
Saturated fat	0.48g
Cholesterol	2.3mg
Fiber	2.6g

Strawberries in Spiced Grape Gelatin

The spicy cinnamon combines with the sun-ripened strawberries to make a dessert for a summer dinner party.

INGREDIENTS

Serves 4

2 cups red grape juice

1 cinnamon stick

1 small orange

1 tablespoon powdered gelatin

2 cups strawberries, chopped,
   plus extra to decorate

1 Pour the grape juice into a pan and add the cinnamon stick. Thinly pare the zest from the orange. Add most of it to the pan but shred some pieces and set them aside for the decoration. Place the pan over very low heat for 10 minutes, then remove the flavorings from the grape juice.

2 Squeeze the juice from the orange into a bowl and sprinkle on the powdered gelatin. When the mixture is spongy, stir into the grape juice until it has completely dissolved. Let the gelatin cool in the bowl until just beginning to set.

3 Stir in the strawberries and quickly put into a 4-cup mold or serving dish. Chill until set.

4 Dip the mold quickly into hot water and invert onto a serving plate. Decorate with strawberries and shreds of orange zest.

NUTRITIONAL NOTES
Per portion:

Calories	85
Fat, total	0.2g
Saturated fat	0g
Cholesterol	0mg
Fiber	1.04g

Chilled Oranges in Syrup

This popular classic is light and refreshing. A perfect dish to serve after a heavy main course.

INGREDIENTS

Serves 4

4 oranges

2¹/₂ cups water

1¹/₂ cups sugar

2 tablespoons lemon juice

2 tablespoons orange-flower water or rose-water

¹/₃ cup unsalted pistachios, shelled and chopped

NUTRITIONAL NOTES

Per portion:

Calories	467
Fat, total	4.9g
Saturated fat	0.59g
Cholesterol	0mg
Fiber	3.1g

1 Peel the oranges with a potato peeler, avoiding the pith.

COOK'S TIP

Almonds could be substituted for the pistachios, if desired, but don't be tempted to increase the amount or you'll raise the level of fat.

2 Cut the peel into strips and boil in fresh water several times to remove the bitterness. Drain on paper towels.

3 Place the water, sugar and lemon juice in a pan. Bring to a boil, add the pared zest and simmer until the syrup thickens. Add the orange-flower or rose-water, stir and then cool.

4 Remove any pith and slice the oranges. Arrange in a serving dish, pour on the syrup and chill for 1–2 hours. Serve with pistachios.

Grapes in Grape-yogurt Gelatin

This light, refreshing combination makes a great special-occasion dessert but takes very little time to make.

INGREDIENTS

Serves 4

1³/4 cups white seedless grapes

scant 2 cups unsweetened white grape juice

1 tablespoon powdered gelatin

¹/2 cup low-fat yogurt

1 Set aside four tiny bunches of grapes for decoration. Pull the rest off their stems and cut them in half.

2 Divide the grapes among four stemmed glasses and tilt the glasses on one side, propping them firmly in a bowl of ice.

3 Heat the grape juice in a pan until almost boiling. Remove it from heat and sprinkle the gelatin on the surface, stirring until it dissolves.

4 Pour half the grape juice over the grapes and let set.

5 Cool the remaining grape juice until on the verge of setting, then stir in the low-fat yogurt.

6 Stand the set glasses upright and pour in the yogurt mixture. Chill to set, then decorate the rim of each glass with grapes, and serve.

NUTRITIONAL NOTES

Per portion:

Calories	113
Fat, total	0.4g
Saturated fat	0.16g
Cholesterol	1.3mg
Fiber	0g

COOK'S TIP

For an easier version, stand the glasses upright rather than at an angle—then they can be put in the refrigerator to set rather than packed with ice in a container.

Fresh Citrus Gelatin

Fresh fruit gelatins really are worth the effort—they're packed with fresh flavor, natural color and vitamins.

Serves 4

3 medium oranges

1 lemon

1 lime

1¼ cups water

6 tablespoons sugar

1 tablespoon powdered gelatin

extra slices of citrus fruit,
 to decorate

1 With a sharp knife, cut all the peel and white pith from one orange and carefully remove the segments. Arrange in the bottom of a 3¾-cup mold or dish. Chill.

2 Remove some shreds of citrus zest with a zester and reserve them for decoration. Grate the remaining zest from the lemon and lime and one orange. Place all the grated zest in a pan, with the water and sugar.

3 Heat gently, without boiling, until the sugar has dissolved. Take off the heat. Squeeze the juice from all the rest of the fruit and stir into the pan.

4 Strain the hot liquid into a measuring cup to remove the zest. You should have about 2½ cups of liquid; if necessary, make up the amount with hot water. Sprinkle the gelatin on the liquid and stir until it has dissolved.

COOK'S TIP

To speed up the setting of the fruit segments in gelatin, stand the dish in a bowl of ice. Or, if you're short on time, simply stir the segments into the liquid gelatin, pour into a serving dish and set it all together.

5 Pour a little of the gelatin onto the orange segments and chill until set. Let the remaining gelatin at room temperature to cool but not set.

6 Pour the remaining cooled gelatin into the dish and chill until set. To serve, turn out the gelatin and decorate it with the reserved citrus zest shreds and extra slices of citrus fruit.

NUTRITIONAL NOTES
Per portion:

Calories	137
Fat, total	0.2g
Saturated fat	0g
Cholesterol	0mg
Fiber	2.1g

Orange-blossom Gelatin

The natural fruit flavor of fresh orange juice in this smooth gelatin has a wonderful cleansing quality.

INGREDIENTS

Serves 4

1/3 cup sugar

2/3 cup water

1 ounce powdered gelatin

2 1/2 cups fresh orange juice

2 tablespoons orange-flower water

NUTRITIONAL NOTES

Per portion:

Calories	135
Fat, total	0g
Saturated fat	0g
Cholesterol	0mg
Fiber	0.2g

1 Place the sugar and water in a small saucepan and heat gently to dissolve the sugar. Pour into a heatproof bowl and let cool.

2 Sprinkle the gelatin on the surface of the syrup. Let stand until it has absorbed all the liquid.

3 Gently melt the gelatin over a saucepan of simmering water until it becomes clear and transparent. Let cool. When the gelatin is cold, mix it with the orange juice and orange-flower water.

4 Wet a mold and pour in the gelatin. Chill in the refrigerator for at least 2 hours or until set. Turn out to serve.

Ground Rice Pudding

This delicious and light ground rice pudding, flavored with almonds, is the perfect end to a spicy meal.

INGREDIENTS

Serves 4–6

1/2 cup coarsely ground rice

2 tablespoons ground almonds

4 green cardamom pods, crushed

3 3/4 cups low-fat milk

6 tablespoons sugar

1 tablespoon rose water

1 tablespoon crushed pistachios and silver leaf
   (optional) to decorate

1 Place the ground rice and almonds in a saucepan with the green cardamoms. Add 2 1/2 cups milk and bring to a boil over medium heat, stirring occasionally.

2 Add the remaining milk and cook over medium heat for about ten minutes or until the rice mixture thickens to the consistency of a creamy chicken soup.

3 Stir in the sugar and rose water and continue to cook for another 2 minutes. Serve garnished with pistachios and silver leaf, if desired.

NUTRITIONAL NOTES

Per portion:

Calories	201
Fat, total	8.78g
Saturated fat	2.57g
Cholesterol	14.70mg
Fiber	0g

Clementine Gelatin

This gelatin has a clear fruity taste and can be made extra special by adding a little white rum or Cointreau.

Serves 4

12 clementines

clear unsweetened white grape juice
(see method for amount)

1 tablespoon powdered gelatin

2 tablespoons sugar

4 tablespoons half-fat crème fraîche,
for topping

VARIATION

Use ruby grapefruit instead of clementines, if you prefer. Squeeze the juice from half and segment the rest.

1 Squeeze the juice from eight of the clementines and pour it into a bowl. Make up to 2½ cups with the grape juice, then strain the juice mixture through a fine sieve.

2 Pour half the juice mixture into a pan. Sprinkle the gelatin on top, leave for 5 minutes, then heat gently until the gelatin has dissolved. Stir in the sugar and remaining juice; set aside.

3 Pare the zest very thinly from the remaining fruit and set it aside. Using a sharp knife, cut between the membrane and fruit to separate the citrus segments. Discard the membrane and pith.

4 Place half the segments in four dessert glasses and cover with some of the liquid fruit gelatin. Place in the refrigerator to set.

5 Arrange the remaining segments on top. Pour in the remaining gelatin and chill until set. Cut the clementine zest into shreds. Serve the gelatins topped with a spoonful of crème fraîche and clementine zest shreds.

NUTRITIONAL NOTES

Per portion:

Calories	142
Fat, total	2.5g
Saturated fat	1.4g
Cholesterol	15.8mg
Fiber	1.5g

Mexican Lemony Rice Pudding

Rice pudding is popular all over the world in many different guises. This Mexican version is light and attractive.

INGREDIENTS

Serves 4

½ cup raisins

½ cup short-grain
   (pudding) rice

1-inch strip of pared lime or
   lemon zest

1 cup water

2 cups skim milk

1 cup sugar

¼ teaspoon salt

1-inch piece cinnamon stick

1 egg yolk, well beaten

1 tablespoon low-fat spread

2 teaspoons toasted sliced almonds
   to decorate

orange segments to serve

3 Discard the cinnamon stick. Drain the raisins well. Add the raisins, egg yolk and low-fat spread, stirring constantly until the spread has been absorbed, the raisins evenly distributed and the pudding is rich and creamy.

4 Cook the pudding for a few more minutes. Put the rice into a serving dish and let cool. Decorate with the toasted sliced almonds and add a few orange segments to each serving.

NUTRITIONAL NOTES

Per portion:

Calories	450
Fat, total	4.9g
Saturated fat	0.88g
Cholesterol	53mg
Fiber	1.4g

1 Put the raisins into a small bowl. Cover with warm water and set aside to soak. Put the rice into a saucepan together with the pared lime or lemon zest and water. Bring slowly to a boil, then lower the heat. Cover the pan and simmer gently for about 20 minutes or until all the water has been absorbed.

2 Remove the zest from the rice and discard it. Add the milk, sugar, salt and cinnamon stick. Cook, stirring, over very low heat, until the milk has been absorbed. Do not cover the pan.

Fragrant Rice with Dates

Moroccan rice puddings are sprinkled with either nuts and honey or wrapped in pastry. This is a low-fat version.

INGREDIENTS

Serves 4

1/2 cup short-grain (pudding) rice

about 3 3/4 cups skim milk

2 tablespoons ground rice

1/4 cup sugar

2 tablespoons ground almonds

1 teaspoon vanilla extract

1/2 teaspoon almond extract

a little orange-flower water (optional)

2 tablespoons chopped dates

2 tablespoons unsalted, pistachios, finely chopped

1 Place the rice in a saucepan with 3 cups of the milk and gradually heat until simmering. Cook, uncovered, over very low heat for 30–40 minutes, until the rice is completely tender, stirring frequently.

2 Blend the ground rice with the remaining milk and add to the pan, stirring. Slowly bring back to a boil and cook for 1 minute.

3 Stir in the sugar, ground almonds, vanilla and almond extracts and orange-flower water, if using. Cook until the pudding is thick and creamy.

4 Pour into serving bowls and sprinkle with the chopped dates and pistachios to decorate. Let cool before serving.

NUTRITIONAL NOTES

Per portion:

Calories	270
Fat, total	4.8g
Saturated fat	0.55g
Cholesterol	4.5mg
Fiber	0.4g

Rice Pudding with Mixed Berry Sauce

*A compote of red berries contrasts
beautifully with creamy rice pudding
for a richly flavored cool dessert.*

INGREDIENTS

Serves 6

low-fat spread, for greasing

2 cups short-grain (pudding) rice

scant 1 1/2 cups skim milk

pinch salt

2/3 cup light brown sugar

1 teaspoon pure vanilla extract

2 eggs, beaten

grated zest of 1 lemon

1 teaspoon lemon juice

2 tablespoons low-fat spread

strawberry leaves, to decorate

For the sauce

2 cups strawberries, hulled
    and quartered

2 cups raspberries

1/2 cup sugar

grated zest of 1 lemon

3 Dot the surface of the rice mixture with the spread. Bake for 50 minutes, until the rice is cooked and creamy.

4 Meanwhile, mix the berries and sugar in a saucepan. Stir over low heat until the sugar has dissolved and the fruit is becoming pulpy.

5 Transfer to a bowl and stir in the lemon zest. Cool, then chill the sauce until needed.

6 Remove the rice pudding from the oven. Let cool. Serve with the berry sauce. Decorate with fresh strawberry leaves.

NUTRITIONAL NOTES

Per portion:

Calories	474
Fat, total	4.9g
Saturated fat	0.95g
Cholesterol	65.5mg
Fiber	1.4g

1 Preheat the oven to 325°F. Grease a deep 8-cup baking dish. Add the rice to boiling water and boil for 5 minutes. Drain. Transfer the rice to the prepared baking dish.

2 Combine the milk, salt, brown sugar, vanilla, eggs, lemon zest and juice. Pour onto the rice and stir.

Fresh Fruit with Caramel Rice

This creamy rice pudding with a crisp caramel crust sounds wickedly indulgent but is relatively low in fat.

INGREDIENTS

Serves 4

generous 1/4 cup short-grain (pudding) rice

low-fat spread, for greasing

5 tablespoons brown sugar

pinch of salt

14-ounce can light evaporated milk made up
   to 2¹/2 cups with water

2 crisp apples

1 small fresh pineapple

2 teaspoons lemon juice

1 Preheat the oven to 300°F. Wash the rice under cold water. Drain well and put into a lightly greased soufflé dish.

2 Add 2 tablespoons of the sugar to the dish, with the salt. Pour in the diluted evaporated milk and stir gently. Bake for 2 hours, then let cool for 30 minutes.

3 Meanwhile, peel, core and cut the apples and pineapple into thin slices, then cut the pineapple into chunks. Toss the fruit in lemon juice, coating thoroughly, and set aside.

4 Preheat the broiler and sprinkle the remaining sugar on the rice. Broil for 5 minutes to caramelize the sugar. Let stand for 5 minutes to harden the caramel. Serve with the fresh fruit.

NUTRITIONAL NOTES

Per portion:

Calories	309
Fat, total	4.6g
Saturated fat	2.51g
Cholesterol	34mg
Fiber	2.8g

Rice Fruit Sundae

Cook a rice pudding on top of the stove instead of in the oven for a light creamy texture. Serve cold, topped with fruits.

INGREDIENTS

Serves 4

¹/₃ cup short-grain (pudding) rice

2¹/₂ cups skim milk

1 teaspoon pure vanilla extract

¹/₂ teaspoon ground cinnamon

2 tablespoons sugar

1³/₄ cups strawberries, raspberries
   or blueberries, to serve

1 Put the rice, milk, vanilla extract, cinnamon and sugar into a medium-sized saucepan. Bring to a boil, stirring constantly, and then turn down the heat so that the mixture barely simmers.

2 Cook the rice for 30–40 minutes, stirring occasionally, until the grains are soft. Put into a bowl and let the rice cool, stirring occasionally. Chill the rice in the refrigerator.

NUTRITIONAL NOTES

Per portion:

Calories	169
Fat, total	3.3g
Saturated fat	0.1g
Cholesterol	3mg
Fiber	0.9g

3 Just before serving, stir the rice and spoon into four sundae dishes. Top with the prepared fruit.

VARIATION

Instead of simple pudding rice try using a Thai fragrant or jasmine rice for a delicious natural flavor. For a firmer texture, an Italian arborio rice makes a good pudding too. You could also use other toppings, such as toasted, chopped hazelnuts or toasted coconut. Another fruit combination could be mango, pineapple and banana for a fresh tropical taste.

Summer Pudding

Summer pudding is an annual treat, and need not be high in fat if you avoid serving it with cream.

INGREDIENTS

Serves 6

1 loaf of white crusty bread,
   1–2 days old, sliced

6 cups fresh red currants

6 tablespoons sugar

4 tablespoons water

4 cups mixed berries, plus extra to decorate

sprig of mint, to decorate

juice of 1/2 lemon

NUTRITIONAL NOTES

Per portion:

Calories	272
Fat, total	1.6g
Saturated fat	0g
Cholesterol	0mg
Fiber	7.6g

1 Trim the crusts from the bread slices and cut a round to fit in the bottom of a 6-cup pudding mold. Line the mold with bread slices, overlapping them slightly. Reserve enough to cover the top of the basin. Mix the red currants with 1/4 cup of the sugar and the water in a saucepan. Heat gently, lightly crushing the berries. When the sugar has dissolved, remove from heat.

2 Put the red currant mixture into a food processor and process until smooth. Press through a fine sieve set over a bowl. Discard the pressed fruit pulp left in the strainer.

3 Put the mixed berries in a bowl with the remaining sugar and the lemon juice. Stir well.

4 One at a time, remove the cut bread pieces from the mold and dip them in the red currant purée. Replace to line the mold evenly.

5 Spoon the berries into the lined mold, pressing them down evenly. Top with the reserved cut bread slices, which have been dipped in the red currant purée.

6 Cover the mold with plastic wrap. Set a small plate, just big enough to fit inside the rim of the mold, on top of the pudding. Weigh it down with cans of food. Chill in the refrigerator for 8–24 hours.

7 To turn out, remove the weights, plate and plastic wrap. Run a knife between the mold and the pudding to loosen it. Invert onto a serving plate. Decorate with a sprig of mint and a few berries. Serve in wedges.

Autumn Pudding

Here is an autumn version of the traditional summer pudding, served with apples, plums and blackberries.

INGREDIENTS

Serves 6

1 pound apples

1 pound plums, halved and pitted

2 cups blackberries

4 tablespoons apple juice

sugar or honey, to sweeten (optional)

8 slices of whole-wheat bread, crusts removed

mint sprig and blackberry, to decorate

half-fat crème fraîche, to serve (optional)

3 Spoon the fruit into the mold with enough juice to moisten.

4 Set aside any remaining juice. Cover the fruit completely with bread. Fit a plate on the top, resting just below the rim and stand the mold in a larger bowl to catch any juice. Weight the plate and chill overnight.

5 Turn the pudding out on a plate and pour the reserved juice onto any areas that have not absorbed the juice. Decorate with the mint sprig and blackberry. Serve with crème fraîche, if desired.

1 Quarter the apples, remove the cores and peel, and slice them into a saucepan. Add the plums, blackberries and apple juice. Cover and cook gently for 10–15 minutes, until tender. Sweeten, if necessary, with a little sugar or honey.

2 Line the bottom and sides of a 5-cup pudding mold with slices of bread, cut to fit. Press together tightly.

NUTRITIONAL NOTES

Per portion:

Calories	141
Fat, total	1.1g
Saturated fat	0.17g
Cholesterol	0mg
Fiber	5.4g

Two-tone Yogurt Ring with Tropical Fruit

A light and colorful dessert with a truly tropical flavor, combining mango, kiwi and Cape gooseberries together.

Serves 6

3/4 cup tropical fruit juice

1 tablespoon powdered gelatin

3 egg whites

2/3 cup low-fat yogurt

finely grated zest of 1 lime

For the filling

1 mango

2 kiwis

10–12 Cape gooseberries,
   plus extra to decorate

juice of 1 lime

1 Pour the tropical fruit juice into a small pan and sprinkle the powdered gelatin on the surface. Heat gently until the gelatin has completely dissolved.

NUTRITIONAL NOTES

Per portion:

Calories	87
Fat, total	0.5g
Saturated fat	0.13g
Cholesterol	1mg
Fiber	2.3g

2 Whisk the egg whites in a grease-free bowl until they hold peaks. Continue whisking hard, gradually adding the yogurt and lime zest.

3 Continue whisking hard and pour in the hot gelatin mixture in a steady stream, until evenly mixed.

4 Quickly pour the mixture into a 6¼-cup ring mold. Chill the mold in the refrigerator until set. The mixture will separate into two layers.

5 Halve, pit, peel and dice the mango. Peel and slice the kiwi. Remove the husks from the Cape gooseberries and cut them in half. Toss all the fruits in a bowl and stir in the lime juice.

6 Run a knife around the edge of the ring to loosen the mixture. Dip the pan quickly into hot water, then turn it out onto a serving plate. Spoon all the prepared fruit into the center of the ring, decorate with the reserved Cape gooseberries and serve immediately.

VARIATION

Any mixture of fruit works in this recipe, depending on the season. Try using apple juice in the ring mixture and fill it with luscious, red summer berries.

Fruited Rice Ring

This looks beautiful turned out of a ring mold, but you can stir the fruit into the rice and serve in individual dishes.

2 Meanwhile, mix the dried fruit and orange juice in a pan and bring to a boil. Cover, then simmer very gently for about 1 hour, until tender and no liquid remains.

3 Remove the cinnamon stick from the rice and stir in the sugar and orange zest, mixing thoroughly.

4 Put the fruit in a lightly oiled 6¼-cup ring mold. Spoon on the rice, smoothing down firmly. Chill.

5 Run a knife around the edge of the mold and turn out the rice carefully onto a serving plate.

INGREDIENTS

Serves 4

5 tablespoons short-grain (pudding) rice

3¾ cups low-fat milk

1 cinnamon stick

1½ cups dried mixed fruit

1½ cups orange juice

3 tablespoons sugar

finely grated zest of 1 small orange

low-fat oil, for greasing

1 Mix the rice, milk and cinnamon stick in a large pan and bring to a boil. Lower the heat, cover and simmer, stirring occasionally, for about 1½ hours, until no liquid remains.

NUTRITIONAL NOTES
Per portion:

Calories	343
Fat, total	4.4g
Saturated fat	2.26g
Cholesterol	15.75mg
Fiber	1.07g

Dried Fruit Fool

This light, fluffy dessert can be made with a single dried fruit—try dried peaches, prunes, apples or apricots.

INGREDIENTS

Serves 4

1¼ cups dried fruit, such as apricots, peaches, prunes or apples

1¼ cups fresh orange juice

1 cup low-fat fromage frais

2 egg whites

fresh mint sprigs, to decorate

NUTRITIONAL NOTES

Per portion:

Calories	180
Fat, total	0.63g
Saturated fat	0.06g
Cholesterol	0.5mg
Fiber	4.8g

1 Put the dried fruit in a saucepan, add the orange juice and heat gently until boiling. Lower the heat, cover and simmer gently for 3 minutes.

2 Cool slightly. Put into a food processor or blender and process until smooth. Stir in the fromage frais.

3 Whisk the egg whites in a grease-free bowl until stiff enough to hold soft peaks, then slowly fold into the fruit mixture until it is all combined.

4 Spoon into four stemmed glasses or one large serving dish. Chill for at least 1 hour. Decorate with the mint sprigs just before serving.

COOK'S TIP

To make a speedier fool, leave out the egg whites and simply swirl together the fruit mixture and fromage frais.

Passion Fruit and Apple Foam

Passion fruit have a delicious flavor that lifts this simple apple dessert. You could use two finely chopped kiwi instead.

INGREDIENTS

Serves 4

1 pound apples
6 tablespoons unsweetened apple juice
3 passion fruit
3 egg whites
1 red-skinned apple, to decorate
1 teaspoon lemon juice

1 Peel, core and roughly chop the apples. Put them in a pan with the apple juice.

2 Bring the liquid to a boil, then lower the heat and cover the pan. Cook gently, stirring occasionally, until the apple is very tender.

3 Remove from heat and beat the apple mixture with a wooden spoon until it forms a fairly smooth purée (or purée the apple in a food processor, if you prefer).

4 Cut the passion fruit in half and scoop out the flesh. Stir into the apple purée to mix thoroughly.

5 Place the egg whites in a grease-free bowl and whisk until they form soft peaks. Fold them into the apple mixture. Spoon the apple foam into four serving dishes. Let cool.

6 Thinly slice the red-skinned apple and brush the slices with lemon juice to prevent them from browning. Arrange the slices on top of the apple foam and serve cold.

COOK'S TIP

It is important to use a good apple, such as a Bramley, for this recipe, because its fluffy texture breaks down easily into a purée. You can use hard apples but will probably have to purée them in a food processor.

NUTRITIONAL NOTES
Per portion:

Calories	80
Fat, total	0.2g
Saturated fat	0g
Cholesterol	0mg
Fiber	2.9g

Raspberry and Mint Bavarois

A sophisticated dessert that can be made a day in advance to impress guests at a special dinner party.

INGREDIENTS

Serves 6

4 cups fresh or thawed frozen raspberries

2 tablespoons confectioners' sugar

2 tablespoons lemon juice

1 tablespoon finely chopped fresh mint

2 tablespoons powdered gelatin

5 tablespoons boiling water

1 1/4 cups low-fat custard

1 cup low-fat plain yogurt

fresh mint sprigs, to decorate

2 Press the purée through a sieve to remove the raspberry seeds. Pour into a measuring cup and stir in the mint.

5 Mix the custard and low-fat yogurt in a bowl and stir in the remaining fruit purée. Dissolve the rest of the gelatin in the remaining boiling water and stir it in quickly.

1 Reserve a few raspberries for decoration. Place the remaining raspberries in a food processor. Add the confectioners' sugar and lemon juice and process into a smooth purée.

3 Sprinkle 1 teaspoon of the gelatin over 2 tablespoons of the boiling water, stirring until it has dissolved. Stir into 2/3 cup of fruit purée.

6 Pour the raspberry custard into the mold and chill it until it has set completely. To serve, dip the mold quickly into a bowl of hot water and then turn it out on a serving plate. Decorate with the reserved raspberries and the mint sprigs.

NUTRITIONAL NOTES
Per portion:

Calories	131
Fat, total	2.4g
Saturated fat	1.36g
Cholesterol	4.1mg
Fiber	1.9g

4 Pour this into a 4-cup mold, and chill in the refrigerator until just setting. Tilt the mold to swirl the setting gelatin around the sides, and chill until set completely.

COOK'S TIP

You can make this dessert using frozen raspberries, which have good color and flavor. Let them thaw at room temperature, and use any juice in the gelatin.

Raspberry and Cranberry Gelatin

INGREDIENTS

Serves 6–8

4³/4-ounce envelope raspberry gelatin

²/3 cup boiling water

1 cup raspberry and cranberry juice

1 cup fresh strawberries

²/3 cup raspberries (fresh or frozen)

1 large red-skinned apple, cored and chopped

NUTRITIONAL NOTES
Per portion:

Calories	276
Fat, total	3.8g
Saturated fat	2.4g
Cholesterol	11mg
Fiber	2.7g

1 Break up the gelatin into a heat-proof measuring cup and pour in the boiling water. Stir until completely dissolved. Pour in the raspberry and cranberry juice and leave until the gelatin is beginning to set.

2 Halve or quarter the strawberries, depending on their size. If using frozen raspberries, leave them in the freezer until you want the gelatin to set. Prepare the apple at the last moment.

3 Have ready a pretty 5-cup mold, rinsed out with cold water. When the gelatin is beginning to thicken, stir in the fruits. (With frozen raspberries it will set almost immediately, so you have to work quickly.) Spoon into the mold and chill until set.

4 Turn out the gelatin onto a serving plate and serve with custard, fromage frais or frozen yogurt.

Blackberry and Apple Romanoff

INGREDIENTS

Serves 6–8

3–4 tart apples, peeled, cored and chopped

3 tablespoons sugar

1 cup half-fat double cream

1 teaspoon grated lemon zest

6 tablespoons plain yogurt

4–6 crisp meringues, roughly crumbled

2 cups blackberries (fresh or frozen)

whipped cream, a few blackberries and mint leaves, to decorate

1 Line a 4–5-cup freezerproof pudding mold with plastic wrap. Toss the apples into a pan with 2 tablespoons sugar and cook for 2–3 minutes or until softening. Mash with a fork and let cool.

2 Whip the cream and fold in the lemon zest, yogurt, the remaining sugar, the apples and meringues.

3 Gently stir in the blackberries, then put the mixture into the lined freezerproof pudding mold and freeze for 1–3 hours.

4 Turn out onto a plate and remove the plastic wrap. Decorate with whirls of cream, blackberries and mint.

NUTRITIONAL NOTES
Per portion:

Calories	148
Fat, total	7.0g
Saturated fat	4.3g
Cholesterol	17mg
Fiber	1.7g

Clementines in Cinnamon Caramel

The combination of sweet yet sharp clementines and caramel sauce with a hint of spice is divine.

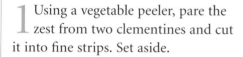

Serves 4

8–12 clementines, about 1–1 1/4 pounds

1 cup sugar

1 1/4 cups warm water

2 cinnamon sticks

2 tablespoons orange-flavored liqueur

1/4 cup shelled, unsalted pistachios

1 Using a vegetable peeler, pare the zest from two clementines and cut it into fine strips. Set aside.

2 Peel the clementines, removing all the pith but keeping each fruit intact. Put the fruits in a heatproof serving bowl.

3 Gently heat the sugar in a pan until it dissolves and turns a rich golden brown. Immediately turn off the heat.

4 Protecting your hand with a dish towel, carefully pour in the warm water (the mixture will bubble and splutter). Bring slowly to a boil, stirring, until the caramel has completely dissolved.

5 Add the shredded peel and cinnamon sticks, then simmer for 5 minutes. Stir in the orange liqueur.

6 Cool the syrup for 10 minutes, then pour it over the clementines. Cover the bowl, cool, then chill for several hours or overnight.

7 Blanch the unsalted pistachios in boiling water. Drain, cool and remove outer skins. Decorate the clementines by sprinkling the nuts on top. Serve immediately.

NUTRITIONAL NOTES
Per portion:

Calories	328
Fat, total	3.5g
Saturated fat	0.42g
Cholesterol	0mg
Fiber	1.4g

Yogurt with Apricots and Pistachios

Drain yogurt overnight to make it thick and more luscious. Add honeyed apricots and nuts for an exotic yet simple dessert.

Serves 4

2 cups low-fat yogurt

3/4 cup dried apricots, snipped

1 tablespoon honey

2 teaspoons roughly chopped unsalted
   pistachios, plus extra for sprinkling

ground cinnamon, for sprinkling

3 Add the yogurt to the apricot mixture, then add the nuts. Spoon into sundae dishes, sprinkle on a little cinnamon and nuts and chill.

NUTRITIONAL NOTES
Per portion:

Calories	164
Fat, total	4.5g
Saturated fat	2g
Cholesterol	5.5mg
Fiber	2.8g

2 Discard the yogurt whey. In a saucepan cover the apricots with water, simmer to soften. Drain, cool, then put into a bowl and add the honey.

1 Place yogurt in a sieve over a bowl. Drain overnight in the refrigerator.

Raspberries and Fruit Purée

Three fruit purées, swirled together, make a kaleidoscopic garnish for a nest of raspberries.

Serves 4–6·

1 cup raspberries

1/2 cup red wine

confectioners' sugar, for dusting

For the decoration

1 large mango, peeled and chopped

14 ounces kiwi, peeled and chopped

1 cup raspberries

confectioners' sugar, to taste

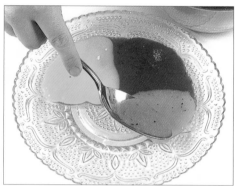

1 Place the raspberries in a bowl with the red wine and let macerate for about 2 hours.

2 Purée separately in a food processor, the mango, kiwi, and the remaining raspberries, adding water if necessary. Press each purée through a sieve into a bowl. Sweeten the purées with sifted confectioners' sugar.

3 Spoon each purée onto a serving plate, separating the kiwi and mango with the raspberry purée as if creating a four-wedged pie. Gently tap the plate on the work surface to settle the purées against each other.

4 Using a skewer, draw a spiral outward from the center of the plate to the rim. Drain the macerated raspberries, dust them heavily with confectioners' sugar and pile them in the center of the purées.

NUTRITIONAL NOTES

Per portion:

Calories	154
Fat, total	0.9g
Saturated fat	0g
Cholesterol	0mg
Fiber	6.7g

Caramel Flan with Fresh Fruit

A creamy caramel dessert is a wonderful way to end a meal. It is light and delicious, and this recipe is very simple.

INGREDIENTS

Serves 6
Caramel
2 tablespoons sugar
2 tablespoons water

Custard
6 medium eggs
4 drops vanilla extract
1/2 cup sugar
3 cups low-fat milk
fresh fruit for serving

1 To make the caramel, place the sugar and water in a heatproof dish and place in a microwave. Cook for 4 minutes on high or until the sugar has caramelized. Alternatively, melt in a pan until pale gold in color. Pour into a 5-cup soufflé dish. Let cool.

2 Preheat the oven to 350°F. To make the custard, break the eggs into a medium mixing bowl and whisk until frothy.

6 Loosen the custard from the side of the dish with a knife. Place a serving dish on top of the soufflé dish and invert, giving a gentle shake.

7 Arrange any fruit of your choice around the caramel and serve.

3 Stir in the vanilla and gradually add the sugar, then the milk, whisking continuously.

4 Pour the custard over the top of the caramel.

5 Cook in the preheated oven for 35–40 minutes. Remove from the oven and let cool.

NUTRITIONAL NOTES
Per portion:

Calories	229
Fat, total	7.40g
Saturated fat	2.77g
Cholesterol	201.25mg
Fiber	0g

Crimson Pears

Poached pears in red wine are among the simplest of sweet treats but look really spectacular.

INGREDIENTS

Serves 4

1 bottle of red wine

3/4 cup sugar

3 tablespoons honey

juice of 1/2 lemon

1 cinnamon stick

1 vanilla bean, split lengthwise

2-inch piece of pared orange zest

1 whole clove

1 black peppercorn

4 firm, ripe pears

low-fat plain yogurt, to serve (optional)

mint leaves, to decorate

1 In a large saucepan combine the wine, sugar, honey, lemon juice, cinnamon, vanilla bean, orange zest, clove and peppercorn. Heat gently, stirring, until the sugar dissolves.

2 Meanwhile, peel the pears, leaving the cores and stems intact. Slice a small piece off the bottom of each pear so it will stand upright.

3 Gently place the pears in the wine mixture. Simmer uncovered for 20–35 minutes, until the pears are evenly cooked and just tender.

4 With a slotted spoon, gently transfer the pears to a bowl. Continue to boil the poaching liquid until reduced by about half. Put into a bowl and let cool.

5 Strain the cooled liquid over the pears. Chill for at least 3 hours.

6 Place the pears in serving dishes, spoon on the liquid and decorate with a mint leaf. Serve solo or with low-fat yogurt.

NUTRITIONAL NOTES

Per portion:

Calories	398
Fat, total	0.2g
Saturated fat	0g
Cholesterol	0mg
Fiber	3.3g

Apple Foam with Blackberries

This lovely light dish is perfect if you want a dessert but nothing too rich or too filling.

INGREDIENTS

Serves 4

2 cups blackberries

2/3 cup unsweetened
   apple juice

1 teaspoon powdered gelatin

1 tablespoon honey

2 egg whites

1 Place the blackberries in a pan with 4 tablespoons of the apple juice and heat gently until the fruit is soft. remove from heat, cool, then chill.

2 Sprinkle the gelatin onto the remaining apple juice in a small pan and stir over low heat until dissolved. Stir in the honey.

3 Whisk the egg whites until they hold stiff peaks. Continue whisking hard and pour in the hot gelatin mixture gradually, until well mixed.

4 Quickly spoon the foam into rough mounds on individual plates. Chill. Serve with the blackberries and juice spooned around.

NUTRITIONAL NOTES

Per portion:

Calories	49
Fat, total	0.2g
Saturated fat	0g
Cholesterol	0mg
Fiber	1.7g

Sensational Strawberries

Strawberries release their finest flavor when moistened with a sauce of raspberries and passion fruit.

Serves 4

2 cups raspberries, fresh or frozen

3 tablespoons sugar

1 passion fruit

6 cups small strawberries

cookies, to serve (optional)

1 Mix the raspberries and sugar in a saucepan and heat gently until the raspberries release their juices. Simmer for 5 minutes. Let cool.

2 Cut the passion fruit in half and scoop out the seeds and juice into a small bowl.

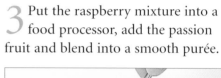

3 Put the raspberry mixture into a food processor, add the passion fruit and blend into a smooth purée.

4 Press the purée through a fine nylon sieve placed over a bowl to remove the seeds.

5 Fold the strawberries into the sauce, then spoon into four stemmed glasses. Serve with the cookies, if desired, but these will increase the total fat content of the dessert.

NUTRITIONAL NOTES

Per portion:

Calories	115
Fat, total	0.5g
Saturated fat	0g
Cholesterol	0mg
Fiber	4.2g

Crunchy Fruit Layers

This simple, almost instant, dessert contrasts smooth and crunchy textures. Other fruits can equally well be used.

INGREDIENTS

Serves 2

1 peach or nectarine

1 cup muesli

2/3 cup low-fat plain yogurt

1 tablespoon jam

1 tablespoon fruit juice

1 Remove the pit from the peach or nectarine and cut the fruit into bite-size pieces with a sharp knife.

2 Divide the fruit evenly between two tall glasses, reserving a few pieces for decoration.

3 Sprinkle the muesli on the fruit in an even layer, then top with the low-fat yogurt.

4 Stir the jam and the fruit juice together in a cup, then drizzle the mixture onto the yogurt. Decorate with the reserved peach or nectarine pieces and serve immediately.

NUTRITIONAL NOTES

Per portion:

Calories	227
Fat, total	2.7g
Saturated fat	0.98g
Cholesterol	3.0mg
Fiber	3.6g

Berry Pavlova

There is a lot of sugar in meringues, but for special occasions this is the queen of desserts.

Serves 4

4 egg whites

pinch salt

3/4 cup sugar

2 tablespoons red currant jelly

1 tablespoon rose water

1 1/4 cups low-fat plain yogurt

4 cups mixed berries, such as blackberries, blueberries, red currants, raspberries or loganberries

2 teaspoons sifted confectioners' sugar

1 Preheat the oven to 275ºF. Oil a baking sheet. Whisk the egg whites with a pinch of salt in a spotlessly clean bowl, until they are white and stiff. Slowly add the sugar and keep whisking until the mixture forms stiff, glossy peaks.

NUTRITIONAL NOTES

Per portion:

Calories	302
Fat, total	3.9g
Saturated fat	2.37g
Cholesterol	5.3mg
Fiber	3.1g

2 Spoon the meringue into a 10-inch round on the baking sheet, making a slight indentation in the center to give it a swirled rim. Bake for 1–1 1/2 hours, until the meringue is firm. Keep checking, as the meringue can easily overcook and brown. Transfer the meringue to a serving plate.

3 Melt the red currant jelly in a small heatproof bowl resting over hot water. Cool slightly, then spread the jelly in the center of the meringue. Gently mix the rose water with the low-fat yogurt and spoon into the center of the meringue. Pile the fruits on top and dust with confectioners' sugar.

Figs with Ricotta Cream

Fresh, ripe figs are full of natural sweetness. This simple recipe makes the most of their beautiful, intense flavor.

Serves 4

4 ripe, fresh figs

1/2 cup ricotta cheese

3 tablespoons half-fat crème fraîche

1 tablespoon honey

1/2 teaspoon pure vanilla extract

freshly grated nutmeg, to decorate

COOK'S TIP

The honey can be omitted and replaced with a little artificial sweetener.

1 Using a small sharp knife, trim the stems from the figs. Make four cuts through each fig from the stem-end, cutting them almost through but being careful to leave them joined at the bottom.

2 Place the figs on serving plates and open them out.

3 In a bowl, mix the ricotta cheese, crème fraîche, honey and vanilla.

4 Spoon a little ricotta cream mixture onto each plate and sprinkle with grated nutmeg to serve.

NUTRITIONAL NOTES	
Per portion:	
Calories	97
Fat, total	5.0g
Saturated fat	3.04g
Cholesterol	26.2mg
Fiber	0.8g

Low-fat
Pastries,
Cakes & Pies

⋄ ✦ ⋄

Spiced Mango Phyllo Fingers

Mangoes have a wonderful texture and look great simply sliced and fanned out next to these phyllo fingers.

INGREDIENTS

Serves 8

4 mangoes

6 phyllo pastry sheets

7 tablespoons butter, melted

3 tablespoons light brown sugar

4 teaspoons ground cinnamon

confectioners' sugar, for dusting

1 Preheat the oven to 400°F. Set the most perfect mango aside for the decoration. Peel the remaining mangoes and slice the flesh. Cut the flesh across into 1/8-inch thick slices.

2 Keeping the rest of the phyllo covered with a damp cloth, lay one sheet on a baking sheet and brush with melted butter. Mix the brown sugar and cinnamon and sprinkle one-fifth of the mixture on the phyllo. Lay a sheet of phyllo on top and repeat for the other 5 sheets, ending with a phyllo sheet.

NUTRITIONAL NOTES
Per portion:

Calories	207
Fat, total	5.0g
Saturated fat	2.75g
Cholesterol	11.5mg
Fiber	3.6g

3 Brush the top phyllo sheet with butter, trim off the excess pastry and lay the sliced mango in neat rows across the layered phyllo, to cover it completely. Brush with reserved butter and bake for 30 minutes. Let cool on the baking tray, then cut into fingers.

4 Slice the flesh from either side of the pit of the reserved mango. Cut each piece in half lengthwise. Make four long cuts, almost to the end, in each quarter. Dust with confectioners' sugar. Put on a plate and carefully fan out the slices. Serve with the mango fingers.

Phyllo Rhubarb Chiffon Pie

Phyllo pastry is low in fat and is easy to bake. Keep a package in the freezer, ready to make impressive desserts like this one.

Serves 3

1¼ pounds pink rhubarb

1 teaspoon allspice

finely grated zest and juice of 1 orange

1 tablespoon sugar

1 tablespoon low-fat spread

3 sheets phyllo pastry, thawed if frozen

VARIATION

Other fruit such as apples, pears, peaches, cherries or gooseberries can be used in this pie—try it with whatever is in season.

1 Preheat the oven to 400°F. Trim the leaves and ends from the rhubarb sticks and chop them into 1-inch pieces. Place them in a medium-sized mixing bowl.

2 Add the allspice, orange zest and juice and sugar; toss well to coat evenly. Put the rhubarb into a 4-cup pie pan.

3 Melt the spread and brush over the phyllo sheets. Crumple the phyllo loosely and arrange on the filling.

4 Place the pan on a baking sheet and bake the pie for 20 minutes, until golden brown. Reduce the heat to 350°F and bake for 10–15 more minutes, until the rhubarb is tender. Serve warm.

NUTRITIONAL NOTES
Per portion:

Calories	118
Fat, total	3g
Saturated fat	0.65g
Cholesterol	0.3mg
Fiber	2.4g

Apricot and Pear Phyllo Roulade

This is a very quick way of making a strudel—normally very time consuming to do—but it tastes delicious!

Serves 6

1/2 cup dried apricots, chopped

2 tablespoons apricot conserve

1 teaspoon lemon juice

1/3 cup light brown sugar

2 pears, peeled, cored and chopped

2 tablespoons sliced almonds

2 tablespoons low-fat spread, melted

8 sheets phyllo pastry, thawed if frozen

1 teaspoon confectioners' sugar, for dusting

1 Put the apricots, apricot conserve, lemon juice, brown sugar and pears into a pan and heat for 5–7 minutes.

2 Remove from heat and cool. Mix in the sliced almonds. Preheat the oven to 400°F. Melt the low-fat spread completely.

3 Lightly grease a baking sheet. Layer the pastry on the baking sheet, brushing each layer with the melted low-fat spread.

4 Spoon the filling down the phyllo, keeping it to one side of the center and within 1 inch of each end. Lift the other side of the pastry up by sliding a spatula underneath.

5 Fold this pastry over the filling, tucking the edge under. Seal the ends neatly and brush all over with spread again. Bake for 15–20 minutes, until golden. Dust with confectioners' sugar and serve hot, cut into diamonds.

NUTRITIONAL NOTES

Per portion:

Calories	190
Fat, total	4.1g
Saturated fat	0.54g
Cholesterol	0.1mg
Fiber	2.6g

Apricot Parcels

These phyllo parcels are a good way to use up mincemeat and marzipan that have been in your cupboard since Christmas!

NUTRITIONAL NOTES

Per portion:

Calories	234
Fat, total	4.4g
Saturated fat	1.1g
Cholesterol	3.7mg
Fiber	1.5g

2 Place an apricot half, hollow up, in the center of each pastry star. Mix the mincemeat, crushed macaroons and marzipan and spoon a little of the mixture into the hollow in each apricot.

3 Top with another apricot half, then bring the corners of each pastry together and squeeze to make a gathered purse.

4 Place the purses on a baking sheet and brush each with a little melted spread. Bake for 15–20 minutes or until the pastry is golden and crisp. Lightly dust with confectioners' sugar to serve.

INGREDIENTS

Serves 8

12 ounces phyllo pastry, thawed if frozen

2 tablespoons low-fat spread, melted

8 apricots, halved and pitted

4 tablespoons luxury mincemeat

12 macaroons, crushed

2 tablespoons grated marzipan

confectioners' sugar, for dusting

1 Preheat the oven to 400°F. Cut the phyllo into thirty-two 7-inch squares. Brush 4 of the squares with melted spread and stack them, giving each layer a quarter turn forming a star shape. Repeat to make 8.

COOK'S TIP

If you have run out of mincemeat, use mixed dried fruit instead.

Phyllo Fruit Scrunchies

*Quick and easy to make, these pastries
are ideal to serve as snacks. Eat them
warm or they will lose their crispness.*

INGREDIENTS

Serves 6

5 apricots or plums

4 sheets phyllo pastry, thawed if frozen

4 teaspoons low-fat spread, melted

1/3 cup brown sugar

2 tablespoons sliced almonds

confectioners' sugar, for dusting

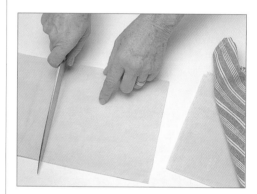

1 Preheat the oven to 375°F. Halve
the apricots or plums, remove the
pits and slice the fruit. Cut the phyllo
pastry into twelve 7-inch squares. Pile
the squares on top of each other and
cover with a damp cloth to prevent
them from drying out.

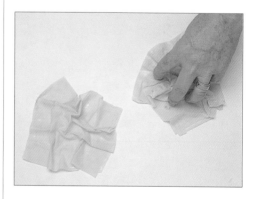

2 Remove one square of phyllo and
brush it with melted spread. Lay a
second phyllo square on top, then, using
your fingers, mold into folds. Quickly
make five more scrunchies in the same
way so that the pastry does not dry out.

3 Arrange a few slices of fruit in the
folds of each scrunchie, then
sprinkle generously with the brown
sugar and almonds.

4 Place the scrunchies on a baking
sheet. Bake for 8–10 minutes, until
golden brown, then loosen the
scrunchies from the baking sheet with
a spatula and transfer to a wire rack.
Dust with confectioners' sugar and
serve immediately.

NUTRITIONAL NOTES

Per portion:

Calories	132
Fat, total	4.19g
Saturated fat	0.63g
Cholesterol	0mg
Fiber	0.67g

Plum Phyllo Pockets

Ricotta-filled plums, baked in phyllo pastry, provide a wonderful mix of sweet and savory tastes for the palate.

INGREDIENTS

Serves 4

1/2 cup low-fat ricotta cheese

1 tablespoon light brown sugar

1/2 teaspoon ground cloves

8 large, firm plums, halved and pitted

8 sheets phyllo pastry, thawed if frozen

sunflower oil, for brushing

confectioners' sugar, for dusting

1 Preheat the oven to 425°F. Mix the low-fat ricotta cheese, brown sugar and ground cloves to make a firm paste.

2 Sandwich the plum halves together with a spoonful of the cheese mixture. Stack the phyllo pastry sheets and cut into 16 pieces, each 9 inches square. Brush each piece with oil and place them diagonally over each other.

3 Place a plum on each phyllo pastry square, lift up the sides and pinch the corners together. Place on a baking sheet. Bake for 15–18 minutes, until golden, then dust with confectioners' sugar.

NUTRITIONAL NOTES

Per portion:

Calories	188
Fat, total	1.87g
Saturated fat	0.27g
Cholesterol	0.29mg
Fiber	2.55g

Tropical Fruit Phyllo Clusters

These fruity phyllo clusters are ideal for a family treat or a dinner party dessert. They are delicious either hot or cold.

INGREDIENTS

Serves 8

1 banana, sliced

1 small mango, peeled, pitted and diced

lemon juice, for sprinkling

1 small apple, coarsely grated

6 fresh or dried dates, pitted and chopped

1/3 cup dried pineapple, chopped

1/3 cup golden raisins

1/3 cup light brown sugar

1 teaspoon ground allspice

8 sheets phyllo pastry, thawed if frozen

2 tablespoons sunflower oil

confectioners' sugar, for dusting

NUTRITIONAL NOTES

Per portion:

Calories	197
Fat, total	3.58g
Saturated fat	0.44g
Cholesterol	0mg
Fiber	2.31g

1 Preheat the oven to 400°F. Line a baking sheet with nonstick baking parchment. In a medium-sized mixing bowl, toss the banana slices and diced mango in lemon juice to prevent discoloration.

2 Add the apple, dates, pineapple, golden raisins, sugar and spice to the bowl and mix well.

3 To make each fruit cluster, cut each sheet of phyllo pastry in half crosswise to make two squares or rectangles (16 pieces in total). Lightly brush two pieces of pastry with oil and place one on top of the other at a 45° angle to form a star shape.

COOK'S TIP

To prevent phyllo pastry from drying out and crumbling, cover with a damp cloth before brushing with the oil.

4 Spoon some fruit filling into the center, gather the pastry up over the filling and secure with string. Place the cluster on the prepared baking sheet and lightly brush all over with oil.

5 Repeat with the remaining pastry squares and filling to make a total of 8 fruit clusters. Bake for 25–30 minutes, until golden brown and crisp.

6 Carefully snip and remove the string from each cluster and serve hot or cold, dusted with confectioners' sugar.

Red Currant Phyllo Baskets

Phyllo pastry is low in fat and needs only a fine brushing of oil before use; a light oil such as sunflower is the best choice.

Serves 6

3 sheets phyllo pastry, thawed if frozen

1 tablespoon sunflower oil

1¹/2 cups red currants

1 cup low-fat plain yogurt

1 teaspoon confectioners' sugar

1 Preheat the oven to 400°F. Cut the sheets of phyllo pastry into eighteen 4-inch squares.

2 Brush each phyllo square very thinly with oil, then arrange three squares in each of six small muffin tin cups, placing each one at a different angle so that they form star-shaped baskets. Bake for 6–8 minutes, until crisp and golden. Lift the baskets out carefully and let them cool on a wire rack.

3 Set aside a few sprigs of red currants on their stems for decoration and string the rest. Stir the red currants into the low-fat yogurt.

4 Spoon the yogurt into the phyllo baskets. Decorate with the reserved sprigs of red currants and sprinkle them with the confectioners' sugar to serve.

NUTRITIONAL NOTES

Per portion:

Calories	80
Fat, total	3.8g
Saturated fat	1.35g
Cholesterol	2.3mg
Fiber	1g

Phyllo Fruit Baskets

Crisp phyllo teamed with fruit in a strawberry yogurt cream makes a fine finish for a summer meal.

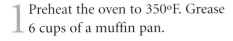

INGREDIENTS

Serves 6

4 large or 8 small sheets of phyllo pastry, thawed if frozen

5 teaspoons low-fat spread, melted

1 cup low-fat plain yogurt

4 tablespoons whole-fruit strawberry jam

1 tablespoon Curaçao or other orange liqueur

1 cup seedless red grapes, halved

1 cup seedless green grapes, halved

1 cup fresh pineapple cubes

2 cups raspberries

2 tablespoons confectioners' sugar

6 small sprigs of fresh mint, for decorating

1 Preheat the oven to 350°F. Grease 6 cups of a muffin pan.

2 Stack the phyllo sheets and cut into twenty-four 4½-inch squares.

NUTRITIONAL NOTES

Per portion:

Calories	207
Fat, total	4.6g
Saturated fat	1.84g
Cholesterol	3.2mg
Fiber	1.4g

3 Lay 4 squares of pastry in each of the 6 muffin tins, rotating to make star-shapes. Press the phyllo firmly down.

4 Brush the pastry baskets lightly with melted low-fat spread. Bake for 5–7 minutes, until the pastry is crisp and golden. Cool on a wire rack.

5 In a bowl, mix the yogurt with the strawberry jam and liqueur.

6 Just before serving, spoon a little of the cream mixture into each pastry basket. Top with the fresh fruit. Sprinkle with confectioners' sugar and decorate each basket with a small sprig of mint.

Phyllo-topped Apple Pie

With its scrunchy topping and only a small amount of low-fat spread, this makes a really light and healthy dessert.

INGREDIENTS

Serves 6

2 pounds Bramley or other apples

6 tablespoons sugar

grated zest of 1 lemon

1 tablespoon lemon juice

¹/₂ cup golden raisins

¹/₂ teaspoon ground cinnamon

4 large sheets phyllo pastry, thawed if frozen

2 tablespoons low-fat spread, melted

confectioners' sugar, for dusting

1 Peel, core and dice the apples. Place them in a saucepan with the sugar and lemon zest. Drizzle on the lemon juice. Bring to a boil, stir well, then cook for 5 minutes or until the apples soften.

2 Stir in the golden raisins and cinnamon. Spoon the mixture into a 5-cup pie dish and level the top. Let cool.

NUTRITIONAL NOTES
Per portion:

Calories	199
Fat, total	2.5g
Saturated fat	0.56g
Cholesterol	0.3mg
Fiber	1.9g

3 Preheat the oven to 350ºF. Place a pie funnel in the center of the fruit. Brush each sheet of phyllo with melted spread. Scrunch up loosely and place on the fruit to cover.

4 Bake for 20–30 minutes, until the phyllo is golden. Dust the pie with confectioners' sugar before serving.

VARIATION

To make phyllo crackers, cut the greased phyllo into 8-inch wide strips. Spoon a little of the filling along one end of each strip, leaving the sides clear. Roll up and twist the ends to make a cracker. Brush with more melted low-fat spread; bake for 20 minutes.

Pineapple and Strawberry Meringue

This is a gooey meringue that doesn't usually hold a perfect shape, but it has a wonderful marshmallow-like texture.

INGREDIENTS

Serves 6

5 egg whites, at room temperature

pinch of salt

1 teaspoon cornstarch

1 tablespoon distilled malt vinegar

few drops of vanilla extract

1¼ cups sugar

1 cup low-fat plain yogurt

6 ounces fresh pineapple, cut into chunks

1⅓ cups fresh strawberries, halved

strawberry leaves, to decorate (optional)

1 Preheat the oven to 325°F. Line a baking sheet with nonstick baking parchment.

2 Whisk the egg whites in a large grease-free bowl until they hold stiff peaks. Add the salt, cornstarch, vinegar and vanilla; whisk again until stiff.

NUTRITIONAL NOTES

Per portion:

Calories	247
Fat, total	2.2g
Saturated fat	1.31g
Cholesterol	2.9mg
Fiber	0.7g

3 Gently whisk in half the sugar, then carefully fold in the rest. Spoon the meringue onto the baking sheet and swirl into an 8-inch round with the back of a large spoon.

4 Bake for 20 minutes, then reduce the temperature to 300°F and bake for 40 more minutes.

5 While still warm, transfer the meringue to a serving plate, then let cool. To serve, top with yogurt, pineapple chunks and halved strawberries. Decorate with strawberry leaves, if you have them.

COOK'S TIP

You can also cook this in a deep, 8-inch loose-bottomed cake pan that is greased and lined.

Nectarine and Hazelnut Meringues

Sweet nectarines and yogurt paired with crisp hazelnut meringues make a really superb dessert.

INGREDIENTS

Serves 5

3 egg whites

¾ cup sugar

½ cup chopped hazelnuts, toasted

1¼ cups low-fat plain yogurt

1 tablespoon sweet dessert wine

2 nectarines, pitted and sliced

fresh mint sprigs, to decorate

VARIATIONS

Use apricots instead of nectarines if you prefer, or you could try this with a raspberry topping.

1 Preheat the oven to 275ºF. Line two large baking sheets with nonstick baking parchment. Whisk the egg whites in a grease-free bowl until they form stiff peaks. Gradually whisk in the sugar a spoonful at a time until the mixture forms a stiff, glossy meringue.

2 Fold in two thirds of the hazelnuts, then spoon five large ovals onto each baking sheet. Sprinkle the remaining hazelnuts onto five of the meringue ovals. Flatten the remaining five ovals.

3 Bake the meringues for 1–1¼ hours, until dry, carefully lift them off the baking parchment and cool completely.

4 Mix the yogurt lightly with the dessert wine. Spoon some of this mixture onto each of the plain meringues. Arrange a few nectarine slices on each. Put each meringue on a dessert plate with a hazelnut-topped meringue. Decorate each portion with mint sprigs and serve the meringues immediately.

NUTRITIONAL NOTES
Per portion:

Calories	293
Fat, total	4.9g
Saturated fat	2.34g
Cholesterol	4.2mg
Fiber	1.4g

Blackberry Brown Sugar Meringue

A brown sugar meringue looks very effective, especially when contrasted with a dark topping.

INGREDIENTS

Serves 6

1 cup light brown sugar

3 egg whites

1 teaspoon distilled malt vinegar

1/2 teaspoon vanilla extract

For the topping

2 tablespoons crème de cassis

3 cups blackberries

1 tablespoon confectioners' sugar, sifted

1 1/4 cups low-fat plain yogurt

small blackberry leaves, to decorate (optional)

1 Preheat the oven to 325°F. Draw an 8-inch circle on a sheet of nonstick baking parchment, turn over and place on a baking sheet.

2 Spread out the brown sugar on a second baking sheet and dry in the oven for 8–10 minutes. Sieve to remove lumps.

3 Whisk the egg whites in a clean grease-free bowl until stiff. Add half the dried brown sugar, 1 tablespoon at a time, whisking well after each addition. Add the vinegar and vanilla, then fold in the remaining sugar.

4 Spoon the meringue onto the circle, leaving a central hollow. Bake for 45 minutes, turn off the oven but leave the meringue in the oven with the door slightly open, until cold.

5 In a bowl, sprinkle crème de cassis onto the blackberries. Let macerate for 30 minutes.

6 When the meringue is cold, peel off the baking parchment, carefully, and transfer the meringue to a serving plate. Stir the confectioners' sugar into the low-fat yogurt and spoon into the center.

7 Top with the blackberries and decorate with small blackberry leaves, if desired. Serve immediately.

NUTRITIONAL NOTES

Per portion:

Calories	199
Fat, total	2.6g
Saturated fat	1.58g
Cholesterol	3.5mg
Fiber	1.8g

Floating Islands in Hot Plum Sauce

The plum sauce for this dessert can be made in advance, and reheated just before you cook the meringues.

INGREDIENTS

Serves 4

1 pound red plums
1¼ cups unsweetened apple juice
2 egg whites
2 tablespoons concentrated apple juice
freshly grated nutmeg

1 Halve the plums and discard the pits. Place them in a wide pan with the unsweetened apple juice.

2 Bring to a boil, lower the heat, cover and simmer gently for 15–20 minutes or until the plums are tender.

COOK'S TIP

Concentrated apple juice is a useful sweetener, or use a little honey.

3 Meanwhile, place the egg whites in a grease-free bowl and whisk them until they hold soft peaks.

4 Gradually whisk in the concentrated apple juice, whisking continuously until the meringue holds fairly firm peaks.

NUTRITIONAL NOTES

Per portion:

Calories	77
Fat, total	0.3g
Saturated fat	0g
Cholesterol	0mg
Fiber	1.7g

5 Using a tablespoon, scoop the meringue mixture into the gently simmering plum sauce. You may need to cook the "islands" in two batches.

6 Cover and let simmer gently for 2–3 minutes, until the meringues are just set. Serve straight away, sprinkled with a little freshly grated nutmeg.

VARIATION

Add an extra dimension to this dessert by using a fruit liqueur such as Calvados, apricot brandy or Grand Marnier instead of the concentrated apple juice.

Raspberry Vacherin

Meringue rounds filled with orange-flavored fromage frais and raspberries make a perfect dinner-party dessert.

INGREDIENTS

Serves 6

3 egg whites

3/4 cup sugar

1 teaspoon chopped almonds

confectioners' sugar, for dusting

raspberry leaves, to decorate (optional)

For the filling

3/4 cup low-fat cream cheese

1 tablespoon honey

1 tablespoon Cointreau or other
orange-flavored liqueur

1/2 cup low-fat fromage frais

2 cups raspberries

1 Preheat the oven to 275°F. Draw an 8-inch circle on each of two pieces of nonstick baking parchment. Turn the paper over so the marking is on the underside and use it to line two heavy baking sheets.

NUTRITIONAL NOTES
Per portion:

Calories	248
Fat, total	2.22g
Saturated fat	0.82g
Cholesterol	4mg
Fiber	1.06g

2 Whisk the egg whites in a grease-free bowl until very stiff, then gradually whisk in the sugar to make a stiff meringue mixture.

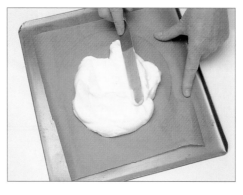

3 Spoon the mixture onto the circles on the prepared baking sheets, spreading the meringue evenly to the edges. Sprinkle one meringue round with the chopped almonds.

4 Bake for 1½–2 hours, then lift the meringues off the baking sheets, peel away the paper and cool on a wire rack.

5 To make the filling, cream the soft cheese with the honey and liqueur in a bowl. Fold in the fromage frais and raspberries, reserving three of the best for decoration.

6 Place the plain meringue round on a board, carefully spread with the filling and top with the nut-covered round. Dust with confectioners' sugar, transfer to a serving plate and decorate with the reserved raspberries, and a sprig of raspberry leaves, if desired.

COOK'S TIP

When making the meringue, whisk the egg whites until they are so stiff that you can turn the bowl upside-down without them falling out.

Baked Blackberry Cheesecake

This light, low-fat cheesecake is best made with wild blackberries, but cultivated ones will do.

INGREDIENTS

Serves 5

low-fat spread, for greasing

3/4 cup low-fat cottage cheese

2/3 cup low-fat yogurt

1 tablespoon whole-wheat flour

2 tablespoons light brown sugar

1 egg

1 egg white

finely grated zest and juice of 1/2 lemon

13/4 cups fresh or thawed frozen blackberries

2 Place the cottage cheese in a food processor and process until smooth. Alternatively, rub it through a sieve, to obtain a smooth mixture.

5 Run a knife around the edge of the cheesecake, and then turn it out. Remove the lining paper, and place the cheesecake on a warm serving plate.

1 Preheat the oven to 350ºF. Lightly grease and bottom-line a 7-inch sandwich cake pan.

3 Stir in the yogurt, flour, sugar, egg and egg white. Add the lemon zest, juice and blackberries, reserving a few for decoration.

6 Decorate the cheesecake with the reserved blackberries, and serve it while still warm.

COOK'S TIP

If fresh blackberries are not in season, you can use canned blackberries. Choose those canned in natural juice, and drain the fruit well before adding it to the cheesecake batter.

4 Put the mixture into the prepared pan and bake it for 30–35 minutes or until it is just set. Turn off the oven and leave for another 30 minutes.

NUTRITIONAL NOTES

Per portion:

Calories	95
Fat, total	1.9g
Saturated fat	0.77g
Cholesterol	41.5mg
Fiber	1.4g

Tofu Berry Cheesecake

Strictly speaking, this isn't a cheesecake at all, as it is made with tofu – but who would guess?

INGREDIENTS

Serves 6

For the crust

2 tablespoons low-fat spread

2 tablespoons unsweetened apple juice

2½ cups bran flakes or other high-fiber cereal

For the filling

1½ cups silken tofu

1 cup low-fat yogurt

4 tablespoons apple juice

1 tablespoon powdered gelatin

For the topping

1½ cups mixed summer berries, such as strawberries, raspberries, red currants and blackberries

2 tablespoons red currant jelly

2 tablespoons hot water

2 Make the filling. Place the tofu and yogurt in a food processor and process until smooth. Pour the apple juice into a cup and sprinkle the gelatin on top. Leave until spongy, then place over hot water until melted. Stir quickly into the tofu mixture.

3 Spread the tofu mixture onto the chilled crust. Chill until set. Remove the tart pan, place the "cheesecake" on a serving plate. Arrange the fruits on top.

4 Melt the red currant jelly with the hot water. Let it cool, then spoon onto the fruit to serve.

NUTRITIONAL NOTES
Per portion:

Calories	163
Fat, total	4.4g
Saturated fat	0.93g
Cholesterol	1.6mg
Fiber	3.2g

1 For the crust, place the low-fat spread and apple juice in a pan and heat them gently until the spread has melted. Crush the cereal and stir it into the pan, mixing well. Put into a 9-inch round tart pan and press down firmly. Let set.

Angelfood Cake

Serve this light-as-air cake with low-fat fromage frais—it makes a perfect dessert.

3 Gently fold in the flour mixture with a large metal spoon. Spoon into an ungreased 10-inch angelfood cake pan, smooth the surface and bake for 45–50 minutes, until the cake springs back when lightly pressed.

4 Sprinkle a sheet of waxed paper with sugar and set an egg cup in the center. Invert the cake pan on the paper, balancing it on the egg cup. When cold, the cake will drop out of the pan. Transfer to a plate, dust with confectioners' sugar, or decorate and serve.

INGREDIENTS

Serves 10

1/3 cup cornstarch

1/3 cup all-purpose flour

8 egg whites

1 cup sugar, plus extra
    for sprinkling

1 teaspoon pure vanilla extract

confectioners' sugar, for dusting

1 Preheat the oven to 350ºF. Sift both flours onto a sheet of waxed paper.

2 Whisk the egg whites in a large grease-free bowl until very stiff, then gradually add the sugar and vanilla, whisking until the mixture is thick and glossy.

NUTRITIONAL NOTES

Per portion:

Calories	139
Fat, total	0.08g
Saturated fat	0.01g
Cholesterol	0mg
Fiber	0.13g

COOK'S TIP

Make a lemony icing by mixing 1 1/2 cups confectioners' sugar with 1–2 tablespoons lemon juice. Drizzle onto the cake and decorate with Cape gooseberries.

Chocolate and Orange Angelfood Cake

This light-as-air cake with its fluffy icing is virtually fat-free, yet it tastes heavenly and looks great too.

INGREDIENTS

Serves 10

¼ cup all-purpose flour

2 tablespoons unsweetened cocoa powder

2 tablespoons cornstarch

pinch of salt

5 egg whites

½ teaspoon cream of tartar

½ cup sugar

pared zest of 1 orange, blanched, to decorate

For the icing

scant 1 cup sugar

5 tablespoons water

1 egg white

2 Add the sugar to the egg whites a spoonful at a time, whisking for a few minutes each time. Sift a third of the flour and cocoa mixture onto the meringue and gently fold in with a spatula. Repeat the procedure, sifting and folding in the flour and cocoa mixture twice more. times.

5 Whisk the egg white in a grease-free bowl until soft peaks occur. Add the syrup in a thin stream, whisking constantly. Continue to whisk until very thick and fluffy.

1 Preheat the oven to 350ºF. Sift the flour, cocoa powder, cornstarch and salt together three times. Beat the egg whites in a large grease-free bowl until foamy. Add the cream of tartar, then whisk into soft peaks.

3 Spoon the mixture into a nonstick 8-inch ring mold and level the top. Bake for 35 minutes or until springy when lightly pressed. Turn upside-down on a wire rack and let cool in the pan. Remove the pan.

6 Spread the icing on the top and sides of the cooled cake. Sprinkle the orange zest on the top of the cake and serve.

COOK'S TIP

Do not over-beat the egg whites. They should form soft peaks to allow for expansion during cooking.

4 Make the icing. Put the sugar in a pan with the water. Stir over low heat until dissolved. Boil until the syrup reaches a temperature of 250ºF on a sugar thermometer, or when a drop of the syrup makes a soft ball when dropped into a cup of cold water. Remove from heat.

NUTRITIONAL NOTES
Per portion:

Calories	153
Fat, total	0.27g
Saturated fat	0.13g
Cholesterol	0mg
Fiber	0.25g

Cinnamon Apple Gâteau

Make this lovely cinnamon-spiced cake for an autumn celebration when apples are at their best.

INGREDIENTS

Serves 8

3 eggs

1/2 cup sugar

3/4 cup all-purpose flour

1 teaspoon ground cinnamon

For the filling and topping

4 large apples

4 tablespoons honey

1 tablespoon water

1/2 cup golden raisins

1/2 teaspoon ground cinnamon

1 1/2 cups low-fat cream cheese

4 tablespoons low-fat fromage frais

2 teaspoons lemon juice

3 tablespoons smooth apricot jam, warmed

fresh mint sprigs, to decorate

2 Sift the flour and cinnamon onto the egg mixture and carefully fold in. Pour into the prepared pan and bake for 25–30 minutes or until the cake springs back when lightly pressed. Slide a spatula between the cake and the pan to loosen the edge, then turn the cake onto a wire rack to cool.

3 To make the filling, peel, core and slice three of the apples and put them in a saucepan. Add 2 tablespoons of the honey and the water. Cover and cook over low heat for about 10 minutes, until the apples have softened. Add the golden raisins and cinnamon, stir well, replace the lid and let cool.

1 Preheat the oven to 375ºF. Grease and line a 9-inch layer cake pan. Place the eggs and sugar in a bowl and whisk until thick and mousse-like (when the whisk is lifted, a trail should remain on the surface of the mixture for at least 15 seconds).

4 Put the cream cheese in a bowl with the remaining honey, the fromage frais and half the lemon juice. Beat until the mixture is smooth.

5 Halve the cake horizontally, place the bottom half on a board and drizzle on any liquid from the apple mixture. Spread with two-thirds of the cheese mixture, then top with the apple filling. Fit the top of the cake in place.

6 Swirl the remaining cheese mixture on top of the cake. Core and slice the remaining apple, sprinkle with the remaining lemon juice and use to decorate the cake edge. Brush the apple with apricot jam and decorate with mint sprigs.

NUTRITIONAL NOTES
Per portion:

Calories	244
Fat, total	4.05g
Saturated fat	1.71g
Cholesterol	77.95mg
Fiber	1.5g

Peach Jelly Roll

A feather-light cake with a filling of peach jam—delicious as a snack or a dinner-party dessert.

INGREDIENTS

Serves 6–8

low-fat spread, for greasing

3 eggs

1/2 cup sugar

3/4 cup all-purpose flour, sifted

1 tablespoon boiling water

6 tablespoons peach jam

confectioners' sugar, for dusting (optional)

NUTRITIONAL NOTES

Per portion:

Calories	178
Fat, total	2.45g
Saturated fat	0.67g
Cholesterol	82.5mg
Fiber	0.33g

1 Preheat the oven to 400ºF. Grease a 12 × 8-inch jelly roll pan and line with nonstick baking parchment. Combine the eggs and sugar in a bowl. Whisk until thick and mousse-like (when the whisk is lifted, a trail should remain on the surface of the mixture for at least 15 seconds).

2 Carefully fold in the flour with a large metal spoon, then add the boiling water in the same way.

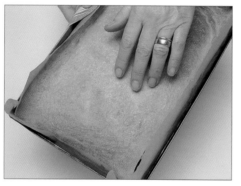

3 Spoon into the prepared pan, spread evenly to the edges and bake for 10–12 minutes, until the cake springs back when lightly pressed.

4 Spread a sheet of waxed paper on a flat surface, sprinkle it with sugar, then invert the cake on top. Peel off the lining paper.

5 Neatly trim the edges of the cake. Make a neat cut two-thirds of the way through the cake, about 1/2 inch from the short edge nearest you.

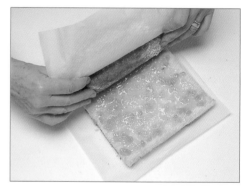

6 Spread the cake with the peach jam and roll up quickly from the partially cut end. Hold in position for a minute, making sure the seam is underneath. Cool on a wire rack. Decorate with icing (see Cook's Tip) or simply dust with confectioners' sugar before serving.

COOK'S TIP

Decorate the jelly roll with icing. Put 4 ounces icing in a piping bag fitted with a small writing nozzle and pipe lines on top of the jelly roll.

Apricot and Orange Roulade

This elegant dessert is very low in fat, so serving it with plain yogurt or fromage frais would not be disastrous.

Serves 6

low-fat spread, for greasing
4 egg whites
1/2 cup sugar
1/2 cup all-purpose flour
finely grated zest of 1 small orange
3 tablespoons orange juice

For the filling
1/2 cup dried apricots, roughly chopped
2/3 cup orange juice

To decorate
2 teaspoons confectioners' sugar, for sprinkling
shreds of pared orange zest, to decorate

1 Preheat the oven to 400ºF. Grease a 9 × 13-inch jelly-roll pan and line it with nonstick baking parchment. Grease the paper.

COOK'S TIP

Make and bake the cake a day in advance and keep it cool, rolled in the paper. Fill with the fruit purée 2–3 hours before serving. The cake can also be stored frozen.

2 Place the egg whites in a large grease-free bowl and whisk them they hold soft peaks. Gradually add the sugar, whisking hard each time.

3 Fold in the flour, orange zest and juice. Spoon the mixture into the prepared pan and spread it evenly.

4 Bake for 15–18 minutes or until the cake is firm and pale gold in color. Turn out onto nonstick baking parchment, and roll it up loosely from one short side. Let cool.

5 Make the filling. Place the apricots in a pan, with the orange juice. Cover the pan and let simmer until most of the liquid has been absorbed. Purée the apricots in a food processor.

6 Unroll the roulade and spread with the apricot mixture. Roll up, arrange strips of paper diagonally across the roll, sprinkle lightly with lines of confectioners' sugar, remove the paper and sprinkle on shreds of pared orange zest. Serve in slices.

NUTRITIONAL NOTES
Per portion:

Calories	154
Fat, total	0.3g
Saturated fat	0.01g
Cholesterol	0mg
Fiber	1.5g

Lemon Chiffon Cake

Lemon mousse provides a tangy filling for this light lemon cake, which is simple to prepare.

Serves 8

low-fat spread, for greasing

2 eggs

6 tablespoons sugar

grated zest of 1 lemon

$1/2$ cup all-purpose flour, sifted

thinly pared lemon zest, cut in shreds

For the filling

2 eggs, separated

6 tablespoons sugar

grated zest and juice of 1 lemon

2 tablespoons water

1 tablespoon powdered gelatin

$1/2$ cup low-fat fromage frais

For the icing

1 cup confectioners' sugar, sifted

1 tablespoon lemon juice

2 Bake for 20–25 minutes, until the cake springs back when lightly pressed in the center. Turn onto a wire rack to cool. Once cold, split the cake in half horizontally and return the lower half to the clean cake pan. Set aside.

3 Make the filling. Put the egg yolks, sugar, lemon zest and juice in a bowl. Beat with a hand-held electric beater until thick, pale and creamy.

1 Preheat the oven to 350°F. Grease and line an 8-inch loose-bottomed cake pan. Whisk the eggs, sugar and lemon zest until thick and mousse-like. Gently fold in the flour, then turn the mixture into the prepared pan.

4 Pour the water into a small heatproof bowel and sprinkle the gelatin on top. Leave until spongy, then place over simmering water and stir until dissolved. Cool slightly, then whisk into the yolk mixture. Fold in the fromage frais. When the mixture begins to set, quickly whisk the egg whites to soft peaks. Fold a spoonful into the mousse mixture to lighten it, then fold in the rest.

5 Pour the lemon mousse onto the cake in the pan, spreading it to the edges. Set the second layer of cake on top and chill until set.

6 Slide a spatula between the pan and the cake to loosen it, then transfer to a serving plate. Make the icing by adding enough lemon juice to the confectioners' sugar to make a mixture thick enough to coat the back of a wooden spoon. Pour onto the cake and spread to the edges. Decorate with the lemon zest.

NUTRITIONAL NOTES

Per portion:

Calories	202
Fat, total	2.81g
Saturated fat	0.79g
Cholesterol	96.41mg
Fiber	0.2g

Tia Maria Gâteau

A feather-light coffee cake with a creamy liqueur-flavored filling and a hint of ginger.

INGREDIENTS

Serves 8

low-fat spread, for greasing

3/4 cup all-purpose flour

2 tablespoons instant coffee powder

3 eggs

1/2 cup sugar

coffee beans, to decorate (optional)

For the filling

3/4 cup low-fat cream cheese

1 tablespoon honey

1 tablespoon Tia Maria

1/4 cup stem ginger,
    roughly chopped

For the icing

2 cups confectioners' sugar, sifted

2 teaspoons coffee extract

1 tablespoon water

1 teaspoon unsweetened cocoa powder

2 Whisk the eggs and sugar in a bowl until thick (when the whisk is lifted, a trail should remain on the batter's surface for 10–15 seconds).

3 Gently fold in the flour mixture with a metal spoon, being careful not to knock out any air. Turn the mixture into the prepared pan. Bake for 30–35 minutes or until it springs back when lightly pressed. Turn onto a wire rack and let cool completely.

4 Make the filling. Mix the cream cheese with the honey in a bowl. Beat until smooth, then stir in the Tia Maria and the chopped stem ginger.

1 Preheat the oven to 375ºF. Grease and line an 8-inch deep round cake pan. Sift the flour and coffee powder together onto a sheet of waxed paper.

5 Split the cake in half and sandwich them with the Tia Maria filling.

6 Make the icing. Mix the confectioners' sugar and coffee extract with enough of the water to make an icing that will coat the back of a wooden spoon. Spread three-quarters of the icing on the cake. Stir the cocoa powder into the remaining icing until smooth. Spoon into a piping bag fitted with a writing nozzle and pipe the mocha icing onto the coffee icing. Decorate with coffee beans, if desired.

NUTRITIONAL NOTES
Per portion:

Calories	226
Fat, total	3.14g
Saturated fat	1.17g
Cholesterol	75.03mg
Fiber	0.64g

Low-fat Custards, Soufflés & Mousses

◆ ◆ ◆

Bread and Golden Raisin Custard

An old favorite gets the low-fat treatment and proves a great success.

INGREDIENTS

Serves 4

1 tablespoon low-fat spread

3 thin slices of bread, crusts removed

2 cups skim milk

1/2 teaspoon allspice

3 tablespoons brown sugar

2 eggs, whisked

1/2 cup golden raisins

freshly grated nutmeg

a little confectioners' sugar, for dusting

1 Preheat the oven to 350°F. Lightly grease an ovenproof dish. Spread the bread with low-fat spread and cut into small pieces.

2 Place the bread in several layers in the prepared dish.

3 Whisk the skim milk, allspice, brown sugar and eggs in a large mixing bowl. Pour the mixture onto the bread, to cover. Sprinkle on the golden raisins and stand for 30 minutes.

4 Grate a little nutmeg on top and bake for 30–40 minutes, until the custard is just set and golden. Serve sprinkled with confectioners' sugar.

NUTRITIONAL NOTES

Per portion:

Calories	246
Fat, total	5g
Saturated fat	1.37g
Cholesterol	99.2mg
Fiber	0.7g

Poppyseed Custard with Red Fruit

Poppyseeds add a nutty flavor to this creamy custard without increasing the amount of fat too much.

INGREDIENTS

Serves 6

low-fat spread, for greasing

2¹/2 cups skim milk

2 eggs

1 tablespoon sugar

1 tablespoon poppyseeds

1 cup each of strawberries, raspberries and blackberries

1 tablespoon light brown sugar

4 tablespoons red grape juice

1 Preheat the oven to 300ºF. Grease a soufflé dish very lightly with low-fat spread. Heat the milk until just below the boiling point, but do not boil. Beat the eggs in a bowl with the sugar and poppyseeds until creamy.

2 Whisk the milk into the egg mixture until very well mixed. Stand the prepared soufflé dish in a shallow roasting pan, then pour in hot water from the kettle to come halfway up the sides of the dish.

VARIATION

If you don't like poppyseeds, sprinkle the surface of the custard with freshly grated nutmeg or ground cinnamon instead.

3 Pour the custard into the soufflé dish and bake in the preheated oven for 50–60 minutes, until the custard is just set and golden on top.

4 While the custard is baking, mix the fruit with the brown sugar and fruit juice. Chill until ready to serve with the warm baked custard.

NUTRITIONAL NOTES
Per portion:

Calories	109
Fat, total	3.1g
Saturated fat	0.69g
Cholesterol	66.2mg
Fiber	1.3g

Orange Yogurt Brûlées

Luxurious treats, much lower in fat than classic brûlées, which are made with cream, eggs and lots of sugar.

INGREDIENTS

Serves 4

2 oranges

2/3 cup low-fat plain yogurt

4 tablespoons half-fat crème fraîche

3 tablespoons sugar

2 tablespoons light brown sugar

1 With a sharp knife, cut off all the peel and white pith from the oranges and segment the fruit, removing all the membrane.

2 Place the fruit in the bottom of four individual flameproof dishes. Mix the yogurt and crème fraîche and spoon onto the oranges.

3 Mix the two sugars and sprinkle them evenly on the tops of the dishes.

4 Place the dishes under a preheated, very hot broiler for 3–4 minutes or until the sugar melts and turns a rich golden brown. Serve warm or cold.

NUTRITIONAL NOTES
Per portion:

Calories	154
Fat, total	3.8g
Saturated fat	2.35g
Cholesterol	15.8mg
Fiber	1.4g

Tofu Berry Brûlée

Brûlée is usually out-of-bounds on a low-fat diet, but this version is perfectly acceptable, as it uses tofu.

INGREDIENTS

Serves 4

11-ounce package silken tofu

3 tablespoons confectioners' sugar

2 cups red berries, such as raspberries, strawberries and red currants

about 5 tablespoons brown sugar

NUTRITIONAL NOTES

Per portion:

Calories	180
Fat, total	3.01g
Saturated fat	0.41g
Cholesterol	0mg
Fiber	1.31g

1 Mix the tofu and confectioners' sugar in a food processor or blender and process until smooth.

COOK'S TIP

Choose silken tofu, as it gives a smoother texture than firm tofu in this type of dish. Firm tofu is better for cooking in chunks.

2 Stir in the berries, then spoon into a 3¾-cup flameproof dish. Flatten the top.

3 Sprinkle the top with brown sugar to cover evenly. Place under a very hot broiler until the sugar melts and caramelizes. Chill before serving.

Passion Fruit Brûlée

Fruit brûlées are usually made with heavy cream, but plain yogurt works just as well.

INGREDIENTS

Serves 4

4 passion fruit

1¼ cups low-fat plain yogurt

½ cup light brown sugar

1 tablespoon water

COOK'S TIP

Watch the caramel closely. It is ready when it darkens to a rich golden brown. At this stage it will be very hot, so protect your hand and pour it with great care.

1 Cut the passion fruit in half, using a very sharp knife. Use a teaspoon to scoop out all the pulp and seeds and divide among four ovenproof ramekins.

2 Spoon equal amounts of the yogurt on the fruit and smooth the surface level. Chill for at least 2 hours.

3 Put the sugar in a small saucepan with the water and heat gently, stirring, until the sugar has melted and caramelized. Pour onto the yogurt; the caramel will harden within 1 minute. Keep the brûlées in a cool place until ready to serve.

NUTRITIONAL NOTES
Per portion:

Calories	139
Fat, total	3.8g
Saturated fat	2.37g
Cholesterol	5.3mg
Fiber	0.5g

Mango and Ginger Clouds

The sweet, perfumed flavor of ripe mango combines beautifully with ginger, and this dessert makes the most of them.

INGREDIENTS

Serves 6

3 ripe mangoes

3 pieces stem ginger, plus 3 tablespoons
   syrup from the jar

1/2 cup silken tofu

3 egg whites

6 unsalted pistachios, chopped

3 Whisk the egg whites in a grease-free bowl to form soft peaks. Fold them lightly into the mango mixture.

4 Spoon the mixture into wide dishes or glasses and chill before serving, sprinkled with the pistachios.

NUTRITIONAL NOTES	
Per portion:	
Calories	141
Fat, total	1.9g
Saturated fat	0.21g
Cholesterol	0mg
Fiber	3.9g

1 Cut the mangoes' flesh off the pits, remove the peel and chop.

2 Put the mango flesh in a food processor and add the ginger, syrup and tofu. Process until smooth. Spoon into a bowl.

NOTE

Raw or lightly cooked egg whites should be avoided by young children and women during pregnancy.

Raspberry Passion Fruit Swirls

If passion fruit is not available, this simple dessert can be made with raspberries alone.

2 Place alternate spoonfuls of the raspberry pulp and the fromage frais mixture into stemmed glasses or serving dishes.

3 Stir lightly to create a swirled effect. Decorate each dessert with a whole raspberry and a sprig of fresh mint. Serve chilled.

INGREDIENTS

Serves 4

2¹/2 cups raspberries

2 passion fruit

1²/3 cups low-fat fromage frais

2 tablespoons sugar

raspberries and fresh mint sprigs,
   to decorate

COOK'S TIP

Over-ripe, slightly soft fruit can be used in this recipe. Use frozen raspberries when fresh are not available, but thaw them first.

1 Using a fork, mash the raspberries in a small bowl until the juice runs. Place the fromage frais and sugar in a separate bowl. Halve the passion fruit and scoop out the seeds. Add to the fromage frais and mix well.

NUTRITIONAL NOTES
Per portion:

Calories	110
Fat, total	0.47g
Saturated fat	0.13g
Cholesterol	1mg
Fiber	2.12g

Chocolate Vanilla Timbales

You really can allow yourself the occasional chocolate treat, especially if it's a dessert as light as this one.

INGREDIENTS

Serves 6

1¹/2 cups skim milk

2 tablespoons unsweetened cocoa powder, plus extra, for sprinkling

2 eggs, separated

1 teaspoon pure vanilla extract

3 tablespoons sugar

1 tablespoon powdered gelatin

3 tablespoons hot water

For the sauce

¹/2 cup low-fat plain yogurt

¹/2 teaspoon pure vanilla extract

1 Mix the milk and cocoa powder in a pan; stir over medium heat until the milk boils. Beat the egg yolks, vanilla and sugar in a bowl, until smooth. Pour in the chocolate milk, beating well.

2 Return the mixture to the pan and stir constantly over low heat, without boiling, until it thickens slightly and is smooth. Dissolve the gelatin in the hot water and then quickly stir it into the milk mixture. Let it cool until on the point of setting.

3 Whisk the egg whites in a grease-free bowl until they hold soft peaks. Fold them quickly into the chocolate milk mixture, then divide among six individual molds. Chill until set.

4 To serve the timbales, run a knife around the edge of each mold, dip the molds quickly into hot water and turn out onto serving plates. For the sauce, stir the yogurt and vanilla together, then spoon onto the plates. Sprinkle the sauce with cocoa powder just before serving.

NUTRITIONAL NOTES

Per portion:

Calories	118
Fat, total	4.1g
Saturated fat	1.89g
Cholesterol	66.7mg
Fiber	0.7g

Peach and Ginger Paskha

This low-fat version of the Russian Easter favorite is made with peaches and stem ginger.

INGREDIENTS

Serves 4

1 1/2 cups low-fat cottage cheese

2 ripe peaches or nectarines

scant 1/2 cup low-fat natural yogurt

2 pieces stem ginger in syrup, drained and chopped, plus 2 tablespoons syrup from the jar

1/2 teaspoon pure vanilla extract

To decorate

1 peach or nectarine, peeled and sliced

2 teaspoons slivered almonds, toasted

1 Drain the cottage cheese and rub it through a sieve into a bowl. Pit and roughly chop the fruit.

2 In a bowl, mix the chopped peaches or nectarines, the low-fat cottage cheese, yogurt, stem ginger, syrup and vanilla.

3 Line a new, clean flower pot or a strainer with a piece of clean, fine cloth such as cheesecloth.

NUTRITIONAL NOTES

Per portion:

Calories	147
Fat, total	2.9g
Saturated fat	0.89g
Cholesterol	5.3mg
Fiber	1.1g

4 Put in the cheese mixture, wrap over the cloth and weight down. Leave over a bowl in a cool place to drain overnight. Unwrap the cloth and invert the paskha onto a plate. Decorate with fruit slices and almonds.

COOK'S TIP

For individual paskhas, line four to six ramekins with the clean cloth and divide the mixture among them.

Strawberry Rose-petal Paskha

This lighter version of a traditional Russian dessert is ideal for dinner parties—make it a day or two in advance.

INGREDIENTS

Serves 4

1¹/2 cups low-fat cottage cheese

³/4 cup low-fat natural yogurt

2 tablespoons honey

¹/2 teaspoon rose-water

2¹/2 cups strawberries

handful of scented pink rose petals,
    to decorate

VARIATION

Use small porcelain heart-shaped molds with draining holes for a pretty alternative.

1 Drain any liquid from the cottage cheese. Put the cheese into a sieve, using a wooden spoon to rub it through the sieve into a bowl. Stir the yogurt, honey and rose-water into the cheese.

2 Roughly chop about half the strawberries and fold them into the cheese mixture.

3 Line a new, clean flowerpot or a sieve with fine muslin and put the cheese mixture in. Drain over a bowl for several hours, or overnight.

4 Invert the flowerpot or sieve onto a serving plate, turn out the paskha and lift off the muslin. Cut the remaining strawberries in half and arrange them around the paskha. Sprinkle on the rose petals. Serve the paskha chilled.

NUTRITIONAL NOTES

Per portion:

Calories	133
Fat, total	1.6g
Saturated fat	1g
Cholesterol	6.1mg
Fiber	0.8g

Lemon Hearts with Strawberry Sauce

These elegant little hearts are perfect for a romantic celebration, such as a Valentine's Day dinner.

INGREDIENTS

Serves 6

3/4 cup low-fat cottage cheese

2/3 cup half-fat crème fraîche

1 tablespoon sugar

finely grated zest of 1/2 lemon

2 tablespoons lemon juice

2 teaspoons powdered gelatin

2 egg whites

low-fat spread, for greasing

For the sauce

2 cups fresh or frozen and thawed strawberries, plus extra to decorate

1 tablespoon lemon juice

2 Pour the lemon juice into a small heatproof bowl and sprinkle the gelatin on the surface. When it has sponged, place the bowl over a pan of hot water and stir until dissolved.

5 Spoon the mixture into six lightly greased, individual heart-shaped molds, and chill the molds until set.

1 Press the cottage cheese through a sieve into a bowl. Beat in the crème fraîche, sugar and lemon zest.

3 Quickly stir the gelatin into the cheese mixture, mixing it in evenly.

4 Beat the egg whites in a grease-free bowl until they form soft peaks. Quickly fold them into the cheese mixture with metal spoon.

6 Make the sauce. Mix the strawberries and lemon juice in a food processor or blender and process until smooth. Pour the sauce onto serving plates and invert the lemon hearts on top of the sauce. Decorate with slices of strawberry.

COOK'S TIP

Don't worry if you don't have heart-shaped (coeur à la crème) molds. Simply use individual fluted molds—or even ordinary teacups.

NUTRITIONAL NOTES

Per portion:

Calories	94
Fat, total	4.2g
Saturated fat	2.60g
Cholesterol	27.7mg
Fiber	0.4g

Souffléed Rice Pudding

The fluffy egg whites in this rice pudding make the portions more substantial, without adding lots of extra fat.

INGREDIENTS

Serves 4

1/3 cup short-grain (pudding) rice

3 tablespoons honey

3 cups low-fat milk

1 vanilla bean or 1/2 teaspoon vanilla extract

2 egg whites

1 teaspoon freshly grated nutmeg

1 Place the rice, honey and milk in a heavy or nonstick pan and bring the milk to a boil. Add the vanilla bean, if using.

2 Lower the heat, cover and simmer over the lowest possible heat for 1–1 1/4 hours, stirring occasionally to prevent sticking, until most of the liquid has been absorbed.

3 Remove the vanilla bean, or, if using vanilla, add this to the rice mixture now. Set the pan aside, so that the mixture cools slightly. Preheat the oven to 425°F.

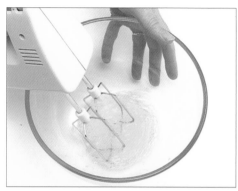

4 Place the egg whites in a grease-free bowl and whisk until they hold soft peaks when the whisk is lifted.

5 Using a metal spoon or spatula, fold the egg whites evenly into the rice mixture, then put into a 4-cup ovenproof dish.

6 Sprinkle with grated nutmeg and bake for 15–20 minutes, until the pudding has risen well and is golden brown. Serve hot.

NUTRITIONAL NOTES

Per portion:

Calories	186
Fat, total	3.7g
Saturated fat	1.88g
Cholesterol	13.1mg
Fiber	0g

COOK'S TIP

If desired, use skim milk instead of low-fat, but watch it when it is simmering, as with so little fat it tends to boil over very easily.

Cinnamon and Apricot Soufflés

Don't expect this to be difficult simply because it's a soufflé—it really couldn't be easier.

INGREDIENTS

Serves 4

low-fat spread, for greasing

all-purpose flour, for dusting

3 eggs

1/2 cup apricot spread

finely grated zest of 1/2 lemon

1 teaspoon ground cinnamon, plus extra
   to decorate

NUTRITIONAL NOTES

Per portion:

Calories	134
Fat, total	4.1g
Saturated fat	1.15g
Cholesterol	144.4mg
Fiber	0g

1 Preheat the oven to 375ºF. Lightly grease four individual soufflé dishes and dust them lightly with flour.

VARIATION

Other fruit spreads would be delicious in this soufflé. Try peach or blueberry for a change.

2 Separate the eggs and place the yolks in a bowl with the fruit spread, lemon zest and cinnamon.

3 Whisk hard until the mixture is thick and pale in color.

4 Place the egg whites in a grease-free bowl and whisk them until they form soft peaks when the whisk is lifted from the bowl.

5 Using a metal spoon or spatula, gradually fold the egg whites evenly into the yolk mixture.

6 Divide the soufflé mixture among the prepared dishes and bake for 10–15 minutes, until well-risen and golden brown. Serve immediately, dusted with a little extra ground cinnamon.

COOK'S TIP

Puréed fresh or well-drained canned fruit can be used instead of the apricot spread, but make sure that the mixture is not too wet or the soufflés will not rise properly.

Fluffy Banana and Pineapple Soufflé

This light, low-fat soufflé looks very impressive but is really very easy to make, especially with a food processor.

INGREDIENTS

Serves 6

2 ripe bananas

1 cup low-fat cottage cheese

15-ounce can pineapple chunks or pieces in juice

4 tablespoons water

1 tablespoon powdered gelatin

2 egg whites

1 Tie a double band of nonstick baking parchment around a 2½-cup soufflé dish, to come approximately 2 inches above the rim.

2 Peel and chop one banana and, with the cottage cheese, blend it in a food processor until smooth.

3 Drain the pineapple and reserve a few pieces for decoration. Add the remainder to the mixture and process until finely chopped.

4 Pour the water into a small heatproof bowl and sprinkle the gelatin on top. Leave until spongy, then place the bowl over hot water, stirring occasionally, until all the gelatin has dissolved.

5 Whisk the egg whites in a grease-free bowl until they hold soft peaks, then fold them lightly and evenly into the mixture. Put the mixture into the prepared dish, smooth the surface and chill it in the refrigerator, until set.

6 When the soufflé has set, carefully remove the paper collar. Decorate the soufflé with the reserved slices of banana and chunks of pineapple.

NUTRITIONAL NOTES
Per portion:

Calories	106
Fat, total	0.6g
Saturated fat	0.37g
Cholesterol	1.9mg
Fiber	0.7g

Hot Blackberry and Apple Soufflés

It's always worth freezing a bag of blackberries to have on hand for treats such as this delicious soufflé.

3 Put a spoonful of the fruit purée into each prepared dish and smooth the surface. Set the dishes aside.

4 Whisk the egg whites in a large grease-free bowl until they form stiff peaks. Very gradually whisk in the remaining sugar to make a stiff, glossy meringue mixture.

5 Fold in the remaining fruit purée and spoon the flavored meringue into the prepared dishes. Level the tops with a spatula, and run a table knife around the edge of each dish.

6 Place the dishes on the hot baking sheet and bake for 10–15 minutes until the soufflés have risen well and are lightly browned. Dust the tops with confectioners' sugar and serve immediately.

INGREDIENTS

Serves 6

low-fat spread, for greasing

2/3 cup sugar, plus extra for dusting

3 cups blackberries

1 Bramley or other large apple, peeled, cored and finely diced

grated zest and juice of 1 orange

3 egg whites

confectioners' sugar, for dusting

1 Preheat the oven to 400°F and heat a baking sheet. Grease six 2/3-cup soufflé dishes and dust with sugar.

2 In a pan, cook the blackberries, diced apple, orange zest and juice for 10 minutes. Press through a sieve into a bowl. Stir in 1/4 cup of the sugar. Set aside to cool.

COOK'S TIP

Running a table knife around the edge of the soufflés before baking helps them to rise evenly without any part sticking to the rim of the dishes.

NUTRITIONAL NOTES

Per portion:

Calories	138
Fat, total	0.3g
Saturated fat	0.5g
Cholesterol	0mg
Fiber	2.7g

Souffléed Orange Semolina

If you've never cooked with semolina,
treat yourself to a taste of this version.

INGREDIENTS

Serves 4

1/4 cup semolina

2 1/2 cups low-fat milk

2 tablespoons brown sugar

1 large orange

1 egg white

NUTRITIONAL NOTES
Per portion:

Calories	158
Fat, total	2.67g
Saturated fat	1.54g
Cholesterol	10.5mg
Fiber	0.86g

1 Preheat the oven to 400°F. Put the semolina in a nonstick pan and add the milk and sugar. Stir over medium heat until thickened and smooth. Remove from heat.

COOK'S TIP

When using the zest of citrus fruit, scrub the fruit thoroughly before use, or buy unwaxed fruit.

2 Scrub the orange zest and pare a few long shreds of zest, save for decoration. Finely grate the remaining zest. Cut all the peel and white pith from the orange and separate the flesh into equal segments. Stir the segments into the semolina, with the orange zest.

3 Whisk the egg white in a grease-free bowl until stiff, then fold lightly and evenly into the mixture. Spoon into a 4-cup ovenproof dish and bake for 15–20 minutes, until risen and golden brown. Sprinkle on the orange shreds and serve.

Quick Apricot Blender Parfaits

One of the quickest desserts you could make—and also one of the prettiest with its delicate swirl of creamy apricot.

INGREDIENTS

Serves 4

14-ounce can apricot halves in juice

1 tablespoon Grand Marnier or brandy

¾ cup low-fat plain yogurt

1 tablespoon sliced almonds

3 Alternately spoon fruit purée and yogurt into four tall glasses or glass dishes, swirling them together slightly to give a marbled effect.

4 Lightly toast the almonds until they are golden. Let them cool slightly and then sprinkle them on top of each whip. Serve immediately.

1 Drain the juice from the apricots and place the fruit and liqueur in a blender or food processor.

2 Process the apricots until smooth.

NUTRITIONAL NOTES

Per portion:

Calories	88
Fat, total	4.4g
Saturated fat	1.38g
Cholesterol	3.1mg
Fiber	0.9g

Prune and Orange Custards

A simple dessert, made in minutes. It can be served right away, but it is best chilled before serving.

Serves 4

1 1/2 cups dried prunes

2/3 cup orange juice

1 cup low-fat yogurt

shreds of thinly pared orange zest,
    to decorate

1 Remove the pits (if any), then roughly chop the prunes. Place them in a pan with the orange juice.

2 Bring the juice to a boil, stirring. Lower the heat, cover and simmer for 5 minutes, until the prunes are tender and the liquid is reduced by half.

3 Remove from heat, let cool slightly, then beat well with a wooden spoon, until the fruit breaks down to a rough purée.

4 Transfer the mixture to a bowl. Stir in the yogurt, swirling the yogurt and fruit purée together lightly, to give an attractive marbled effect.

5 Spoon the mixture into stemmed glasses or individual serving dishes, smoothing the tops.

6 Top each pot with a few shreds of thinly pared orange zest, to decorate. Chill before serving.

COOK'S TIP

This dessert can also be made with other dried fruit, such as apricots or peaches. If using dried apricots, try the unsulfured variety for a rich color and flavor. For a special occasion, add a dash of brandy or Cointreau with the yogurt.

NUTRITIONAL NOTES

Per portion:

Calories	125
Fat, total	0.7g
Saturated fat	0.28g
Cholesterol	2.3mg
Fiber	3.2g

Gooseberry Cooler

Gooseberries are one of the less common summer fruits, so they're well worth snapping up when you can get them.

INGREDIENTS

Serves 4

4 cups fresh or frozen gooseberries
1 small orange
1 tablespoon honey
1 cup low-fat cottage cheese

NUTRITIONAL NOTES
Per portion:

Calories	93
Fat, total	1.4g
Saturated fat	0.56g
Cholesterol	3.1mg
Fiber	3.4g

1 Trim the gooseberries and place them in a medium-sized saucepan. Finely grate the zest from the orange and squeeze out all of the juice; then add the orange zest and juice to the pan. Cover the pan and cook gently, stirring occasionally, until the fruit is completely tender.

2 Remove from heat and stir in the honey. Purée the gooseberries with the cooking liquid in a food processor until almost smooth. Cool.

3 Press the cottage cheese through a sieve, or process it in a food processor, until smooth. Stir half the gooseberry purée into the cheese.

4 Spoon the cheese mixture into four serving dishes or glasses. Top each with a spoonful of the gooseberry purée. Serve chilled.

Grape Cheese Custards

A deliciously cool dessert of low-fat cream cheese and honey, topped with sugar-frosted grapes as decoration.

INGREDIENTS

INGREDIENTS

Serves 4

1¼ cups black or green seedless grapes, plus tiny bunches

2 egg whites

1 tablespoon sugar

finely grated zest and juice of ½ lemon

1 cup low-fat cream cheese

3 tablespoons honey

2 tablespoons brandy (optional)

NUTRITIONAL NOTES

Per portion:

Calories	135
Fat, total	3g
Saturated fat	1.2g
Cholesterol	0.56mg
Fiber	0g

1 Brush the tiny bunches of grapes lightly with egg white and sprinkle with sugar to coat. Let dry.

2 In a bowl, mix the lemon zest and juice, cheese, honey and brandy if using. Chop the remaining grapes and stir them into the mixture.

3 Whisk the egg whites in a grease-free bowl until stiff enough to hold soft peaks. Fold the whites into the grape mixture, then spoon into four serving glasses.

4 Top with the sugar-frosted grapes and serve chilled.

Apricot Delight

A fluffy mousse bottom with a layer of fruit gelatin on top makes this dessert doubly delicious.

Serves 8

2 14-ounce cans apricots in
   natural juice

4 tablespoons fructose

1 tablespoon lemon juice

1½ tablespoons powdered gelatin

15 ounces low fat ready-to-serve custard

⅔ cup low-fat yogurt, strained

To decorate

1 batch yogurt piping cream

1 apricot, sliced

1 sprig of fresh apple mint

2 Drain the apricots, reserving the juice. Put the drained apricots in a food processor or blender. Add the fructose and 4 tablespoons of the apricot juice. Blend into a smooth purée.

3 Measure 2 tablespoons of the apricot juice into a small bowl, add lemon juice, then sprinkle on 2 teaspoons of the gelatin. Let sit for 5 minutes.

4 Stir the gelatin into half the apricot purée and pour into the pan. Chill in the refrigerator for 1½ hours.

5 Sprinkle the remaining 1 tablespoon gelatin onto 4 tablespoons of the apricot juice. Soak and dissolve as before. Mix the remaining purée with the custard, yogurt and gelatin. Pour onto the layer of set fruit purée and chill in the refrigerator for 3 hours.

6 Dip the cake pan into hot water for a few seconds and unmold the dessert onto a serving plate. Decorate with yogurt piping cream, the sliced apricot and a sprig of fresh apple mint.

1 Line the bottom of a 5-cup heart-shaped or round cake pan with nonstick baking parchment.

COOK'S TIP

Don't use a loose-bottomed cake pan for this recipe, as the mixture may seep through before it sets.

NUTRITIONAL NOTES
Per portion:

Calories	155
Fat, total	0.63g
Saturated fat	0.33g
Cholesterol	0mg
Fiber	0.9g

Low-fat
Fruit Salads

◆ ◆ ◆

Strawberries with Cointreau

Strawberries at the height of their season are one of summer's greatest pleasures. Try this unusual way of serving them.

INGREDIENTS

Serves 4

1 unwaxed orange

3 tablespoons sugar

5 tablespoons water

3¹/₂ cups strawberries, hulled

3 tablespoons Cointreau or other
   orange-flavored liqueur

1 cup low-fat plain yogurt

1 With a vegetable peeler, remove wide strips of zest from the orange, being careful to avoid the pith. Stack two or three strips at a time and cut into very thin julienne strips.

2 Mix the sugar and water in a small saucepan. Heat gently, swirling the pan occasionally until the sugar has dissolved. Bring to a boil, add the julienne strips, then simmer for 10 minutes. Remove the pan from heat and let the syrup cool.

3 Reserve four strawberries for decoration and cut the rest lengthwise in halves or quarters. Put them in a bowl. Stir the Cointreau or chosen liqueur into the syrup and pour it onto the fruit. Add the orange zest. Set aside for at least 30 minutes or for up to 2 hours.

NUTRITIONAL NOTES
Per portion:

Calories	155
Fat, total	3.2g
Saturated fat	1.97g
Cholesterol	4.4mg
Fiber	1.2g

4 Whip the yogurt, then sweeten to taste with a little strawberry syrup.

5 Spoon the chopped strawberries into glass serving dishes and top with dollops of the sweetened yogurt. Decorate with strawberries.

Fresh Figs with Honey and Wine

Fresh figs are naturally sweet, and taste wonderful in a honeyed wine syrup. Any variety can be used in this recipe.

INGREDIENTS

Serves 6

scant 2 cups dry white wine

1/3 cup honey

1/4 cup sugar

1 small orange

8 whole cloves

1 pound fresh figs

1 cinnamon stick

bay leaves, to decorate

For the sauce

1 1/4 cups low-fat plain yogurt

1 teaspoon pure vanilla extract

1 teaspoon sugar

1 Put the wine, honey and sugar in a heavy saucepan and heat gently until the sugar dissolves.

2 Stud the orange with the cloves and add to the syrup with the figs and cinnamon. Cover and simmer until the figs are soft then let cool.

3 Flavor the low-fat yogurt with the vanilla and sugar. Spoon it into a serving dish. Transfer the fruit to another serving dish. With a sharp knife cut one or two of the figs in half, if desired, to show off their pretty centers. Decorate with the bay leaves and serve with the yogurt.

NUTRITIONAL NOTES

Per portion:

Calories	201
Fat, total	2.7g
Saturated fat	1.58g
Cholesterol	3.5mg
Fiber	1.5g

Persian Melon Cups

This typical Persian dessert uses delicious, sweet fresh fruits flavored with rosewater and a hint of aromatic mint.

INGREDIENTS

Serves 4

2 small melons

2 cups strawberries, sliced

3 peaches, peeled and cut into small cubes

1 bunch of seedless grapes, about 8 ounces

2 tablespoons sugar

1 tablespoon rosewater

1 tablespoon lemon juice

crushed ice

4 sprigs of mint, to decorate

COOK'S TIP
∽

If you don't have a melon baller, scoop out the melon flesh using a large spoon and then cut into bite-size pieces.

1 Carefully cut the melons in half and remove the seeds. Scoop out the flesh with a melon baller, being careful not to damage the skin. Reserve the melon shells for later.

2 Reserve four strawberries and slice the rest. Place in a bowl with the melon balls, the peaches, grapes, sugar, rosewater and lemon juice.

3 Put fruit into the melon shells and chill in the refrigerator for 2 hours.

4 To serve, sprinkle with crushed ice and decorate each melon shell with a whole strawberry and a sprig of mint.

NUTRITIONAL NOTES
Per portion:

Calories	137
Fat, total	0.4g
Saturated fat	0g
Cholesterol	0mg
Fiber	3.2g

Fragrant Mandarins with Pistachios

Mandarins, tangerines, clementines, mineolas: any of these lovely citrus fruits could be used for this dessert.

INGREDIENTS

Serves 4

10 mandarins

1 tablespoon confectioners' sugar

2 tablespoons orange-flower water

1 tablespoon chopped pistachios

3 Mix the reserved mandarin juice, confectioners' sugar and orange-flower water and pour it onto the fruit. Cover the dish and place in the refrigerator for at least an hour to chill.

4 Blanch the shreds of zest in boiling water for 30 seconds. Drain and cool on paper towels, then sprinkle them on the mandarins, with the pistachios, to serve.

1 Pare a little mandarin zest and cut into fine shreds. Squeeze the juice from two mandarins and set it aside.

2 Peel the remaining fruit, removing all the pith and place in a bowl.

NUTRITIONAL NOTES

Per portion:

Calories	91
Fat, total	2.2g
Saturated fat	0.25g
Cholesterol	0mg
Fiber	2g

Orange and Date Salad

This Moroccan dessert is simplicity itself, yet it is wonderfully fresh-tasting and light at the end of a rich meal.

INGREDIENTS

Serves 6

6 oranges

1–2 tablespoons orange-flower water or rosewater (optional)

lemon juice (optional)

2/3 cup pitted dates

scant 1/2 cup pistachios

1 tablespoon confectioners' sugar, plus extra for dusting

1 teaspoon toasted almonds

3 Chop the dates and almonds and sprinkle onto the salad with the confectioners' sugar. Chill for 1 hour.

4 Just before serving, sprinkle the salad with the toasted almonds and a little extra confectioners' sugar.

NUTRITIONAL NOTES
Per portion:

Calories	147
Fat, total	4.3g
Saturated fat	0.45g
Cholesterol	0mg
Fiber	3.5g

1 Peel the oranges with a sharp knife, removing all the pith. Cut into segments, catching the juice in a bowl. Place in a serving dish.

2 Stir in the juice from the bowl, with a little orange-flower or rosewater, if using, and sharpen with lemon juice, if desired.

COOK'S TIP

Use fresh dates, if you can, although if you can't get hold of them dried dates are delicious in this salad, too.

Fresh Fruit Salad and Almond Curd

This is a wonderfully light Chinese dessert usually made from agar-agar or isinglass, although gelatin can be used.

2 In a separate saucepan, dissolve the sugar in the remaining water over the heat. Add the milk and the almond extract. Blend well, but do not boil.

3 Pour the agar-agar, isinglass or gelatin mixture into a large serving bowl. Add the flavored milk gradually, stirring constantly. When cool, put in the refrigerator for 2–3 hours to set. To serve, cut the curd into small cubes and spoon into a serving dish or into individual bowls. Spoon the fruit salad onto the curd and serve.

NUTRITIONAL NOTES
Per portion:

Calories	117
Fat, total	1.2g
Saturated fat	0.75g
Cholesterol	5.3mg
Fiber	0g

INGREDIENTS

Serves 6

¹/₄ ounce agar-agar or isinglass
    or 1 ounce gelatin
about 2¹/₂ cups water
¹/₄ cup sugar
1¹/₄ cups low-fat milk
1 teaspoon almond extract
fresh fruit salad

1 In a saucepan, dissolve the agar-agar or isinglass in about half of the water over low heat. This will take at least 10 minutes. If using gelatin, follow the instructions on the envelope.

Fresh Pineapple with Coconut

This refreshing dessert can also be made with canned pineapple, and it is very simple to make and light to eat.

INGREDIENTS

Serves 4

1 fresh pineapple, about
  1 1/2 pounds, peeled
few slivers of fresh coconut
1 1/4 cups unsweetened pineapple juice
4 tablespoons coconut liqueur
1-inch piece stem ginger, plus
  3 tablespoons syrup from the jar

3 Thinly slice the stem ginger and add to the pan with the ginger syrup. Bring just to a boil, then simmer gently until the liquid is slightly reduced and the sauce is fairly thick.

4 Pour the sauce onto the pineapple and coconut, let cool, then chill in the refrigerator before serving.

1 Peel and slice the pineapple, arrange in a serving dish and sprinkle the coconut slivers on top.

2 Place the pineapple juice and coconut liqueur in a saucepan and heat gently.

NUTRITIONAL NOTES
Per portion:

Calories	177
Fat, total	2.2g
Saturated fat	1.55g
Cholesterol	0mg
Fiber	2.2g

Perfumed Pineapple Salad

Prepare this fruit salad ahead to give the fruit time to absorb the perfumed flavor of the orange-flower water.

INGREDIENTS

Serves 4

1 small ripe pineapple

1 tablespoon confectioners' sugar

1 tablespoon orange-flower water, or
   more if desired

2/3 cup fresh dates, pitted and quartered

2 cups fresh strawberries, sliced

a few fresh mint sprigs, to serve

1 Cut the skin from the pineapple and, using the tip of a vegetable peeler, remove as many brown "eyes" as possible. Quarter the pineapple lengthwise, remove the core from each wedge, then slice.

2 Lay the pineapple slices in a shallow glass serving bowl. Sprinkle with confectioners' sugar and drizzle on the orange-flower water.

COOK'S TIP

Orange-flower water is available at Middle Eastern food stores or good delicatessens.

3 Add the dates and strawberries to the pineapple, cover and chill for at least 2 hours, stirring once or twice. Serve, decorated with a few mint sprigs.

NUTRITIONAL NOTES

Per portion:

Calories	127
Fat, total	0.4g
Saturated fat	0g
Cholesterol	0mg
Fiber	2.9g

Pineapple Crush

The sweet flavors of pineapple and lychees combine well with richly scented strawberries.

INGREDIENTS

Serves 4

2 small pineapples

4 cups strawberries

14-ounce can lychees

3 tablespoons kirsch or white rum

2 tablespoons confectioners' sugar

1 Remove the crown from both pineapples by twisting sharply. Reserve the leaves for decoration.

VARIATION

You could use other tropical fruit such as mango, papaya or guava as well as the pineapple.

NUTRITIONAL NOTES
Per portion:

Calories	251
Fat, total	0.7g
Saturated fat	0g
Cholesterol	0mg
Fiber	5.2g

2 Cut the fruit in half diagonally with a large serrated knife.

3 Cut around the flesh inside the skin with a small serrated knife, keeping the skin intact. Remove the core from the pineapple.

4 Chop the pineapple and combine with the strawberries and lychees, being careful not to damage the fruit.

5 Combine the kirsch or rum with the confectioners' sugar, pour onto the fruit and freeze for 45 minutes.

6 Turn the fruit out into the pineapple skins and decorate with the pineapple leaves. Serve chilled.

COOK'S TIP

A ripe pineapple will resist pressure when squeezed and will have a sweet, fragrant smell. In winter, freezing conditions can cause the flesh to blacken.

Pineapple Wedges with Allspice and Lime

Fresh pineapple is easy to prepare and always looks festive, so this dish is perfect for easy entertaining.

2 Loosen the flesh on each wedge by sliding a knife between the flesh and the skin. Cut the flesh into slices, leaving it on the skin.

3 Using a sharp-pointed or canelle knife, remove a few shreds of zest from the lime. Squeeze out the juice.

INGREDIENTS

Serves 4

1 ripe pineapple, about 1³/4 pounds

1 lime

1 tablespoon dark brown sugar

1 teaspoon ground allspice

1 Cut the pineapple lengthwise into quarters and remove the hard core from each wedge.

4 Sprinkle the pineapple with the lime juice and zest, sugar and allspice. Serve immediately, or chill for up to an hour.

NUTRITIONAL NOTES

Per portion:

Calories	96
Fat, total	0.5g
Saturated fat	0.03g
Cholesterol	0mg
Fiber	2.3g

Papaya and Mango Medley with Frozen Yogurt

Tropical fruit with mango frozen yogurt makes a wonderful dessert. Buy very ripe fruit for this dessert.

Serves 4

2 large ripe mangoes, total weight
     about 1 1/2 pounds

1 1/4 cups low-fat plain yogurt

8 dried apricots, halved

2/3 cup unsweetened orange juice

1 ripe papaya, about 11 ounces

1 Take one thick slice from one of the mangoes and, while still on the skin, slash the flesh with a sharp knife in a criss-cross pattern to make cubes.

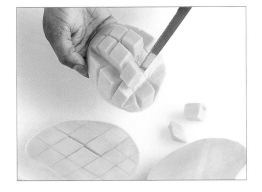

2 Turn the piece of mango inside-out and cut the cubed flesh from the skin. Place in a bowl, mash into a pulp with a fork, then add the yogurt and mix well. Spoon into a freezer tub and freeze for 1–1 1/2 hours, until half frozen.

3 Meanwhile, put the apricots and orange juice in a pan. Bring to a boil, then simmer until the apricots are soft, adding a little water, if needed, so that the apricots remain moist. Remove from heat and set aside to cool. Peel, pit and chop the mangoes.

4 Halve the papaya, and remove the seeds and peel. Dice the flesh and add to the mango. Pour on the apricot sauce.

5 Stir the mango yogurt a few times. Serve the fruit topped with the mango yogurt.

NUTRITIONAL NOTES
Per portion:

Calories	231
Fat, total	4.3g
Saturated fat	2.44g
Cholesterol	5.3mg
Fiber	7.5g

Pineapple and Passion Fruit Salsa

Serve this fruity salsa solo or as a filling for halved baby cantaloupes. Either way, it is a cool and refreshing dessert.

INGREDIENTS

Serves 6

1 small fresh pineapple
2 passion fruit
2/3 cup low-fat plain yogurt
2 tablespoons light brown sugar
meringues, to serve (optional)

1 Cut off the top and bottom of the pineapple so that it will stand firmly on a cutting board. Using a large sharp knife, slice off the peel.

2 Use a small sharp knife to carefully cut out the eyes from around the pineapple.

VARIATION

Use low-fat fromage frais instead of the yogurt, if desired.

3 Slice the pineapple and use a small pastry cutter to stamp out the tough core. Finely chop the flesh.

4 Cut the passion fruit in half, remove the seeds and scoop out the pulp into a bowl.

NUTRITIONAL NOTES

Per portion:

Calories	82
Fat, total	1.5g
Saturated fat	0.79g
Cholesterol	1.8mg
Fiber	1.3g

5 Stir in the chopped pineapple and yogurt. Cover and chill.

6 Stir in the brown sugar just before serving the salsa. Serve with meringues, if desired.

Grapefruit Salad with Campari and Orange

The bittersweet flavor of Campari combines especially well with citrus fruit for this sophisticated dessert.

INGREDIENTS

Serves 4

2/3 cup water

3 tablespoons sugar

4 tablespoons Campari

2 tablespoons lemon juice

4 grapefruit

5 oranges

4 sprigs fresh mint

COOK'S TIP

When buying citrus fruit, choose brightly colored varieties that feel heavy for their size.

1 Bring the water to a boil in a small saucepan, add the sugar and simmer until dissolved. Cool in a metal tray, then add the Campari and lemon juice. Chill until ready to serve.

2 Peel the grapefruit and oranges. Working over a bowl, to catch the juice, cut the fruit into segments. Add them to the bowl, stir in the Campari syrup and chill again.

3 Spoon the salad into four dishes and finish with a sprig of fresh mint.

NUTRITIONAL NOTES

Per portion:

Calories	182
Fat, total	0.4g
Saturated fat	0g
Cholesterol	0mg
Fiber	5.3g

Muscat Grape Frappé

The flavor and perfume of the Muscat grape is rarely more enticing than when captured in this icy-cool salad.

2 Remove the seeds from the grapes with a pair of tweezers. If you have time, peel the grapes.

3 Scrape the frozen wine with a tablespoon to make a fine ice. Combine the grapes with the ice and spoon into four shallow glasses.

INGREDIENTS

Serves 4

1/2 bottle Muscat wine, Beaumes de Venise, Frontignan or Rivesaltes

2/3 cup water

4 cups Muscat grapes

COOK'S TIP

To make this frappé alcohol-free, substitute 1 1/4 cups apple or grape juice for the wine.

1 Pour the wine into a stainless-steel or nonstick tray, add the water and freeze for 3 hours or until solid.

NUTRITIONAL NOTES

Per portion:

Calories	155
Fat, total	0g
Saturated fat	0g
Cholesterol	0mg
Fiber	1g

Cool Green Fruit Salad

A sophisticated, simple fruit salad, which would look wonderful served on a bed of crushed ice.

INGREDIENTS

Serves 6

3 Ogen or Galia melons

1 cup green seedless grapes

2 kiwis

1 star fruit, plus extra slices to garnish

1 green-skinned apple

1 lime

3/4 cup unsweetened sparkling grape juice

3 Thinly pare the zest from the lime and cut it in fine strips. Blanch in boiling water for 30 seconds, and then drain them and rinse them in cold water. Squeeze the juice from the lime and pour it onto the fruit. Toss lightly.

4 Spoon the prepared fruit into the reserved melon shells; then chill the shells until required. To serve, spoon the sparkling grape juice onto the fruit and sprinkle with lime zest. Decorate with slices of star fruit.

1 Halve the melons and scoop out the seeds. Keeping the shells intact, scoop out the flesh and cut into bite-size cubes. Reserve the melon shells.

2 Cut any large grapes in half. Peel and chop the kiwi. Slice the star fruit and set aside a few slices for decoration. Core and slice the apple and place in a bowl, with the melon, grapes and kiwi.

NUTRITIONAL NOTES

Per portion:

Calories	91
Fat, total	0.4g
Saturated fat	0.00g
Cholesterol	0.0mg
Fiber	1.6g

Blackberry Salad with Rose Granita

The blackberry is a member of the rose family and combines especially well with rosewater.

INGREDIENTS

Serves 4

2¹/2 cups water

²/3 cup sugar

petals from 1 fresh red rose, finely chopped

1 teaspoon rosewater

2 teaspoons lemon juice

4 cups blackberries

confectioners' sugar, for dusting

For the meringue

2 egg whites

¹/2 cup sugar

2 Preheat the oven to 275°F. Line a baking sheet with six layers of newspaper and cover with nonstick baking parchment.

4 Spoon the meringue into a piping bag fitted with a ¹/2-inch plain nozzle. Pipe the meringue in lengths on the lined baking sheet. Dry in the bottom of the oven for 1¹/2–2 hours.

1 Bring ²/3 cup of the water to a boil in a stainless-steel or enamel saucepan. Add the sugar and chopped rose petals, then lower the heat and simmer for 5 minutes. Strain the syrup into a deep metal tray, add the remaining water, the rosewater and lemon juice; let cool. Freeze the mixture for approximately 3 hours or until solid.

3 Make the meringue. Whisk the egg whites in a grease-free bowl until they form soft peaks. Whisk in the sugar, a little at a time, then continue to whisk until the meringue forms stiff peaks when the whisk is lifted out of the bowl.

5 Break the meringue into 2-inch lengths and place three or four lengths on each of four large plates. Pile the blackberries next to the meringue. With a tablespoon, scrape the granita finely. Shape into ovals and place on the meringue. Dust with confectioners' sugar and serve immediately.

COOK'S TIP

Serve the dessert as soon as possible after piling the granita on the meringue, or the meringue will soon get soggy.

NUTRITIONAL NOTES

Per portion:

Calories	310
Fat, total	0.2g
Saturated fat	0g
Cholesterol	0mg
Fiber	3.5g

VARIATION

Other berries such as blueberries, raspberries or loganberries would work equally well with this dessert.

Blueberry and Orange Salad Meringues

What could be prettier than this simple salad of delicate blueberries, oranges and meringues flavored with lavender?

INGREDIENTS

Serves 4

6 oranges

3 cups blueberries

8 sprigs fresh lavender

For the meringue

2 egg whites

1/2 cup sugar

1 teaspoon fresh lavender flowers

2 Spoon the meringue into a piping bag fitted with a 1/4-inch plain nozzle. Pipe small buttons of meringue onto the prepared baking sheet. Dry the meringue near the bottom of the oven for 1 1/2–2 hours.

4 Arrange the segments on four plates, fanning them out.

1 Preheat the oven to 275ºF. Line a baking sheet with six layers of newspaper and cover with nonstick baking parchment. Whisk the egg whites in a large grease-free bowl until they hold soft peaks. Add the sugar a little at a time, whisking thoroughly after each addition. Fold in the lavender flowers.

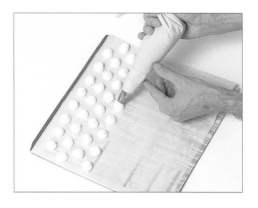

3 To segment the oranges, remove the peel from the top, bottom and sides with a serrated knife. Loosen the segments by cutting with a paring knife between the flesh and the membranes, holding the fruit over a bowl to catch the juice.

5 Combine the blueberries with the lavender meringues and pile inthe center of each plate. Decorate with sprigs of lavender and serve immediately.

NUTRITIONAL NOTES

Per portion:

Calories	198
Fat, total	0.3g
Saturated fat	0g
Cholesterol	0mg
Fiber	3.5g

COOK'S TIP

Lavender is used in both sweet and savory dishes. Always use fresh or recently dried flowers, and avoid artificially scented bunches that are sold for dried flower displays.

VARIATION

You could use blackberries or firm raspberries with fresh rosemary leaves and flowers for this dessert. You would also make 3-inch circles of meringue instead of small buttons and layer the berries in between circles of meringue.

Mixed Fruit Salad

A really good fruit salad is always refreshing, especially when it comes bathed in fresh orange and lemon juices.

1 Place the fresh orange and lemon juices in a large serving bowl.

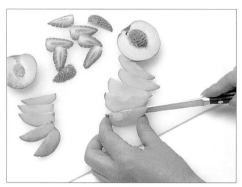

2 Prepare all the fruits by washing or peeling them as necessary. Cut them into bite-size pieces. Halve the grapes and remove any seeds. Core and slice the apples. Pit and slice larger fruit and leave small berries whole. As soon as each fruit is prepared, add it to the juices in the bowl.

3 Taste the salad, adding sugar if needed. Liqueur can also be added, if desired. Cover the bowl and put it in the refrigerator for at least 2 hours. Mix well before serving.

INGREDIENTS

Serves 4

juice of 3 large sweet oranges

juice of 1 lemon

1 banana

1–2 apples

1 ripe pear

2 peaches or nectarines

4–5 apricots or plums

1 cup black or green grapes

1 cup strawberries or raspberries

any other fruits in season

sugar, to taste (optional)

2–3 tablespoons Kirsch, Maraschino
   or other liqueur (optional)

COOK'S TIP

For an herb infused flavor add chopped fresh herbs, try pineapple mint, lemon balm or borage flowers.

NUTRITIONAL NOTES
Per portion:

Calories	133
Fat, total	0.4g
Saturated fat	0.03g
Cholesterol	0mg
Fiber	3.8g

Spiced Fruit Platter

The spicy sour flavor of chat masala may seem a little strange at first, but this Indian dessert can become addictive!

INGREDIENTS

Serves 6

1 pineapple

2 papayas

1 small melon

juice of 2 limes

2 pomegranates

chat masala, to taste

sprigs of fresh mint, to decorate

NUTRITIONAL NOTES

Per portion:

Calories	102
Fat, total	0.5g
Saturated fat	0g
Cholesterol	0mg
Fiber	4.8g

1 Peel the pineapple. Remove the core and any remaining "eyes," then cut the flesh lengthwise into thin wedges. Peel the papayas, cut them in half, and then into thin wedges. Halve the melon and remove the seeds from the middle. Cut it into thin wedges and remove the skin.

2 Arrange the fruit on six individual plates and sprinkle with the lime juice. Cut the pomegranates in half and scoop out the seeds, discarding any pith. Sprinkle the seeds onto the fruit. Serve, sprinkled with a little chat masala to taste. Sprinkle on a few sprigs of mint, to decorate.

Ruby Fruit Salad

After a rich main course, this port-flavored fruit salad is light and refreshing. Use any fruit available.

INGREDIENTS

Serves 8

1 1/4 cups water

1/2 cup sugar

1 cinnamon stick

4 cloves

pared zest of 1 orange

1 1/4 cups port

2 oranges

1 small ripe Ogen, Charentais or
  honeydew melon

4 small bananas

2 apples

2 cups seedless grapes

1 Put the water, sugar, spices and pared orange zest into a pan and stir over low heat to dissolve the sugar. Then bring to a boil, lower the heat, cover and simmer for 10 minutes. Let cool, then add the port.

NUTRITIONAL NOTES
Per portion:

Calories	212
Fat, total	0.2g
Saturated fat	0.04g
Cholesterol	0mg
Fiber	1.9g

2 Strain the liquid into a bowl. With a sharp knife, cut off all the skin and pith from the oranges. Then, holding each orange over the bowl to catch the juice, cut it into segments, and drop them into the syrup. Squeeze the remaining pulp to release any juice.

3 Cut the melon in half, remove the seeds and scoop out the flesh or cut it in small cubes. Add it to the syrup.

4 Peel the bananas and cut them diagonally in 1/2-inch slices. Quarter and core the apples and cut the wedges in small cubes. Leave the skin on, or peel them if it is tough. Halve the grapes if large or leave them whole. Stir all the fruit into the syrup, cover with plastic wrap and chill for an hour before serving.

Winter Fruit Salad

A colorful, refreshing and nutritious fruit salad, this makes an excellent choice for a winter buffet.

2 Segment the oranges, catching any juice in the bowl, then add the orange segments and pineapple to the fruit juice mixture.

3 Core and chop the apples and pears and add them to the bowl.

4 Stir in the plums, dates and apricots. Cover and chill for several hours. Decorate with fresh mint sprigs to serve.

INGREDIENTS

Serves 6

8-ounce can pineapple cubes in fruit juice

scant 1 cup fresh orange juice

scant 1 cup unsweetened apple juice

2 tablespoons orange- or
    apple-flavored liqueur

2 tablespoons honey (optional)

2 oranges, peeled

2 green-skinned apples

2 pears

4 plums, pitted and chopped

12 fresh dates, pitted and chopped

$1/2$ cup dried apricots

fresh mint sprigs, to decorate

1 Drain the pineapple, reserving the juice in a large serving bowl. Add the orange juice, apple juice, liqueur and honey, if using, and stir.

NUTRITIONAL NOTES

Per portion:

Calories	227
Fat, total	0.37g
Saturated fat	0g
Cholesterol	0mg
Fiber	5.34g

Mixed Melon Salad

Several melon varieties are combined with strongly flavored wild or woodland strawberries for a delicious salad.

INGREDIENTS

Serves 4

1 cantaloupe or charentais melon

1 Galia melon

2 pounds watermelon

1½ cups wild strawberries

4 sprigs fresh mint

NUTRITIONAL NOTES
Per portion:

Calories	91
Fat, total	0.7g
Saturated fat	0g
Cholesterol	0mg
Fiber	2.7g

1 Cut the cantaloupe or charentais melon, Galia melon and watermelon in half.

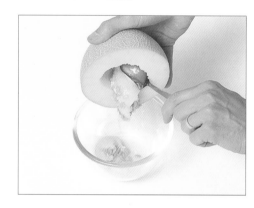

2 Using a spoon, scoop out the seeds from the cantaloupe or charentais, and the Galia.

3 With a melon scoop, take out as many balls as you can from all three melons. Mix them in a large bowl, cover and put the bowl in the refrigerator. Chill for 2–3 hours.

4 Just before serving, add the wild strawberries and mix lightly. Spoon into four stemmed glass dishes.

5 Decorate with sprigs of mint and serve immediately.

Fresh Fruit with Mango Sauce

*This bright, flavorful sauce is easy to
prepare and turns a simple fruit salad
into something very special.*

INGREDIENTS

Serves 6

1 large ripe mango, peeled, pitted and chopped

zest of 1 unwaxed orange

juice of 3 oranges

sugar, to taste

2 peaches

2 nectarines

1 small mango, peeled

2 plums

1 pear or 1/2 small melon

juice of 1 lemon

2 heaping tablespoons wild strawberries
    (optional)

2 heaping tablespoons raspberries

2 heaping tablespoons blueberries

small mint sprigs, to decorate

1 In a food processor fitted with a
metal blade, process the large
mango until smooth. Add the orange
zest, juice and sugar to taste and
process again until very smooth. Press
through a sieve into a bowl and chill
the sauce.

2 Peel the peaches if desired,
then slice and pit the peaches,
nectarines, small mango and plums.
Quarter the pear and remove the core
and seeds, or, if using, slice the melon
thinly and remove the peel.

3 Place the sliced fruits on a large
plate, sprinkle with lemon juice
and chill, covered with plastic wrap,
for up to 3 hours before serving.
(Some fruits may discolor if cut too far
ahead of time.)

4 To serve, arrange the sliced fruits
on individual serving plates, spoon
the berries on top, drizzle with a little
of the mango sauce and decorate with
the mint sprigs. Serve the remaining
sauce separately.

NUTRITIONAL NOTES

Per portion:

Calories	229
Fat, total	0.6g
Saturated fat	0g
Cholesterol	0.0mg
Fiber	4.9g

Marzipan Figs with Dates

*Sweet Mediterranean figs and dates
combine well with crisp apples.
A hint of almond unites the flavors.*

INGREDIENTS

Serves 4

6 large apples

juice of 1/2 lemon

1 cup fresh dates

1 ounce white marzipan

1 teaspoon orange-flower water

4 tablespoons low-fat yogurt

4 green or purple figs

4 almonds, toasted

1 Core the apples. Slice thinly and cut into fine matchsticks. Use lemon juice to prevent them from browning.

2 Remove the pits from the dates and cut the flesh into fine strips, then mix with the apple matchsticks in a bowl.

3 Soften the marzipan with orange-flower water and combine with the low-fat yogurt. Mix well.

4 Pile the apples and dates in the center of four plates. Remove the stem from each of the figs and cut the fruit into quarters without slicing the bottom. Squeeze the bottom with the thumb and forefinger to open the fruit.

5 Place a fig in the center of the salad, spoon in the yogurt filling and decorate each portion with a toasted almond.

NUTRITIONAL NOTES

Per portion:

Calories	210
Fat, total	3.1g
Saturated fat	0.15g
Cholesterol	0.6mg
Fiber	5.4g

Dried Fruit Salad with Summer Berries

*This is a wonderful combination of fresh
and dried fruit. In the winter you can
use frozen raspberries or blackberries.*

INGREDIENTS

Serves 4

$^1/_2$ cup dried apricots

$^1/_2$ cup dried peaches

1 fresh pear

1 fresh apple

1 fresh orange

$^2/_3$ cup mixed raspberries and blackberries

$2^1/_2$ cup water

1 cinnamon stick

$^1/_4$ cup sugar

1 tablespoon honey

1 Soak the apricots and peaches in
water for 1–2 hours, until plump,
then drain and halve or quarter.

2 Peel and core the pear and apple
and cut into cubes. Peel the orange
with a sharp knife, removing all the
pith, and cut into wedges. Place all the
fruit in a large saucepan with the
raspberries and blackberries.

NUTRITIONAL NOTES

Per portion:

Calories	190
Fat, total	0.4g
Saturated fat	0g
Cholesterol	0.0mg
Fiber	5.1g

3 Add the water, the cinnamon,
sugar and honey.

4 Bring to a boil, then cover the pan
and simmer very gently for 10–12
minutes, until the fruit is just tender,
stirring occasionally.

Tropical Fruit Salad

Like all nuts, coconut is a significant source of fat, so go easy on the strips used to decorate this delicious salad.

INGREDIENTS

Serves 4–6

1 medium pineapple, about 1 pound, 5 ounces

14-ounce can guava halves in syrup

2 medium bananas, sliced

1 large mango, peeled, pitted and diced

4 ounces stem ginger, plus 2 tablespoons of the
   syrup from the jar

4 tablespoons thick coconut milk

2 teaspoons sugar

1/2 teaspoon freshly grated nutmeg

1/2 teaspoon ground cinnamon

a few fine strips of coconut, to decorate

1 Peel, core and cube the pineapple, and place in a serving bowl. Drain the guavas, reserving the syrup, and chop. Add the guavas to the bowl with half the sliced banana and the mango.

2 Chop the stem ginger and add to the fruit mixture.

3 Pour 2 tablespoons of the ginger syrup, and the reserved guava syrup, into a blender or food processor. Add the remaining banana slices with the coconut milk and the sugar. Blend into a smooth purée.

NUTRITIONAL NOTES

Per portion:

Calories	340
Fat, total	1.8g
Saturated fat	0.83g
Cholesterol	0mg
Fiber	8.1g

4 Pour the banana and coconut mixture onto the tropical fruit. Add a little grated nutmeg and a sprinkling of cinnamon on top. Serve chilled, decorated with fine strips of coconut.

Melon and Strawberry Salad

This colorful fruit salad can be served either as a dessert or as a refreshing appetizer before a meal.

Serves 4

1 Galia melon

1 honeydew melon

1/2 watermelon

2 cups fresh strawberries, halved if large

1 tablespoon lemon juice

1 tablespoon honey

1 tablespoon water

1 tablespoon chopped fresh mint

2 Mix the lemon juice, honey and water in a bowl and stir into the fruit.

3 Sprinkle the chopped mint on the fruit and serve.

NUTRITIONAL NOTES

Per portion:

Calories	139
Fat, total	0.84g
Saturated fat	0g
Cholesterol	0mg
Fiber	2g

1 Prepare the melons by cutting them in half and scraping out the seeds. Use a melon baller to scoop out the flesh into balls or a knife to cut it into cubes. Place these in a fruit bowl and add the fresh strawberries.

Papaya and Green Grapes with Mint Syrup

*This wonderful combination of textures
and flavors makes the perfect dessert to
follow a spicy main course.*

INGREDIENTS

Serves 4

2 large papayas

2 cups seedless green grapes

juice of 3 limes

1-inch piece fresh ginger root, peeled and
   finely grated

1 tablespoon honey

5 fresh mint leaves, cut into thin strips, plus
   extra whole leaves, to decorate

1 Peel the papaya and cut into small
cubes, discarding the seeds. Cut the
grapes in half.

2 In a bowl, mix the lime juice,
grated ginger, honey and shredded
mint leaves.

3 Add the papaya and grapes and
toss well. Cover and set in a cool
place to marinate for 1 hour.

4 Serve in a large dish or individual
stemmed glasses, garnished with
the whole fresh mint leaves.

NUTRITIONAL NOTES

Per portion:

Calories	120
Fat, total	0.2g
Saturated fat	0g
Cholesterol	0mg
Fiber	4.4g

Papaya Skewers with Passion Fruit Coulis

Tropical fruits make a simple, exotic dessert. The passion fruit flesh can be used without puréeing or sieving.

INGREDIENTS

Serves 6

3 ripe papayas

10 passion fruit or kiwis

2 tablespoons fresh lime juice

2 tablespoons confectioners' sugar

2 tablespoons white rum

lime slices, to garnish

NUTRITIONAL NOTES

Per portion:

Calories	94
Fat, total	0.3g
Saturated fat	0g
Cholesterol	0mg
Fiber	4.1g

3 Press the fruit pulp through a sieve placed over a bowl; discard the seeds. Add the lime juice, confectioners' sugar and rum, then stir the coulis well until the sugar has dissolved.

4 Spoon a little coulis onto plates and place the skewers on top. Scoop the flesh from the remaining passion or kiwi and spoon on. Serve immediately, garnished with lime slices.

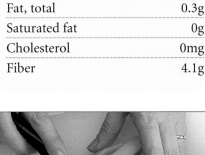

1 Cut the papayas in half and scoop out the seeds. Peel them and cut the flesh into even-size chunks. Thread the chunks onto six bamboo skewers.

2 Halve eight of the passion fruit or kiwi and scoop out the flesh. Purée the flesh for a few seconds in a blender of food processor.

Three-fruit Compote

Mixing dried fruits with fresh ones makes a good combination, especially if flavored with orange-flower water.

INGREDIENTS

Serves 6

1 cup dried apricots

1¼ cups water

1 small ripe pineapple

1 small ripe melon, about 1 pound

1 tablespoon orange-flower water

mint sprigs, to decorate

NUTRITIONAL NOTES

Per portion:

Calories	86
Fat, total	0.4g
Saturated fat	0g
Cholesterol	0mg
Fiber	3.2g

2 Peel and quarter the pineapple, cut the core from each quarter and discard. Cut the flesh into chunks.

3 Cut the melon in half and out the seeds. Working over a bowl to catch the juices, scoop balls from the flesh. Add the juices into the apricots.

4 Put the apricots, with the juices, into a bowl. Stir in the orange-flower water. Add the pineapple and melon and mix all the fruits gently.

5 Pour into a serving dish or individual dishes. Decorate with a mint sprig and chill before serving.

1 Put the apricots into a saucepan and pour in the water. Bring to a boil, then lower the heat and simmer for 5 minutes. Let cool.

VARIATION

A good fruit salad doesn't have to consist of a mixture of fruits. For a delicious red fruit salad, try berries with sliced plums, or for green fruits, try apple, kiwi and green grapes.

Apricot and Banana Compote

This compote is delicious with low-fat custard or ice cream. Served for break-fast, it makes a tasty start to the day.

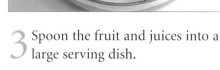

3 Spoon the fruit and juices into a large serving dish.

4 Serve immediately, or cover and chill for several hours first. Sprinkle with sliced almonds just before serving.

INGREDIENTS

Serves 4

1 cup dried apricots

1¹/4 cups unsweetened orange juice

2/3 cup unsweetened apple juice

1 teaspoon ground ginger

3 medium bananas, sliced

¹/4 cup toasted sliced almonds

1 Put the apricots in a saucepan with the fruit juices and ginger and stir. Cover, bring to a boil and then simmer gently for 10 minutes, stirring.

2 Set aside to cool, leaving the lid on. Once the compote is cool, stir in the sliced bananas.

COOK'S TIP

Use other combinations of dried and fresh fruit, such as prunes or figs and apples or peaches.

NUTRITIONAL NOTES
Per portion:

Calories	241
Fat, total	4.18g
Saturated fat	0.37g
Cholesterol	0mg
Fiber	4.91g

Spiced Fruits Jubilee

Based on the classic Cherries Jubilee, this is a great way to use a glut of pitted fruit. The spiced syrup is a delicious bonus.

2 Add the fruit, cover the pan and simmer for 5 minutes. Drain the fruit and set it aside; return the syrup to the pan. Boil it, uncovered, for 2 minutes or until thick and syrupy.

3 Put the arrowroot in a small bowl and stir in 2 tablespoons of the brandy. Stir the mixture into the syrup. Continue cooking and stirring, until the sauce thickens. Return the fruit to the pan.

4 If serving with ice cream, place a scoop in each serving bowl and spoon the hot fruit on top. Warm the remaining brandy in a small pan, then set it on fire. For maximum dramatic effect, ladle it onto the fruit at the table.

INGREDIENTS

Serves 6

1/2 cup sugar

thinly pared zest of 1 lemon

4 whole cloves

1 cinnamon stick

1 1/4 cups water

8 ounces tart red plums, pitted and sliced

8 ounces nectarines, pitted and chopped

2 cups cherries, pitted

1 teaspoon arrowroot

5 tablespoons brandy

low-fat vanilla ice cream, to serve (optional)

1 Put the sugar, lemon zest, cloves, cinnamon stick and water in a pan. Bring to a boil, stirring, then simmer for 5 minutes. Lift out the spices with a slotted spoon and discard.

NUTRITIONAL NOTES
Per portion:

Calories	151
Fat, total	0.1g
Saturated fat	0g
Cholesterol	0mg
Fiber	1g

Italian Fruit Salad and Ice Cream

Macerated fruit is delectable on its own, and also make a wonderful ice cream.

INGREDIENTS

Serves 6

8 cups mixed fruits, such as strawberries, raspberries, loganberries, red currants, blueberries, peaches, apricots, plums and melons

juice of 6–8 oranges

juice of 1 lemon

1 tablespoon liquid pear and apple concentrate

4 tablespoons very low-fat fromage frais

2 tablespoons orange-flavored liqueur (optional)

fresh mint sprigs, to decorate

3 Set half the macerated fruit aside to serve as it is. Purée the remainder in a blender or food processor.

4 Gently warm the pear and apple concentrate and stir it into the fruit purée. Whip the fromage frais and fold it in, then add the liqueur, if using.

NUTRITIONAL NOTES
Per portion:

Calories	60
Fat, total	0.2g
Saturated fat	0.01g
Cholesterol	0.1mg
Fiber	3.2g

5 Churn in an ice-cream maker. Alternatively, place in a container and freeze until ice crystals form around the edge, then beat until smooth. Repeat once or twice, then freeze until firm. Soften slightly before serving decorated with mint. Serve accompanied by the macerated fruit.

1 Prepare the fruit according to type. Cut it into reasonably small pieces, large enough to hold their shape.

2 Put the fruit pieces in a serving bowl and pour in enough orange juice to cover. Add the lemon juice, stir gently, cover and chill for 2 hours.

Low-fat Ices & Sorbets

◆ ◆ ◆

Red Currant and Raspberry Coulis

A dessert sauce to serve with meringues and fruit sorbets. Make it pretty with a decoration of fresh flowers and leaves.

3 Blend the cornstarch with the orange juice, then stir into the fruit purée. Transfer to a saucepan and bring to a boil, stirring continuously, and cook for 1–2 minutes, until smooth and thick. Leave until cold.

4 Spoon the sauce onto each plate. Drip the cream from a teaspoon to make small dots evenly around the edge. Draw a toothpick through the dots to form heart shapes. Scoop or spoon sorbet into the middle and decorate with flowers.

INGREDIENTS

Serves 6

2 cups red currants

4 cups raspberries

1/2 cup confectioners' sugar

1 tablespoon cornstarch

juice of 1 orange

2 tablespoons cream

edible flowers, to decorate

1 Strip the red currants from their stems. Place them in a blender with the sugar and raspberries, and blend into a purée.

2 Press the fruit mixture through a fine sieve into a bowl and discard the seeds and pulp.

NUTRITIONAL NOTES
Per portion:

Calories	81
Fat, total	1.2g
Saturated fat	0.6g
Cholesterol	0mg
Fiber	3.2g

Christmas Cranberry Bombe

*This alternative to Christmas pudding is
light and low in fat, but still very festive
and luxurious.*

INGREDIENTS

Serves 6

1 cup buttermilk

4 tablespoons low-fat crème fraîche

1 vanilla bean

2 eggs

2 tablespoons honey

2 tablespoons chopped angelica

2 tablespoons mixed citrus peel

2 teaspoons sliced almonds, toasted

For the sorbet center

1 1/2 cups fresh or frozen cranberries

2/3 cup fresh orange juice

finely grated zest of 1/2 orange

1/2 teaspoon allspice

1/4 cup brown sugar

1 Heat the buttermilk, crème fraîche
and vanilla bean until the mixture is
almost boiling. Remove the vanilla bean.

NUTRITIONAL NOTES

Per portion:

Calories	153
Fat, total	4.6g
Saturated fat	1.58g
Cholesterol	75.5mg
Fiber	1.5g

2 Place the eggs in a heatproof bowl
over a pan of hot water and whisk
until they are pale and thick. Pour in
the heated buttermilk in a thin stream,
whisking hard. Continue whisking
over the hot water until the mixture
thickens slightly.

3 Whisk in the honey and then cool.
Spoon the mixture into a freezer
container and freeze until slushy, put
into a bowl and stir in the chopped
angelica, citrus peel and almonds.

4 Pack into a 5-cup pudding mold
and hollow out the center. Freeze
until firm.

5 Meanwhile, make the sorbet
center. Put the cranberries, orange
juice, zest and allspice in a pan and
cook gently until the cranberries are
soft. Set some cranberries aside for
decorating. Add the sugar to the rest,
then purée in a food processor until
almost smooth, but still with some
texture. Let cool.

6 Fill the hollowed-out center of
the bombe with the cranberry
mixture, smooth over and freeze until
firm. To serve, let soften slightly at
room temperature, then turn out
and serve in medium-sized slices,
decorated with the reserved cranberries.

Berry Salad Ice Cream

What could be more cooling on a hot summer day than fresh summer berries, lightly frozen in this irresistible ice cream?

INGREDIENTS

Serves 6

6 cups mixed summer berries, such as
   raspberries, strawberries, black currants
   or red currants
2 eggs
1 cup low-fat plain yogurt
3/4 cup red grape juice
1 tablespoon powdered gelatin

1 Reserve half the fruit for the decoration; purée the rest in a food processor, then sieve it over a bowl to make a smooth purée.

VARIATION

You could use other combinations of summer fruit such as apricots, peaches and nectarines, with apple or orange juice for a more delicate ice cream.

NUTRITIONAL NOTES
Per portion:

Calories	116
Fat, total	3.9g
Saturated fat	1.69g
Cholesterol	66.8mg
Fiber	3.6g

2 Separate the eggs, whisk the yolks and the yogurt into the fruit purée.

3 Heat the grape juice until almost boiling, then remove it from heat. Sprinkle the gelatin on the grape juice and stir to dissolve the gelatin completely.

COOK'S TIP

Red grape juice has a good flavor and improves the color of the ice, but if it is not available, use cranberry, apple or orange juice instead.

4 Whisk the dissolved gelatin mixture into the fruit purée. Cool, then pour the mixture into a freezerproof container. Freeze until half-frozen and slushy in consistency.

5 Whisk the egg whites in a grease-free bowl until stiff. Quickly fold them into the half-frozen mixture.

6 Return the ice cream to the freezer and freeze until almost firm. Scoop into individual dishes and decorate with the reserved berries.

Frozen Apple and Blackberry Terrine

This pretty, three-layered terrine can be frozen, so you can enjoy it at any time of year.

Serves 6

1 pound apples

1¼ cups sweet cider

1 tablespoon honey

1 teaspoon pure vanilla extract

scant 2 cups fresh or frozen and
    thawed blackberries

1 tablespoon powdered gelatin

2 egg whites

fresh apple slices and blackberries,
    to decorate

1 Peel, core and chop the apples and place them in a pan with half the cider. Bring the cider to a boil, then lower the heat, cover the pan and let the apples simmer gently until tender.

2 Put the apples into a food processor and process into a smooth purée. Stir in the honey and vanilla. Add half the blackberries to half the apple purée, and process again until smooth. Sieve to remove the seeds.

3 Heat the remaining cider until almost boiling, then sprinkle on the gelatin and stir until the gelatin has dissolved completely. Add half the gelatin mixture to the apple purée and half to the blackberry purée.

4 Let both purées cool until almost set. Whisk the egg whites until they are stiff. Quickly fold them into the apple purée. Remove half the purée to another bowl. Stir the remaining whole blackberries into half the apple purée, and then put this into a 7½-cup loaf pan, packing it down firmly.

5 Top with the blackberry purée and spread it evenly. Finally, add a layer of the plain apple purée and smooth it evenly. If necessary, freeze each layer until firm before adding the next.

6 Freeze until firm. When ready to serve, remove from the freezer and let stand at room temperature for about 20 minutes to soften. Serve in slices, decorated with fresh apple slices and blackberries.

VARIATION

For a quicker version the mixture can be set without the layering. Purée the apples and blackberries together, stir the dissolved gelatin and whisked egg whites into the mixture, turn the whole thing into the pan and let the mixture set.

NUTRITIONAL NOTES
Per portion:

Calories	83
Fat, total	0.2g
Saturated fat	0g
Cholesterol	0mg
Fiber	2.6g

Key Lime Sorbet

Cool and refreshing, this traditional sorbet is ideal for serving after a curry or any spicy dish.

INGREDIENTS

Serves 4

1¼ cups sugar

2½ cups water

grated zest of 1 lime

¾ cup fresh key lime juice

1 tablespoon fresh lemon juice

2 tablespoons confectioners' sugar

lime shreds, to decorate

1 In a small heavy saucepan, dissolve the sugar in the water, without stirring, over medium heat. When the sugar has dissolved, boil the syrup for 5–6 minutes. Remove from heat and let cool.

2 Mix the cooled sugar syrup and lime zest and juice in a bowl. Stir well. Sharpen the flavor by adding the lemon juice. Stir in the confectioners' sugar.

3 Freeze the mixture in an ice-cream maker, following the instructions of the machine's manufacturer. Decorate with lime shreds.

NUTRITIONAL NOTES

Per portion:

Calories	300
Fat, total	0g
Saturated fat	0g
Cholesterol	0mg
Fiber	0g

COOK'S TIP

To make ice cream by hand, pour the mixture into a freezerproof container and freeze until softly set, about 3 hours. Spoon into a food processor and process until smooth. Return the mixture to the freezer container and freeze again until set. Repeat this process 2 or 3 times, until a smooth consistency is obtained.

Ruby Grapefruit Sorbet

On a hot day, nothing slips down more easily than a smooth sorbet. This one looks as good as it tastes.

INGREDIENTS

Serves 8

3/4 cup granulated sugar

1/2 cup water

4 cups strained freshly squeezed
    ruby grapefruit juice

1 tablespoon fresh lemon juice

1 tablespoon confectioners' sugar

mint leaves, to decorate

1 In a small heavy saucepan, dissolve the sugar in the water over medium heat, without stirring. When the sugar has dissolved, boil the syrup for 3–4 minutes. Remove from heat and let cool.

2 Pour the cooled sugar syrup into the grapefruit juice. Stir well. Taste the mixture and adjust the flavor by adding the lemon juice or the confectioners' sugar, if necessary, but do not make it over-sweet.

NUTRITIONAL NOTES
Per portion:

Calories	133
Fat, total	0.1g
Saturated fat	0g
Cholesterol	0mg
Fiber	0g

3 Pour the mixture into a metal or plastic freezer container and freeze for about 3 hours or until softly set.

4 Remove from the container and chop roughly into 3-inch pieces. Place in a food processor and process until smooth. Return the mixture to the freezer container and freeze again until set. Repeat this freezing and chopping process 2 or 3 times, until a smooth consistency is obtained.

5 Alternatively, freeze the sorbet in an ice-cream maker, following the manufacturer's instructions. Serve, decorated with mint leaves.

Mango Sorbet with Mango Sauce

After a heavy meal, this Indian specialty makes a refreshing dessert. Remove from the freezer 10 minutes before serving.

INGREDIENTS

Serves 4

5 cups mango pulp

1/2 teaspoon lemon juice

grated zest of 1 orange and 1 lemon

4 egg whites

1/4 cup sugar

1/2 cup low-fat plain yogurt

1/2 cup confectioners' sugar

1 In a large, chilled bowl that can safely be used in the freezer, mix half of the mango pulp with the lemon juice and the grated citrus zest.

NUTRITIONAL NOTES

Per portion:

Calories	259
Fat, total	1.7g
Saturated fat	0.79g
Cholesterol	1.8mg
Fiber	5.9g

2 Whisk the egg whites in a grease-free bowl to soft peaks and fold into the mango mixture with the sugar. Cover, and freeze for at least 1 hour.

3 Remove the sorbet from the freezer and beat again. Transfer to an ice-cream container, and freeze until solid.

4 Lightly whisk the yogurt with the confectioners' sugar and the remaining pulp. Spoon into a bowl and chill for 24 hours. Scoop individual servings of sorbet. Cover with mango sauce.

Lychee and Elderflower Sorbet

The flavor of elderflowers is famous for bringing out the extract of gooseberries, and it complements lychees wonderfully.

Serves 4

3/4 cup sugar

1 2/3 cups water

1 1/4 pounds fresh lychees, peeled and pitted

1 tablespoon undiluted elderflower cordial

cookies, to serve (optional)

NUTRITIONAL NOTES

Per portion:

Calories	249
Fat, total	0.1g
Saturated fat	0g
Cholesterol	0mg
Fiber	0.9g

1 Heat the sugar and water until the sugar has dissolved. Then boil for 5 minutes and add the lychees. Lower the heat and simmer for 7 minutes. Remove from heat and let cool.

2 Purée the fruit and syrup. Place a sieve over a bowl and press the purée through it with a spoon.

3 Stir the elderflower cordial into the strained purée, then pour the mixture into a freezerproof container. Freeze for approximately 2 hours, until ice crystals start to form around the edges.

4 Remove the sorbet from the freezer and process briefly in a food processor or blender to break up the crystals. Repeat this process twice more, then freeze until firm.

5 Transfer to the refrigerator for 10 minutes to soften slightly before serving in scoops. Cookies can be served with the sorbet but aren't really necessary. If you do serve them, remember that they will increase the fat content of the dessert.

Plum and Port Sorbet

This is a grown-up sorbet, but you can use red grape juice instead of port, if you prefer.

INGREDIENTS

Serves 6

2 pounds ripe red plums, halved
   and pitted

6 tablespoons sugar

3 tablespoons water

3 tablespoons ruby port or red wine

cookies, to serve (optional)

1 Put the plums in a pan with the sugar and water. Stir over low heat until the sugar has melted, then cover and simmer gently for about 5 minutes, until the fruit is soft.

2 Put into a food processor and purée until smooth, then stir in the port or wine. Cool completely, then put into a container that can safely be used in the freezer, and freeze until firm around the edges.

3 Spoon into the food processor and process until smooth. Return to the freezer and freeze until solid.

4 Soften slightly at room temperature then serve in scoops, with cookies, if desired, but they will add fat content.

NUTRITIONAL NOTES
Per portion:

Calories	166
Fat, total	0.25g
Saturated fat	0g
Cholesterol	0mg
Fiber	3.75g

Raspberry Sorbet with a Berry Garland

This stunning fresh fruit and herb garnish creates a bold border for the scoops of sorbet.

INGREDIENTS

Serves 8

3/4 cup sugar

1 cup water

1 pound fresh or thawed
   frozen raspberries

strained juice of 1 orange

For the decoration

1 bunch mint

selection of berries, including strawberries,
   raspberries, red currants and blueberries

1 Heat the sugar with the water in a saucepan, until dissolved, stir occasionally. Bring to a boil, then set aside to cool. Purée the raspberries with the orange juice, then sieve, to remove any seeds.

2 Mix the syrup with the puréed raspberries and pour into a suitable container for the freezer. Freeze for 2 hours or until ice crystals form around the edges. Whisk until smooth, then return to the freezer for 4 hours.

3 About 30 minutes before serving, transfer the sorbet to the refrigerator to soften slightly. Place a large sprig of mint on the rim of a serving plate, then build up a garland, using more mint sprigs.

4 Leaving on the leaves, cut the strawberries in half. Arrange on the mint with the other fruit. Place the fruits at different angles and link the leaves with strings of red currants. Place scoops of sorbet in the center.

NUTRITIONAL NOTES

Per portion:

Calories	158
Fat, total	0.4g
Saturated fat	0g
Cholesterol	0mg
Fiber	3.4g

Black Currant Sorbet

If not serving immediately, cover this black currant sorbet tightly and freeze it again, for up to one week.

INGREDIENTS

Serves 4

scant $1/2$ cup sugar

$1/2$ cup water

4 cups black currants

juice of $1/2$ lemon

1 tablespoon egg white

1 Mix the sugar and water in a small saucepan. Heat gently, stirring until the sugar dissolves, then boil the syrup for 2 minutes. Remove the pan from heat and set aside to cool.

2 Remove the black currants from the stems by pulling them through the tines of a fork. Wash thoroughly and drain.

3 Using a metal blade, process the black currants and lemon juice until smooth. Or, chop the black currants coarsely, then add the lemon juice. Stir in the sugar syrup.

4 Press the purée through a sieve to remove the seeds.

5 Pour the black currant purée into a nonmetallic dish that can safely be used in the freezer. Cover the dish with plastic wrap or a lid and freeze until the sorbet is almost firm but still slushy.

6 Cut the sorbet into pieces and process in a food processor until smooth. With the machine running, add the egg white through the feeder tube and process until well mixed. Put the sorbet back into the dish and freeze until almost firm. Chop the sorbet again and process until smooth. Serve immediately.

NUTRITIONAL NOTES

Per portion:

Calories	132
Fat, total	0g
Saturated fat	0g
Cholesterol	0mg
Fiber	4.1g

Mango and Lime Sorbet in Lime Shells

This richly flavored sorbet looks pretty served in the lime shells, but is also good served in traditional scoops.

INGREDIENTS

Serves 4

4 large limes

1 ripe mango

1 1/2 teaspoons powdered gelatin

2 egg whites

1 tablespoon sugar

strips of pared lime zest, to decorate

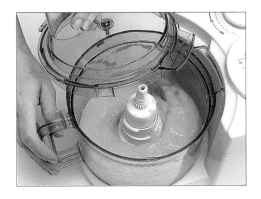

1 Slice the top and bottom off each lime. Squeeze the juice, keeping the shells intact, then scrape out the shell.

2 Halve, pit, peel and chop the mango. Purée in a food processor with 2 tablespoons of the lime juice.

3 Sprinkle the gelatin onto 3 tablespoons of the lime juice in a small heatproof bowl. Set aside until spongy, then place over a pan of hot water and stir until the gelatin has dissolved. Stir it into the mango mixture.

4 Whisk the egg whites in a grease-free bowl until they hold soft peaks. Whisk in the sugar. Fold the egg white mixture quickly into the mango mixture. Spoon the sorbet into the lime shells. Any leftover sorbet can be frozen in small ramekins.

NUTRITIONAL NOTES

Per portion:

Calories	83
Fat, total	0.4g
Saturated fat	0g
Cholesterol	0mg
Fiber	2.3g

5 Place the filled shells in the freezer until the sorbet is firm. Overwrap the shells in plastic wrap. Before serving, let the shells stand at room temperature for about 10 minutes; decorate them with knotted strips of pared lime zest.

Watermelon Sorbet

A slice of this refreshing sorbet is the perfect way to cool down on a hot day. Ensure that the watermelon is perfectly ripe.

INGREDIENTS

Serves 6

1/2 small watermelon, about 2 1/4 pounds

6 tablespoons sugar

4 tablespoons unsweetened cranberry juice or water

2 tablespoons lemon juice

sprigs of fresh mint, to decorate

3 Mix the sugar and cranberry juice or water in a saucepan and stir over low heat until the sugar dissolves. Bring to a boil, then lower the heat and simmer for 5 minutes. Let the sugar syrup cool.

5 Put the sorbet into a chilled bowl and whisk to break up the ice crystals. Return to the freezer for another 30 minutes, whisk again, then put into the melon shell and freeze until solid.

1 Cut the watermelon into six equal-size wedges. Scoop out the pink flesh, discarding the seeds but reserving the shell.

4 Put the melon flesh and lemon juice in a blender and process to a smooth purée. Stir in the sugar syrup and pour into a freezer-proof container. Freeze for 3–3 1/2 hours or until slushy.

6 Carefully remove the sorbet-filled melon shell from the freezer and turn it upside down. Use a sharp knife to separate the segments, then quickly place them on individual plates. Decorate with mint sprigs and serve.

2 Select a bowl that is about the same size as the melon and which can safely be used in the freezer. Line it with plastic wrap. Arrange the melon skins in the bowl to re-form the shell, fitting them together snugly so that there are no gaps. Put in the freezer.

NUTRITIONAL NOTES
Per portion:

Calories	125
Fat, total	0.52g
Saturated fat	0g
Cholesterol	0mg
Fiber	0.26g

COOK'S TIP

Watermelon seeds make a delicious and nutritious snack if toasted in a medium oven until brown and hulled to remove the outer shell.

Rhubarb and Orange Sorbet

Pink rhubarb, with sweet oranges and honey—the perfect summer sorbet. Add more honey or sugar if needed, to taste.

Serves 4

12 ounces pink rhubarb

1 orange

1 tablespoon honey

1 teaspoon powdered gelatin

orange slices, to decorate

NUTRITIONAL NOTES
Per portion:

Calories	38
Fat, total	0.1g
Saturated fat	0g
Cholesterol	0mg
Fiber	2g

1 Trim the rhubarb and slice into 1-inch lengths. Place the rhubarb in a nonreactive pan.

2 Finely grate the zest from the orange and squeeze out the juice. Add about half the orange juice and the grated zest to the rhubarb in the pan and simmer until the rhubarb is just tender. Stir in the honey.

3 Heat the remaining orange juice and stir in the gelatin to dissolve. Stir it into the rhubarb. Put the whole mixture into a rigid container that can safely be used in the freezer; freeze for about 2 hours or until slushy.

4 Remove the mixture from the freezer, put into a bowl and beat well to break up the ice crystals. Freeze until firm. Soften slightly at room temperature before serving in scoops, decorated with orange slices.

Orange Ice with Strawberries

Juicy oranges and really ripe strawberries make a flavorful ice that does not need any additional sweetening.

INGREDIENTS

Serves 4

6 large juicy oranges

3 cups ripe strawberries

finely pared strips of orange zest,
    to decorate

NUTRITIONAL NOTES

Per portion:

Calories	124
Fat, total	0.4g
Saturated fat	0g
Cholesterol	0mg
Fiber	5.6g

1 Squeeze the juice from the oranges and pour into a shallow freezer-proof bowl. Freeze until ice crystals form around the edge of the mixture, beat thoroughly and freeze again. Repeat this process at 30-minute intervals over a 4-hour period.

2 Halve the strawberries and arrange them on a serving plate. Scoop the ice into serving glasses, decorate with strips of orange zest and serve immediately with the strawberries.

COOK'S TIP

The ice will keep for up to 3 weeks in the freezer. Sweet ruby grapefruits or deep red blood oranges can be used for a different flavor and color.

Frozen Oranges

These little sorbets served in the fruit shell are easy to eat—just the thing for serving at a barbecue picnic.

NUTRITIONAL NOTES

Per portion:

Calories	167
Fat, total	0.3g
Saturated fat	0g
Cholesterol	0mg
Fiber	4.3g

3 Grate the zest of the six remaining oranges and add this to the syrup. Squeeze the juice from the oranges, and from the reserved flesh. There should be 3 cups. Add water, if necessary.

4 Stir the orange juice into the syrup, with the remaining lemon juice and water. Pour the mixture into a shallow container that can safely be used in the freezer. Freeze for 3 hours.

5 Turn the mixture into a bowl, and whisk to break down the ice crystals. Return to the freezer container and freeze for 4 more hours, until firm, but not solid.

6 Pack the mixture into the orange shells, mounding it up, and set the "hats" on top. Freeze until ready to serve. Just before serving, make a hole in the top of each "hat," using a skewer, and push in a bay leaf as decoration.

INGREDIENTS

Serves 8

2/3 cup sugar

juice of 1 lemon

scant 1 cup water

14 oranges

8 fresh bay leaves, to decorate

1 Put the sugar in a heavy pan. Add half the lemon juice, then pour in 1/2 cup of the water. Heat gently, stirring occasionally, until the sugar has dissolved, then bring to a boil, and boil for 2–3 minutes, until the syrup is clear. Let cool.

2 Slice the tops off eight of the oranges, to make "hats." Scoop out the flesh from inside each, taking care not to damage the shell, and set it aside. Put the empty orange shells and the "hats" on a baking sheet and place in the freezer until needed.

COOK'S TIP

Use crumpled aluminum foil to keep the shells upright on the baking sheet.

Fresh Orange Granita

A granita is like an Italian ice, but coarser and quite grainy in texture. It makes a refreshing dessert after a rich meal.

INGREDIENTS

Serves 6

4 large oranges

1 large lemon

2/3 cup sugar

2 cups water

cookies, to serve (optional)

pared strips of orange and lemon zest,
    to decorate

1 Thinly pare the orange and lemon zest, avoiding the white pith, and set aside for the decoration. Cut the fruit in half and squeeze the juice into a bowl. Set aside.

2 Heat the sugar and water in a heavy saucepan, stir until the sugar dissolves. Bring to a boil, and boil without stirring, until a syrup forms. Remove from heat, add the orange and lemon zest and shake the pan. Cover and let cool.

3 Strain the sugar syrup into a shallow freezer container, and add the fruit juice. Stir well, then freeze, uncovered, for 4 hours, until slushy.

COOK'S TIP

Slice orange and lemon zest into thin strips. Blanch for 2 minutes, refresh in cold water and dry.

4 Remove the half-frozen mixture from the freezer and mix with a fork, return to the freezer and freeze again for 4 hours or until frozen hard.

5 To serve, turn into a bowl and let soften for about 10 minutes, break up again and pile into long-stemmed glasses. Decorate with the orange and lemon zest. Serve with cookies, if desired, but the fat content must be taken into account.

NUTRITIONAL NOTES
Per portion:

Calories	139
Fat, total	0.2g
Saturated fat	0g
Cholesterol	0mg
Fiber	1.6g

Lemon Granita

Nothing is more refreshing for dessert on a hot summer's day than a fresh lemon granita.

INGREDIENTS

Serves 4

2 cups water

1/2 cup granulated sugar

2 large lemons

NUTRITIONAL NOTES
Per portion:

Calories	114
Fat, total	0g
Saturated fat	0g
Cholesterol	0mg
Fiber	0g

1 In a large saucepan, heat the water and sugar together over low heat until the sugar dissolves. Bring to a boil, stirring occasionally. Remove from heat and let cool.

2 Grate the zest from one lemon, then squeeze the juice from both. Stir the grated zest and juice into the sugar syrup. Place it in a shallow container or freezer tray, and freeze until solid.

3 Plunge the bottom of the frozen container or tray in very hot water for a few seconds. Turn the frozen mixture out, and chop it into large chunks.

4 Place the mixture in a food processor fitted with metal blades, and process until it forms small crystals. Spoon into serving glasses.

Coffee Granita

A granita is a cross between a frozen drink and a flavored ice, and can be made at home with the help of a food processor. The consistency should be slushy, not solid.

INGREDIENTS

Serves 4

2 cups water

1/2 cup sugar

1 cup very strong espresso coffee, cooled

NUTRITIONAL NOTES
Per portion:

Calories	115
Fat, total	0g
Saturated fat	0g
Cholesterol	0mg
Fiber	0g

1 Heat the water and sugar together gently until the sugar dissolves. Bring to a boil, stirring occasionally. Remove from heat and let cool.

2 Stir the coffee and sugar syrup together. Place it in a container and freeze until solid. Plunge the bottom of the frozen container or tray in very hot water. Turn the mixture out, and chop into chunks.

3 Place the mixture in a food processor and process until it forms small crystals. Spoon into tall glasses and serve.

COOK'S TIP

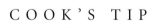

To store a granita, pour the processed mixture back into a container, cover, and freeze again. Let thaw slightly before serving.

Index